LEGEND

A RANDOM HOUSE BOOK published by Random House New Zealand
18 Poland Road, Glenfield, Auckland, New Zealand

For more information about our titles go to www.randomhouse.co.nz

A catalogue record for this book is available from the National Library
of New Zealand

Random House New Zealand is part of the Random House Group
New York   London   Sydney   Auckland   Delhi   Johannesburg

First published 2013

© 2013 text Paul Goldsmith; images of phases of manufacturing at the
Gallagher Group plant in Hamilton, ranging from tool and die making,
through to plastic and electronics on pages 9, 33, 59, 87, 119, 147, 193, 231,
267, 293, 325, 357 and 393, Jane Ussher; images on pages 31, 399 and 406
also Jane Ussher; all other images Gallagher private collection.

The moral rights of the author have been asserted

ISBN 978 1 77553 333 8
ePub 978 1 77553 337 5

This book is copyright. Except for the purposes of fair reviewing no part
of this publication may be reproduced or transmitted in any form or by
any means, electronic or mechanical, including photocopying, recording
or any information storage and retrieval system, without permission in
writing from the publisher.

Design: Carla Sy
Front cover image: Jane Ussher
Back cover and inside flap images: Gallagher private collection

Printed in China by Everbest Printing Co Ltd

This title is also available as an eBook

LEGEND

From electric fences to global success:
The Sir William Gallagher Story

PAUL GOLDSMITH

RANDOM HOUSE
NEW ZEALAND

CONTENTS

Foreword
Rt Hon. Mike Moore   6

Introduction
'FOR FUN AND PROFIT' — THE GALLAGHER STORY   8

Chapter one
INHERITANCE   32

Chapter two
YOUNG BILL GALLAGHER: 1941–62   58

Chapter three
RESOURCEFUL YOUNG MEN: 1962–70   86

Chapter four
PLAYING DOUBLES: 1971–77   118

Chapter five
THE ELECTRIC FENCES TAKE OVER: 1977–85   146

Chapter six
SURVIVAL: 1985–89   192

Chapter seven
REGAINING MOMENTUM: 1989–95   230

Chapter eight
STALLING: 1996–99   266

Chapter nine
A NEW DIRECTION: 1999–2001   292

Chapter ten
THE ROAD TO BUCKINGHAM
PALACE: 2002–06   324

Chapter eleven
THE RELENTLESS DRIVE FOR
INNOVATION: 2006 AND BEYOND   356

POSTSCRIPT   392

ENDNOTES   407

ACKNOWLEDGEMENTS   412

INDEX   413

Foreword

The Gallagher story is a unique New Zealand, even global, story. I'm pleased it's being told because it's inspirational, and speaks to courage, risk, innovation and perspiration.

I first met Bill, now Sir William, when he accompanied me as New Zealand Trade Minister on a number of trade missions to many countries. Bill was one of the stars on these missions, which at the time were a unique way of promoting New Zealand and its products.

The idea was to organise a military aircraft and to visit markets that exporters thought could use the presence of a minister to get appointments and to attract the attention of buyers and decision-makers. We had over 40 business people on some missions. My memories of Bill were of his consistent good humour, his availability and advice to other Kiwis who were not so experienced, and his eagerness to be a team player. He is an economic patriot.

The Gallagher Group, led by Bill, is the best in the world in its field. They started building electric fences for Kiwi farmers and now are leaders in a number of product areas, including security, service stations — that is, petrol distribution — and a host of creative ideas. They are in dozens of countries, from the Middle East to Eastern Europe, and from Latin America to Australia and North America.

Bill is a charismatic leader who leads from the front. He is always on the road, always taking risks, always seeking improvement. Beneath that rough exterior there is a rough interior.

When he speaks no one doubts where he came from and where he stands. The fact that he has been honoured by governments, both Labour and National, speaks to the high esteem in which he is held by leaders of all political persuasions.

I doubt if he will ever slow down; the man is a legend. We all have Bill Gallagher stories like the one when Bill was knifed while on a trade mission. None of us was really worried; we also had a good veterinary surgeon on the mission so we knew she would be right.

If New Zealand had another 100 Bill Gallaghers we would be the richest, most decent, best-natured nation on earth. He is a Kiwi hero.

Mike Moore
Former Prime Minister of New Zealand
Former Director General of the World Trade Organisation
New Zealand Ambassador to the United States

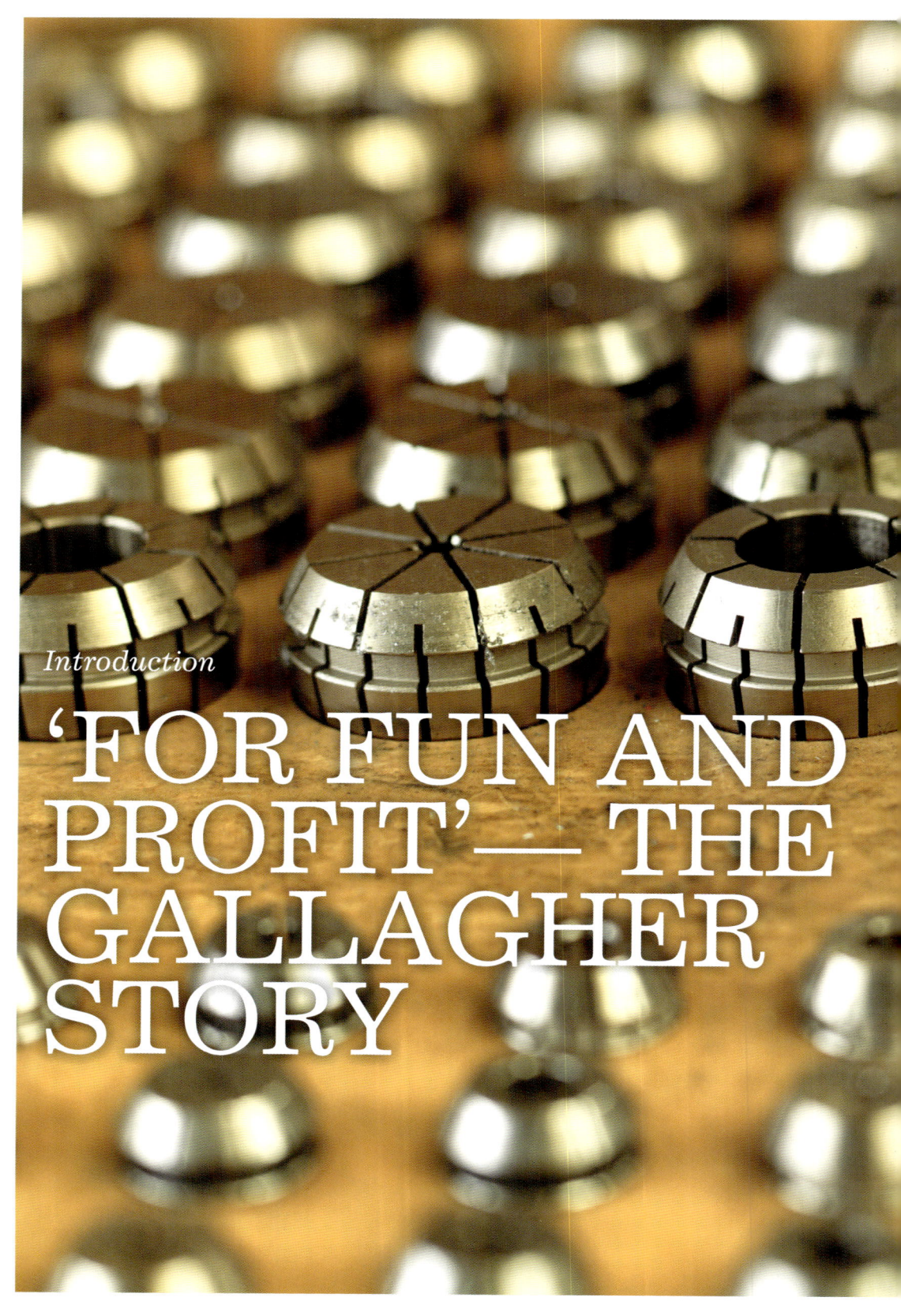

Introduction

'FOR FUN AND PROFIT'— THE GALLAGHER STORY

Introduction

'FOR FUN AND PROFIT' — THE GALLAGHER STORY

The second time Bill Gallagher was mugged he was on Zeedijk Road in Amsterdam's red light district, an area famous for its colourful nightlife. It was a chilly evening in March 1988. Bill, wearing a beige Peter Sellers-style trench coat, was 'looking around'. Out of the shadows a dark figure emerged and demanded his wallet. Bill was going to cooperate, but as he fumbled for his wallet two other men rushed in and he was stabbed through the left hand and twice in the chest. Fortunately the knife aimed directly at his heart hit a rib and failed to penetrate.

Bill saw red and, raising his right hand, knocked the men and their knives out of the way. Big steps were taken fast up the canal. Bill stumbled into a bar, shouting he'd been stabbed, and was thrown a paper towel then pointed toward the door. Next he reached a rundown chicken bar, dripping 'plenty of tomato sauce' on the counter. Again he was waved back outside, but this time toward two nearby policemen, who packed him off to hospital. It was a narrow escape. As the local inspector took his statement a few hours later, he told Gallagher that he had had two stabbings in his district that night: 'The other guy didn't make it.'

In March 1988 Bill Gallagher was a 47-year-old electric fence manufacturer from Hamilton. As he lay in his Dutch hospital bed he was agitated, not so much because of his recent brush with death, but because he knew that he was due in Turkey six days later to join a New Zealand Exporters mission, led by Trade Minister Mike Moore. And before that he faced what was likely to be a boisterous meeting with his Dutch distributors, Veldman & Dijkstra, a couple of hours' drive to the north, followed by a call on a French polywire manufacturer in Lyon. First thing the next morning, ignoring stern protests from his doctors, he checked himself out of the hospital, wheeling two intravenous drips across the carpark to Erik Dijkstra's waiting car before a nurse disconnected him.

Six days and several plane trips later Gallagher touched down in Ankara, determined not to miss the business opportunity presented by the New Zealand minister's visit. He proudly showed his wounds to anyone interested, but drew the line when one of his colleagues on the mission, Jock Allison, offered to take out his stitches on the bus. Allison was an agricultural consultant from Dunedin who taught veterinary surgery.

After four days scooting around Turkey, meeting potential distributors and learning about the market, Gallagher flew to Sri Lanka. He had hosted Gamini Dissanayake, the Sri Lankan Minister of Agriculture, at the Gallagher Group's Hamilton factory six months earlier and was determined to take up a return invitation. Much flattering attention followed his landing in Colombo, and he was soon travelling to the island's far north with President JR Jayawardene's party. There were two helicopters, and the president was in the other one. When they reached their destination the president's chopper swooped down fast, while Gallagher's hovered around. They were in Tamil Tiger territory, the president had survived an assassination attempt the previous year, and with the thud-thud-thud of the chopper in his brain it slowly dawned on the New Zealander that his machine was the decoy. Mercifully, no shots were fired.

Throughout the trip Gallagher took every opportunity to convince the Sri Lankans of the eminent suitability of his company's electric fence as a means to prevent marauding elephants trampling over villages. He'd tell anyone who would listen how his fences were already keeping elephants out of palm-oil plantations in Malaysia, bears out of honey bee hives in Alberta, wildebeest from dairy herds in Kenya, and wild pigs out of crops in Holland.

In Colombo he met the author Arthur C Clarke, who as well as writing science fiction shared Gallagher's love of scuba diving. In 1964 he had published a diving classic, *The Treasure of the Great Reef*, about his adventures with friends on the Great Basses Reef, 10 miles off Sri Lanka's southern coast, in the Bay of Bengal. The reef was littered with wrecks, and in 1961 Clarke's group had found a horde of silver rupees dating from 1702. Wide-eyed at Clarke's stories, Gallagher wanted to look at this reef, though his hand was still bandaged from the stabbing and the puncture wound in his chest had not fully mended. He found Cedric Martynstein, a retired Sri Lankan naval commander, hired a chopper, and the following day fluked dead calm conditions over the usually roiling and treacherous shoal. A day or two later he finally arrived back in Auckland, happily bearing a couple of trinkets. Within a few years, sadly, both Gamini Dissanayake and Cedric Martynstein had been killed, victims of Sri Lanka's civil war.

It would be an exaggeration to say that this was a typical fortnight for Bill Gallagher, but in terms of its frenetic pace and Gallagher's sense of purpose it wasn't at all out of character. This was the essential Bill Gallagher: on the hoof, spending 80 to 100 nights overseas each year as he peddled his wares to a world that was surprisingly receptive; night after night on the road, usually knocking off a country a day. 'We're not "here today and gone tomorrow",' he'd laugh; 'we're "here today and gone tonight".' His pattern was to plot a wobbly three-week course around the world, taking in as many stops as was physically possible, and repeating the exercise four or five times a year. Since virtually every night was spent in a new hotel, it was difficult to have his laundry done. By the third week of each trip he'd be looking somewhat dishevelled. Like a rock star ceaselessly touring, the never-ending sales trip has been his drug, with the very occasional stolen day for his primary indulgence, diving. By 1988 Bill Gallagher had been living this way for 13 years.

Twenty-four years later, aged 71, and now knighted, Sir William Gallagher is still doing it. And for most of the past 20 years his wife, Lady Judi, has travelled with him. Illnesses, injuries and life's everyday dramas are inconveniences to be shrugged aside for conversations with the next distributor or another potential customer. The itinerary for his September 2011 trip, for example, was enough to give any normal person the stitch: Bangkok (one day), Bangalore,

Ahmedabad, Mumbai, New Delhi (four days), Copenhagen (one day), Stockholm (one day), road trip from Aberdeen to London stopping in a dozen centres (five days), Orlando, Florida, for a trade show (three days) and Kansas City for a Gallagher regional managers' conference (three days). Day after day of airport check-ins, traffic jams and the challenge of finding the next hotel. Some flights were reasonably pleasant; others, such as the leg from New Delhi to Copenhagen, leaving India at 2am and transiting through Vienna seven hours later, were stinkers. This extraordinary effort is devoted to one purpose: to generate more demand for his products.

By 2012 the product mix extended well beyond what was on offer in the 1980s. Back in the 1980s he had been peddling agricultural electric fencing, the product that had made the name Gallagher famous in New Zealand and throughout the pastoral farming world. His father, Bill Gallagher senior, had started making electric fences for the local market in the late 1930s. But it had been Bill and his brother John who had grasped the commercial potential of the technological changes pioneered by a New Zealand scientist in the 1960s which lifted the power output of energisers by several orders of magnitude and revolutionised their utility. In the 1970s the Gallaghers took this product to the world, and by the 1980s the best markets outside their home country were Australia, northern Europe, the British Isles, North America, southern Africa and Japan. Yet Gallagher also made countless visits to Latin American countries and throughout South East Asia and eastern Europe in search of entrepreneurial distributors who might take on the challenge of marketing his goods.

And everywhere he went he encountered barriers to trade, ranging from duties in excess of 100 per cent in Argentina and India to the more subtle technical barriers favoured in Europe. He saw how warped the global agricultural market had become after decades of protectionism. When New Zealand eliminated its subsidies for agriculture in 1985, Gallagher understood clearly the central importance of productivity gains in making subsidy-free pastoral farming possible. He became a missionary, preaching the gospel of how modern electric fencing could significantly increase the productivity of pastoral farming, thus doing away with the need for subsidies and offering the promise of sustainably feeding a growing world.

New Zealand farmers had pioneered the practice of subdividing paddocks cheaply using temporary electric fencing and moving stock regularly to maximise the pasture growth and nutrition. Gallagher and his team showed farmers from Denmark's Jutland Peninsula to Wisconsin how they could do the same. Permanent electric fencing, meantime, could save farmers a fortune in comparison to traditional fencing because it required fewer posts, less wire and less maintenance.

By the turn of the century, with Gallaghers' energisers and electric fencing accessories well established in agricultural markets, Bill Gallagher's focus shifted to the rapidly expanding security side of the business. This had grown out of informal efforts in the 1980s to use electric fences to secure car yards and other commercial premises. Gallagher spied what he thought was a magnificent opportunity, and during the 1990s the R&D team developed sophisticated perimeter security and monitoring systems under the PowerFence brand. Gallaghers' UK subsidiary achieved notable success in introducing the product to the British market.

In 1999 Gallagher seized an opportunity to expand his security offering when PEC Ltd, a struggling New Zealand technology company, came up for sale. PEC had developed the Cardax access control system in the early 1980s, and since then had achieved a measure of international success. Knitting together electric fencing on the perimeter and access control at the points of entry, Gallagher saw the potential of a unique solution to take to the market. Over the following few years he poured millions of dollars into R&D to build on the robust Command Centre that drove the Cardax system and to plug perimeter fencing and other security applications into a single security offering. Now he had another world-beating product to take to the market.

I witnessed Sir William in full flight in September 2011, giving his pitch to a couple of influential security consultants in a hot little office in a modest, low-level block in Chembur, Mumbai. It had taken most of the day to get there through Mumbai's chaotic traffic, but once Gallagher sat down the fatigue fell from him as he recounted stories of how his product had developed; how farmers in South Africa had first wanted electric fences around their houses with a voltage alarm attached, before extending them out to the paddocks; how in the mid-1990s National Grid in the UK had had problems with thieves smashing down the steel palisade fences around its substations to steal copper wiring, which was not only annoying in itself but also dangerous, because the next morning children could wander through the holes in the fence. The Gallagher PowerFence had put a stop to that nonsense. 'And the best thing about the product' — he was really warming up now — 'is that it produces very few false alarms. We've got a fence installed on a very high-security site in the US, which I'm not allowed to identify, where the PowerFence is one of three layers on the perimeter. And a few years ago they had a big storm and the two other layers went into alarm. The security guys assumed that our fence must also have been knocked out of action, even though it had sent no warning or message. So they sent a few burly marines to check it out. Well, it was working all right. That really sat them on their bums!'

And with stories like these, Gallagher painted a picture of a great product that exceeded expectations and did things that people had previously thought impossible, and of a company driven by a man who believes passionately in his products.

The day before his Mumbai visit, Sir William had been in Ahmedabad, addressing a crowd of some 200 security people who had turned out to hear his presentation on 'Emerging Trends in Perimeter and Integrated Access Security'. They had gathered in the St Laurn Hotel, a reasonably modern complex rising out of the wild streets of Ahmedabad, with its shanty towns, cows in the middle of the road, young girls carrying bricks on their heads, rubbish, mangy dogs and mud. The contrasts of India are striking for the western observer, but the security business is growing in leaps and bounds, and the audience was interested. Some may have struggled with Gallagher's broad Kiwi accent, but they laughed at his jokes. 'I was asked by one guy whether electric fencing is legal for security in India,' he started out; 'I said, "It's around your Parliament Buildings in Delhi. And, of course, your politicians wouldn't do anything illegal, would they?"'

At the end of the presentation, Gallagher's Indian partner, Vishnu Narain, organised the usual party trick, where a mobile electric fence unit is turned on. A dozen or so people formed a chain, holding hands, with the last person touching a wire. When, after much coaxing and goading, the first person was persuaded to grab another wire, everyone leapt about as the shock came through, roaring with laughter. Once they're convinced that while the shock is an effective deterrent it won't kill anyone, Gallagher and his team have won half the battle.

And on it goes. As Gallagher says, 'India is a thrill to visit and a thrill to leave.' On to Copenhagen, Stockholm, then Aberdeen, where Gallagher was driven an hour or so north to St Fergus, where four large terminals are laid out side by side along the shoreline, capturing North Sea gas that comes onshore from pipes starting kilometres out to sea. Around 25 per cent of Britain's gas supply comes through St Fergus, so it's an important area. All four terminals have Gallagher PowerFence on the perimeter. Gallagher walked around with a security consultant who would be involved in tendering for dozens of other sites of Critical National Infrastructure. Most of these sites will have their security specifications upgraded over the next few years. The consultant was given the full Gallagher history and a sense of Gallagher's determination to stay one step ahead of the 'bad guys'.

All this charging about is tiring, but Gallagher has the ability to nod off the moment the SatNav has been engaged by Judi, who generally drives, and then to wake up refreshed as she pulls up for the next appointment. Such a regimen is not typical for 70-year-olds. Gallagher carries on because he enjoys it. Early in his career he picked up the phrase used by Robert Townsend, the CEO of Avis: 'If you are not in business for fun or profit, what the hell are you doing here?' That seemed right to him. He tells everyone that he's in business 'for fun *and* profit', adding, 'It's not so good if you have to settle only for one or the other.'

For him, the fun comes with the stimulation of the technological and business challenges and from the people he works with, from his trusted managers like Margaret Comer in Hamilton or Dave Bentley in the UK, to distributors like Bilal Chehime in Lebanon or Vishnu Narain in Bangalore, who he'll see once or twice a year. Each and every one has his or her personal stories, dramas and triumphs, in which Sir William and Lady Judi share. As, indeed, do some of the creatures that are kept in by Gallaghers' product. One of the most interesting of these that the Gallaghers have met is Kanzi, the

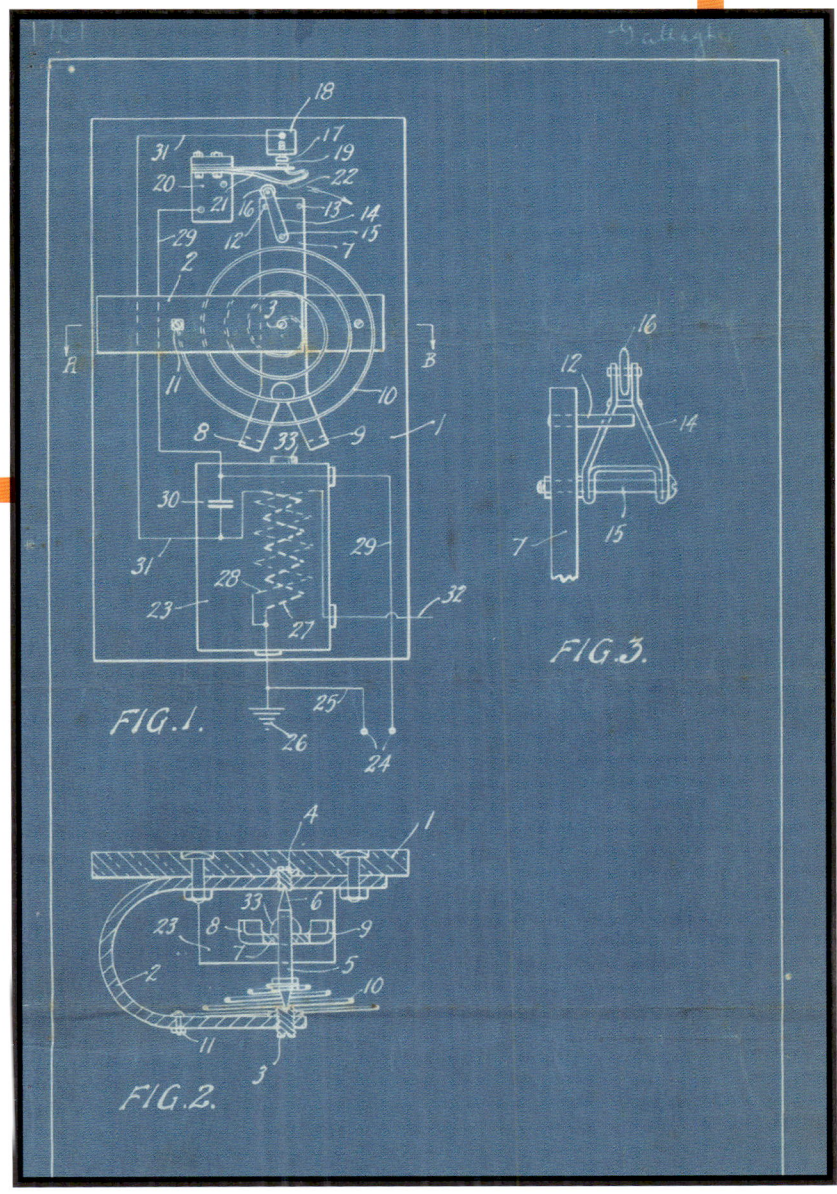

ABOVE The patent that began it all. The Gallagher Group's founder Bill Gallagher senior filed this patent for his electric fence in 1938.

male bonobo, who understands a fair bit of human language but hasn't yet figured out how to get past the Gallagher electric fence at the Great Apes Trust in Des Moines, Iowa.

And there has been plenty of profit over the years. Aside from a brief experiment in the 1990s, the company has remained wholly in the ownership of the family, first with Bill Gallagher senior and later shared between the families of his two sons, John and Bill junior. Profits were fairly modest until the early 1970s, while the company remained a small business, but began to flow from the mid-1970s as the brothers transformed the Gallagher Group into an exporting enterprise with genuine scale and enjoyed 15 years of rapid growth.

In real terms, growth slowed between the mid-1980s and the late 1990s, as the company negotiated changes in government policy for exporters, a rollercoaster currency, ruthless foreign competitors (many of them companies that had been started by former Gallaghers employees or distributors), as well as all the normal problems of privately held companies: health scares, kidnappings, power struggles, marriage break-ups, confidence men and ne'er-do-wells. But through it all the company remained profitable, and as a result, since the late 1980s the Gallaghers have been able to make a significant philanthropic contribution to the Hamilton and New Zealand communities. Growth, meantime, returned after 1999, both in the company's traditional forte of electric fencing and animal management, and also in the new field of security following the acquisition of PEC Ltd.

At the time of writing, the Gallagher Group has annual revenues approaching $200 million. It is one of very few New Zealand companies with an internationally recognised brand, in electric fencing and animal management, and it is striving hard to consolidate its position as a significant player in its segment of the security industry.

This book celebrates the first 75 years of the company's history, since Bill Gallagher senior sold his first home-built electric fence energisers to neighbours from his farm north of Hamilton. Its purpose is to trace the development of the company and to explain the key ingredients of its ongoing success. And since the company's growth has been driven and guided in such large measure by the Gallagher family itself, and in particular by Bill junior (now Sir William), there is a strong element of biography to the tale.

In a sense the company's history falls into two halves. For roughly the first 30 years Bill Gallagher senior was in charge and the company remained a small Hamilton business, employing a dozen or so workers in what was essentially an engineering shop that made various products for the domestic rural economy. A modest company suited Bill senior's modest ambitions; it provided him with the wherewithal to pay for the diesel to fuel his home-made 27 metre launch, food for the table, and the upkeep of the family home beside his workshop. He was happiest with a blowtorch in his hand, piecing together some machinery in a new way, in the hope that it might work better.

Not for the first time in human history, the sons appear to have reacted to their father's lifestyle and career choices and concluded that they would go further. All the Gallagher men were possessed of enormous energy and would naturally work, in some fashion or other, every hour that sleep would not deny them. But Bill junior in particular combined that energy with an entrepreneurial instinct and huge ambition. The Hamilton stage was not big enough for him, and in the 1970s he led the company's entry into the export market and its quest for global leadership in electric fencing, travelling incessantly and doing whatever it took to overcome innumerable obstacles to success.

In part it was a matter of personality. As a schoolboy in 1956 Bill flew to Australia on a DC6. His party went to Sydney's Luna Park, which featured a rollercoaster that was much more vigorous than any he had encountered in New Zealand. After an initial terrifying ride, the 15-year-old concluded that he could either sit at the back and scream or he could grab the front seat on his next go round and from there try to drive it and make it go faster. He adopted the second strategy and had more fun than he'd thought possible. It is an attitude to life that he has never dropped.

Aggression was another of Bill Gallagher junior's hallmark qualities. Gallaghers' Dutch distributor for more than 30 years, Erik Dijkstra, observes: 'New Zealanders generally are too soft to dominate in international business. For the typical Kiwi it's an embarrassment to be best in class at school. The exception is

ABOVE From humble beginnings: the first of the Gallagher energisers, 1938.

rugby, in which most boys want to be the best. And in that case, the All Blacks will do a war dance before the game. They know it's a battlefield out there. But international business is the same. It's a battlefield and you have to treat it that way. And on that score Bill is unusual for a New Zealander in that he's a street fighter; hard and immovable. In all our years working together if we ever had a meeting where there was no conflict, at the end no one would feel pleased. It somehow wasn't proper. And yet we stuck together because alongside the aggression came loyalty.'[1]

This mix of energy, ambition, hunger for excitement and aggression has carried the company a long way, particularly since none of it has diminished over the 40 or so years that Bill Gallagher junior has led the company. Where many such energetic leaders would run out of steam after a decade or two and sell the company to an international competitor, with all the hazards that entails, Gallagher's ambition has been unquenched. He has kept raising the bar, determined to deliver the best products to customers worldwide.

The effort, naturally, extends well beyond one man. John Gallagher was very active in the company from the early 1960s to the late 1980s, laying the groundwork for the North American market in the 1970s and concentrating for a while on the agricultural machinery side of the business. As the primary shareholder alongside Bill, his fundamental contribution has been to maintain the successful ownership structure that has allowed them to take a long-term approach to investment. In the early days the brothers lived relatively frugally and ploughed most of the company's profits back into the business. And to this day, instead of maximising annual profits and dividends, the Gallaghers have been content to invest heavily in R&D.

This 40-year investment has been one of the key ingredients underpinning the company's reputation for innovation, first in electric fencing, but subsequently in perimeter security and access control. And having resisted the urge to raise quick capital on the share market or by bringing in other investors, the Gallaghers have been beholden to no one, other than the banks, which as the years have passed have enjoyed less leverage. This has kept Bill Gallagher

ABOVE The promise of electric fencing: that a single wire can hold back bulls. Electric fencing revolutionised the pasture management of New Zealand's dairy farmers.

free to concentrate solely on his customers, rather than having one eye peering over his shoulder in fear of criticism from investors after a bad year's result.

Beyond the family, Bill Gallagher's initial insight when exports began in earnest was to harness the energies of entrepreneurs in each market the company entered. It took a while to find some of these people, and for every success there were two or three failures. But the best of these — such as David Mullen in Australia and the United States and the Dijkstras in Holland, Bernd Allie in southern Germany, John Lucey in Ireland and Surge Miyawaki in Japan — created significant distributing and marketing businesses in their respective areas that collectively generated the demand for Gallaghers' products around the world.

For a long time, the Gallagher Group was free to concentrate on what it did best — manufacturing innovative products and selling them in New Zealand — while a diverse group of international partners, each with their own 'skin in the game', worked out how best to market Gallaghers' products in their individual countries, with all their local quirks and idiosyncrasies. Over the years the Gallagher Group took minority shareholdings in several of these distribution companies. Thirty-five years later, with Gallaghers' presence in several key markets well established, the strategy has shifted so that the Gallagher Group has taken over the marketing of its products in most of the English-speaking countries. But in the history of the company, the efforts of these distributors can scarcely be overemphasised.

Meanwhile, it is often difficult for a family-run business to transition to a point where professional management can guide the company successfully. With his rare blend of technical skill, business acumen and natural authority in leadership, Bill Gallagher has tended to dominate the scene, and it took a long time to develop a strong second and third tier of management. In the early 1980s Vaughan Jones, a South African-born farmer, had a major impact as sales manager, introducing marketing disciplines to an engineering-orientated company. Then in the late 1980s and early 1990s, Neil Richardson, an Australian management consultant, became the de facto CEO for a few years, though Bill Gallagher retained the title. Richardson introduced a new level of sophistication to many areas of the business, from financial reporting to manufacturing processes

ABOVE Constant innovation has been a key ingredient in Gallaghers' success. The SmartFence, a portable fencing system with a built-in reel, posts and wires, to make it easier for farmers to set up temporary fences quickly and simply. This Gallagher promo shot sets the scene.

and brand consistency. But by 1996 his vision for the company had diverged from Bill Gallagher's, and Richardson departed.

It has only really been with the elevation of Steve Tucker through several senior roles to deputy CEO in the early 2000s that Bill Gallagher has been able to step back from the day-to-day management of the company with confidence. So while Gallagher provides the overall direction of the company and retains a special interest in the still developing security side of the business, he is also free to do what he enjoys most, which is to travel about promoting the business in export markets.

He and Tucker now guide a settled and competent senior management team, the core of which consists of: Steve Hoffman, the sales manager of the company for 20 years, who is now general manager of Gallagher Animal Management; Margaret Comer, Bill Gallagher's executive assistant in the 1980s, who has grown with the company over the decades and has been a key figure as head of Corporate Services for more than a decade; and Curtis Edgecombe, who joined the company in 2005 as general manager of Gallagher Security. Between them, Gallagher and his team are directly responsible for over 600 employees in New Zealand and a further 300-odd overseas, not to mention the owners and employees of the numerous independent companies throughout the world which have built their businesses around Gallagher products.

People make the business, from Sir William at the top projecting a sense of mission, to the new sales rep in Alabama or Abu Dhabi trying to make a name for himself by lifting sales volumes for the forthcoming month. But circumstances are also very important. The stars all fell into alignment at the right time for Gallaghers during the 1970s and early 1980s, the pivotal 15 years for the company. After a decade or so of adventuring as young men, the Gallagher boys were ready to settle down to business just at a time when they had a potentially world-beating product in the BEV II energiser. They had been on hand to build on technological advances pioneered a few years earlier by a New Zealand scientist who worked a few miles down the road, and had made the product a lot more reliable by using Silicon-Controlled Rectifier (SCR) switching, which became affordable only around 1970.

So they had a good product and plenty of desire, and as they set out they struck a sweet spot in New Zealand government policy, when successive administrations introduced ever more generous encouragement for manufacturing exporters. The combination of tax incentives for R&D and export sales promotion, and tax rebates for exports meant that for an extended period Gallaghers paid no company tax, and indeed for several years actually received payments from the tax department equating to a negative tax rate of 15 to 20 per cent. Since the company was quite profitable, this was enormously helpful in that it allowed the Gallaghers to fund rapid growth primarily from retained profits, aided by manageable levels of bank debt, together with some useful finance from a government agency.

Such generous industry policy from government had acquired a bad name by the late 1980s, primarily because it contributed to the massive budget deficits that bedevilled public finances for many years, but also because it produced a vast crop of mostly rotten fruit. Feasting on incentives, many manufacturing exporters that did not have an internationally competitive product and never produced a real operating profit grew bloated without creating genuine wealth.

Gallaghers, by contrast, was among the small minority of such firms that did possess internationally competitive products capable of commanding a premium in the global marketplace. It had set out to be the best in the world in its little niche and it was succeeding. By the time the government support was withdrawn, as it inevitably would be, in the late 1980s, the Gallagher Group was well established and able to survive the difficult transition to unfettered free enterprise.

Having received plenty of encouragement during its establishment years, like any company Gallaghers had many opportunities to lose its edge in the years thereafter. Consistent good performance over an extended period generates brand loyalty, but, as Bill Gallagher is keenly aware, it could easily be unwound by a few mistakes. 'Bad news travels fast,' he warns.

L ooking at the history of the company as a whole, particularly the 40 years since it began to export, some themes emerge that help explain Gallaghers' continued success. First and foremost is the passion for the products demonstrated by the company's principals. Gallaghers' electric fences and subsequent lines are not just products to be sold, numbers on a spreadsheet; at heart they are a means to improve productivity on farms, which benefit consumers and help to reduce the justification for farming subsidies. And in the security field, in combination with access control and a sophisticated command centre, they offer the opportunity to rethink security in an increasingly dangerous world. There's a sense of mission that galvanises everyone involved with the Gallagher brand.

A sustained commitment to R&D and product innovation has distinguished Gallagher equipment for decades. Having set out to be the best at what they do, they recognised that the best would become standard within a few years and so the mantle of leadership had to be reclaimed constantly. The shareholders have forgone greater profits today in the belief that investment in R&D will produce better products, a higher premium in the marketplace and even greater profits down the line. Forty years on, super-sized profits have always been eaten into by yet more R&D and the costs of establishing new parts to the business, but the instinct for long-term investment remains and the Gallagher brand still commands a premium.

In a world where businesses — whether they are manufacturers, distributors or end-users — frequently display all the loyalty of an alley tomcat, Bill Gallagher built his export business on a reputation for loyalty to his distributors, concluding that it was better to suffer periods of poor performance in some markets than to be distrusted. Demand for Gallagher products grew when international distributors felt confident about making a long-term investment in their own businesses and the development of the Gallagher brand in their marketplaces. In an extreme case, Gallagher endured around 15 years of negligible growth in the Indian market under its distributor Ibex before the business began to take off. And so there have been a number of 30-year relationships between the Gallagher Group and key distributors around the world. While the model has changed since the late 2000s, the tradition of loyalty to key partners has remained.

Aside from the boom times of the late 1970s and early 1980s, when the company concentrated solely on shipping the product out the door as fast as possible, Gallaghers' manufacturing history has followed the pattern of all surviving operations operating in free markets worldwide. It has waged a constant battle to improve performance, in order to keep ahead of the jackals of competition that appear constantly in new places around the world. Every aspect of the business, from manufacturing processes to inventory control, factory dispatch, quality controls and the productivity of the R&D section, has been constantly reviewed and rethought to produce more for less. The boring but important investments made in new computer systems every 10 years or so, and their effectiveness, explain in part why Gallaghers has kept ahead of the pack, while others have fallen away.

And finally, Gallaghers' longevity results from maintaining a disciplined and realistic strategic approach over the years, which has helped the company avoid any colossal mistakes. Bill Gallagher took note in 1991 when Michael E Porter, the Harvard Business School professor and author of *The Competitive Advantage of Nations*, came to this country and singled out the electric fencing industry as one of very few New Zealand industries that were genuinely internationally competitive. His advice was, 'If you don't have a competitive advantage, don't compete.'[2] Gallagher knew he had a competitive advantage in electric fencing; it was by no means obvious that he would enjoy a similar advantage with the many other products that people suggested he should add to his range or include in his expansion strategy. Another business professor, Hermann Simon, crystallised Gallagher's thinking perfectly when he said, 'Narrow the speciality and take it wide.'[3]

And so, under Bill Gallagher's management, with the support of his brother John, the approach to expansion has been careful and considered. A contrast may be made with a rival New Zealand company that around the year 2000 boasted of its intention to be a billion-dollar company within a decade and bought up everything in sight in pursuit of that vision, including much dross, and is now smaller than it was a decade ago. Gallaghers' major acquisitions have been in areas that strongly complement its existing strengths. And rather than pursue acquisitions according to some overarching growth strategy, even when the price might not be right, Gallagher has been an opportunist, seizing businesses that add to his range when they've been going cheap without ever betting the farm on the outcome.

Over the course of 50 years in business, Bill Gallagher has slowly expanded his 'circle of competence', to use Warren Buffett's phrase, from agricultural electric fencing to the broader field of animal management systems, incorporating electric fences, gates, weigh-scales and electric identification readers. And he has extended agricultural electric fencing to perimeter security fencing, and from there to access control systems, and on to a flexible and adaptable command centre capable of integrating numerous elements of security made by third parties, such as CCTV or iris scanners. From simply being a tool to control the opening and closing of doors, under Gallagher the Cardax access control system has evolved into a management tool for highly regulated sectors. This began by using swipe cards to operate air bridges at airports, not operating them if the person's training was not up to date, and has extended to a host of applications in the mining industry. Meantime, as part of his acquisition of PEC in 1999 Gallagher picked up a petrol pump manufacturing business, which after some restructuring proved too good to let go. In 50 years, then, he hasn't strayed too far.

Even that relatively modest level of extension has created enormous challenges for the group. It has been hard enough to build and maintain global leadership in the field of agricultural electric fencing, and in elements of the wider field of animal management. Yet this is a niche industry, where for the most part Gallaghers has been able to fly under the radar and avoid attracting extended direct competition from multinational conglomerates with deep pockets. In general, such firms have taken a look and found the industry too small and too difficult to crack into to be worth the effort.

The field of security, however, is an entirely different beast. In access control Gallaghers competes directly with Honeywell, Siemens, United Technologies (UTC), Schneider, General Electric and other multi-billion-dollar corporations, as well as the myriad cheap copiers of their technology trying to cut their lunch on the smaller jobs. The game is much harder, with Gallaghers relying more on responsiveness to clients, flexibility and providing innovative and unique solutions to old problems as a means to create a competitive advantage.

It has enjoyed many great successes. Gallagher gear has been entrusted with securing some of the world's most high-profile sites, from perimeter fencing around Buckingham Palace to access control systems protecting Turkey's crown jewels at Topkapi Palace in Istanbul. But in terms of Bill Gallagher's motto, while the security challenge is providing plenty of fun, after 20 years of development profits are only just starting to flow and are greatly prized. His goal is to be among the largest of the independents on the world stage in the access control and security industries.

In its seventy-fifth year the company is as dynamic as ever, comprising a large team inspired by its leader Sir William Gallagher to take on the world and win. Over four decades from the 1970s the Gallagher Group has progressed from a small family operation to a significant international business with a brand that is recognised globally. In New Zealand it has been the sort of company that politicians and commentators all want to see: a technology-driven exporter that commands a premium in the marketplace.

For most of his career Bill Gallagher has been something of a business hero in this country. The only disappointment, from the New Zealand perspective, is the degree to which Gallagher stands out like an icon, because there are comparatively few similar firms that have remained in business, let alone in local ownership. New Zealand's future depends on dozens of such companies emerging over the next few decades. This story shows that it can be done.

Paul Goldsmith
Auckland
March 2013

ABOVE Sir William in the electronics section of the Gallagher manufacturing plant in Hamilton.

Chapter one

INHERITANCE

By the time Bill Gallagher was conscious of the world around him, in the late 1940s, his father had his own business. He wasn't taking wages; he wasn't working for someone else. Bill Gallagher senior was employing people, making things in a garage in front of his house and selling his creations to tough and demanding customers. And he was quite successful. It was the perfect environment in which to produce an entrepreneur.[1]

In origin, however, the Gallaghers, Irish Catholics from County Roscommon, were farmers and soldiers more than businessmen. Thomas Gallagher (1805–84) had fought his way around the world as a young man with the 51st Yorkshire West Riding Regiment.[2] For a while, between 1839 and 1846, he guarded convicts in Van Diemen's Land, hardly a glamorous assignment. Then he came to New Zealand as one of the Royal New Zealand Fencibles. These were British army pensioners who, in return for being liable for defence work for an agreed period, were given free passage to New Zealand, a cottage and a one acre section, as well as medical and education services and various other perks.

Gallagher landed on Auckland's Mission Bay with his family in January 1848. They were lucky; 46 children had died during

ABOVE The Gallagher-Maher Cottage at the historical Howick village, Auckland. Bill Gallagher's Fencible Regiment-great-great grandfather's family lived in the right-hand half of the cottage.

the voyage out, but theirs had been spared. The family settled in Panmure, and Gallagher was fortunate enough to be demobilised 10 years later without having had to fire a shot.

According to family legend, Thomas's third son, James Gallagher (1840–1920), was beaten by the Catholic priest in Panmure for stealing apples. In disgust he turned to the Anglican Church and drifted away from the rest of the family. For this he was rewarded by striking it rich on the Australian goldfields.[3] In 1877 he had gone to Gympie in Queensland, and taken a twentieth share in a mine. After a quick course in geology in Sydney he took charge of the underground mining operations and found gold.[4] Needing more capital, he and his colleagues formed the North Phoenix Gold Mining Company, which became one of the best dividend-payers among the plethora of such companies in the 1880s.

His English wife, however, thought Gympie too hot, and in late 1881, when she found a snake curled up by the legs of her sleeping baby she insisted they go to New Zealand. Back in Auckland, James Gallagher bought several urban properties and a 343 acre (139 ha) farm at Mauku, near Pukekohe, paying cash for all of them. It was at the farm, up Mauku Creek on a southern arm of the Manukau Harbour, that Alfred was born in 1883. He was their second son and ultimately one of eight children.

Alfred J Gallagher (1883–1975), Bill junior's grandfather, enjoyed an affluent and carefree lifestyle in his youth. The family had a large, comfortable house at Mauku and took long holidays at their summer home at 39 Argyle Street, Herne Bay, a central Auckland suburb. This property had four acres (1.6 ha) running down to a private beach. With a foot in both country and city camps, James Gallagher was dismissive of the country folks, once observing that if Darwin had come to Pukekohe he surely would have found the missing link.[5]

Alfred and his brother George went to the Boer War in 1902, but they arrived too late for any action. On their return their father bought them a 300 acre (121 ha) farm near Te Kowhai, northwest of Hamilton, which the brothers ultimately divided. The property was rough, and over the years they took on some debt to develop it.

At Te Kowhai the Gallagher brothers had as neighbours the Clow family, Scottish migrants who had done pretty well and now possessed a quality 600 acre (243 ha) farm. The brothers snaffled the Clows' two pretty daughters, Alfred marrying Sarah Clow in 1910. Alfred William (Bill) Gallagher was born the following year, the son of farmers on both sides of the family. He was the first of six, with two younger brothers and three sisters following. Barely 70 years after the first Gallaghers had arrived in New Zealand the countryside was teeming with their descendants.

Until the early 1920s, Bill Gallagher's life was very comfortable. At Te Kowhai he and his brothers drifted and explored their way around their and the Clows' farms. All the men were bush mechanics, interested in the rudimentary machinery that was improving the productivity of farming. Alfred J Gallagher was among the first in the district to use milking machines and a power-driven separator.

Farming boomed during the Great War, helped immeasurably by arrangements for bulk government orders from Britain, which stayed in place until 1920. But then Alfred Gallagher made what in hindsight proved to be a bad mistake when he bought a new farm at the height of the market. He paid £12,800 (about $1 million in 2012 terms) for a 400 acre (162 ha) property at Papamoa, near Te Puke. He had probably inherited some money from his father, who died in 1920,[6] and, flush with cash, made a rash decision. Many others were caught up in similar exuberance after so many years of expansion, but in fact it would take another 30 years for farm prices to regain their 1920 levels. Worse, Gallagher had bought his land in summer when it looked good. In winter it was an unprofitable swamp.

By 1927 he was technically bankrupt, but with help from the Clow family and understanding creditors he struggled through for another couple of years before walking off the land one morning in 1929. With some more inherited money and additional borrowings, his wife Sarah bought a better farm, 390 (158 ha) acres on Te Matai Road, Te Puke, and the family 'took everything that wasn't nailed down' up the road to their new home. The humiliation, however, was too much for Alfred, and soon after he set off to Australia to sort himself out and to find money to pay off all his debtors. He divorced Sarah in 1932,[7] although he returned to New Zealand in the late 1930s, taking up farming again, and ultimately he and Sarah would remarry.

Bill Gallagher was 18 when his father left, and he took on much of the responsibility for the family. Not a natural student, he had already left school in Standard Six, in 1926. He had no time for the rote learning of the era; 'You can always find out what you need to know when you need to know it' was his motto. Now, he and his mother were left running a farm as the Great Depression tightened its grip in the early 1930s. There was little money to spare, but Bill and Henry, his younger brother by two years, amused themselves tinkering with machinery and improvising. When the local garage had given up trying to make an old Essex car start, Bill negotiated to take it at the knock-down price of £15 (around $1300 in today's terms) if he could make it work. This he did in no time. At around the same time, Henry had an old Harley-Davidson motorbike, which the brothers 'souped up' so Henry could race it on Mt Maunganui beach. Then they tinkered with the family's old Chandler car, which had been bought in earlier times of affluence but was no longer roadworthy. They put a deck on the back and rigged up a topdressing hopper, which greatly reduced the labour involved in fertilising the farm. When it was no longer good for that task, they used the engine to drive a thresher.

By 1933 the brothers and their mother were making a go of the farm. Notwithstanding the very low commodity prices, they had built a cowshed and were milking a hundred cows. Then disaster struck. Sarah suffered the first of several strokes, which left her incapacitated.[8] The boys struggled on with the help of their uncle, George Clow, but none of it was easy.

Bill's marriage in 1936 to Millie Murray, a young woman from a farm further up Te Matai Road, prompted a reshuffle of the family's affairs. Sarah sold the Te Matai farm and moved her family back to the Te Kowhai/Horotiu area to be near the Clows. Bill was given his share of the proceeds, £1000 (a little under $100,000 in today's terms), and used it to pay a deposit on a 98 acre (40 ha) farm on Speedy Road, Horotiu. With 37 dairy cows on a block of scruffy land, alongside plenty of rabbits, no internal fencing and a sizeable mortgage to service, the set-up wasn't going to make him rich. Just to survive he had to improvise. His neighbour, Roy Jefferies, later observed that 'because Bill didn't have the money to solve his problems, he had to use his brains'.[9]

Coupled with his brains, Bill had prodigious energy. Jefferies noted that Bill worked six days a week from 6am to 9pm. There was a lot to do. Unable to afford one of the tractors that were now coming onto the market, he found an old car and put iron-shod, cleated

RIGHT Bill Gallagher's first improvised tractor, c. 1938.

ABOVE Bill Gallagher takes his family for a spin in his home-made tractor, c. 1946.

wheels on the back to produce a handy machine. With this he hauled a large roller to flatten the scrub, which he then burned, then he pulled a plough to prepare pasture.

Traditional fencing was something else Bill couldn't afford, but he had read that American farmers had started using electrified wire to hold in stock. Since the earliest days of electricity, farmers had been tinkering with the idea of electrifying fencing. In 1889 New Zealand newspapers reported as 'the eighth greatest wonder of the world' a 30 mile long electric fence that a farmer had rigged up on his ranch in Carlston County, southern Kansas, to contain steers.[10]

But it wasn't until the early to mid-1930s that simple electric fencing became available commercially in the United States. The Gengler Electric Fence, for example, manufactured in Milwaukee, Wisconsin, was available from 1934.[11] This caught Bill Gallagher's attention because a single thin wire, held up by light standards, promised much cheaper fencing than the traditional arrangement with four or five thick, and possibly barbed, wires, regular posts and heavy strainers. But there was no way he could buy a finished electric fence product from the United States, and in 1937 they weren't yet available in New Zealand. Bill would have to come up with something himself. He then remembered 'Old Jo', the horse that has subsequently become central to the Gallagher electric fence legend.

Back in their Te Matai Road days, in the early 1930s, the Gallagher brothers had horses, which were used for taking out the cream and for riding. Bill used to get annoyed at the way they would back into fence posts to scratch themselves, frequently breaking the fence in the process. Worse, one horse, Old Jo, had crashed his way into a shed and taken to scratching his hindquarters against the car. Once he had managed to break the hood.[12] One day when Bill and Henry were working on the Harley-Davidson motorcycle and spinning a magneto they heard Old Jo starting once more on his destructive path.

In his rage, holding the magneto, Bill devised a plan to use this basic magnetic generator to create an electric shock sufficient to penetrate Old Jo's thick equine skull. The idea was to rig up a circuit that linked the car to the magneto. When the horse rocked the car, it would trigger a flywheel that Bill had wound up with a rubber band like a model aircraft. The unwinding flywheel would drive the magneto, which in turn would deliver a healthy shock. No one witnessed Old Jo getting his comeuppance, but the flywheel was found unwound and the horse was never again seen near the car. So Bill Gallagher was familiar with the principle of using electric shocks to manage stock.

The question at Speedy Road in 1937 was how to produce an electric fence so Bill could subdivide his property on the cheap. He started out by linking the farm's mains power supply to an old battery B eliminator, which fed 300 volts at a continuous current of 300 milliamps through a mile of circuit. This was dangerous, however, so he then figured out how to make a pulse, using a Y-shaped circuit breaker that flopped back and forth like a piece of clockwork. A short pulse of electricity is safer than a continuous current.

Pleased with his invention, in 1938 Bill filed a patent for his device to create the pulse. This was granted in February 1939.[13] Gallagher's energiser worked reasonably well, especially in the wetter months, when plenty of moisture aided conduction of electricity, but it suffered from the problem of being illegal. A concerned neighbour reported Bill to the authorities, who instructed him to disconnect his device.

Bill Gallagher then turned his mind to a battery-driven device, using an old Ford ignition coil. But because this had high internal resistance, it suffered from a lack of power; the moment any load was put on the fence, such as by a blade of grass, the voltage would drop away to nothing. In Gallagher's vernacular, it had 'no guts'.[14] After some experimentation he found that if he wound heavier wire in the coil, he could produce a greater current. Some time in 1939 he tried selling some of these little units to neighbours. He moved half a dozen of them in short order, 'on a month's trial', and most of his customers eventually paid for them.

His timing was impeccable. The idea of electric fences was still new to New Zealand. In the normal course of events, units might have been imported relatively cheaply from the US, making it difficult for local farmyard tinkerers to compete, something that had been starting to happen in late 1938. In November that year a Palmerston North firm, Abraham & Williams Ltd, was advertising itself as agent for the Prima electric fence, built in the US, and taking the fences to agricultural shows.[15]

Politics intervened, however. The First Labour Government

ran for a second term in office in the general election of November 1938, vowing to introduce 'cradle-to-grave' social security. The voters loved it and returned Labour to power. Many among the business community and the wealthy, however, were horrified at this bounding socialism and the certainty of significant tax rises. There was substantial capital flight in late November and early December, as many with the ability to do so took their money out of the country. Rather than retreat, on 6 December Finance Minister Walter Nash imposed absolute exchange controls and strict import licensing.[16] Competition from imports was thenceforth very limited, if not non-existent. A year later, the commencement of the Second World War cut off shipping for all but essentials, further insulating the economy.

The result was a massive stimulus to local manufacturing of all types and industries. And since electric fences were new technology there was nothing to stop clever bush-engineers throughout the country having a go. While Gallagher was perfecting his working model, Herb Christie, an engineer from Levin, was developing an electric fence that later became the Speedrite brand, alongside several others, no doubt.

Bill Gallagher may not have taken his fences much further, however, if another crisis at home had not prompted a rethink. Millie contracted polio shortly after the couple's second child, John, was born in February 1939. She recovered, but was left with her right arm effectively paralysed. With a two-year-old daughter, May, to cope with already, the new baby proved too great a burden. Within a year John was sent down to Te Puke to stay with Millie's parents, where he would remain for five years. Meanwhile, Millie was greatly limited in her ability to help around the farm.

Gallagher might have pressed on with his farming in these difficult circumstances if he had loved the work, but he didn't. He hated it, later telling his younger son, Bill junior, that being a dairy farmer 'was the last job the good Lord had made; come hell or high water the cows were still waiting at the end of the day and they had to be milked'. Boredom and dissatisfaction compelled him to try something new.

Some time around February or March 1940, Bill Gallagher made a life-changing decision to give up farming. He sold the Speedy Road farm (settling in April) and moved into Hamilton. Renting a building on the corner of Bridge and Grey streets, Hamilton East, he hoped to make a living by building his electric fences and a handful of other products requiring light engineering skills.

Gas producers were one product with a ready market, since severe wartime petrol restrictions were forcing people to improvise to keep their cars on the road. A burner was bracketed onto the side of the car, which burnt charcoal to cook coal, which in turn produced coal gas. It was a relatively simple task to convert car engines to run on the gas. Gallagher bought an old lathe, taught himself how to weld, and got to work making these gas producers. Soon he had a friend, Bill O'Brien, helping him, and for a time his younger brother Vivian (Viv). Gallagher must have been one of the earlier people to start making these devices; the government only caught up with the trade and started licensing manufacturers in September 1940.[17]

The work was more to his taste than milking cows, but the volume wasn't sufficient to generate much of a living. Indeed, the next few years would be unsettled ones for the Gallaghers. War, obviously, was omnipresent. Both Bill's brothers joined up: Henry went into the Royal Australian Air Force as an aircraft engineer, and Vivian joined the New Zealand Air Force and became a pilot. With two children and a disabled wife, who after April 1940 was pregnant with their third child, Bill Gallagher decided against volunteering for active service but made himself available for work on the home front if required.

While he was still trying to make a go of his little Hamilton business, Bill drove his father down to Wellington to visit the Centennial Exhibition, which ran from November 1939 to May 1940. The gas producer on Bill's Ford V8 caught the eye of LF Wallace, the owner of Wallace's Service Station in Wellington. The Ford's performance, using Gallagher's producer, so impressed the Wellingtonian that he drove to Hamilton a short time afterwards to persuade Gallagher and O'Brien to come down to make the contraptions for his customers in the capital. The offer was £6 per week — around $500 in 2012 terms — plus half the profits from their manufacturing venture.

With prospects not particularly good in Hamilton, Gallagher

GALLAGHER ELECTRIC FENCER

This "Gallagher" Electric Fencer is the outcome of two years practical farm experience during wet and dry weather on several Waikato farms. The main place for experiment being the farm of the inventor.

How it operates

It is designed to work hanging on a wall or post in a covered place such as a shed or a weather-proof case. The operating power is drawn from a six volt battery, current being used only when the contact points are pressed together by the roller on the swinging arm.

To operate the machine just clip the two battery clips to the battery, the earth clip to a piece of pipe or some metal driven well into the earth, then connect the insulated fence to be charged to the terminal marked FENCE connection on the machine, and start the machine. Providing the fence is well insulated and not touching earth anywhere the light will flash indicating that the fence wire is charged and that anything standing on earth and touching the fence will get a shock.

Materials in manufacture

Contact points in this machine are high grade tungsten and were made for use in a very reliable English magneto. The cushion spring arm which the roller pushes up to connect the contact points is made from the finest and best clock spring obtainable and is softened to the extent where it will not bend out of shape in operation and so will give years of service. The roller is made of red fibre and this material needs no recommendation. The tripper arm which carries the roller is made of steel and hardened to a degree where it is hard and yet tough enough not to be brittle and runs on a hardened pin. Where it works on the pin it is made with two pockets which are packed with felt to hold oil for long periods. The main arm is pivotted on hardened silver steel pivots and bearings which are adjustable and the bearings are drilled on the other ends and packed with felt to retain oil.

Made by

A. W. GALLAGHER
ROTOTUNA - HAMILTON

N.Z. Patent applied for No. 81476.

ABOVE Bill Gallagher's original selling proposition, 1938.

ABOVE The second edition of Gallagher's selling pamphlet was produced in 1939, with a stamp changing his address the following year.

took his lathe and some other machinery, together with his family and O'Brien, down to Wellington to try his luck with Wallace. Over the course of 10 months he learned a lesson in the perils of loose partnerships. Wallace's accounts were murky, with the profits from the gas producers and occasional electric fences not separated out. Gallagher thought he was being exploited, something he wouldn't stand for. 'Old LF had his hands on the books,' he later groaned.[18] When confronted, Wallace produced the agreement they had signed when Gallagher had come to Wellington, which stated that if Gallagher left he would forfeit the lathe and other gear he had brought down from Hamilton. He'd been hornswoggled. After consulting a lawyer, the 31-year-old Gallagher decided the best tactic was simply to take the gear one Saturday when a friendly worker was in charge. He got away with the heist.

He and O'Brien then set up their own little business in Wellington's Tory Street, installing gas producers and doing other odd jobs, but by mid-1942 they had to admit failure. Bringing Millie, daughter May and the infant Bill junior back to Hamilton, Gallagher set up once more with a little business making gas producers on Seddon Road. Again the business failed. Bill senior later claimed that he had made the mistake of 'employing raw hands', who made too many mistakes.

His salvation came toward the end of 1942 when he was manpowered by the government to work for the Colonial Ammunitions Company (CAC). This was the only pre-war munitions factory in New Zealand, having specialised in .303 cartridges. Its operations had been shifted from Auckland to several buildings scattered around Hamilton, in the interests of security. Gallagher worked in a big plant on Dey Street and tried not to worry when 'Tokyo Rose', the Japanese radio propagandist, said something along the lines of 'we know you've moved the CAC from Auckland to Hamilton, but we're going to move it off the face of the earth'. CAC was a cost-plus enterprise: its owners simply charged the government an agreed profit margin over what they said it cost to make the munitions. For Gallagher, the wages were good. Better still, he learned welding and fitting from experts.

Feeling able to settle down, he had bought a simple house at 63 Seddon Road for £950, equivalent to about $75,000 in today's terms.[19] It was on the edge of an industrial section of town, barely a

ABOVE Delivering an improvised tractor to another happy customer, c. 1942. Note the gas producer on the car, which was Gallagher's most successful product during the war years.

kilometre west of the town centre. In the evenings Bill continued to work on gas producers and the odd electric fence in the garage. Then, in 1944, the government controller shifted him to the Machinery Exchange, a farm machinery repair business in Anglesea Street, only a few hundred metres from home. This provided further good experience, and while he did his duty Gallagher had plenty of time to plan his postwar business moves.

He had a stroke of luck that year when the Seventh Day Adventists offered him a three-quarter acre section over the back fence from his home. This property ran through to Norton Road, a busy light-industrial thoroughfare. They wanted £140 for the block (barely $10,000 in today's terms), which once had had a sawmill on it but was now covered in blackberry bushes and rubbish. This cheap land would provide the site for his next business venture, and this time he would make a success of it.

Gallagher was eventually released from his wartime duties in mid-1945. By then he had worked in his spare time with his aged and now retired father to build a dirt-floor, concrete-walled workshop, 9 x 12 metres, on his new section. It was cheap and cheerful, and his business overheads would be very light. Now everything came together for him. He had polished his light-engineering skills, he had found a handful of capable workers who had been his colleagues during wartime service, he had learned from his earlier business mistakes, and at the conclusion of the war the market was hungry for his goods.

At first, with petrol still in short supply, there was strong demand for his gas producers. 'I just couldn't make enough of them,' he said later.[20] But he also made a few electric fences and some of his improvised tractors, using old cars. He had found a way to make the gearbox more robust. The first flush of serious success, however, came in 1948 when Gallagher started making spinning topdressers. These had a cast-iron base and gearbox, then sheet-metal funnels 1 metre high, and were mounted on the back of a trailer or truck tray. He had been repairing the most popular model then on the market with monotonous regularity, and concluded that he could do the country a favour by designing a more reliable one. His brothers, Viv and Henry, had returned to Hamilton in 1945 and

BELOW Bill Gallagher's first attempt at a display stand at the Winter Show in 1949 was fairly rudimentary.

TOP Mass production of Gallagher's spinning topdressers at Norton Road, c. 1949.

ABOVE The Gallagher topdresser used a sprocket on one of the trailer's wheels to drive the spinner. The early electric fencer sits on the trailer to the left.

1947, respectively, and were now working alongside him.[21] Together they made a fresh design for the topdresser, with a robust feeding mechanism at the bottom. They went so far as to patent the design.[22]

Gallagher employed a former CAC colleague, John Major, to develop and run a simple assembly line for the topdresser, which passed through five pairs of hands as it moved along the line. The machine quickly found favour with Waikato farmers, who were pouring back onto the land after the war and enjoying good prices for their produce. Having started at a rate of four topdressers a month, the business was eventually turning out 50 a month. During the off-season months, from April to July, when demand for the topdressers fell off, they concentrated on making electric fences.

For a while it was a very relaxed family operation. Viv had an English wife, Molly, who arrived a year after he had returned from the war, and was somewhat shocked to find herself sitting in the so-called office, with mud under her feet and invoices mixed up amongst the machinery.[23] Viv built a house, a wooden structure really, behind the workshop. Chickens wandered around. If they wandered too close to the machinery one of the workers would repel them with a 'swift blast of Gallagher orange', the primer paint that would become the signature colour for the company.[24] The brothers and the men would amuse themselves during slack months of the year playing practical jokes, which invariably involved some sort of electric shock.

It was a strange time in which to be successful. Most of Gallagher's records for this period have been lost, but scattered papers include Bill's 1951 tax return which shows he declared an income of £5496 (around $300,000 in 2012 terms, measured against the Consumers Price Index). He was operating as a sole trader, not having formed a company. But out of this income he paid £2250 tax. There were a lot of exemptions in the tax code at the time, which had lowered his average tax rate to 41 per cent. However, for every pound that he had earned over £3700 in 1951 he paid income and social security taxes at a rate of 73.5 per cent.[25] The tax rate had been even worse in 1950 and the previous few years. There wasn't much incentive to expand the business when the government left a man with only a quarter of each additional pound in profit.

Humans naturally respond to such powerful incentives. Gallagher could have avoided a lot of tax by setting up a company and cleverly using trusts, but that road didn't seem to interest him. In fact, he didn't get around to forming a company until 1963, after his sons had joined the business. In the short term, his response was to pay his key staff generous bonuses. Norm Gera, the man in charge of the electric fences, recalled receiving a bonus of £400 one year, the equivalent of around $25,000 in today's terms. The logic was simple. If Gallagher tried to keep the £400 for himself, he lost around £300 of it to the government. Gera, with a much smaller income, which attracted much lower rates, would have kept most of it.

This approach appears to have annoyed Gallagher's brothers. Perhaps he wasn't as generous to them with his bonuses. In late 1950 they argued that Bill should have been ploughing his profits back into plant and machinery in order to reduce his tax bill, rather than giving it away. They could have been right, but Bill resented the advice. It was his business and he would do as he saw fit. The argument crystallised things for the brothers and led them to go their separate ways.

In truth, the three brothers were too similar in their personalities to work together for too long — all three were strong, independent-minded and entrepreneurial. Henry and Viv went on to establish Galco Products in Lincoln Street, which made electric fences and other farm machinery. They soon parted, however, and Viv established Vogal Engineering at 21 Norton Road, which took the electric fencing side, as well as making drain-diggers, slashers and his own tractor-mounted topdresser.[26] After a short period of hurt feelings the three brothers settled down to good working relationships, avoiding direct competition with each other. Viv and Molly continued to live in the family compound at 22A Norton Road.

The flaw in Henry and Viv's suggestion to plough profits back into the business, in order to grow it, was that in New Zealand around 1950 there was very little point in growing your company. With taxes above 70 per cent, it was almost irrational to take on the extra stress of building a larger organisation. It provides an answer to the question posed by an American visitor in the 1950s who was bewildered by New Zealand, attitudes to work: 'Why,' David Ausubel asked, 'do New Zealanders, by American standards, display so little ambition, enterprise and initiative in pursuing a livelihood while exhibiting almost unbelievable energy, enthusiasm

BELOW *Seddon Park* takes shape on the front lawn at Seddon Road, Hamilton, 1949.

ABOVE Hamiltonians gathered to witness the launching of Bill Gallagher's *Seddon Park* into the Waikato River, 15 December 1951.

and resourcefulness in such pursuits as sport, gardening and "do it yourself" projects?'[27] The tax regime reflected the prevailing 'Jack's as good as his master' egalitarianism that was a reaction to the hierarchies of Britain, of which, no doubt, there were many reminders during the war. Eddie Leaf, who joined Gallagher in 1950 to work on the lathe, captured the sentiment of his workmates when he paid Bill Gallagher the highest accolade of the time, describing him as 'totally unassuming, truly modest, no skite, a good Kiwi'.[28]

Gallagher exemplified the Kiwi culture that Ausubel found so strange. Just as his business was taking off, he threw himself into a much more important project: building a boat. Earlier, in 1946, he had constructed a 5 metre trailer boat. Fashioned from 16-gauge steel, *Taboo* was 'heavy as hell', ugly and slow. But it served a useful purpose on some early family camping trips to Raglan, Tauranga and Whangamata. In 1949 Gallagher was inspired to do something better when he and a camping friend saw an impressive launch at Whangamata. 'Well, Bill,' his friend sighed, 'you and I will never own a boat like that.'[29] That fellow may have had no prospects, but Gallagher clearly felt he could foot it with anyone. Jokingly he told friends that he would design and build his own launch simply by blowing up a toy boat to size, but quietly he also investigated the designs of overseas steel-hulled pleasure craft.

Having come up with a design that met Marine Department approval standards for a 50 foot heavy displacement hull, he laid the keel on 29 October 1949. Over the next two years a great steel beast, not much smaller than Gallagher's home, took shape on his front lawn. Gallagher did much of the welding himself, engaging friends and staff to help him on the weekend. He found two Gardner 5LW five-cylinder, 60 hp diesel engines for £130 apiece, formerly from London buses. Eventually they would propel the 24 ton boat to a top speed of eight knots.

In December 1951 Gallagher's 'floating bach' was ready to launch. This must have been the most exciting thing that had happened in Hamilton since the New Zealand Wars, because large crowds gathered beside the route along which he hauled the great boat towards the Waikato River. A *Waikato Times* reporter captured the moment:

> Hydraulic brakes, operated from the launch, and a
> rope from the bows and around a tree held the boat

as she was prepared for her final plunge. After a cup of tea for all hands, the last of the fittings . . . were removed, the hydraulic brakes on the trailer were eased off and the rope released. The vivid orange boat slid stern first into the water. Soon the whirring of a starter motor was heard from the engine room . . . and a diesel motor burst into life. Several perfect smoke rings shot from the funnel.[30]

After a week of on-water preparations, the *Seddon Park*, named after the local cricket ground, set off on her maiden voyage downriver to the Tasman Sea on 24 December. Forty-seven passengers crammed the decks as far as Mercer, then Gallagher and three other brave souls — his brother Henry and two Gallagher employees, Charlie Beckett and Horace Hough — carried on toward the heads. Sensibly they used a pilot to take them down the river, but at the mouth it was 'blowing like blazes'.

They had to wait four days before it was safe to go over the bar. Having made it out, Gallagher wrote in the log: 'Anchored about 2 miles out, sea rough as hell, all sea sick (awful), ship behaves very well in the rough'. The next morning they discovered it took one and a half hours to wind in the anchor by hand winch. It then took four and a half hours to sail through rough seas the 50 kilometres to their destination, Raglan Harbour. No doubt with his heart in his mouth, Gallagher skippered his new boat past Raglan's rough bar into the calm of the harbour 'to a great reception' from friends and family.

Bill Gallagher senior was 40. After years of frenetic activity with mixed results, he had settled on a modestly successful business formula and, like most of his countrymen, was living for the weekends.

ABOVE The Gallagher energiser, mid-1950s.

2

YOUNG BILL GALLAGHER: 1941–62

Chapter two

YOUNG BILL GALLAGHER: 1941–62

Watching the *Seddon Park* slip into the Waikato's swift current in December 1951 was 10-year-old Bill Gallagher junior. His family was led by a man with prodigious energy and zeal, and the young boy had good reason to feel confident about life. 'It was an exciting time,' he remembers. 'No one else in town had anything like the *Seddon Park*. From our front lawn, as Dad built it, it looked like the bow overhung the footpath. The main rugby ground wasn't far away, so you'd have huge crowds walking past this massive boat on a Saturday afternoon and everyone was talking about it. My job, with my brother John, was to chip slag off the welds. Dad was obsessed with it, though at the time I thought it was pretty natural.

'I remember him putting down the $3/16$ inch thick plate for the front deck on 28 October 1950, then ducking off to see Mum in hospital where my younger sister Olive had been born, before rushing back to weld it into place. Taking it to the launch spot, he'd thought everything through; he'd built the trailer with its great axle and hydraulic brakes; he'd planned his route, past the Post Office, through the centre of town. It was brilliant.'

The family compound at Seddon Road provided a wonderful, secure environment for Bill and his older brother John, who had rejoined the family in 1945 after a spell with his grandparents to lighten the burden for his mother. Their Uncle Viv lived down the back and, according to Bill senior, 'could talk the leg off an iron pot'. He warned his sons never to visit Viv at 3pm, 'since you'd write off the afternoon'. But a 5pm visit was always enjoyable. Uncle Henry, who lived a mile away on Killarney Road, was more like Bill senior in that he was quieter and more considered in his comments.

Since their father worked all hours of the day and evening in the workshop or on his boat, the boys were often left to do their own thing. They were drawn to the great blackberry bush that spread its tentacles over most of the section. Long planks of timber lay around, over which people walked to cross the hazard. In season, they'd eat the blackberries. If the boys were lucky they would chance across the nest of one of their father's chickens that had escaped into the bush. That would be a 'bonza' find for a young boy, since he might get a dozen eggs in one hit, for which his father would pay good money.

To amuse themselves the boys dug underground huts in remote parts of the blackberry; then they dug one across the road amid a prolific grove of gorse bushes. Carefully concealing their hole with boards, they would slide in with candles to do whatever boys did in dark holes — such as smoking cane, which was 'bitter and horrible, but strangely enjoyable'. Fortunately they never set the dry gorse on fire. Less sensible perhaps was the hut they built under the house, by the chimney, once more lit by candles. When Bill told his Aunt Molly, his confidante on such things, about their hideaway she encouraged them to desist.

The boys seldom came unstuck, but they did so on one of their earlier entrepreneurial ventures. Good money was to be made by returning empty soft-drink bottles to the shop — threepence for an empty. Bill noticed a great stash of empties under the Frankton Town Hall and became expert at regularly extracting bottles to sell at the local shop, always keeping the volume sufficiently small to avoid suspicion. But eventually they were sprung and reported to the police. Bill suffered the humiliation of being doubled on the policeman's bicycle (sitting on the crossbar) down to the station. The brothers had to fill out some forms and pay restitution of four shillings and sixpence (equivalent to a few weeks' pocket money) before going home to receive 'a good hiding' from their father. Their sister May remembers being told of Bill, 'He's a good leader, but of the bad boys.'[1]

Aunt Molly also wondered if her nephews were going to come to a bad end, but she soon saw that the bottle episode, and their father's uncompromising response, was a formative experience for them as they learned right from wrong.[2] Coming from England, it had been a shock for her to see the boys always running around in bare feet, regardless of their mother's pleas, when for her bare feet had always been a sign of desperate poverty. John she found reserved, but Bill clearly had a strong personality: 'He was always running everywhere, never walked when he could run. Red-faced, with large round glasses, shirt always hanging out and bare feet. He was open and friendly, and incredibly cheeky. We had ducks, and I remember one time one of our ducks laid an egg over on the Gallaghers' property. Bill's little face appeared over the fence. "I've got your egg," he said, "but the law says if it's on our property we're legally entitled to keep it." As an eight- or nine-year-old he'd spend hours talking to my husband, always about machinery. Viv said, "That boy's got potential." You could just see the burning ambition in him, and I'd wonder to myself where on earth it had come from.'[3]

From their home the boys would set off for Whitiora School. Their shoes would be stowed in the letter box, hidden from their mother, and they'd cross Hinemoa Park, with frost cracking between their toes in the winter, before negotiating their way along a couple of blocks to reach the school on Willoughby Street. Often they would encounter an old lady, whom they nicknamed 'Coffee and Bun' because every day she would walk down to the railway station to wait for her son to come back from the war; she'd have her coffee and bun and return home sadly along the same route.

At school Bill didn't do much to exert himself. He'd had a slow start, having been sick for a while. Nobody is quite sure what the problem was; not polio, but some sort of paralysis that led to an extended period in hospital. This put his reading and spelling well back and left him a year behind his age group. Since his eyesight wasn't good, he couldn't see the blackboard until he was given glasses. Then these were constantly being broken. Once those problems were sorted out he still didn't have any inclination to work. As a result he failed Standard Two and had to repeat it. His teacher that year was Alan 'Ponty' Reid, who also happened to be the Waikato and All Black halfback, although Gallagher in no way blames him for his failure. Between 1951 and 1953 Waikato twice held the Ranfurly Shield, the pinnacle of New Zealand provincial rugby. Bill and John Gallagher, meantime, made some good money selling tin 'Mooloo' badges to supporters walking past their house on their way to the matches.

Bill Gallagher started his final year at primary school in 1953, aged 12, two years older than many of his classmates. This had the upside of lending him extra weight and strength in the ceaseless schoolyard fights of the era. Like most boys he lived for the weekends, many of which were spent at Raglan after the *Seddon Park* was moored there at the end of 1951. Since Millie didn't much care for the boat — the constant rolling wasn't easy to handle with only one functioning arm, and she couldn't swim — Bill senior rented baches for a while before buying a steep but cheap section on Rose Street, overlooking the harbour. He and a friend played around with a bulldozer to make the section less steep, then he built a rough home. Restrictions on building materials were still in place following the war, which meant the house was one bedroom short.

The boys learnt to swim in Raglan Harbour, the freedom of the era allowing them to take chances and learn at their own pace. John Gallagher remembers an old tyre next to the wharf which they'd throw into the water then try to retrieve before they ran out of breath.[4] The brothers used an old tin boat with a sail made from sacks to chase stingrays across the harbour. But the primary purpose of their visits was to take the big boat over the bar on fishing expeditions. And the fish were plentiful. The ship's log notes that on 10 February 1952, for instance, 280 fish were caught. But John Gallagher is sure that the record for one day was 700, with 20 fishermen on board. Their father paid twopence a fish, so the boys worked quite hard. The surplus would be sold at the wharf or to a local fish and chip shop. Almost as much time was spent maintaining the vessel as was spent at sea. The boys watched, and sometimes helped, as their father regularly overhauled the engine, scraped back the hull and carried out other tedious tasks.

The payoff came soon enough, however. After a little more than a year teaching himself basic seamanship around Raglan, and surviving a few 'memorable experiences' on the bar, Bill Gallagher

RIGHT Bill Gallagher junior's first brush with publicity, December 1953.

STOOD ON BROKEN BOTTLE

Boy in Hospital

(O.C.) HAMILTON, Sunday

When he stood on a broken beer bottle at Mt Maunganui on Thursday evening, William Gallagher, aged 12, of Seddon Road, Hamilton, severed the Achilles tendon at the back of his heel. He was admitted to the Tauranga Hospital.

The bottle was lying about 100 yards north of Salisbury Wharf, on a sloping bank between the road and the beach.

The lad's father, Mr A. W. Gallagher, said his son was expected to be in hospital about three weeks. For some time afterwards he would only be able to hobble.

"People do not appreciate how great a menace broken bottles are," he added. "If parents learn what happened to my boy it may help to protect other children."

Mr Gallagher said he would like to see the Courts punish people who break bottles and leave the fragments lying about. When this was referred to the Hamilton police, they said that under the powers given them by the Police Offence Act they would prosecute anyone detected leaving glass in a public place.

William Gallagher

set off in March 1952 with his young family and a couple of other crewmates on their first real voyage, south to New Plymouth. Two things stood out for young Bill on that journey. At New Plymouth his father took on 1000 gallons of diesel at a cost of £87 10s, equivalent to around $4500 today. Since there was a refinery there, fuel was cheaper than elsewhere, and quite sweet-smelling. The second thing that struck Bill was at the wharf, where they saw a diver working on the piles. He had a copper hard-hat, rubber suit and a pipe pumping air down from the surface. Both Bill and John were fascinated.

It was a while before they attempted another lengthy journey. A year later, in March 1953, according to the log they 'caught a big roller' going out, just past the bar. Bill had taken all the usual precautions, waiting for high tide, then gunning it once the big waves had passed, but was caught out by an extra big one straggling behind the set. Suddenly they found a huge wall of water coming at them, which smashed three of the four front windows and left several of those on board, including John Gallagher and Horace Hough, with cuts. Generally, going out was the easy part; coming in was hairy because the boat was so slow that the sea easily outran it, raising the danger of the craft broaching (turning sideways and rolling).

In December 1953, however, Gallagher mustered the courage to set off with the family around North Cape and down the east coast to Mt Maunganui. He had taught himself, from books, how to swing a compass to discover the deviation from true magnetic north caused by the steel of the boat, and figured he could navigate safely. Young Bill missed the return trip after finding himself laid up in Tauranga Hospital for three weeks. He had stood on a broken bottle on the beach and severed his Achilles tendon, but at least this afforded him his first piece of publicity, since the local newspaper found the incident newsworthy.

The following summer they were even more adventurous, sailing south from Raglan to spend January 1955 in the Marlborough Sounds. Their stop-off in Wellington was sufficiently novel to warrant a good-sized picture in the *Dominion* and the story 'Bound for Sunny Nelson and the Sounds'.[5] 'Launch becomes floating home for large family', the newspaper gushed. Of the five Gallagher children on board, Edna, aged two, was the youngest, followed by four-year-old Olive. Sensibly, perhaps, Millie and the girls had flown to Wellington,

E
N
R
ave
ted
s to
last

es
pt

nu-
es-
at-
ing
iki,
iti,
the
ep in
duled
Mr. 1.
go is
previ-
other,
break
ad of
n the
le in
the
tions
ever,
le in
f the
W.
loped
ndon
three
Tai-

BOUND FOR SUNNY NELSON AND THE SOUNDS

THE SKIPPER AND "CREW" of the diesel launch Seddon Park at Queen's Wharf, Wellington, yesterday. All from Hamilton, they hope to cross Cook Strait today for a fortnight's fishing, cruising, and "general lazing round." The three girls are, from left, Gwen Reynard, Glynne Darlington, and May Gallagher. Others, from left, Mr. H. Hough, Mrs. A. W. Gallagher, Mr. A. W. Gallagher (skipper), Billy Gallagher, Don Gallagher, Mr. A. J. Gallagher, and, in front, Edna and Olive Gallagher.

SEARCH FOR VARIETIES OF STONE FRUIT

Fruit research workers are seeking new varieties of stone fruit in New Zealand. The search may end in someone's backyard.

Most varieties of deciduous fruits do not "come true" from seed. The seedlings differ in some characters from their parents and differ from one another. Sometimes a seedling is superior to the parents and may be introduced as a new variety. Many of the older peach, apricot, plum and cherry varieties originated by chance in this way.

Launch Becomes Floating Home For Large Family

A launch that looks like a "home" has attracted attention at Queen's Wharf, Wellington, over the last few days. She is the 30-ton Seddon Park, built by her owner, Mr. A. W. Gallagher, on the front lawn of his home in Hamilton. This undertaking took three years.

The Seddon Park is 50 feet long, 14 feet wide, has a welded steel hull

England And

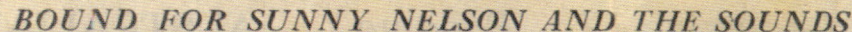

ABOVE The *Dominion* reports on the Gallagher family's travels, January 1955.

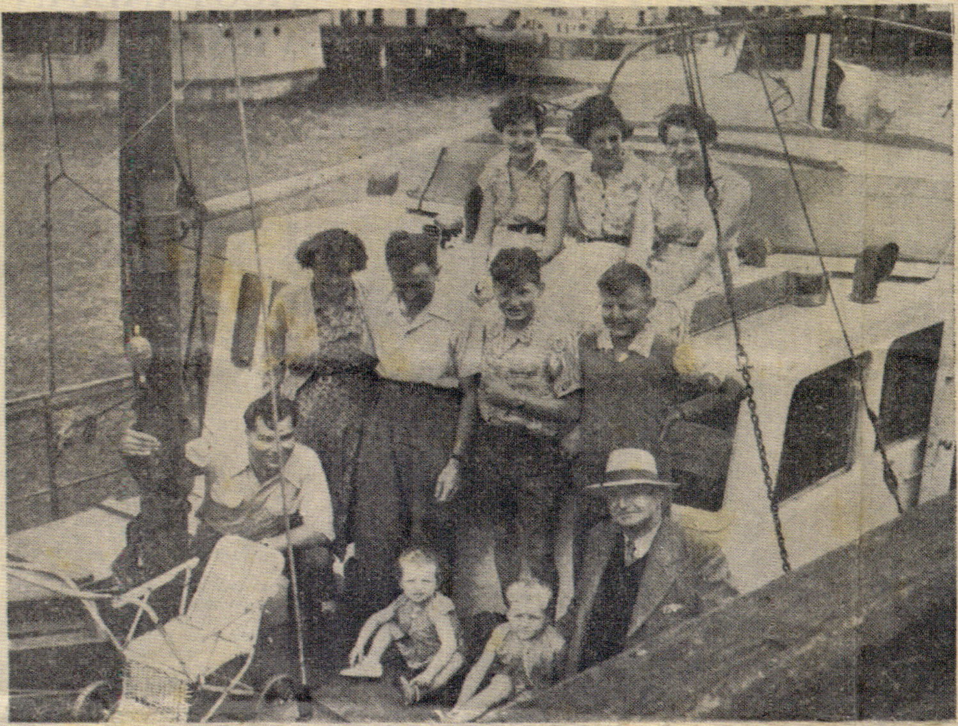

limiting their exposure on board to the Cook Strait crossing.

Safely across the strait, Gallagher took the boat up the Wairau River to Blenheim, where crowds of onlookers peered at what he called his 'floating bach'. He didn't court publicity, he was just doing what he wanted to be doing, but he was happy to talk to local newspapers when they came around. Young Bill was most fascinated by the immense bone yards around the Wairau bar: 'I found it an amazing scene, like a cattle slaughter-yard, with all these enormous bones laying around. Moa bones included. Locals told us the story of how the ancient Maori would drive the big birds down on to the bar and slaughter them there. I also loved collecting eggs and there were endless supplies there of seagull and tern eggs, with the nests of gulls among the terns, which I found strange given that the seagulls are predators of the terns. With my little box Brownie I took hundreds of photos.'

After that voyage the *Seddon Park* was moored in Auckland, on the Tamaki river near Panmure. Gallagher thought the Hauraki Gulf would be better for sailing than Raglan, with its tricky bar and the boring coastline thereabouts.

By the time young Bill Gallagher arrived at Maeroa Intermediate School in February 1954 he had a full swag of adventurous stories to tell. After two uneventful years at Maeroa, in 1956 he carried on to Hamilton Technical High School (now Fraser High), a large school then on the edge of Hamilton's CBD, a short distance from the Gallaghers' home. Bill was 15 years old (as opposed to the usual 13), but to his surprise he was put in the top class, 'Engineering 3A'. To his greater surprise he came second in the class in its first set of exams.

This encounter with academic success transformed his outlook. Education had not featured prominently in the family's history to that point. Bill senior had been obliged by family circumstances to leave school at the age of 12. Viv, who everyone regarded as a natural scholar, had cut short his schooling, aged 14, to help his father break in a farm. None of Bill senior's generation had attended university. Bill junior's older sister May educated herself in a different way by leaving home in 1956, aged 19, to spend three years in Europe. John had left Hamilton Tech as soon as he could, aged 15, to begin an apprenticeship as a fitter and turner with the engineering firm Mullan & Noy Ltd.[6]

Now, suddenly, young Bill Gallagher discovered the joys of academic learning. It was the competitive instinct more than anything that kept him engaged. Looking back, he remembers that he relaxed a bit in the second half of the third form and, to his annoyance, came fourth. The following year he knuckled down in the first half of the year and came top, only to relax again. When he reached School Certificate at the end of the fifth form, he did well in all his subjects except English, which he barely passed. The following year he gave that attention and topped his year for English. 'I learnt a work ethic at secondary school,' he says. 'I gained such great gratification in coming second in class that I wanted more of it, and since we had a group of six or so of us in the top class, all vying like hell to come out on top, I became pretty competitive.'

By the time Bill reached the upper sixth, the final year of secondary school, it was 1960 and he was 19. He was deputy head prefect for the first half of the year, then head prefect after Brian Henderson left halfway through the year. He had developed a good relationship with the principal, Les Day — nicknamed Akki Day by the boys — a notoriously enthusiastic proponent of corporal punishment. Gallagher thinks he gained Day's respect after a vigorous argument over a science exam result. Gallagher had been given 96 out of 100 and wanted to know why. He had been marked down for a defective definition of relative velocity. The boy fought tooth and nail, arguing that his definition was perfectly adequate, and gained his victory after mediation with Les Day.

All in all, Hamilton Tech was a comfortable, amenable environment out of which the young man had no particular desire to extract himself. He had gained his University Entrance by the end of the sixth form, and the following year was preparing for university. He says his mother supported his staying on for that final year; by implication, his father was a bit sceptical.

Meantime, much of Gallagher's learning continued to take place back at Seddon Road and on the water. At home the family role models remained hard-working men of initiative and independence, who made their living by employing other men and giving customers what they wanted. For Bill Gallagher senior there was little separation between work and home life. Through the 1950s he didn't grow the business particularly, keeping it steady at around eight employees, but it was sufficient to maintain a successful little unit. He was a quiet man, but there was no question who was boss. The story is told of one worker, Dick Kemp, arguing with Gallagher about how something should be done. Eventually Gallagher asked, 'Are you working for me or for yourself?' 'For you,' was the sheepish reply. 'In that case, you'll do it this way!'

But both Gallagher and his workers took fierce pride in their work. The story of the bull was frequently related; how Horace Hough had been told by a farmer that his bull had no fear of electric fences until he encountered the Gallagher electric fence, which after 1952 packed a bit more punch than many of its rivals. 'The bull slightly touched it with his hindquarter, looked a little bemused, then very gingerly touched the wire with his tongue, did a somersault which landed him on his back, after which he refused to move from the centre of the paddock for some time.'

Casting his eyes a bit further, young Bill would see his uncles also living on their wits as independent businessmen. Viv was more ambitious than Bill senior, and by the late 1950s had grown Vogal Engineering to the point where he was employing around 15 staff. His topdresser was connected to the three-point linkage of the tractor, driven by its PTO (power take-off). Over time it outsold Bill's trailer-mounted topdresser, which used a sprocket on one of the trailer's wheels to drive the spinner. The Vogal Electric Fence, with a blue box as against Gallagher's orange, also sold pretty well. Eventually, Bill lost the battle for the topdressers — the market moved to the tractor PTO model — but he never gave way on the electric fences.

To keep his business ticking along, Bill Gallagher migrated increasingly to general metal work, such as gates and cattle stops, with a speciality in hay barns. The barns particularly were big-ticket items that sold in the mid-1950s in a range between £400 and £1100 (around $18,000–$50,000 in 2012 terms). Meanwhile, Uncle Henry's Galco Engineering continued to prosper, making calf bails, rotary clotheslines, custom balustrading for houses, and many other such products.

Old Alfred Gallagher, Bill senior's father, visited the Seddon Park compound regularly. After Sarah's death he remarried and lived in Tauranga. His new wife, Mary (Dot) Clark, was the aunt of Tom Clark, a thrusting Auckland businessman who was growing the family brick and pipe business and its crockery offshoot, Crown Lynn.

With business being the most natural thing in the world in the extended Gallagher clan, it wasn't long before young Bill and his brother John were looking for their own way into the action. After their brush with the law over the stolen bottles, they had sought out more conventional methods, such as paper runs. And their father provided a variety of jobs. Bill spent many holidays sitting in a hammock cutting wires into strips of a particular length for electric fence units. He was paid threepence for 100 strips. 'It was a perfect education,' he recalls, 'since I learnt some basics by trial and error. To keep the lengths consistent I needed to have a sample one, otherwise the length would creep over time.'

But the young brothers' first serious money-spinner, and indeed their entrance into business on their own account, grew out of their new hobby, scuba diving. Its origins went back to 1954, when their sister May had a boyfriend, Gary Williams, who lived at Cooks Beach, on the Coromandel Peninsula. On weekend visits the brothers would go snorkelling with gloves, masks and flippers, looking for crayfish, even in wintertime. Before diving they would light a large bonfire of driftwood on the beach to warm themselves when they got out. It was good fun mostly, although less so for John one time when, running back to the fire after the dive, he found a pile of ashes and the bones of a watch to one side. It was all that was left of his clothes.

After a year or so of skin-diving the brothers were ready to take the next step. Scuba gear was just becoming available, and so in January 1956 the boys saved up and ordered an Atlas Aqualung through Cannes, a Hamilton sports store. It had been made in Auckland, by Auckland Automotive Engineers. They took it for its first outing at Te Kaha, on a family camping trip around East Cape. Over the next few days both Bill and John taught themselves how to use it and managed to catch a few crayfish. Immediately they were hooked on the new sport and thereafter spent every spare moment diving. Nothing would get in the way of a diving expedition, even if it meant leaving home at 3am on Saturday morning. The usual pattern, however, was to leave after school on Friday. Bill and John would borrow their father's old Jowett Bradford light truck and drive to Whangamata or somewhere else on the Coromandel Peninsula. A favoured spot was Sailors Grave Bay, just north of Tairua, although it meant negotiating a slippery clay track in the old Bradford, with predictable results. The Bradford, however, was not to be despised. In a 'power dive' on a downhill on the open road they would get the old beast up to 70 mph.

Soon enough the boys found they were freezing during their dives, so they saved up for a Heinke drysuit, rubber with a cloth backing and seals at the neck, wrists and waist. They kept warm by layering six woollen jerseys underneath it, supplemented by three or four woolly socks with the ends chopped off on their arms, since most of the sleeves on the jerseys had worn through. Dressed this way, they could dive, off and on, for hours and remain tolerably warm. But they couldn't go very deep. At around 15 metres, large wrinkles would develop in the suit, like those on an elephant's legs, and it would become too difficult to move their arms.

An old friend of their father's, Jack Poole, was a member of the Waikato Underwater Club and an early diver. Often he would come along as the brothers' boat man. They would potter around harvesting the plentiful crayfish that were then within easy reach. Before they thought of taking down a bag, they would simply dive until they had a crayfish in each hand, return to the boat, throw the crays over the top, and repeat the exercise until they ran out of air.

There was good money to be made in this. They would limp home to Hamilton late on Sunday evening and sell their crayfish to a local fish shop for two shillings and twopence a pound, live weight, a little over $5 in 2012 terms. The average weighed close to two pounds. Since there were no limits to how much they could gather, a good catch of 100 or so crayfish — six coal sacks — could net them more than $1000 in today's terms. This would comfortably cover their petrol and the not inconsiderable costs of their diving equipment.

hile the boys were developing their business skills, their father was deep into his next boat project. It had become painfully clear that the stubby and slow *Seddon Park*

was no good for substantial voyages. Flicking through the pages of *Rudder* magazine in 1956, Gallagher read about the *Lampooner*, a 66 foot (20 metre) motor launch that could do 20 knots with 200 hp. That was the sort of thing he needed. He wrote to its designer, L Francis Herreshoff of Boston, and for US$100 Herreshoff agreed to send him the hull line drawing.[7] Gallagher would design everything else himself. Then he discovered an abandoned Fairmile motor launch for sale in Tauranga: if he could pick that up cheaply enough he could strip it for parts and save himself a lot of money.

While travelling to Tauranga he found the *Tiare*, a 112-footer, laid on a mooring up one of the arms of the harbour. A bollard had taken a big piece out of the side, and over the two years it had been on the mooring water had penetrated the deck so that the stringers, the horizontal beams, had turned to mush. But it had all the gear: two Cummins 150 hp engines, propellers, shafts and pumps. Gallagher bought it for £800, equivalent to around $30,000 today, then sailed it to Raglan where it could be stripped more conveniently. John and Bill were two of the six-man crew, and Bill remembers as 'somewhat scary' sailing around North Cape in a leaky boat with the pumps going full bore and the hull timbers moving around underneath them over the rotten stringers.

It was soon obvious that the *Tiare*'s parts, excellent though they were, were too heavy for a 66 foot boat, so Gallagher asked Herreshoff to scale up his design to 88 feet (27 metres). The magnificent project got underway in January 1957 when Gallagher laid the keel on the back lawn of 20 Norton Road, adjoining the workshop. The result, the *Hamutana* (a Maori transliteration of Hamilton), would be ready to launch in September 1958. 'Sleek and graceful', it looked like the plaything of a millionaire. Gallagher wasn't anywhere near so wealthy, but he stretched each dollar a long way, so much so that he managed to release some capital by upgrading from the *Seddon Park* to the *Hamutana*.

In February 1957, not knowing quite what to do with the *Seddon Park*, he had taken out a commercial fishing licence and employed a skipper to start trawling out of Raglan. Young Bill went out with them some weekends, using a hand line with four hooks. It was dangerous work and Bill senior became something of an amateur surgeon, pushing deeply lodged hooks through fingers then taking the barb off with wire cutters. But commercially the venture was

ABOVE Gallagher workmen, c. 1953. Back row, from left: Jim Bryant, Horace Hough, Norm Gera, Bob Shaw. Front row, from left: Isaac Beckett, Bill Smith, Bill Gallagher, George Wilson.

a flop, and Gallagher ended up selling the boat to KM Snowden of Ngaruawahia for £6500 (about $300,000 today).

By comparison, Gallagher calculated that by the time he had finished the *Hamutana* it owed him a mere £6000. Young Bill and John had participated in the meticulous scavenging operation that had made this possible. They spent a lot of time unscrewing portholes from the *Tiare* and polishing them up to be used on the *Hamutana*, cutting bits of plywood from the *Tiare* to fit in with the *Hamutana*'s design, or simply collecting copper rivets for reuse. Gallagher lifted the Fairmile's wheel-house in its entirety onto his new boat, which would confuse many boat-spotters over the years. The Fairmiles had been built for the navy during the war, so Gallagher was able to find spare parts for Cummins engines at 'giveaway' prices at the Devonport Naval Yard.

Gallagher employed friends and devoted one or two of his workshop employees to the boat-building task for more than a year. The boat was fully electric, with electric winches, fridges and a separate 230 volt alternator. John and Bill both did plenty of welding. It's impossible to tell now whether there was any confusion or overlap between the costs of building the boat and Gallagher's business. Bill thinks his father was generally very principled about tax, but did overhear him say once, 'I obey the law as long as it's reasonable; but if it's too stupid that's another matter.' In 1958 the top personal tax rate was still 67.5 per cent. More than anything, however, Gallagher was a very determined man. He wanted to build this great boat and nothing would get in the way of the achievement. Millie Gallagher, sitting alone each night, knitting awkwardly using her lame arm as a crook, happily lived a quiet life.

Launching the 28 ton *Hamutana* on an overcast spring Sunday morning, 14 September 1958, provided another public spectacle. The *Waikato Times* described it as the 'best free show in years'.[8] Literally hundreds of Hamiltonians lined the streets and the banks of the Waikato River to see the beast, painted beautifully in white, lumber down the same route as the *Seddon Park*. They had to lop some branches from nearby oak trees to manoeuvre the boat into position, entertaining the crowd, who watched an enthusiastic helper sitting on the branch as he began to saw himself off.

This time, however, the launching was a shambles. Gallagher's home-made trailer sank into soft ground near the boat-launching

THIS PAGE On 14 September 1958 the launching of the Gallagher's new boat, the *Hamutana*, via Hamilton's Victoria Street, provided the 'best free show' in town for years.

ramp and wouldn't be budged until a bulldozer pulled it out. Then, when launched over the edge, the *Hamutana* became stuck on the bank. John and Bill pulled on their scuba gear and dived into the river, but couldn't see anything for the mud. In a display of civic cooperation unthinkable today, the Hamilton Fire Brigade hosed away the mud on the bank. Meantime, the Hydro-Electric Department arranged to release more water from dams upstream overnight, and the rising river waters soon floated her.

Bill Gallagher's dream was to sail the *Hamutana* around the world. The first step was an expedition that October around North Cape to park the boat at Panmure. The trip must have given him pause for thought, though, because he nearly rolled the new ship attempting a foolhardy entry into the Kaipara Harbour in rough weather. They were caught nearly side-on by a huge wave. Gallagher recorded in the log that the green water on the port side was above the top of the wheel-house, and as it crashed over it broke the glass in the door and put it on top of the wheel-house. Fortunately the boat righted itself.

Undeterred, that summer the Gallagher men sailed the length of the country as far south as Cape Saunders on the Otago Peninsula. Now with a world-class diving platform, the boys concentrated seriously on their diving. Recreation and business, however, were always intertwined, and their passion for diving led to a fresh business venture. Throughout 1958 they had devoted any spare time to making diving gear. Diving regulators, the set of valves and tubes that feed the air from the diver's gas cylinder to the mouthpiece in a controlled way, were expensive to buy and it was difficult to find replacement parts. The brothers started experimenting with ways to make their own replacements and eventually began crafting their own full sets of equipment.

Bill Gallagher recalls: 'I began to fiddle with spun copper and silver, learnt how to drive a lathe, and began to make things. We could use Dad's workshop after hours and punched out a few valves. It was extremely crude, but it led to our first business on the side, while I was entering the sixth form. The hardest part was to find a suitable compressed-air tank, which had to be imported. But other than that, we made the backpacks, just a piece of sheet metal and a harness hose clips, regulators from spun copper and the rest. No one used pressure gauges then.

'There were no regulations at the time and not much could go wrong. We made these sets and used them. But of course they used to leak, and so we'd be forever tapping and fiddling with them before a dive, which tended to spook other people. I remember getting ready to dive into an underwater cave at Cold Water Creek, Waitomo, and pulling my home-made regulator to bits to stop it leaking, leading one of our diving mates to bail out of the adventure. Over my last two years at school we made around 20 sets and sold most of them to Dad's friends, underwater club members and through word of mouth.'

John Young, a well-known New Zealand diver, started diving in 1958. He met the Gallaghers and saw their copies of regulators, but there was no way that he would have bought one.[9]

Filling the air cylinders was another expense for the diver. Bill and John knew they could save themselves some money, and make a bit besides, by buying their own compressor. They imported a second-hand Hamworthy compressor from England, and it arrived in April 1959 while John was away on his three months of compulsory military training at Papakura. He had been diving at Ruapuke, near Raglan, one weekend and had got so wet and cold that he came down with pneumonia. This ruled him out of the last week of camp, so he spent the time fiddling with the new compressor. Now the Gallagher brothers — Bill still a schoolboy — were filling tanks for local diving enthusiasts most Thursday and Friday evenings, and the profits supported their lives of adventure. At a time when the typical school teacher didn't have a cheque book, Bill could be found at the back of the class casually writing out cheques for his business activities.

Their father, however, was still the primary provider, and for the summer of 1959/60 he was planning their most exciting trip to date: they would cross the Tasman. Bill junior and his father spent months studying navigation and charts, and plotting their course. They set off after Christmas and reached Lord Howe Island on New Year's Eve, having averaged 11.75 knots. A boat came out and guided them through a hole in the reef, and once on the island the locals showed the New Zealanders a great time. Although Bill senior was a teetotaller, he didn't stop his sons getting stuck into the beer. Bill junior was already well acquainted with apple cider, the drink of choice at student parties, but this was a new experience.

Millie and the girls joined the menfolk in Brisbane and the family spent the next few weeks cruising down the Pacific coast to Sydney. Bill took a hitchhiking trip inland from Coff's Harbour to find Viv Clow, one of his Gallagher relatives, who lived on a farm at Currabubula, near Tamworth. He was struck by the primitive conditions on the farm, where a diesel generator was used to provide electricity. The boys' sister May met them in Sydney, having come back from Europe overland with a guy she had met, travelling mostly on a scooter they had bought in Italy.

The Gallaghers left Sydney Harbour on 2 February 1960 with Bill junior navigating. A simple but serious error in his calculations, however (adding the magnetic variation instead of subtracting it), sent them 30 degrees off-course. Fortunately his father noticed that night that the stars were in the wrong place, and they were able to correct for the mistake without significant embarrassment. Young Bill started his final year at school a few days late, but with more stories to tell.

Enjoying a 'nice, lazy time' at school in 1960, Bill concentrated on his diving and business activities. Wade Doak had begun publishing the magazine *Dive*, which included photos and stories about the Poor Knights Islands, offshore from Whangarei. The Gallagher brothers joined a small but devoted group who made the pilgrimage to the area on weekends. They met Kelly Tarlton and other enthusiasts, who egged each other on to try new things and to plumb new depths (60 metre dives were not unusual). The Gallaghers bought underwater cameras and were learning the tricky art of taking photos that captured the brilliantly coloured sea life in all its intensity. Back home, a little more money could be made from the odd salvage job around Hamilton or at Raglan. Someone might have dropped an anchor or a piece of useful gear in the river or the harbour, and the Gallagher boys would dive for it. Roose Shipping Company, sand dredgers on the Waikato, was an early client.

The Gallagher brothers' early enterprise, at bottom, was driven by the desire to raise money for new toys or, tackling the problem from the other side, by their desire to get their hands on new toys

TOP On the *Hamutana* upon arrival from Sydney at Auckland Harbour, 8 February 1960. From left to right: Millie Gallagher, Bill Gallagher senior, Edna Gallagher, Ralph Reynolds, Bernard (no surname given), May Gallagher, Olive Gallagher, Norm Cook, Bill Gallagher junior, John Gallagher.

BELOW 'Shivering in Tauranga', *Bay of Plenty Times*, 1963.

"It's colder here," was the reaction of the crew of the Hamutana to a cool Tauranga morning. They are from left, Ralph Reynolds, Bill Gallagher, Edna (11), Mr Gallagher and Olive (13).

on the cheap. It was the latter impulse that led to their first formal business, Gallagher Underwater Supplies Ltd. Wetsuits were slowly becoming available, and were much to be preferred over the cumbersome drysuits. But they were very expensive. Young Bill concluded that the best way to get hold of reasonably priced wetsuits was to import them himself. In New Zealand's highly regulated economy, that required an import licence from the Department of Trade and Industry. And if they were going to go to the trouble of getting a licence, it might as well be for diving gear generally. They could also import single-hose regulators that were less likely to leak under pressure than their home-made arrangements.

Obtaining an import licence was difficult. Since these conferred near monopolies on their holders, they tended to be jealously guarded by incumbents. Any newcomer struggled to crack into the racket. With the help of their local MP, Lance Adams-Schneider, who had taken the Hamilton seat in a May 1959 by-election, they succeeded. At first they would simply operate their little business from home, but Bill senior was planning a new showroom on the piece of land at 20 Norton Road on which he had built the *Hamutana*. When that was completed the brothers' diving supply company would colonise a small part of the building.

While juggling this new business with diving and more trips on the *Hamutana*, Bill junior started university in March 1961. Given his mechanical bent, and with the ultimate intention of joining his father's business, he resolved on an engineering degree. An intermediate year at the University of Auckland's main campus in central Auckland would be followed by three years of professional papers at the School of Engineering at Ardmore.

At first Gallagher boarded in a little villa in Kowhai Street, Mt Eden, not far from the back end of Eden Park, then he migrated to a student flat in Hepburn Street, Freemans Bay. At Hepburn Street he flatted with Trevor Graham and Brian Henderson, his predecessor as head prefect at Hamilton Tech. Their main entertainment was to go for late-night runs, including one foray across the Harbour Bridge. When they were caught on the return run over the bridge, Gallagher mounted a defence that argued that, since a vehicle is defined as something going faster than walking pace, a running man might be defined as a vehicle. It was a weak reed, but considerable latitude was given to students.

ABOVE Once Bill Gallagher senior had launched the *Hamutana*, he built a showroom for Gallagher Engineering at 20 Norton Road They moved there in September 1961. Bill junior and John Gallagher operated their side business, Gallagher Underwater Supplies, from the same premises.

The academic work didn't come easy for Gallagher, a fact of life that in retrospect he thinks proved useful. 'I'm a relatively slow reader, though I can hold quite a lot. At Auckland I had some smart colleagues. By 4pm they'd be outside playing, while I'd be plodding away at my desk past 9pm. Now, looking back, it's noticeable that a lot of the smarties, who could whizz through the work, didn't achieve much in later life. And I think part of the reason is that they never learnt how to work. Generally, to succeed in the real world a bit of toil is required. Fortunately I had no choice: to get where I wanted I had to develop a work ethic at school and it carried me through. And frankly I enjoyed it.'

The weekends, however, were another matter. Gallagher would hitchhike home to Hamilton, driven not just by a desire to carry on his diving and businesses, or for home-cooking, but also by love. He had met his girlfriend, Jenny Geddes, at Hamilton Tech, where she had been a year ahead of Bill, though they were the same age. She had come to know the family only when the *Hamutana* was launched in September 1958, and she had stood amazed among the gasping crowd as these crazy people lifted power lines down the street so the boat could go under them. Once she became involved with the family, she says she felt special to have a connection to them.[10]

Jenny's father, Sam Geddes, was an engine driver for the railways, so the family had moved around the country over the years, to such towns as Waipukurau and Te Kuiti. After leaving high school she had found a job in the display department of H & J Court Ltd, a large Hamilton department store. Back in town for the weekend, Bill would take her out in the old Bradford truck, sometimes on diving expeditions, although Jenny didn't take to the water, and sometimes to the cinema. The boat had now been shifted to Whitianga, closer to the most interesting diving spots, so that was a frequent destination.

They became engaged in January 1961, when they were both aged 20. Sadly, a week later Jenny's father died suddenly, still in his fifties. Her mother, Rene, who had lived in railway houses all her life, soon had to find a home of her own. Jenny stayed with her mother as together they struggled to come to terms with the shock, and she stayed home while the Gallaghers took the *Hamutana* on an expedition to Norfolk Island the following summer.

The following year, 1962, Bill Gallagher was presented with a dilemma. He was enjoying his engineering studies, now out at Ardmore, but he wouldn't complete them until the end of 1964. At the same time, he was keen to get married sooner rather than later. It would be difficult to persuade Jenny to leave her grieving mother to live with him in Auckland, where they had no real means of supporting themselves while he studied. With a little thought he discovered a way around the problem. Rather than complete his Bachelor of Engineering at Auckland he could shift across to the traditional British qualification from the Institute of Mechanical Engineering. This required two years of university study followed by nine years of part-time but very gruelling and rigorous papers and exams through correspondence. His professor, Alan Titchener, tried to dissuade him, pointing out that most students fell away during the years of study by correspondence. But Gallagher's mind was set; he would leave Ardmore in November 1962 and marry Jenny.

The Ardmore campus was well known for student hijinks, and Bill played an enthusiastic part in these. The hundred or so students, all male, lived in dormitories that had previously been army huts. These were not treated with great respect: a typical prank would involve rigging a barrel of water above a window so that its contents would pour into the dorm when someone opened the window. The victim would find himself sloshing around in six inches of water.[11] Women could be found at the Teachers' Training College down the road, so expeditions were made down there in the middle of the night with improvised aluminium bombs that went off with great explosions after the men had already filled the corridors with smoke.

The students' best talents, however, were applied on April Fool's Day. In 1962 there was much civic controversy over plans to erect a large television aerial on the top of Mt Eden. Gallagher helped a team erect a fake 12 metre tower on the mountain in the middle of the night, which generated much mayhem in the morning and a front-page story in the *New Zealand Herald*.[12] The borough works overseer told reporters that the pranksters had been lucky, since the foundations for one of their girders missed an underground power cable by only a few feet.

With his first professional papers successfully negotiated,

Gallagher left Ardmore in November 1962 and returned to Hamilton to marry Jenny Geddes. Over the previous few months he had bought a house at 97 Seddon Road, a few houses up the road from his parents' place, and beside his Uncle Viv's. It was connected to Gallaghers' larger commercial property through an access way from the back fence that ran past Viv's kiwifruit vines. The house had been lived in for years by an elderly woman, a Mrs Roberts, and it was very run-down. Young Bill had been helped to scratch together a deposit by his father, who had cashed in some building society shares. In the weeks before his wedding Bill put in a modern kitchen and an inside toilet, and generally lifted the house to a very basic standard.

Jenny remembers that they had no money at all: she was 'working for peanuts' as a display artist, while Bill had a job with his father and his various diving businesses on the side, which 'made a bit, but no more than he spent on new diving equipment'. Aside from having access to a beautiful 88 foot (27 metre) boat parked at Whitianga, they were an average hard-grafting young Hamilton couple. Yet to Jenny and most other observers it was obvious that young Bill's determination in life was anything but average. As she says: 'From the moment Bill started working with his father in 1962 his outlook, his challenge, his life was totally focused on growing the company. He was like his father in that his work was also his hobby and his life, but, boy, he was so much more ambitious.'[13]

3
RESOURCEFUL YOUNG MEN: 1962–70

Chapter three

RESOURCEFUL YOUNG MEN: 1962–70

In life you might as well be driving, rather than at the back screaming.

— BILL GALLAGHER JNR

At the end of 1962 Bill Gallagher senior was 51. He was always busy but, at bottom, he was a lifestyler, happy solving problems in the workshop and content to keep his small business ticking over sufficiently to enable him to run his pride and joy, the *Hamutana*, with the utmost economy. In the 12 years or so since his brothers Henry and Viv had left his engineering workshop to set up on their own accounts, Bill Gallagher's business had gone sideways, if not slightly backwards. Figures are sparse, since he was still operating as a sole trader without formal accounts, but the business that delivered him a pre-tax income of £5496 in 1951 (equivalent to around $300,000 in today's terms) still only had a turnover of £33,034 in the year to March 1963 (around $1.2 million in current terms). He would have needed a return of 25 per cent on sales in 1963 to equal the profitability of 1951.

From that modest turnover Gallagher had to pay his eight or so employees, run his workshop, pay for materials, cover his bad debts and all the other costs of business. He was just one of hundreds of such small, independent businessmen who collectively formed the backbone of the New Zealand economy. He had no ambitions to be regarded as a prominent Hamilton businessman. A plaque recognising contributions to a fancy new playground put in by the lake in 1957 provides a lengthy list of the 'business houses' of Hamilton at the time — Firth Concrete, AM Bisley and Co, Roose Shipping, Crittal Engineering, Tapper Construction and the like. Gallagher wasn't in that league, but his business had a good reputation with its customers and he was happy. He wrote later: 'I did alright! But some people say, you must go ahead all the time, or go down. I don't believe that is correct. Had I gone ahead, I would be faced with more overheads, more worries, and probably no more money. It's a different field altogether once you really get out of the workshop, and I've always felt that I was more cut out to being in the workshop and running things that way, rather than leave it to others. Even now I would rather get my hands dirty, than mess around with paper work.'[1]

From the end of 1962, Gallagher's business would also accommodate his two sons. Bill, newly married and with two years of his engineering qualification under his belt, was raring to go. John also returned to the business at the same time. He had finished his apprenticeship with Mullan & Noy in March 1960, then worked with his father for a few months before travelling to England in April 1961 to see the world and to chase a young Welsh girl. He came home, without the girl, at the end of 1962. May, who had married at the end of 1961 and who had a similar personality and temperament to Bill, also wanted to be involved in the business. But her father, in part reflecting the prevailing attitude of the times, discouraged that idea.

Even with just the two boys involved, something positive was called for. The business could not carry on as it was and hope to generate a decent income for what would eventually be three Gallagher families. Bill senior had been planning for this challenge when he had taken out a £2500 mortgage to build a showroom and better office facilities facing Norton Road. These had been completed in 1962 and set the business on a new level, underlining the fact that there was no room for two new passengers. Bill and John would have to generate new income to pay their way. Fortunately, everything they had done in life so far indicated that they would be assets rather than liabilities to their father.

Gallagher had been best known through the 1950s for his trailer-mounted topdressers and his electric fences. By the end of 1962 the topdressers were in decline, outclassed by Viv's tractor-mounted model and others. To replace the lost business Gallagher had turned increasingly from the late 1950s to relatively simple metal work — hay barns, cattle stops, cow bails and farm gates. The problem with that line of business, as Bill junior quickly realised, was its simplicity. It required no significant capital or skills, and so there were few barriers to competition from a large potential pool of under-employed farmers' sons with access to a blowtorch and welder. These amateurs drove down the prices and narrowed profit margins.

On the electric fencing side, the industry was in a state of flux. The Gallagher Electric Fence was one among a dozen or so brands available locally; competitors included Arc-Rite from Marton, the AKO from Hooker & Co of Auckland, Speedrite from Levin, Brown from Waihi, and the Williams Electric Fence system. In 1961 all the fences were basically variations on the same machine that Gallagher and his rivals had been building in the early 1940s, incrementally improved by a series of superficial changes — sturdier boxes and handles and stronger wires — which reduced maintenance costs. They were good for powering temporary fences to contain dairy cows, the most docile of farm animals, and as such were widely used by dairy farmers to divide up larger paddocks for strip-grazing. Beyond that, their use was limited because the energiser couldn't deliver a high-powered pulse beyond a relatively short distance. And if long grass reached the wires the pulse weakened further, or even shorted out. Batteries, meanwhile, had to be regularly recharged and then replaced.

Then two events, the first in February 1961, the second in June 1962, threatened to turn the industry on its head. New Zealand's Electric Wiring Regulations were amended on 20 February 1961 to allow the use of mains power in electric fences. Freed from the constraints of weak batteries, this offered the prospect of permanent and more powerful electric fencing. Then in June 1962 Doug Phillips, one of the scientists at the government-funded Agricultural Research Station at Ruakura, on the outskirts of Hamilton, demonstrated a 'revolutionary departure' from the conventional electric fence with a fresh design that the *Waikato Times* dubbed the 'unshortable electric fence'.[2]

The existing fences typically used car ignition coils to generate the electric pulse on the fence wire. The coil itself had high internal resistance, soaking up much of the energy before it ever hit the fence. It was, in Phillips's words, 'like trying to fill a leaky bucket with a teapot'.[3] His key insight was to see that it could be safe to have a high current if it was only applied for a very short time. And then he figured out how to deliver this power onto the wire by discharging a capacitor, a power storage device that had far less internal resistance than a car ignition coil. Using a transformer, he could hoist the voltage up to a couple of thousand volts either from a 9 volt battery or from a 240 volt mains power plug. Then the capacitor could discharge the full voltage with a strong current onto the wire in a short time pulse.

Carrying on the water analogy, with voltage as pressure and current as flow, the old coil energisers were like having a small pump. They might have produced high pressure, but as soon as the system sprang a leak (for a fence, by having grass touch the wire or poor insulation on the fence post), the pressure dropped away to nothing. Phillips's invention was like having a big flood pump, which, even if you had water squirting everywhere from dozens of leaks, still maintained plenty of pressure in the hose. At the annual Ruakura farmers' field day he demonstrated his invention, using a single energiser in a small wooden box to power a two-wire fence around the entire 55 hectare 'No 1 Dairy Farm'.

The electric fence makers, including the Gallaghers, were highly sceptical of the idea and, in Phillips's recollection, pooh-poohed it vigorously. But once they saw it in action they were worried. Phillips remembers the manager of the Barrier Fence Company driving up from Marton to see what the fuss was about. He took one look at the two-wire fence stretching around the farm and declared it was 'impossible' and that Phillips's claims were 'bullshit'. Kneeling on the ground, he grabbed the fence contemptuously with both hands, and nearly did a full backwards somersault. Without saying a word he shuffled, somewhat jerkily, to his car and drove off. The main criticism now was that the fence was going to kill people. Phillips explained that the shock wouldn't be fatal because the power came only in a short pulse, around 0.3 milliseconds. The zap was of sufficient duration for the central nervous system to react violently, but not long enough to cause any lasting damage to the body.

Bill junior recalls that his father thought the idea was wonderful, in theory. It offered the prospect of electrifying permanent fences cheaply and reliably. Sheep and beef cattle could be drawn into the picture and the entire industry would be expanded enormously. But, though he had ample opportunity, he wasn't prepared to be the guinea pig who would turn a scientist's ideas into a commercial proposition. Phillips, meantime, had given the government the opportunity to take out a patent on his idea, but in typical bureaucratic fashion this wasn't taken up. The Department of Agriculture wasn't interested, and Phillips was told that he was at liberty to take out a patent privately.

Phillips was friendly with Mortie Foreman, the owner of Plastic Products Ltd, a private Hamilton company that made the bulk of New Zealand's ballpoint pens, plastic milking machine parts and squeeze bottles at its new factory in Te Rapa. Crying over his beer one day, Phillips told his friend about his problems, and Foreman responded that, if he patented it, Plastic Products would make the energisers and market them. Foreman would give Phillips a royalty of 5 per cent of the factory price. They had a deal, and Phillips filed for a patent on 15 October 1962.[4]

Plastic Products was a much larger and more sophisticated company than Gallaghers, with 238 staff and a turnover of £750,000 in 1962/63, almost $30 million in today's terms.[5] But its speciality was plastic moulding; electric fences were well outside its field. Phillips had to do most of the electronics himself. Nevertheless, in 1963 Plastic Products launched the Waikato fence, using Phillips's technology. Bill junior recalls that Gallaghers was selling around 500 electric fence energisers a year. Once, in the mid-1950s, it'd had a 'bonza' year and sold 1000. Suddenly, Waikato sold 3000 in its first year, and 'we were very envious'.

It wasn't that Gallagher's business was being destroyed. The demand for the old-style, battery-powered fences for use in strip-grazing dairy herds remained steady. But now the market was being expanded massively into permanent electric fencing for not only dairy but also the sheep and beef industries. Gallaghers was missing out on the opportunity of a lifetime.

A natural division of labour at Gallaghers followed. Bill senior devoted himself to the task of cadging Phillips's ideas to produce his own low-impedance, 'unshortable' fence — which, as it turned out, would take several years. The boys concentrated on reviving the agricultural machinery side of the business.

But first they had to set the business on a more formal footing. Bill Gallagher senior incorporated Gallagher Engineering Ltd as a limited liability private company on 2 May 1963, with a modest £3000 capital. (The Norton Road site was kept separate from the company assets.) Initially Bill senior retained all the shares, but a year later he transferred 500 £1 shares each to John and Bill (giving them 16.6 per cent of the business each). Meantime, Bill junior was convinced they needed ready access to more cash if his plans for expansion were to be realised. To that point his father had had a £1500 overdraft with the Frankton branch of the ANZ Bank, which for no apparent reason the bank wanted paid off. The brothers walked across the road to Aussie Packer, who was the manager at National Bank, and organised a £6000 overdraft (around $250,000 in 2012 terms), secured against their father's assets. 'Dad had pleasure in writing a cheque to close the ANZ account,' Bill junior recalls, and the company now had much more money on hand with which to develop new products.

With every incentive, the boys set about expanding the agricultural machinery side of the business. At first Bill junior threw himself into pumps. One of his father's friends, Stan Southcombe, ran the Dairy Board's bull farm, which was on wet land that had tile drains. He needed a pump. Fresh out of university, Gallagher thought he could design his own axial flow pump, using a small electric motor. He sold it to Southcombe and concluded that there was money to be made in pumps. He 'spent a lot of money' building a concrete testing tank at Norton Road and produced a few six-inch flow pumps for land drainage. He promoted the pumps hard but managed to sell only two.

Looking back, he acknowledges that the episode provided an early business lesson: 'I went onto farms and found that their requirements varied enormously. Our six-inch pump was either too small, too large, or with insufficient lift. That left me with a dilemma. Either I could sell him my pump anyway, which because it wouldn't do the job compromised my integrity and the firm's integrity, or I'd have to point him towards another pump manufacturer. In that case I'd effectively be a salesman for my competition. The lesson I drew from that is that if you're going into a market you need to have the full product range. There was no way I could do that with pumps, and so we bowed out. I have no idea how much the exercise cost us, since we didn't keep any record of productive time and research costs, but it was significant. We did, however, make a little money out of a related side venture: sludge pumps that emptied muck pits in cowsheds. We sold a few of those.'

John's first task was the forage harvester, a reasonably complicated piece of farm machinery that harvested long grass, chopped it up and blew it out the back so that it could be collected to make silage. A few protected local manufacturers — Lilley, Monroe, and Greens — made these machines and they were quite expensive. Bill senior and Viv Gallagher's company, Vogal Engineering, had a joint venture going to produce their own model. The Gallaghers were focused on the rotors, while Vogal concentrated on the gearbox, since Viv had an old Robey-Smith gear-cutter. Progress, however, had been slow.

John took up the task and produced four prototypes following an initial design. But, looking at the completed machines, nobody was particularly pleased with them. Bill senior then had the insight to suggest a much heavier flail, twice the thickness, with a hardened edge and a much heavier rotor. This, when adopted, generated more momentum and much better results.

Bill junior, meanwhile, worked with Viv on making their own gearbox. Their competitors imported theirs, adding to the cost. Bill found a book of involute equations and spent weeks working out the complex mathematics to shape the gear teeth. Then he'd 'tickle' them, for further refinement. The result was ready for the market in 1964. It was marketed independently by Gallaghers and Vogal Engineering; the former painted orange, the latter blue. Bill was fascinated that at the annual A&P show there always seemed to be a larger crowd gathered around the orange machine, although that year the machines were otherwise identical. After a couple of years, the Gallaghers bought their own gear-cutter and began producing a gearbox for themselves, ending the joint venture and starting a period of friendly competition against the Vogal forage harvester. Bill junior was sure that his gearbox was less noisy than Viv's.

The knowledge Bill Gallagher was acquiring on gearboxes could usefully be applied to other pieces of farm machinery. In 1964 he developed a tractor-mounted post-hole digger. The business opportunity was sound, since there was only one model on the market, which was made in the US. The basic task was to take the 500 revs produced by the three-point linkage PTO on the back of the tractor, and to reduce it through a gearbox to around 100 revs to turn the augur. After some fiddling around, Bill discovered that old Ford V8 differential gears in a new cast-iron gearbox would do

ABOVE The Gallagher forage harvester.

the job perfectly, and cheaply. Then they figured out how to make the augurs first by cutting flat steel plate, then stretching it with a big double-action press and heating it with a gas torch to create the helix shape. Proudly demonstrating this beast to his father and the rest of the crew, Bill was embarrassed to discover that he had the augur turning the wrong way, so that it wouldn't dig anything. But that was easily fixed, and soon they were selling hundreds of them. When, after a few years and almost 2000 units, they had exhausted the nation's supply of Ford V8 diff gears from the wreckers, he moved on to Mark 1 Zephyr diff gears.

A similar market opportunity existed with rotary hoes. The Howard rotary hoe, made by an English company, was the only model on the market. These were notorious for breaking down when used in New Zealand's tough conditions, prompting Bill Gallagher senior's observation, 'There's no one so hard on farm machinery as the New Zealand farmer, so you have to make machines that will stand up to rough use.'[6] Old car gears wouldn't work for the rotary hoes — too much power was required and the ratio was not right. Slowly, over a few years, they perfected their own design. Gallaghers sold the machines directly in the North Island, and through AM Bisley and Co in the South Island. The volumes weren't huge, but they were big-ticket items, selling for between $870 and $1280 by the end of the decade ($12,500–$18,500 in 2012 terms).

The forage harvester, post-hole digger and rotary hoe provided a strong foundation for growth in the agricultural machinery side of the business. Bill Gallagher senior, meanwhile, was making progress on the electric fences. Owen Williamson, an old school friend of John's, had a radio shop over the road from Gallaghers called Precision Electronics Ltd (PEL).[7] He had made himself useful to the Gallaghers by providing them with cheap television sets in 1963, the year transmission finally reached Hamilton. Williamson discovered that kitsets for television sets that had a minor fault could be sourced from the UK for £20. Without any trouble, he was able to get them going. They looked rough, with no frame and plenty of tubes and circuit boards poking out the back, but so long as you didn't let any children too close to the back they worked well.

In 1964 the Gallaghers invited Williamson to work with them to develop a low-impedance energiser. The Waikato electric fence was taking the world by storm, being exported to Australia and Ireland,

TOP AND BELOW Along with the forage harvester, the post-hole digger (top) and rotary hoe (bottom) were the mainstays of the agricultural machinery side of Gallaghers' business through the 1960s and 1970s.

but already a major problem was emerging with the design: Waikato used a gas discharge tube to trigger the pulse, but these kept failing. And because of the way the units were built, replacing the tube was no simple matter. Waikato had sold its energisers with a three-year guarantee, and now Plastic Products faced an untidy situation.

Bill Gallagher senior and Owen Williamson used a mercury switch to trigger the pulse. By 1966 they felt they had it working well. It was putting about 5000 volts on the fence, which generated 10 times more energy than the Waikato's 2000 volts. They made an initial run of around 300 and put them on the market as a Gallagher Electric Fence, designed by PEL, with the slogan '10 times more powerful'. There were plenty of advertisements aimed at the sheep and beef farming market, which until that point had been beyond Gallaghers' reach.

Success didn't come so easily, however. The machines used electrolytic capacitors to deliver the energy, but these weren't reliable. Bill junior groans that they had sold 300 with a guarantee and before too long 'had repaired 500'.

The business lesson was more profound, however. The Gallaghers' relationship with Williamson had been entirely informal, and under the strain caused by a product that was seriously threatening Gallaghers' reputation for reliability the partners eventually fell out. Williamson, in turn, wanted greater recognition of his rights as a designer and a partner in the manufacturing process. After some argument they went their separate ways, with Williamson going into business on his own account in 1968. To the Gallaghers' amazement, he proved very capable on his own, and over the years, under different ownership, the PEL electric fence would become a major rival.

One saving grace was that the makers of the Waikato fence were distracted. Plastic Products was sold to Alex Harvey Industries at the end of December 1963, and as a small unit within a larger conglomerate the electric fence business lost its impetus for a while.

Gallaghers, meantime, was back to square one, still with only their old-technology models on the market. Bill junior recalls that after licking his wounds for a while his father had a 'skunk works upstairs' in the evenings with Jack Page, the husband of the office assistant Evelyn Page, who happened to be a very competent electrician working for the dairy company. He had built the transmitting radio for the *Hamutana*, which had enabled them to talk to New Zealand from New Caledonia when no one else could.

By 1969 they had a good mains-powered fence, the Gallagher Model B, ready for the market. But it still relied on a mercury switch, which wasn't particularly reliable with the high internal current running through the energiser (up to 2000 amps). A better alternative was Silicon-Controlled Rectifier (SCR) switching, but in 1966 these cost £12 each, the full retail price of a typical energiser. By 1970, however, the price had come right down and Gallagher produced the BE model (the 'E' standing for electronic), using an SCR switch. This was a much more reliable product.

Meantime, the boys were making steady, if not spectacular, progress on the agricultural machinery. Their new lines had increased the size of the business, so that by the end of 1968 the three Gallagher men were joined by 16 employees. But they weren't making much money. Declared profits for the years between 1964 and 1967 averaged only £2039 per year (around $60,000–$70,000 in today's terms), creeping up to $5069 in 1968 ($75,000). Bill junior now realises that he wasn't handling the pricing well: 'I'd been a hero not moving prices for several years, steadily slicing our margin, then when I tried to move it 10 per cent one year to get back to something realistic the customers started screaming.' The experience taught him to 'have a nibble every year', increasing prices 2 or 3 per cent, which didn't generate so much resentment and retained profitability during a period of gathering inflation.

The American investor Warren Buffett once observed, 'There's no place where we turned the switch. So damn much happens by accident. It does show the value of showing up every day.'[8] The Gallaghers showed up to work one day in October 1967 to find a telex message arrive that launched their exporting career. Fred Cornet from Elder Smith Goldsborough Mort (now Elders) wrote to ask if the Gallaghers could demonstrate their forage harvester at the next Orange Field Day, the oldest annual agricultural demonstraion field day in Australia, held near Orange on the central tablelands of New South Wales. Cornet had been put onto Gallaghers by the New Zealand Trade Commission. The Aussies were showing interest in New Zealand goods now that the New Zealand Australia

Free Trade Agreement (NAFTA) had come into effect, sweeping away duties on agricultural equipment. The only problem was that the show started in two weeks.

Bill junior says his father was highly sceptical about exporting. 'But,' he said to his sons, 'if you boys are willing, you can have a go.' That was all the encouragement they needed. Bill junior scrambled and had one of their half-ton forage harvesters air-freighted to Sydney on a Qantas 707 (the beast wouldn't fit through the cargo door on Air New Zealand's DC8). He followed, turning up at the field day with a big grin and a forage harvester, much to the delight of the man from Elders, who nicknamed him 'GT' Gallagher, after a souped-up sports car of the era.

Young 'GT' managed to sell 20 of his harvesters at the show, and signed Elders as their Australian distributor. While he was there, however, on 21 November 1967, the New Zealand government devalued the dollar 19.45 per cent against the US and Australian dollars. He had agreed on an Australian dollar price and stood to make a windfall extra 20 per cent in New Zealand dollar terms. That wouldn't have been a 'fair crack of the whip' from the Australian perspective, however. Gallagher won a few friends that day, and closed some more sales, by offering to split the difference, lowering the Australian dollar price by 10 per cent.

Thereafter, the Orange Field Days became an annual event for Gallaghers. It was a large and somewhat chaotic show — John Gallagher remembers that the organisers calculated the turnover each year by extrapolating from the number of pies they sold — but, together with the Elders relationship, it provided a beachhead into Australia. Over the following years they introduced the post-hole diggers and rotary hoes, which found a ready market in the Queensland cane industry.

When, in 1968, plans emerged for a big agricultural field day in Hamilton, Bill Gallagher junior immediately saw the value in it. He sat on committees with the driving figures — among them John Kneebone, Ossie James, Don Llewellyn and Vaughan Jones — and Gallaghers was a founding exhibitor at the first 'Fielday' in June 1969. At the time it was called the Waikato Town and Country Festival, and the venue was the Te Rapa Racecourse. The second show was timed to coincide with the Royal visit of March 1970, but thereafter it settled into a winter timeslot, when most farmers had spare time on their hands, and the location moved to Mystery Creek after the festival society purchased land there.

Gallaghers' relatively prominent presence at the first Fieldays underlined its determination to lead the pack and to create a well-recognised brand. There was a lot of activity and prospects were good, but by the end of the 1960s the company had yet to take off. Rudimentary company accounts for Gallagher Engineering Ltd exist from 1969, showing local sales worth $149,000 and exports worth $9000 ($158,000 in total, about $2.3 million in 2012 terms). They were able to pay themselves modest salaries and drive around in reasonable cars; Bill junior roared about in a dark green Chrysler Ranger. But the company declared a modest net profit of $7152 after tax ($100,000 in today's terms). In essence, it remained a small business, albeit one that was growing steadily. Sales grew 15 per cent the following year to reach $182,000 (about $2.5 million adjusted for CPI).

In the eight years since the brothers had joined the business, Gallaghers had doubled in real terms: sufficient to accommodate them as two additional principals, but no more. The relatively slow gradient reflected the life-stages of the Gallagher family. Approaching 60, Bill senior remained happy with a small business that enabled him to pursue his real passion of sailing around in the *Hamurana*. The boys, in their twenties, were more ambitious, but still finding their feet and enjoying the opportunities for adventure that boats and diving provided.

Bill, in particular, had a lot on his plate. His routine, as remembered by his first wife Jenny, is almost unthinkable 50 years later for a young married man: 'Bill went off to the workshop at 7.30am, coming home around 5.30pm. Dinner was at 6 and at 6.30 he'd go into his study to get through his correspondence studies for engineering and that would be it for the evening. I'd take him a cup of coffee around 8.30 and he'd carry on to 10.30 or 11. Like some of the other Gallaghers he has an ability to switch everything else off and concentrate on the task at hand. And the idea was he'd have the weekend off, but something always cropped up and he'd have to make up the study time on Saturday morning. Then he'd take off on Saturday afternoon and dive all Sunday, coming home late in the afternoon. Then back into the study again for Sunday evening.'

Bill kept up this remorseless study routine until 1969, when he finally completed his requirements for membership of the Institute of Mechanical Engineers. There had been eight in the group in Auckland when he sat the final exams; only he and one other, from Christchurch, made it through. He subsequently made little direct use of his mechanical engineering training, but counts it as useful. 'As one guy put it, "The shadow of forgotten knowledge prevents one from being deceived." Pretty quickly I couldn't remember most of my engineering, but in a host of technical fields its disciplines have helped me see if something doesn't add up — in essence, to spot bullshit.'[9]

He did find time to do some things with his new wife. From time to time a group of their friends would hire a hall on a Saturday night and dress it up with palm leaves, fish nets and so forth for a 'Mad Shipwreck Ball'. These could become quite riotous. But diving was Bill Gallagher's primary passion. And for a while there continued to be a business element to it. Gallagher Underwater Supplies carried on in the corner of the Gallagher Engineering showroom throughout the 1960s, until Bill senior persuaded his sons that it was just a distraction. Bill junior remembers, 'One day, after I'd spent two hours talking to a diving friend and sold a cheap spearhead, Father sat us down and asked if we were serious about business or just wanted to play diving.' Bill junior realised his time was more valuably spent on the agricultural machinery, so they sold the business to Marine Services in 1969.

The compressor for filling air tanks was too valuable to let go, however. And the brothers carried on their underwater salvage work. His father had advanced Bill junior's skills in the latter area. In November 1961, while John was overseas, Bill junior and Ralph Reynolds, a friend, launched their first salvage operation from the *Hamutana* using gelignite.[10] They had found a large bronze propeller on the wreck of the *Manaia*, a passenger ship that had gone down near Slipper Island, off the Coromandel coast, in June 1926. It lay in only 6 metres of water. Bill senior recommended a blast of gelignite — which he called the 'Gympie Hammer' in recognition of his grandfather's mining exploits in Gympie, where they'd been enthusiastic blasters. This would loosen all the nuts and bolts, to release the propeller. Bill junior took down half a stick and pressed in an electric detonator. Back on the boat they touched the wires across a 12 volt battery and 'up she went'. They had shaken things sufficiently to extract a couple of quarter-ton blades from the propeller. In February they returned to gather the rest.

Bill remembers, 'We painstakingly unscrewed the remaining nuts with a hammer and chisel, going through a few tanks of air in the process. Later on we learnt to use more gelly to blow them to bits, but back then we were doing it the hard way.' They had agreed to give some money to the owners of the wreck for the salvage rights, but the Gallaghers and Reynolds still harvested a tidy sum for the scrap metal. Bill junior was in the underwater salvage business for both fun and profit.

Having acquired a taste for underwater explosions, Bill was soon looking for more things to light up. When John returned they let it be known around town that they were in the business of underwater demolition as well as general salvage. Their most celebrated job, a couple of years later, was the Raglan concrete footbridge. General contractors had taken out the connecting spans and the Gallaghers were called in to blow out the legs. They dived and laid gelignite, using the battery from the old Bradford truck as the exploder, as their father had taught them.

The first shot didn't do the job, and while they were preparing for the second a Department of Labour safety inspector appeared from nowhere. He was unimpressed with their amateur operation: they needed to get themselves a proper exploder. But after some pleading from Bill, the inspector allowed them one more blast, and to their immense pleasure the whole bridge 'folded like a pack of cards . . . each span across the estuary . . . zoink, zoink, zoink'.[11] After that, the brothers bought an exploder and later went on a two-day Department of Labour course on construction blasting. They were 'instant experts' after that. Meantime, they had successfully modified an oxy-acetylene torch to run underwater so they could cut away any remaining steel reinforcing rods.

The demolition instinct led them in odd directions. They had landed the job of demolishing the old Ngaruawahia railway bridge in September 1962, but the authorities wouldn't let them blow it up since it was hard up against the new one. Forced to use mechanical means to pull it down, they removed the wooden braces in the side trusses, then used a Caterpillar tractor with a winch to roll up the

ABOVE Bill Gallagher and Ralph Reynolds successfully demolishing the Ngaruawahia railway bridge, September 1962.

bridge like a big strip of netting. It was a spectacular sight, but the Gallaghers were in danger of spreading themselves too thin. What *was* their core business again?

Still, throughout the 1960s they usually had an underwater job every second week or so, many of them with a fresh challenge. Pulling himself along a rope through newly laid 1-metre diameter sewerage pipes under Killarney Road in Hamilton to seal the joints with epoxy from the inside, Bill Gallagher felt 'like a piston in a cylinder'. Over the years they picked up plenty of police work, which became 'grizzly and sad' when they had to fish cars and bodies in states of disrepair out of the river. It was scarcely glamorous work, but it was exciting and a great diversion.

Most diving, however, was purely recreational. The *Hamutana* was the base for a great family adventure up to Noumea and the Loyalty Islands between April and June 1964. Bill junior had spent some time yacht-racing with Darcy Gilbert, a friend of his father's who had a 15 metre sloop, the *Naomi N*. They competed in a race up to Noumea with the *Hamutana* tagging along as the mother ship. Millie and Jenny joined the *Hamutana* at Noumea, and after the race the extended family sailed to the Loyalty Islands, then on to the New Hebrides (Vanuatu), where Bill senior was delivering a tractor to a mission station on the south of Santos Island. Bill junior and Ralph Reynolds dived down to the USS *Tucker*, a wrecked American destroyer off Malo Island. Visiting Malekula Island they met local inhabitants who had not had a great deal of exposure to modern civilisation. Bill recalls that five years previously there had been a celebrated cannibalism case. Now the culprit was out of prison and proudly installed as the local policeman. Jenny remembers scrambling up a live volcano on Tanna Island with Bill senior, Bill, Edna and Olive, and experiencing a huge blast when they were near the top, which sent them all racing down the perfect cone of loose cinders in an undignified manner.

Three years later, in April 1967, they returned to Noumea, this time with Bill junior the skipper. Having dived to the wreck of the SS *President Coolidge* off Espiritu Santo and delivered another tractor to a mission station, Bill took the *Hamutana* across to Fiji. Bill senior was struggling with seasickness and flew home from Fiji, entrusting the return of his precious boat to his son. They reached Tauranga on 31 May, carrying among other things a case of Johnnie Walker

Red Label whisky. In their absence the New Zealand government had significantly increased excise taxes on alcohol, but fortunately a friendly Customs officer pointed out that duties didn't apply if the seals of the bottles had been broken and they were 'in use'. That was easily fixed. Then someone suggested to Bill that the combination of whisky and condensed milk was good, which indeed it was — at first.

Bill junior and John took turns going on these lengthy, late autumn South Pacific sojourns during the 1960s. The other would remain at home to keep the business ticking over. They had a similar routine over the summer, when their diving friends Kelly Tarlton, Wade Doak and others mounted serial adventures.[12] In late 1965 John had joined Tarlton and Doak on a trip up to the Three Kings Islands to search for the SS *Elingamite*, a ship that had sunk in 1902 with silver and gold bullion worth £17,320 on board. They found it, and after Christmas 1967 the same group returned, after months of intensive planning, this time having formed a formal syndicate. They successfully recovered 10,000 silver coins; not the untold riches for which they had hoped, but more than enough to cover their costs.[13] As Arthur C Clarke wrote, 'Nothing, except perhaps the landing of a Flying Saucer in one's backyard, is quite so disruptive of everyday life as the discovery of sunken treasure.'[14] Somehow John Gallagher had to return to the humdrum business of agricultural machinery until the next treasure hunt could be arranged.

Weekend adventures helped feed the Gallagher brothers some adrenalin in the meantime. Perhaps the most dramatic of these were their explorations of inundated parts of the Waitomo Caves. Having explored Cold Water Creek within the system in 1958, when Bill was a schoolboy, they were contacted in 1967 by cavers from the New Zealand Speleological Society, who were systematically exploring the Waitomo system and had come to the end of the rope at the Rangitaawa siphon.[15] Wearing 6-millimetre neoprene wetsuits and helmets, and armed with electric torches, compasses and depth gauges, Bill and John Gallagher, together with a diving club friend, Lionel Sylvester, were lowered 100 or so metres on a bouncing and stretching $3/16$ inch wire cable and then felt their way into the massive riddle of stalagmites and stalactites. Over the next few months they also explored the Mangapu Resurgence.

Bill acknowledges that the underwater caving expeditions were 'quite scary'. He was, quite frankly, living dangerously — perhaps worryingly so, since he had become a father when his daughter Janine was born in May 1966. His son Ian would follow, in December 1968.

Trouble seemed drawn to Bill Gallagher. In January 1968 he had taken 24 divers to White Island on the *Hamutana*. The island, which is a live volcano, erupted while they were there. One eyewitness recalled seeing Kelly Tarlton, bare-headed, with no shirt and light sandals on his feet, dancing about, keeping the ash and stones off his head with a bit of corrugated iron.[16] The gleaming white *Hamutana* was coal-black with a thick covering of ash by the time it had gathered the stragglers. Worse, two days later they were nearly bombed by the air force while diving on the Volkner Rocks, just north of White Island.

It was well known that the air force used these rocks for bombing practice, so Gallagher had checked before diving. He was told 'they had nothing coming'. The spokesman added, however, that 'they would pass over before bombing'.[17] Having had the time of his life spearing a 30-kilogram kingfish, Gallagher was out of the water when two Canberra bombers appeared over the horizon and dropped their load on some rocks around 500 metres away. Ten divers were still down, and it was fortunate none were hit.[18] To the irritation of the Gallaghers, Wade Doak went to the *New Zealand Herald* with the story, attracting unwelcome front-page publicity. The response from an RNZAF spokesman the following day, however, suggested the air force's health and safety culture was a bit loose at the time. He pointed out that the five bombs dropped were practice bombs with very low explosive charges, and that there would only have been 'a slight explosion when the bombs went off'. Nobody, evidently, was worried about a direct hit.

The bombing spoilt that trip somewhat, but there were several other successful White Island diving expeditions on the *Hamutana*. Nights were riotous affairs, involving heavy drinking and naked swimming. Flying fish would come from all directions when the spotlight was turned on. Bill junior remembers one genuine skin-diver making 'a suitable noise' when a flying fish 'rattled up between his legs from the rear'. Even better parties could always be found at South East Bay on Mayor Island, where the Tauranga Sports Fishing Club had its rooms. It was a good place to relax after a day's diving. The next morning, if a southerly swell had picked up during the night, the *Hamutana* would be the last to pull out.

In January 1969 Bill Gallagher was lucky to survive a dose of the bends. He had been diving at the Nga Peta Reef out from Whangamata on New Year's Day to a depth of around 115 feet (35 metres). He tells the story: 'I came up normally, but while I was on the surface someone from a nearby boat said a shark was about. I tried a "pull push" over the boat side, but my hand slipped into the boat and I fell back into the water. I thought nothing of it and got into the boat by the ladder, then had another dive. But coming home I had pins and needles in my legs. At home, holding Janine, who was then two, I fell over backwards. I could walk only with jacked knees. Then I made the mistake of going to bed — "he who keeps his head, doesn't understand the problem".

'The next morning I knew I had bubble trouble and rang Tony Slark, a close friend who was a naval surgeon in Auckland. "Get up here quickly," he said, "and don't drive." Though I didn't know it, he told Jenny that I mightn't walk again. So they threw me in the decompression chamber in Auckland. I had 165 feet [50 metres] for two hours, followed by 36 hours' slow recompression. With this my symptoms started to ease. For a start I could urinate once more, which was nice. They stuck a catheter in and an incredible volume came out. It was a funny episode because we couldn't believe that I'd got the bends on that dive. The shake-up I'd had falling on the boat must have started the bubbles forming.'

Not yet 28, Gallagher, by now president of the Waikato Underwater Club, was chastened by the experience, but not fully checked. The death of a close diving buddy, Henry Laison, two years later brought the dangers home more forcefully.

Meantime, after three summers of salvage on the Three Kings, John Gallagher and his syndicate mates had extracted all they could from the *Elingamite*. They were looking for their next wreck. John Pettit, the owner of one of Auckland's more successful nurseries, was part of the *Elingamite* syndicate. After some discussion, he and Kelly Tarlton settled on the SS *General Grant* as their next target. Since it had gone down on the Auckland Islands, 465 kilometres south of New Zealand in treacherous sub-Antarctic waters, they needed a decent

8th January 1969.

Lt. Cmdr. T.H. Wickham,
R.N.Z.N.,
Devonport.

Dear Sir,

    I wish to offer you and your staff my deepest thanks for the effort and trouble you were put to, to cure my compressed air illness.

    I fully appreciate your effort and the expence to the navy in treating a case such as mine.

    It was in understanding the disruption and expense an operation such as this would put you to, and combined with the fact that my fellow diver and I were diving well inside the recognised non decompression limits, that I delayed in contacting Dr. Slark however, as it turned out, this made your job more difficult.

    I am now almost fully recovered, except for a slight numbness in the legs that will pass in time. I fully realise that without treatment I would be a cripple from the waist down.

    My particular thanks to Guy Kidd and Jim Maxwell who were in the chamber with me, also to the team outside to whom I spoke but did not see.

    As president of the Waikato Underwater Club, the secound largest in New Zealand, I have nothing but praise for the work of your section of the navy.

Gratefully Yours,

....
William M. Gallagher.

ABOVE Bill Gallagher was shaken by his dose of the bends but he still had the presence of mind to compose this note of thanks to the officer in charge.

ABOVE The crew of the *Hamutana* en route to the Auckland Islands. From left to right: Bill Gallagher, Kelly Tarlton, Don Lock, John Dearling, John Pettit, Peter Clements, John Gallagher and Len Scherer. The other crew member, John Calcott, took the photo.

boat, so they invited the Gallaghers to take part.[19] Bill wasn't going to miss out on the fun this time, so once they had persuaded their father to let them take the boat, both brothers were involved.

The *General Grant*, 1118 tonnes of American sailing ship, had hit the Auckland Islands on 14 May 1866 on its way to London from Melbourne. Its destruction had been particularly gruesome. On a dark night the wind had dropped away to nothing, leaving the ship helpless as large swells carried it slowly but inexorably toward the high cliffs of one of the islands. By chance it hit a large cave and was sucked into its maw and crushed. Only 15 of the 83 passengers and crew on board reached the island safely, and of these only 10 survived.[20] Rumours of bullion from the Australian goldfields had attracted eight attempts at salvage since 1866, the most recent being in 1955. No one had yet found any sign of the wreck.[21] Tarlton, John Pettit, and John and Bill Gallagher each put $250 into the Historical Wreck Syndicate in December 1969 and, with the utmost secrecy, set about making their plans. In his book *Treasure Below*, Pettit says that his and Tarlton's plan was not to tell the government beforehand but, if they were successful and found treasure, they would slip off to another country and start negotiations with the government from there.[22]

Bill was to be skipper on the voyage to the islands. His father simply told him, 'Don't lose yourselves, and preferably don't lose the ship.' Since the west coast of the islands was uncharted, Bill junior recalls, the boat's insurers 'didn't want to know us'. On weekends he supervised getting the boat ready at Tauranga, while Tarlton undertook detailed research on previous expeditions, studying newspaper articles, the ship's manifest and reports from survivors. Pettit organised the rest of the crew: Peter Clements, Don Lock, Len Scherer, John Dearling and John Calcott (the fourth John on board). They set off on 23 January 1970, encountering their first rough weather after Akaroa. Pettit recalls Dearling asking Bill if he'd had *Hamutana* in rougher water than this. 'Oh yes,' came the reply. 'Where?' Dearling pressed. 'Around this next point,' Gallagher laughed.[23] Encountering gale-strength southwesterlies in Foveaux Strait, they laid up at Stewart Island to wait for the weather to clear.

It proved a fortuitous delay. While sitting at the end of Stewart Island's Patterson Inlet they noticed that a shipwreck was marked on the map. Diving in, they found they were right on top of it, with a huge propeller just waiting to be salvaged. After a fair bit

Afternoo

THE SOUTH

(Incorporating

No. 34,319   25c Weekly — City and Towns   5c Casual Sales   INVERCARGILL, WEDNES

Sea Search For Treasure Fails

Auckland Islands Expedition Returns

Another abortive attempt to find the gold-laden shipwreck of the General Grant in the Auckland Islands' Cave of Death has ended. The 90ft motorized yacht Haumutana sailed into Bluff this morning bearing a disappointed but undefeated crew.

Peering through a porthole recovered from one of the Auckland Island shipwrecks is Don Locke, of Matamata, one of the historical wreck syndicate on the yacht Haumutana, which sailed for Tauranga from Bluff early this afternoon. The 90ft yacht will visit the West Coast sounds on its return to Tauranga.

Members of the historical wrecks syndicate, the nine men from the Auckland-Hamilton area, spent two weeks diving to wrecks, picking up relics and charting the previously uncharted north-west coast of the Auckland Island.

Spokesman for the syndicate, Mr J. Pettit of Auckland, said shortly before the yacht's departure for Tauranga this afternoon that the trip was "an adventure cruise" around the south of the South Island, Stewart Island, and the Auckland Islands, with the focal point being the Cave of Death where the General Grant was wrecked in 1866.

Visiting many of the historical wrecks in the islands area, the divers recovered relics such as portholes and brass fittings for a maritime museum in Paihia, Bay of Islands.

"We searched for the wreck of the General Grant, which is probably the greatest prize in these waters because of its cargo of gold," Mr Pettit said.

"We did about 80 dives on the west coast, and searched the Cave of Death where the ship was wrecked. Other caves were also dived into, if they bore any resemblance to the cave described by the survivors.

"We found no sign of any wreck in any of the caves except for a kedge anchor in the Cave of Death. This was probably put over by one of the ship's boats. It was completely jammed and had cemented itself into the surrounding rock, so we blasted it loose. Kelvin Tarlton and John Dealing used a lifting bag — an underwater parachute filled with compressed air.

"At Erebus Cove we visited the cemetery containing the remains of many shipwrecked survivors who died of starvation on the island. Many of the wooden crosses had rotted away, leaving some names indecipherable," he said.

Mr Pettit and his partner think the General Grant may have dropped her ballast when she was smashed the cave, and this would have caused the wreck float and drift out to sea.

The men were: Messrs Pettit (Auckland), W. Gallagher (Hamilton, skipper) K. Tarlton (Hamilton), Clements (Auckland), Locke (Matamata), L. Shear (Hamilton), J. Dealing (Auckland), and J. Colc (Hamilton).

"We found that there was quite a strong surface current out from the cav while we were diving," added.

The Haumutana carried more than $7000 worth diving equipment, including five 4000lb cylinders of a 59 aqualungs and about wet suits.

She has an electric sto and the men usually have roast meal most nights, beef steaks, preferring to eat a great deal of fish.

Four Years' Gaol

(P.A.)   WELLINGTON

"Those persons who helped the girl and chased a caught the prisoner publicly commended," Justice Beattie said in t Supreme Court today, wh he sentenced Alexand Christie, aged 40, facto worker to four years ga for indecently assaulting girl under 12.

Christie had pleaded guil in the Nelson Magistrate Court and had been commited to the Supreme Court f sentence.

LEFT The *General Grant* expedition was big news in Southland.

of blasting, they hauled it up. Then they found another one, the *Tarawera*, and retrieved the blades from that, and another on Dog Island, the *Waikouaiti*. It was Pettit's job to sell the scrap at Bluff, more than 9 tons of brass in all, collecting a series of fat cheques.[24] Meantime, they had used up their supply of blasting gelatine before they had even headed to the Auckland Islands. Tarlton set off to Invercargill to get some more, returning, as John Gallagher recalled, on the bus, alongside old ladies and school kids, with a 'great big brown paper parcel' of gelignite sitting on his lap.[25] It wasn't for nothing that he was called 'Gelly Kelly'.

Finally the weather cleared sufficiently for them to set off for the Auckland Islands. Although at only 51 degrees south, the equivalent latitude of London in the northern hemisphere, the Auckland Islands have a bleak climate. Even in summer, with nothing between them and Antarctica, the water temperature rarely rises above 11 degrees celcius and the air temperature isn't much better. Enormous swells sweep through. The Gallagher brothers and their crew had heard that during a storm in 1944 waves had swept up over Adams Rocks, which are 118 metres high. Even in relatively good conditions, it was dangerous. Kelly Tarlton wrote, 'On one occasion we surfed down the front of huge waves and were lucky not to broach. The ship was 88 feet long and of deep draught, but the seas were too big to handle from behind.'[26]

Their most perilous moment came when they were trying to find an anchorage on the uncharted west coast, sailing between Disappointment Island and the main island. *The South Pacific Island Pilot* was no use, simply saying not to go there. Tarlton described their plight: 'Across the top near Bristow Rock the seas were tremendous, with overfalls. Bill and John were at the wheel (nothing worries them — they take all emergencies calmly and efficiently) and the *Hamutana* was almost surfing. She took one huge green wave over the side that sent everything flying, including me (fell off my stool). The cold damp mist had come down and reduced the visibility to about 300 yards. We had set a course to take us clear of Column Rocks and suddenly found we had Invercauld Rock on our port side and Column Rocks dead ahead. It took a rapid bit of slowing down and creeping slow ahead in very rough seas to feel our way around. Poor Len Scherer was out in front in all his waterproof gear, freezing in the icy spray.'[27]

Bill Gallagher remembers they faced a choice of carrying on

RIGHT Gallagher and his diving mates were enthusiastic blasters of old wrecks, as they searched for metal for recycling.

through the breakers to calm waters beyond them or going around and risking hitting a rock. They went for the breakers, and the *Hamutana* punched through successfully into a beautiful calm harbour, with wild cattle running along the beach, among rabbits and seals. The cattle, sadly, were too quick to shoot, so the crew had to make do with ship supplies, which involved a lot of tinned peaches. They did, of course, catch plenty of fish and giant Auckland Island crabs.

Their purpose, however, was to find gold, so the next day they went out to the coast and found what they thought was the Cave of Death. John Dearling described the scene: 'Our hearts were beating with excitement and steam came off our breath as the master plan was made. Kelly and I were to dive first, swim into the cave, mark the gold's position and then everyone would help raise it.'[28] If only they had been so lucky. Within five minutes of diving in, their fingers were so cold as to be helpless, powerful currents swept them in, and out, and there was no sign of a ship, let alone gold.

Bill Gallagher had arranged a code with his father. A radio message, 'All the best for your anniversary', would have indicated that they had struck gold. He didn't get to send that message. 'Three days fishing, no crayfish' was all he could send, the meaning being obvious.

John Pettit's description of Bill Gallagher indicates that as captain he tolerated no nonsense. Someone had knocked a copper air vent overboard, but no one took responsibility. When Pettit, as expedition leader, announced it was time to head home, Bill stated firmly that the anchor would not be lifted until the vent had been recovered. Tired and depressed divers had to get their gear on for one last freezing dive.[29]

Spirits were lifted on the way back to Bluff with a couple more successful salvage efforts. They harvested a few more hefty propellers, together with a good collection of surprisingly valuable paua. By the end of their expedition the syndicate members had met their costs entirely and walked away with $400 each, around $5700 in 2012 terms. Pettit was able to buy his wife her first automatic washing machine.

The *General Grant* expedition proved a swansong for the *Hamutana*. Bill Gallagher senior was becoming increasingly susceptible to seasicknesses. 'It was nice going places,' he wrote, 'but sitting down for days on end being tossed around, a bloke began to think well, what a fool I am for being out here. I could be home in an armchair.'[30] Besides, the costs of running the boat were escalating, and he and his two sons were tiring of spending so many weekends in Tauranga pulling engines apart and carrying out other mucky tasks. He sold it to a Samoan ferry operator for $30,000, delivered to Apia.

Gallagher shared out some of the proceeds from the sale of the *Hamutana* to his sons, and Bill junior used the money to buy a section at Whangamata. He had seen some graphic photos of beachfront properties being gouged out by the sea, so he bought one row back, hoping quietly that a few good storms might promote him to the front row. Coastal property was still cheap then, so Gallagher picked up his section for $3000. The family spent the summer there in a caravan while Bill and a bricklayer friend, Doug Bunyan, built a house on it: 2400 concrete blocks, he recalls. It was very simple, but had room underneath for the 5 metre speedboat that would now become the centre of his recreational activities. Bill's daughter Janine recalls that a typical Whangamata weekend consisted of one day on the boat and a day's maintenance on the bach. Bill had a red, spotty towelling hat that had one surface covered in gobs of paint from working under the eaves; the following day he would simply invert it to present the clean surface for boating.

Bill Gallagher junior had his thirtieth birthday in January 1971, while he was working away on his concrete blocks at Whangamata. A lust for gold and adventure still burned within him, but he was sensible enough to acknowledge that scudding around through sub-Antarctic swells in relatively small boats looking for old wrecks was unlikely to yield much of the gleaming stuff. If the swells at the Auckland Islands had been a bit bigger and the fog a bit thicker he might have come unstuck, just as he may have with his dose of the bends, or if his air pipe had snagged on a stalactite and he had dropped his torch somewhere deep in the bowels of the Waitomo Caves. While John, at 32, still remained a carefree bachelor, Bill had a wife and two young children, and there was a limit to how long he could carry on this way.

The matter was simply resolved. Henceforth business would provide Bill Gallagher with both the gold and the adventure.

4
PLAYING DOUBLES: 1971–77

Chapter four

PLAYING DOUBLES: 1971–77

Thomas Edison said invention is 1 per cent inspiration and 99 per cent perspiration, and it's so true. In our experience even once you have a product made and working right you are not even halfway to success; the biggest cost and the usual area of failure is getting it to market.

— BILL GALLAGHER JNR

When forging a life of adventure on the high seas — including blowing things up and searching for gold — in favour of knuckling down to a life of business in a provincial city, it helps if the prospects are good. Bill Gallagher's timing in 1971 was impeccable. The firm's forage harvesters, rotary hoes and post-hole diggers weren't glamorous, but they found a ready market in New Zealand and Australia. In the Gallagher electric fence energiser, meantime, the company had a product that it would eventually realise was as good as anything in the world, if not better. Small, and moderately valuable for its size, the electric fence energiser was a natural export product. Having developed their confidence in Australia, the Gallaghers would spend the next few years extending their nose into world markets, cautiously at first, then helter skelter from 1976.

With the benefit of hindsight, we can now see these years, 1971–77, as the period of transformation for Gallaghers, the company's point of take-off. In this period, it went from being a small, higgledy-piggledy backyard family operation to a rapidly expanding exporter with a scale that was starting to get noticed. In the year to March 1971, Gallagher Engineering Ltd managed sales of $196,000 (around $2.5 million in 2012 terms), of which a mere $15,000 came from exports. Net profit was $5270 ($66,000 today). Six years later, in the year to March 1977, the Gallagher Group generated sales of $2.46 million (around $16 million in 2012 terms), almost exactly half of which were from exports. Net profit was now $193,000 ($1.3 million today).

Sales had grown six-fold in real terms, while profits had soared 20-fold, albeit from a low base. What had been a 30-man operation now employed around 90 in a new, purpose-built factory on Kahikatea Drive. Something resembling a senior management team was now required. Growth was explosive at times: the company's turnover grew by more than 100 per cent between the 1976 and 1977 years. In the Waikato vernacular, they were 'playing doubles'.

The shape of the business was still evolving — in the mid-1970s agricultural machinery still dominated. Gallagher Electronics, a new company established in February 1974 to focus on electric fencing, was growing rapidly, crouched ready to spring into dozens of markets throughout the world. It was full of promise, but in 1977 it was still only half the size of Gallagher Engineering.[1]

Ultimate success was not assured, of course. Many companies fall apart at the seams after an initial burst of rapid growth. But in the early to mid-1970s Gallaghers had heaved itself over a hump to enter the world of serious business. This transformation was not the outcome of a six-year strategic plan written in 1971. No such thing existed, beyond vague thoughts nursed in the breasts of Bill junior and John that they should 'go for it'. Growth came opportunistically and gathered its own momentum. What were the critical ingredients?

First and foremost, the company shifted gear in 1971 when it received the full blast of the brothers' undivided attention, particularly after Bill junior was freed from his earlier distractions. It was never enough just to have good products; there had to be a determination by the company's principals to commercialise their products and take them to the world. Many of the Gallaghers seem to have had a surplus of energy, combined with formidable powers of concentration. Bill senior, however, appears to have found his satisfaction in solving technical problems; he would tinker away until he had a product working well, then he would move on to the next one, happy in his work. As his sons watched, thinking, as most sons do, that they could do better than their 'old man', they saw a huge void in his business efforts. There needed to be as much effort, ingenuity and thought devoted to the task of selling the product and promoting it as there was put in at the workshop. This is what the brothers now provided. The balance of ownership also shifted in their favour. When Gallagher Electronics was established the two brothers and their father each had a third share.

The relationship between the brothers, John and Bill junior, lay at the core of the enterprise. The previous generation of Gallagher brothers — Bill senior, Viv and Henry — had been too similar in personality to work together successfully; with all three being independent-minded leaders they quickly clashed. John and Bill Gallagher junior, by contrast, were polar opposites. From childhood it was clear that Bill junior was massively driven, a natural leader, with plenty of aggression and few self-doubts, while John was quieter, less confrontational, and good at smoothing ruffled feathers. The combination was a good one, since between them they covered most of the personality traits required for a successful operation, and, because John recognised his younger brother's extra fire and ambition, they avoided a potentially destructive contest for domination. Bill junior assumed the role of general manager, while John was content to be sales manager.

It helped that in the early 1970s the rural economy in New Zealand was clipping along nicely. With good products and an active presence at Fieldays and other farm markets, and a good reputation for reliability, the Gallagher products — the Rotohoe (including the Dreadnought Rotohoe for the heaviest work), post-hole digger and forage harvesters — were all selling well. Most farmers owned their own equipment, and with money in their pocket, particularly in 1973 and 1974 when commodity prices were high, they opened their cheque books.

The electric fences were also now reliable and selling well on the local market. In 1971 Gallaghers introduced the BEV mains energiser, the 'V' being for 'voltage dependent resister', which they had added to limit the output to less than 5000 volts, which was

BELOW One of Gallaghers' many efforts to make it easier to erect a temporary fence.

the law in New Zealand at the time. The following year they put an injection-moulded plastic case on it and called it the BEV II. This became their most famous model (and prompted many distributors and farmers to assume that Bill Gallagher had a stroppy wife called Beverley), and it won an award at the 1972 Fieldays at Mystery Creek. But other models were also popular. The E12 had a 12 volt wet battery unit, and was designed for permanent fences up to 35 kilometres long in remote places with no power supply. The KM2, in contrast, was a lightweight, portable and weatherproof unit designed for short, temporary lines. This was the model beloved by farmers using intensive strip-grazing methods. The next breakthrough model, the Super 60, was ready for the New Zealand market in 1976. This had twice the power of the BEV II and was designed for permanent electric fences 'subject to high challenge from vegetation, animals and long distance'. Gallaghers initially called the Super 60 the 'Sheep Energiser', in the hope of shifting the still prevalent perception that electric fences couldn't penetrate the wool on a sheep's flank.

In Australia, meantime, they hadn't progressed too far from the beachhead Bill junior had established in November 1967. In the year to March 1971 they still managed only $15,000 worth of business. From then on, Bill junior devoted himself more vigorously to the task. Elders continued to handle the agricultural machinery, and at various points, in different states at different times, Gallagher products were in hot demand. For a while the beef industry was booming and its farmers were buying plenty of forage harvesters, but in 1975 beef incomes collapsed and so did Gallaghers' machinery sales.

Bill junior didn't fight it. He accepted that the money had left that industry and there was no point in wasting resources in a vain attempt to restore his earlier turnover. Looking around, he saw that the sugar industry was thriving in Queensland. Here he enjoyed a stroke of luck. Three up-and-coming young Elders executives had been given the task of developing the Queensland business and were keen to make their mark. In December 1974 they approached Gallaghers for sole distribution rights to the Rotohoe in Queensland for use in the sugar plantations.[2] Within a short time they were sending four or five container-loads of Rotohoes per month to Queensland.

Elders was selling another firm's electric fence energisers,

ABOVE Gallaghers' standard publicity shot for their energiser, 1950–70.

so when the Gallaghers felt their energiser was ready for export, Bill junior had to find a new agent. On his first trip to Australia for the Orange Field Day in 1967 he had met Bob Piesse, a well-known electric fence innovator from Melbourne. They had chatted and Piesse had followed up with an offer to distribute Gallaghers' energisers in Australia. At that stage Bill turned him down, saying they weren't ready for export.[3] By August 1970, however, he was feeling more confident and sent Piesse details of the BE model's performance.

Gallagher recalls, 'Bob Piesse was the only guy I'd met who, when I talked about our energiser holding 2000 volts into 500 ohms, knew what I was talking about and understood its significance.' Ohms is a measure of resistance, which runs on an inverted scale. So in terms of an electric fence, 1,000,000 ohms represents a fairly light load but a high resistance; 500 ohms represents quite a heavy load (and small resistance), the equivalent of plenty of grass on the wire; 50 ohms represents a wire completely covered in foliage. Gallagher told Piesse that his machine delivered 4500 volts at 1 megaohm, 1800 volts at 500 ohms, and 900 volts at 50 ohms. Unused to praising New Zealanders, Piesse did manage to observe that such figures were 'quite exciting'. He had measured the performance of the Waikato E2, the second-generation Waikato energiser that Piesse regarded as 'easily the best performer on the market' and which enjoyed the largest market share in Australia. It could manage only 600 volts at 500 ohms and nothing whatsoever at 50.[4]

Earlier in 1970, Piesse had joined forces with Norman W Hutchinson & Sons, a long-established Melbourne merchant house, primarily focused on steel. Their subsidiary, WH Billings Ltd, handled electric fences and manufactured their own low-powered energisers. They were keen to distribute Gallaghers' machines, and so by early 1971 the firm's energisers reached the Australian market, trading first as the Supremo Electric Fence Energiser. With their extra power, Gallaghers' energisers soon enjoyed a strong following from the big sheep stations that needed long fences to keep out kangaroos and dingoes, as well as hold in the sheep. By the year to March 1975 Billings was selling 2000 energisers annually, and rising. At around $50 each, that represented $100,000 worth of business (approaching $1 million in 2012 terms).

An inventive and active promoter, Piesse also encouraged the

Gallaghers to think beyond simply producing energisers. Farmers need to buy plenty of other accessories to have a good electric fence — wires, fence posts, reels, voltmeters and insulators especially. Slowly they pieced together the important elements, and by 1975 they were offering a more comprehensive package than any of their competitors in Australia.

Gallaghers' rapid progress in the early to mid-1970s was being powered by Bill's ambition and focus, quality products, the generally buoyant economic conditions, and by the assistance of some good distributors in Australia. But there was another important element: Gallaghers enjoyed very supportive government policies in New Zealand.

Britain's entry to the EEC on 1 January 1973, which had long been feared, ended New Zealand's open access to its largest market. During the 1960s Keith Holyoake's government had been lending a little bit of assistance to manufacturing exporters, in the hope of reducing the country's excess reliance on earnings from the old staples of wool, dairy products and meat. In the early 1970s, with the EEC threat materialising, that tendency accelerated and the tax system was used selectively to encourage new industries to earn export dollars. With the first oil shock in 1973, which sent oil prices soaring and prompted a massive deterioration in New Zealand's terms of trade in 1974, the search for new export industries became increasingly desperate and more and more generously encouraged.

As the Gallaghers felt their way into exporting they realised that they were doing precisely what the politicians wanted during a time of great national anxiety. Bill Gallagher recalls: 'As rapidly growing manufacturing exporters, we were heroes in the 1970s. The officials in Wellington really treated us royally; there was nothing they wouldn't do for us. And we picked up the vibes and this spurred us into doing more exporting. Too right it did. We grasped the opportunities that presented themselves and responded positively.'

In the year to March 1973 they had paid tax at a rate of 21 per cent on their net profits; that was nothing like the horrors that Bill senior had experienced in the late 1940s and 1950s, but nor was it negligible. Over the next few years, more generous depreciation rates and an 'increased exports incentive', which gave tax deduc-

Gift to Field Days Society

able so that attractive, efficient services could be provided in the national interest.

CONSIDERABLE

"The leeway to be made up," he said, "is considerable. The achievements of the Department over the past year have shown what can be done to carry an increased quantity of goods; much more can be accomplished as modern rolling stock is provided and outmoded techniques eliminated."

ATTENDANCE AT THE NEW ZEALAND NATIONAL FIELD DAYS held at Mystery Creek on the last three days of last week has been set at 36,000. In this picture, taken there, Mr William Gallagher of the Frankton engineering firm and family is seen as he presented the Field Days Society with a new rotary hoe, manufactured by his firm. Accepting it on behalf of the Society was Dr D. R. Llewellyn, president of the Society and vice-chancellor of the University of Waikato. He is standing at the extreme right of the picture. Mr Vaughan Jones, secretary manager of the Society, is seen extreme left, by Mr Gallagher.

REGISTERED AT POST OFFICE HEADQUARTERS WELLINGTON, AS A NEWSPAPER.

ABOVE Bill Gallagher was an early and consistent supporter of the Waikato Fieldays and was never shy of some publicity.

tions if a firm increased its volume of exports, reduced that taxation to zero.⁵ Gallaghers was able to keep every cent of the $193,000 net profit it earned in the year to March 1977. And the Gallaghers knew they needed to keep expanding their exports in order to continue enjoying the tax holiday. The incentives were a world away from those operating in the 1950s.

On top of that, other little veins of assistance could profitably be mined. In 1974 Bill Gallagher had gone to a manufacturing engineers conference in Queenstown where Warren Freer, the Minister of Trade and Industry, complained that the government had put in place an Industry Research and Development expansion scheme, 'but very little use was being made of it'. It offered a government grant based on a percentage of any increase in a company's R&D spending, on the condition that a university graduate in science was employed. Gallagher looked into the scheme and saw that it could mean moving beyond their current practice of 'doing R&D on a shoestring in a relatively amateur, unprofessional manner' — using the proverbial knife and fork to fiddle with things on the kitchen table in the evenings — toward a formal, methodical programme of research. Bill himself qualified as the graduate, so he filled out the forms and the firm received a grant of $8493 in the 1974/75 year (around $80,000 in 2012 terms).⁶

The scheme lasted only three years, but Gallagher credits this early seed funding with opening his eyes to the value of methodical R&D. He wrote later: 'In the struggling days of forming a company, a large expenditure in R&D is sometimes difficult to justify, particularly if accountants have any influence . . . a few technical boffins in the back room can eat a lot of funds and in the short term produce very little results for the bottom line. And if the answer is to produce results this year, as it is in many public companies, R&D is probably something you can do without. [But when the scheme] gave us encouragement, we started doing it on a sounder basis and found it was a paying proposition.'⁷

During those three years, the little R&D department began work on a solar-powered electric fence and on electric fence theory. Their prototype of the former won an award at the New Zealand National Fieldays in 1975, although the high cost of the solar panel made it a difficult commercial proposition in the short term. The theory, meantime, which sought to understand the physics of the fence as effectively a transmission line, proved invaluable over the years. Another research project developed a modular circuit construction for the standard BEV II mains energiser, which was of huge practical assistance since it made maintenance and the replacement of faulty or lightning-damaged parts simple.

The scheme lasted just long enough for Bill Gallagher to see the commercial value gained from R&D, so that even after the grant had been removed the company continued to increase its spending in this area. A culture of research-informed innovation had been embedded, which he now counts as one of the decisive factors in the company's subsequent international success.

As for any rapidly growing firm, finding sufficient money to finance expansion was a constant challenge. By the early 1970s it was obvious that Bill senior's backyard, with a few additions onto Norton Road, was no longer adequate. The premises had a nice family feel: Bill's young children, Janine and Ian, ran around in the evenings and weekends when their father was often to be found in the workshop, usually underneath welding goggles and other gear. The rule was that if they saw sparks flying, they had to wait on the grass. Janine remembers that if they annoyed him too much, he'd simply drop them down a large forage harvester chute that was lying on the ground, from which it was impossible to climb out.[8] But, even with the blackberry and chooks long gone, with more than 40 people on site it was badly overcrowded. Machinery and boxes spilled out all over the footpath when containers were being filled for export.

As early as 1971 Bill junior had begun looking for a new site. He had found a good one outside the city limits, but the council refused permission for its industrial use on the grounds that there was plenty of industrial land inside the city. Gallagher launched into the press, grumbling about the high price of land in Hamilton and threatening to move to Huntly if something didn't turn up.[9] This prompted a few offers, but no progress was made until 1974, when a local builder and developer, Vince Moss, offered them 2.68 acres (just over 1 ha) on Kahikatea Drive. It was part of a 10 acre (4 ha) block he planned to subdivide. Comprising swampy peat land, it was close to the city on an arterial road that was

ABOVE Bill Gallagher senior in a characteristic pose.

ABOVE A new manufacturing site for Gallagher Engineering on Kahikatea Drive, 1976.

developing into a western bypass of the city, and the rail line was handy.

The eventual cost of the land was just under $40,000, and it would cost a further $156,000 to put the first factory on it. Bill senior didn't want to know about such an investment, leaving his sons to do it themselves. Bill junior and John formed a partnership for the purpose, then Bill 'wore out his knees' grovelling to bankers to find the money. Eventually he persuaded the Norwich Insurance Company to come to the party.

In his enthusiasm to get things underway he had engaged an engineer to begin on the complicated task of building a floating foundation on the peat, even before Moss had completed the paperwork on his subdivision. The Gallaghers had signed a sale and purchase agreement that was conditional on the subdivision. This state of affairs dragged on for several months, raising the temperature somewhat, since the brothers had paid a deposit on the land and were spending thousands each month building furiously on land they didn't own. Norwich, naturally, declined to hand over any of its money until the legal niceties were observed. Fortunately the Gallaghers' faith in Moss was rewarded and everything was straightened out so that they actually owned the factory and single-level office block that was completed in January 1976. But for several months through 1975, cash was in very short supply.

In such circumstances, being able to retain all the company's profits in order, ultimately, to fund the new land and buildings was very handy. But a company doubling in size in some years had a voracious appetite, needing cash for additional plant and machinery, as well as for simple working capital. Critically, further government assistance became available at a helpful stage. In April 1974 Gallaghers obtained an export suspensory loan from the state-owned Development Finance Corporation (DFC). This was the best sort of loan — one that you didn't have to pay back in full. At a time when the shareholders' funds in the company were limited, the DFC lent the Gallagher Group $100,000 in order to buy plant and machinery.[10] No commercial bank would have given them the money. And if they achieved certain export growth targets, which Bill Gallagher knew they could meet 'standing on their head', 40 per cent of the loan would be written off. All in all, Gallagher remembers that the DFC cash 'gave us a real lift'.

While showing John Hunn, the DFC's general manager, over the building site in late 1974, Bill 'almost rubbed him out' by pulling out into traffic on Kahikatea Drive in his Chrysler. Looking into the sun, he had missed seeing an oncoming car and very narrowly avoided a ghastly accident.

Events were passing in something of a blur during this period. For as well as building factories, shifting production and expanding their Australian market, the Gallaghers were now looking further afield for markets, encouraged by all the government assistance on offer.

Long-haul exporting had begun with Bill senior being at a loose end. Having sold his beloved *Hamutana* at the end of 1970, he was ready, after a couple of years holidaying onshore in New Zealand, for something more adventurous. With 150 per cent tax-deductibility for export market development travel costs, it made sense to combine some work with travel and go somewhere new. In 1973 he and Millie set off for an extended tour of the UK. Buying a Morris Oxford 1100 and a little caravan, they trundled around attending agricultural shows throughout the country, gathering intelligence about the state of the electric fence industry. What he saw was sufficient to convince the former exporting sceptic that a magnificent opportunity lay before them, and over the summer he signed up Rutland Electrics as Gallaghers' British distributor. The company was owned by Les Dickinson, who had a whiteware shop in Oakham, Rutland, about 150 kilometres north of London. The first consignment of 32 units was sent in August 1973.[11]

Bill junior, meantime, had been concentrating on Australia. And each year, during the August school holidays, he would take his family on a trip somewhere in the South Pacific, where he would scout about for a few sales. In Fiji, the Cook Islands and Samoa, these trips were relaxing. Further to the west, things could get a little more exciting. In New Caledonia one year they were driving home late one evening after a day's diving when they encountered a roadblock. Some of the indigenous Kanak people who wanted independence had been 'causing trouble' and the gendarmes wanted to know what these travellers were doing. Fumbling his French, Gallagher mixed up 'tourist' with 'terrorist', and found himself hauled out while the gendarmes took everything out of the car, kids and all, to satisfy themselves that there was nothing untoward going on. Orders from the South Pacific were just sufficient to persuade the taxman that his trips did indeed have some business merit, but no more.

By 1975 Bill junior was ready to see the rest of the world. After a year on the job in the UK, Les Dickinson had managed to sell only 200 energisers and hadn't been in a rush to pay his bills. Bill set off in late June to see what the problem was, taking Jenny on what would be a serious overseas trip. It didn't turn out quite as Jenny imagined: 'It was very business-orientated. We picked up Mum and Dad's caravan, which was pretty run-down — it was good enough for them, therefore it was good enough for us. And we travelled around a succession of big shows, where Bill would work all day at the fair and I'd wander around. And in between the shows we toured around contacts he'd made, in this blimmin' caravan. Finally, we ditched the caravan and drove up to Scotland to visit more people, staying in B&Bs. We went through Edinburgh, where my family had come from. I said to Bill, "Can we stop?" He said, sure, we were at a red traffic light. "OK, now we're off." He wasn't interested in being a tourist; he was there for business.'[12]

They stayed for a while with Les Dickinson in Oakham. Between talking to Dickinson and countless farmers and distributors around the country, Gallagher realised how different the market was to what he had experienced in New Zealand and Australia: 'It was relatively easy to wow them in the UK with something exciting and different, but they wouldn't talk to their neighbour about it. Normally when you're trying to sell something radically different you convince the farm leaders, knowing that they'd talk about it. But it didn't happen in the UK; there wasn't the word-of-mouth vector that we'd come to expect.'

However, he expected the native English to devise a marketing plan that worked. They were advertising nationally, and Gallagher expected results. He had been approached separately by Dan Cherrington, a well-connected young farmer from Noss Mayo, near Plymouth, Devon. His father, John Cherrington, had been the leader of the Farmers' Union, so the family was very politically aware, with wide networks. While travelling in New Zealand Dan had visited the Gallagher factory and been impressed. Back at his Devon farm he arranged with Dickinson to sell some E12 models in the south of England and had quickly sold 40.

Gallagher travelled down to Plymouth, rambled about in the

sun, did some diving on the southern coast, and concluded that Cherrington was just the man he needed to sharpen up Rutland Electrics' performance. So, on the spot, in August 1975 he signed up Cherrington as Gallaghers' distributor south of the M4 and of the Thames east of London, with Dickinson retaining the north of England and the Midlands. Now that he faced competition, Dickinson became lively, and soon the two distributors were locked in a fierce battle, arguing over who had rights to the M4 itself.

After that first international trip of consequence, Bill caught fire. He took off all over the world, opening new fronts from Japan to Argentina, casting his bread on the waters not knowing what would come back. The main stops on the way to the UK in 1975 were Indonesia and the United States. After Britain he skipped across to Denmark to attend a show in Herning, Jutland, and down to Limoges in France, where he signed up Elpa Services as the distributor for France as well as Spain, Switzerland and Italy. In Argentina he met Vicente Casares, who was keen to sell Gallaghers' energisers, but import duties were prohibitive. The only way around the problem was for Casares to manufacture them in Argentina under licence. Vicente Casares junior was sent to New Zealand in 1976 to learn the recipe, as it were.

Meanwhile a Japanese company, Surge Miyawaki Co Ltd, had shown interest in the electric fences. Bill called in to see them and travelled up to Hokkaido to spread the gospel among dairy farmers. He also returned to the UK and Denmark in 1976, this time meeting Poul Dalgaard in Copenhagen. The young Dane, still in his early twenties, had been trading horses and antiques in the UK. He had heard about the Gallagher fences and made contact. Bill met Dalgaard at the Kong Frederik Hotel and spent an evening talking to him over a series of cognacs. Seeing an entrepreneurial spark in the 2 metre tall 'Great Dane', Gallagher drew up a distributor's agreement on the plane home. Within 10 days of their meeting, in October 1976, Dalgaard was signed up and intent on building a business from his home patch near Roskilde.

John Gallagher, meanwhile, had been concentrating on the US. Back in 1974 he had been to a Toastmasters International convention in Anaheim, California, taking his new bride,

TOP Bill Gallagher senior enjoying his later years marketing electric fences during the English summer.

ABOVE Bill Gallagher's strategy was to find energetic businessmen to market his fences around the world. In Denmark he found Poul Dalgaard, pictured left.

Glenice (they had married in September 1972). After the convention they drove up the West Coast, visiting their contacts and others supplied by New Zealand's trade officials: Customs agents, freighters, feedstores, dealers, distributors and machinery businesses — anyone who might help point them in the right direction. Then they flew to Chicago and spent some time driving around the Midwest, 'visiting farms, looking at who was doing what, and finding what electric fences were available'. To his amazement John found that the industry had scarcely developed at all in a technological sense since the 1930s. 'The Americans,' he recalls, 'operated a system where the all-powerful seller squeezed the manufacturers to death, forcing prices down constantly, leaving no money in the industry for R&D and the development of new products.'[13] As a result the electric fence 'chargers' — as the Americans called them — were dirt cheap but, compared with the high-powered Gallagher models, not very effective.

Another wonderful opportunity appeared to beckon. John adopted the US market as his challenge and went back for three-week visits twice a year for the next few years to get it established. It wasn't as easy as he had hoped: 'I had a real problem getting distributors and farmers to see what they could do with a high-powered fence. All the American manufacturers made wild advertising claims, that they could power fences for 20 miles, etc, but the reality was that two blades of grass would kill it. We had to convince them that it actually was possible. And then we wanted $147 for one of our units, when the highest cost American one was $49 and the lowest could be picked up for just $11.50. So it wasn't straightforward.'[14]

After several knock-backs he managed to sign up a nationwide distributor in 1975, only for the arrangement to fall over in short order. Henry Swayze, an architect turned small-time lifestyle farmer in Vermont, approached the firm and was granted the distribution rights for his small state later in the year.

Freezing in Chicago on a Friday afternoon in late January 1976, after several more demoralising weeks making little progress, John Gallagher looked at a card that he had from a man in San Antonio, Texas. Figuring that at least it would be warmer there, close to the Mexican border, he resolved on one last try before going home. He spent a weekend on Art Snell's farm, pitching hay. Over the

ABOVE American distributor Art Snell translated the Gallagher message into American.

following months Snell took a few models and sold them. When John returned to Snell's farm six months later, he was met by the statement, delivered in a strong Texan drawl: 'John, we are onto something here.' He had tried out all the US fence chargers and found them wanting; Gallaghers' technology was way ahead of anything else. In January 1977 Art Snell signed on as Gallagher's sole distributor for 35 states, and after more than four years the Gallaghers at last felt they were making progress. But as John Gallagher told a New Zealand newspaper at the time, he found the Americans hard to read: 'American businessmen can lull you with backslapping and hospitality. When you think a deal is all sewn up, nothing happens.' A large part of the job was simply to convince them that coming from New Zealand, a country two-fifths the size of Texas, with a climate somewhat like Montana, you could still be serious businessmen.[15]

And the Americans still weren't rushing to pay a huge premium for the New Zealand energisers over the cheaper domestic models. One of Snell's catalogues pitched the Gallagher electric fences as offering effective animal and predator control for less money than conventional fencing, asserting that protection from 'coyotes, wild hogs, deer, rabbits, bears and varmints can now be achieved'. Coyotes, in particular, were the scourge of sheep farmers, so, drawing on assistance from the Australian Bob Piesse, John Gallagher and Snell started working with a university in Denver to design a coyote-proof fence. They began experiments in North Dakota and Kansas in 1977; early results were promising and offered great opportunities for propaganda.

As a result of all this activity, global export receipts from energisers more than trebled from $151,000 in the year to March 1976 to $476,000 in the year to March 1977 ($3.3 million in 2012 terms). A further healthy rise was expected through the rest of 1977. Many new territories didn't yet amount to much; Canada, for example, only took around 50 energisers a year. Australia still dominated, but the UK was rising and the US offered great hope.

But none of it was easy. Every country had its obstacles. In Argentina, the main problem was how to get the money out. (That was an issue in most markets.) In England, as in many places, Gallaghers faced ingrained conservatism among farmers. Cherrington wrote, 'Talking to the average British farmer about mains electric fencing is like suggesting a trip to the moon.'[16] They could get their heads around the battery-powered models, but he predicted that a major effort would be required to launch the BEV II. The logistics of getting energisers to distant parts of the world were also demanding. Art Snell was soon complaining about energisers arriving in Texas with solder connections broken, no doubt in transit. The offending connections were easily redesigned to be more robust, but it was just another thing to worry about. The major achievement of the company at this time was that it managed to hold itself together over this period of rapid expansion without any major disasters.

Importantly, by 1977 Bill junior had stitched together a much more robust organisation than had existed in 1971. For a start, the 90-odd staff members now had room to move. From early 1976 the engineering side of the business spread out over its large new factory floor, and in the early months of 1977 work began on a new building for the electronics business. The company's organisational structure, meantime, had also evolved. In the 1960s it had been flat and flexible, but as the workforce grew, basic structures had to emerge.

By 1972 Bill junior and John both ranged over both sides of the business. Beneath them, Eddie Smith was responsible for the machine and welding shops, which formed the bulk of the agricultural side of the business, while Jim Dudek, a Polish immigrant, ran the electronics department. As the volume of products rose rapidly, more attention was given to cost control, assembly design, and storage and dispatch systems. An experienced English production engineer, Colin Standing, joined the team at the end of 1972, working with Pat McQuillan, an ex-air-force man who looked after the accounts and established a numbering system for components on the production floor. But it would be fair to say that during the mid-1970s the emphasis was on growing the export market as fast as possible and building the products as fast as they could sell them. Despite the formation of a Production Committee and a Technical Committee, production and maintenance costs were guessed at rather than finely calculated. Bill junior devoted his full attention to expansion; questions of efficiency could be dealt with later.

At Norton Road the company had mostly kept under the radar. It wasn't until 1974, when it had nearly 50 staff, that Ralph Savage, a local Engineers' Union secretary, wandered onto the site. Bill junior recalls, 'His eyeballs nearly dropped out; all these workers

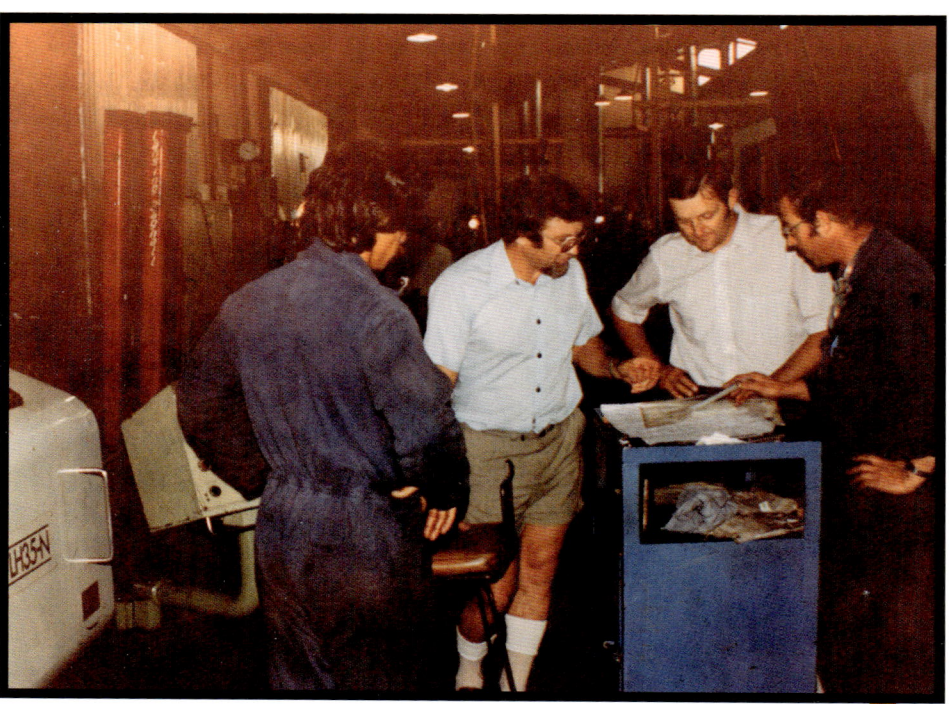

THIS PAGE Brothers Bill and John Gallagher worked closely through the 1970s, both on the factory floor (top) and in the constant round of publicity shoots for the latest products (bottom).

and not a single union member.' By law union membership was compulsory so Gallaghers had no option, once sprung, but to join up. Working on the principle that if you can't fight it, you might as well join it, Bill junior joined the union as well. While many large-scale engineering companies were wracked with industrial relations strife, Gallaghers was small enough and retained sufficient family atmosphere to avoid serious problems.

At a time when 'us and them' attitudes were the norm between workers and bosses, it was a huge advantage to have three Gallagher men working on site and undeniably passionate about their products. Bill senior remained at his happiest in the workshop. And although Bill junior and John increasingly focused on sales and travelled a lot, they remained equally at home in the workshop. A striking demonstration of this commitment was Bill junior's insistence on moving house when the factory relocated to Kahikatea Drive. He wanted to be able to see the factory from home, and so he found a section at 40 Kowhai Street, on a slight rise a few hundred metres north of the factory. Janine remembers that when her father arrived home, usually late in the evening, he would sit in his chair in the lounge from which he could see down, across Gower Park, to the workshop. If he spied anyone wandering around, he'd be off in a flash to see what was going on.

On the evening of 29 June 1977 he gazed out the window to see flames coming from his beloved engineering factory, where electric fences were being produced while the new electronics factory was nearing completion. Jenny rang the fire brigade while Bill charged down the stairs. The factory suffered extensive damage.

Bill junior's passion for the company wasn't surprising. The world seemed ripe with opportunity. The size of that opportunity was brought home to him during a visit to Budapest in April 1977. Gallagher was there to represent the Australian Standards Committee at a meeting of the International Commission on rules for the approval of Electrical Equipment's (CEE) Technical Committee for Electric Fences. This was the body that set standards for electric fence energisers in Europe and, since it was the best organised in the world, the body that had the most influence internationally.

Back in 1974 Gallagher had got wind that the CEE was developing a new standard that included a proposal to limit the power internally rather than limiting the output, since output was seen as difficult to measure. This would have been very restrictive for Gallaghers and highly disadvantageous, while potentially more dangerous for users. The process, however, was slow and convoluted, so Gallagher had plenty of time to put together a New Zealand Standards Committee, comprising representatives from the eight major local manufacturers, in order to review the New Zealand standard and comment on the CEE draft.

Bill's travels through Europe in 1975 and 1976 powerfully reinforced the importance of good international standards, given the real dangers of technical barriers to trade. In Europe, quite simply, there wasn't any trade. No foreigners had yet broken in; the Germans weren't in Holland, the Danes weren't in Germany or Sweden, nobody crossed borders because each country had quirks in its own standards that made it too difficult. Gallagher saw this as a challenge rather than an obstacle, and reasoned that if he worked within the CEE system at least he would understand fully how it worked and he might increase his chances of breaking into the fortresses. When the CEE declared as one of its objects the removal of technical barriers to trade, Bill Gallagher was sufficiently naïve, at first, to believe they were serious.

While New Zealand had no status with the CEE, Australia enjoyed observer status. And so Gallagher persuaded the Australian Standards Committee to send him as their representative to the next big meeting, to be held in Budapest on 26–27 April 1977. He drove in from Vienna, a little unsettled on his first trip to a communist country at the feeling of being in a prison camp. On the official programme for the CEE meeting, Bill Gallagher was listed as General Manager, Gallagher Electronics Ltd, Hamilton, New Zealand, Australia. Curiously, it was only the Swedes who asked him at the cocktail function on the first night when New Zealand had joined Australia. Nobody else seemed at all surprised, and being from Australia had the advantage of his being seated at the front, alongside Austria and Belgium.

As a garrulous Australian he proposed many changes to the draft standard, which improved prospects for Gallaghers considerably, but his moment of epiphany came when he heard the German delegation making its submission. Here were the leaders in the electric fencing field in Germany, a country renowned for its technology, and they were proposing things that Bill Gallagher knew didn't work. He recalls: 'It was like a blinding flash. I realised how far advanced we were and that we really did have a world-beater on our hands. The Germans produced nice theoretical papers showing how little current you needed to stop animals. But they had answered the wrong question. The real issue was how much current you needed to get past vegetation and still have sufficient power to stop animals. They'd missed the point entirely. Their most powerful energiser had a hundredth of the power of our torch battery strip-grazing energiser, which we considered our play one. We had to get hold of the market before these bunnies woke up.'

In New Zealand Gallaghers would sell nearly 4000 energisers in 1977. If the company could break through technical trade barriers and farmer conservatism worldwide to achieve similar levels of penetration in the massive northern hemisphere markets, finding a few gold bars on a sunken ship would look like chicken feed.

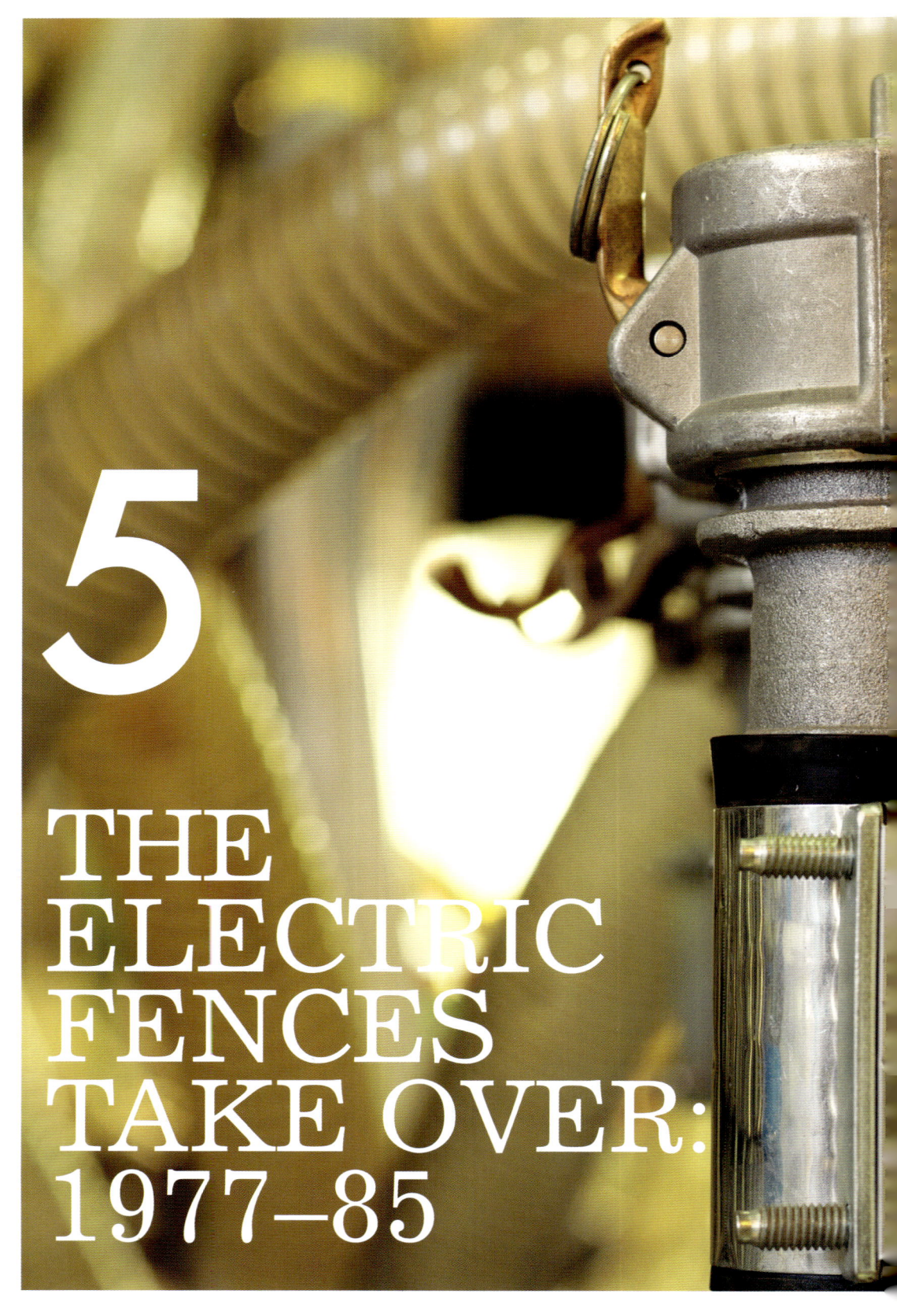

5
THE ELECTRIC FENCES TAKE OVER: 1977–85

Chapter five

THE ELECTRIC FENCES TAKE OVER: 1977–85

Late one dark, stormy night in the spring of 1977 the Dijkstra family was sitting around the fire at its farm in Holland's far north when they heard someone tapping at the window. 'Who the hell could that be?' they wondered. No one knocks on the window in Holland. The Dijkstra farm was in the middle of nowhere, in the countryside beyond Groningen; it was raining, there were no lights outside. Dutch visitors would simply enter the out-buildings and make their way inside.

As the family let the bedraggled stranger in, he introduced himself as Bill Gallagher. One of the Dijkstras had written to him, and now he was here from New Zealand to talk about his electric fences.

The Dijkstras' interest in Gallagher electric fences had been sparked a few months earlier by a memorable shock. Dooitze Dijkstra had been scouting for pedigree sheep in Scotland, and wanted to cross an electric fence to look at some lambs. He saw it was covered in long grass and from his knowledge of electric fences was certain that it would have long since shorted out, offering no threat. Swinging his leg over the wire he received the shock of his life in a most inconvenient spot. As his son Erik says, 'Totally impressed by what had hit him, my father was anxious to discover its cause. It was simply not possible that he'd been zapped by a fence so covered with grass.' He found the farmer and was shown the Gallagher BEV II energiser. Dooitze Dijkstra returned to Holland without his sheep, but he had two Gallagher energisers.

Back home, he showed his new purchase to his brother-in-law and business partner John Veldman. Immediately they saw a business opportunity. Having started off as farmers with 100 hectares, which was quite large for a Dutch farm, Veldman and Dijkstra had branched out into various entrepreneurial schemes over the years. They traded sheep and had a meat works. Knowing that the leading Dutch electric fence, Koltec, was weak and ineffectual the moment foliage grew around it, they were sure that this new and much more powerful beast would find a ready market among Dutch sheep farmers, who faced considerable costs with their traditional fencing.

Looking at the label, they saw the energisers came from New Zealand, a country about which they knew nothing. They wrote to Gallaghers, asking for more information. And it was in response to that letter that Bill Gallagher turned up on a chilly April night. On his way back to New Zealand from London, he had flown into Amsterdam and hired a car, but driving north he had been so overwhelmed with tiredness that he had pulled over for a sleep beside the road. Hence his late-night arrival.

Inside, he started telling the Dijkstras all about the company and its origins, and why its energisers were so good. Dooitze's English wasn't so good then, but Erik and his younger brother Meindert had enough to gain a handle on the story. Another visit from Gallagher followed in October, and Veldman & Dijkstra took the distribution rights for Holland.

Erik, who was not long out of school but already well equipped with a strong personality and infectious sense of humour, was given the task of growing the enterprise. In January 1978 he flew to Hamilton to spend three months learning about the business. He recalls: 'Bill had built up the story about Gallaghers' fame quite high, so when I arrived at Auckland airport and the officials asked what I was planning to do in New Zealand I said confidently I was going to see Gallagher. "Who? What?" they asked me. I thought everyone in the country would know him. Eventually they found

Gallaghers of Kahikatea Drive, Hamilton, in the phone book. So that was a disappointment; he'd somewhat oversold his fame.

'I got over that shock and then started my education in fencing and efficient New Zealand farming, including my "masters of fencing" from Ben Hickey, a Gallagher distributor from north of Whangarei who put fences on the most amazing hillsides. New Zealand was so isolated; I almost had to ask permission from the operator to ring Holland. They'd ring back an hour later with a connection, then once you were on you finished every sentence with "over" and waited for the reply, all costing $15 a minute.

'But I loved it. I'd been thinking about studying economics when I returned to Holland, but by the end of that summer I'd forgotten all about that, I was so thrilled by what I'd seen — the strip-grazing systems that applied in New Zealand, made possible by efficient electric fencing. I felt like a disciple returning home to preach the new gospel.'[1]

The electric fence distributing company, Veldman & Dijkstra, was established in May 1978 with Erik its first employee. At first he followed his father around. Dooitze sold farmers sheep and Erik came along behind, selling energisers and erecting fences for them. The value proposition was powerful. Instead of a netting fence with heavy posts dug into the ground every 4 metres, requiring constant maintenance because the sheep made it their mission in life to try to knock the fence over, Erik sold them a Gallagher energiser for 450 guilders (10 times the price of the local energiser). But now the fence needed only five wires, droppers only every 10 metres, and a heavy post every 50 metres. And once it was up, it required very little maintenance. 'Only a fool wouldn't buy a Gallagher fence,' Erik told his potential customers. 'The world is changing, if you want to survive in five years you need to be more efficient, you need one of these. Get with it.' In the year to June 1979 he sold 1503 energisers.

Over the next few years the business grew and grew, so that both Dooitze Dijkstra and John Veldman dropped most of their other activities and concentrated on the Gallagher electric fences. Six years later, in the calendar year 1984, Gallaghers exported $1.07 million worth of goods to Veldman & Dijkstra, equivalent to around $3.2 million in 2012 terms. It represented around 11 per cent of Gallagher Electronics' total exports that year, which wasn't a bad effort for a comparatively small part of Europe. In real terms, exports to Veldman & Dijkstra in 1984 were the equivalent of Gallaghers' entire electric fence exports in 1977.

The Dutch story was replicated in many other countries around the world over the same period, usually, but not always, on a smaller scale, and it was these business relationships that propelled Gallaghers forward in the late 1970s and early 1980s. Bill Gallagher junior summed it up in a 1984 speech: 'Even when a product is made and is working right, the job is not even half complete. The largest part of the money and a considerable amount of the effort is required to place the product in the hands of the end user.'[2]

And the best marketers of electric fences, he had found, were local people with a farming background, who happened also to be dynamic entrepreneurs. The trick was to find these people. A large measure of Gallaghers' success over these years lay in Bill's impressive hit rate in finding excellent distributors in a range of markets, who themselves were powerfully motivated to grow the business rapidly. With the demand for Gallagher energisers generated by these people Gallaghers could genuinely claim to be a global leader in electric fencing by the early 1980s.

The company's figures spoke for themselves. Sales of $2.7 million in the year to March 1978 ($16.5 million in 2012 terms) grew to $20 million in the year to March 1984 (around $60 million today). Meantime, a $202,000 after-tax profit in 1978 (equivalent to around $1.2 million in 2012) was transformed to $2.2 million in 1984 (around $6.5 million today). Growth had been reasonably steady, although it had surged in 1979, when the company had once more been 'playing doubles'.

At the same time, the shape of the company was changing significantly. Almost all the growth after 1978 came from Gallagher Electronics, the electric fence side of the business. Gallagher Engineering, the agricultural machinery business, stagnated. While its turnover doubled between 1978 and 1984, that only just kept pace with the rapid inflation of those years. By 1984 it was contributing only 15 per cent of the group's turnover, most of it in New Zealand, and less than 7 per cent of the profits. Meantime, the electric fence business had grown in scope. Accessories — from hardwood fence posts to plastic insulators and voltmeters — had become increasingly important, particularly in New Zealand. At home, energisers accounted for only 15 per cent of the turnover; abroad it was closer to 50:50, energisers to accessories. Gallaghers wasn't just selling electric fences, it was marketing animal containment systems.

If those were the broad commercial trends of the period, the constant was the continuance of a highly supportive local regime. New Zealand government assistance to manufacturing exporters was at its zenith, having gone up another notch in 1978, which an increasingly worried National government had dubbed Export Year. Until then the combination of increased export incentives, export market expenditure, investment allowances, generous depreciation rates and other schemes meant that the company had not paid any substantial tax for several years. Now, in 1978, a tax credit scheme was introduced which made cash payments for increased manufacturing exports. Twenty per cent of increased exports were non-assessible for tax, so if your exports increased by a $1 million, $200,000 was non-assessible for tax, resulting (with a 45 per cent company tax rate) in a $90,000 tax credit. The beauty of the scheme, from the point of view of export companies, if not other taxpayers, was that if the company's tax bill was zero after all the other factors, then a cheque for $90,000 would arrive in the mail.

This was magic for Gallaghers in 1978, which otherwise was not a great year. Gallagher Engineering actually lost $11,000 for the year, after sales in New Zealand fell for the first time in more than a decade and stiff competition in rotary hoes in Australia had sliced margins. Gallagher Electronics' profit, meantime, was a modest $40,000. However, a cheque for $175,000 from Inland Revenue transformed the situation, hoisting the group's after-tax profit from $29,000 to a much more acceptable $204,000. A crash in the Queensland sugar cane industry fouled things up the following year, but in the early 1980s the company was receiving cheques from the tax department equivalent to negative tax rates ranging from 20 to 45 per cent.

It was a wonderful period to be a New Zealand manufacturing exporter. But it didn't take much imagination, given the country's slide into chronic budget deficits, financed by ever more desperate overseas borrowing, to see that the good times couldn't last forever. Bill Gallagher's response, in good farming tradition, was to make hay while the sun shone. He tore about frantically trying to grasp as much territory as possible while conditions favoured him, and before the competition had a chance to catch up or fight back.

Having discovered that shipping to Australia was often more expensive than shipping to Europe, he felt no constraints in casting his net far and wide. The basic strategy that evolved has been dubbed the 'sow and reap' approach by one commentator.[3] Working on the philosophy that 'everywhere is on the way' if one is travelling between New Zealand and Europe, Bill called in on new countries on every journey, finding local entrepreneurs in each place who were prepared to have 'their own skin in the game'. He didn't spend money on market research or any such extravagance; he would go to agricultural field days and shows, talk to a few people and then take a punt. Then the new distributor was left to stand or fall on their own account. Some stood, some ran, some fell, and Bill would focus his attention on those who were promising, visiting them regularly thereafter to encourage and motivate them. And as the business took root in a dozen or so markets, a strong global enterprise began to develop.

Bill was cunning in the way he tried to minimise the financial risks of such rapid expansion. He wrote in 1978:

> It is extremely desirable to sell the initial consignment to the new agent, thus ensuring his financial stake in the product. The usual approach is for the agent to ask for consignment stock [only paid for if they sell it] and in my experience this is almost fatal, and to be agreed to only as a very last resort. The successful answer in my experience to the request for consignment stock is to give extended terms. The norm is 90 days but sometimes a special initial 180 days could be offered . . . the major advantage is that it puts the agent on his mettle to move the product and not just let more important things take precedence with his time. It is not very difficult to talk the agent into 180 days, as if he does not think that he can sell the product within six months you are probably speaking to the wrong agent.[4]

This was all very well, but first they had to gain access to the market. This was straightforward in Britain, Australia and the US, but it wasn't easy in parts of Europe. For all the Dijkstras' enthusiasm in Holland, Gallaghers' energisers would get nowhere if they could not first storm past the gates of technical barriers to trade to become the first foreign manufacturer to sell to the Dutch market.

It was Bill's conclusion that since his company needed to produce energisers that complied with international standards it 'would help no end to take an active part in writing those standards'. This was why Gallagher had gone to the CEE meeting in Budapest in April 1977, a week or so after he had first met the Dijkstras. His efforts to derail a German attempt to skew the revamped standards away from high-powered energisers, such as those Gallaghers was producing, were very successful. Gallagher achieved several important modifications to the draft at Budapest, and if all went well these would be approved at the next meeting, scheduled for April 1978 in Brussels.

During the Budapest meeting Gallagher had listened intently to MH Huizinga, the Dutch Secretary-General of the CEE, who gave what the New Zealander thought was a 'pious' speech on how the organisation's purpose was to remove technical barriers to trade. 'However,' Gallagher recalls, 'when our company went to gain our electrical approval in Holland, the obstacles and barriers and criticisms they raised on the product were almost totally impossible, so that we believed no practical product could meet such requirements, least of all the local product already on the market.'

The trouble had started when Erik Dijkstra was given the task of taking the BEV II to KEMA, the Dutch testing agency in Arnhem. The visit was a fiasco, as Dijkstra recalls: 'I wasn't allowed into the testing room, but no sooner had they plugged it into the socket than there was a big explosion and the entire testing room filled with smoke and fire. There was nothing left of their testing equipment. The engineer came out all black, just like in the movies. "Mr Dijkstra, do I have to explain to you why this energiser will not pass the test?" I said, "Yes, of course, you need to give me a report, based on some criteria."

'Eventually after much shouting they sent me something that I forwarded on to Bill. He comes back, "They're joking; they're interpreting the standard wrong." I'm now the middleman. I tell KEMA that they're interpreting it wrong. "Are you telling me, Mr Dijkstra, after I've been testing energisers for more than 20 years, that I don't know the standard, but some guy from New Zealand knows better?" No progress, until the next time Bill comes over [and] we return to Arnhem and he has a long discussion with the engineer. Then he has an argument with the engineer's boss over the standards. In that meeting, Bill was able to convince the chief of that department, who had been there 20 years, that he was interpreting the regulation wrong. It was amazing. And then he showed him why the equipment blew up and what he needed to do.'[5]

Gallagher's visit was in April 1978. A fortnight earlier he had been to Brussels, where the less intrusive new European standard was agreed at the CEE Technical Committee meeting in the Bedford Hotel. Bill Gallagher had previously written a long letter to Huizinga outlining all the problems he had been having with Dutch regulators, a copy of which had been sent to the president of the CEE, who was from Sweden. And at a cocktail function in Brussels the Swede asked Gallagher how he was getting on with the Dutch. Bill replied that he didn't know, but he would soon find out. So he was applying pressure on the Dutch from all angles — arguing directly with KEMA, forcing Huizinga to explain why his country was dragging its feet, and embarrassing him among his peers. Gallagher recalls: 'A guy from Canada had taught me over a beer how to deal with the technical public service bureaucracy. From the point of view of the bureaucratic test engineer, the least risky position is not to reach a decision, and this can be achieved by making things difficult. But if the applicant is persistent, the next least risky and troublesome decision is to decline to give approval, in which case normally only the applicant is disappointed, whereas approval is likely to have all the local manufacturers up in arms.

'So the best strategy for me as an applicant was to make granting approval the least uncomfortable decision. If they said no, now they'd have to explain themselves to CEE's secretary general and president, who were interested. I also had the New Zealand embassy involved and I'd defeated their arguments at KEMA. So the two basic lessons on technical barriers are these: if the international rules are no good, get on to the rules; and once the rules are OK, if the application is still a problem, then it requires considerable effort, pressure and manoeuvring to have them applied favourably.'

The Dutch gave up the fight midway through 1978 and the Dijkstras were free to get started. Gallaghers' energisers, meantime, enjoyed a distinct advantage since the local manufacturers had been working to the old interpretation of the standards. It would take them a few years to catch up.

Veldman & Dijkstra made the most of its power advantage. One of its early jobs was to erect a wild-pig-proof fence for the Dutch government. For years wild pigs had been damaging crops in the south of Holland, near the German border. The government was compensating farmers for the damage caused and it was costing a lot. Erik Dijkstra and his team went down there to fence quite a large area, at least 800 hectares, and to their surprise the local farmers, who benefited nicely from the compensation payments, helped them enthusiastically. 'I soon discovered,' Dijkstra says, 'that they thought the whole thing was a joke; there was no way this two-wire fence was going to stop the pigs.'

Attitudes changed abruptly, however, when the fence was completed and it did indeed work. The local farmers saw their compensation payments disappearing and, worse, realised that they would actually have a harvest to gather, which was much more time-consuming than banking the annual government cheque. Two weeks later, however, Dijkstra had a call from a government officer saying that his fence didn't work: 'I went down and, sure enough, it had been sabotaged, very deviously. Shorting wires, painted the colour of the wood, had been laid close to the post. I fixed it and mentioned the handiwork to the government. A day or two later it started shorting again. This time I asked Gallagher New Zealand for a system to monitor the fence that would give an alarm immediately if there was a shortage. This was Bill's latest device. We had a staff member of the Forestry Commission monitoring it from a nearby barn, and, because we knew where it was likely to happen, the police swooped and caught a farmer red-handed.

'The farmers didn't take this very well and ostracised the forestry guy, who had worked with them for years. When they found out where we were monitoring it from, the barn was burnt down. Then someone's house was burnt down; it was pandemonium. The government now refused any further compensation payments, some people were imprisoned and the story filled national newspapers for a while. Not bad advertising.'[6]

Other tactics in Holland were less newsworthy but equally effective. The Dijkstras' primary task was to demonstrate to farmers the strength of the Gallagher energiser. Most trade shows were held indoors, but at the one annual field day Veldman & Dijkstra hired two circus elephants from Belgium and kept them behind a two-wire fence in the middle of the show. This impressed many farmers, but, as Erik Dijkstra recalls, it also offered an opportunity for bush-fighting tactics against his competition: 'The man in charge of the elephants had to walk them twice a day, so that they could urinate. We were talking about up to 100 litres that smelt repulsive. And I was fascinated to learn that they could do this on command. So I asked him to take the elephants past the stand of our competitor Koltec, so they could "by accident" pee on the place. They trundled along and Koltec were very pleased to see these elephants coming to their stand with a horde of farmers following, until 100 litres of urine poured out all over the place. And in the summer heat their display reeked to high heaven for the rest of the show.'[7]

Poul Dalgaard, Gallaghers' Danish distributor, was an equally inventive showman. He devised the 'Shock Tunnel' as a gimmick for his stall at agricultural shows. Inquisitive farmers were drawn through a round doorway into a black tunnel, constructed simply from black-painted plywood. Around a few corners it was pitch black. When the intrepid visitor trod on a mat, the energiser was engaged, lighting a circuit that produced a large spark and crack across a potato. It was a cheap thrill that created plenty of interest and gave him some Danish headlines about the 'strongest electric fence in the world', followed by some more when it was closed down by the fire brigade.[8]

Sweden was another country that offered good prospects but was well defended by technical barriers. Its standard was so restrictive that Bill Gallagher thought it was impossible to make an effective electric fence that complied. He battled away but made progress only after September 1980 when Björn Lundvall, the former president of LM Ericsson, was killed in Östergötland when his family Saab hit an elk that leapt out of the woods onto the road.

ABOVE Erik Dijkstra used circus elephants to demonstrate the power of the Gallagher electric fence.

Gallagher argued that it was time Sweden adopted a new standard along the lines of the new CEE specifications; no one had been killed by a high-powered electric fence, but the absence of effective fences, such as along highways through the forests, was costing Swedish lives. The argument worked, and Gallaghers was the first foreign manufacturer to enter the Swedish market. In a country where vigorous spring growth wreaked havoc with traditional electric fences, Gallaghers' first distributor, Lundex, benefited from substantial pent-up demand. In the year to March 1982 exports to Sweden approached $400,000 (7 per cent of that year's export total, and $1.3 million in 2012 terms).

The Germans were equally restrictive. Bill Gallagher had been making a nuisance of himself at German trade fairs, asking local fence manufacturers if he could test their machines. 'They'd think I meant grabbing the wire and taking a few pulses,' he recalls. 'But when I'd whip out a set of resisters and a digital voltmeter their faces would change.' The most powerful mains energiser he could find gave 300 volts on a 1000 ohm load. He would happily report to his customers that his lowest-powered dry-battery, strip-grazing model, the KM2, gave 3000 volts on the same load (100 times the energy). The usual reaction from a German farmer then was to say, 'Well, if it's so powerful why doesn't it kill everything in sight?' And Gallagher would have to explain that the very short pulse, less than 0 0003 of a second, meant that there'd be no lasting damage.

Yet after more than a year of trying he still hadn't received approval from VDE, the German government electrical testing house, which was based near Frankfurt airport. Gallagher recalls the frustration: 'We had gone through about 12 tests, and they'd put up an objection. We'd put up another sample; they'd knock it down. We finally got to the end, and then they found fresh faults in samples three layers back in the process. I went over there. "Right," I said, "that's it: either you are incompetent, since you didn't find the faults first time round, or you're being obstructive. I want to see the chief." He was away and wouldn't be back for 10 days. "No trouble," I said; "I'll be back in 10 days." And that fixed it. "It was all a misunderstanding," they now said. Sometimes you have to show aggression. Once you have them on the back foot you have to go hard. The Germans don't like being accused of incompetence.'

STATENS JORDBRUGSTEKNISKE FORSØG
Bygholm, 8700 Horsens. Telf. 05 - 62 31 99

SjF Meddelelse   Nr. 6

Ordinær prøve   Gruppe 11 c nr. 1
1979

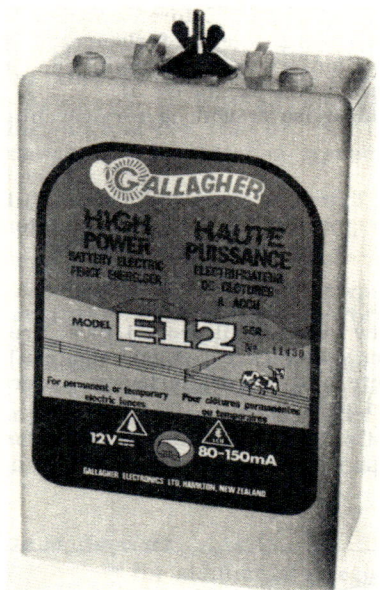

Gallagher akkumulatorhegn
type E 12

Fabrikant: **Gallagher Electronics,** Hamilton, New Zealand.

Anmelder: **Van Hollands Agentur,** 4420 Regstrup.
Tlf. 03 - 47 11 47.

Pris: **650** kr. excl. afgift, april 1979.

ABOVE Even the Swedes were enthusiastic users of the Gallagher energiser.

It wasn't so easy to find a good distributor in Germany, however. The first, Wolfgang Cords, operated out of Bremen starting in 1981, but he failed to make sufficient progress. Bill Gallagher then gave Veldman & Dijkstra free rein in the north of Germany. Erik Dijkstra remembers their first trip across the border: 'We had 15 energisers, and when the border guard stopped us he looked in the trunk. "What are you doing with these?" he said. "Oh, we're just showing them to farmers." "Why do you need 15?" We bluffed our way through; 15 different kinds of energiser, or something. We sold them all during the day, but we asked the farmers for the boxes back. And lo and behold, when we came back through the border the same guy was still working. He must have been working 12 hours. He saw us. "Please open the trunk." He saw the boxes, prodded them and of course they were empty. He thought he had us, but we weren't stupid. "But did you check to see if the boxes were empty this morning?" He had to admit that he hadn't. So he smiled and said, "OK, I can't prove it. But I'm going to write your names down and every time you cross this border, I'm going to open every little box you have." And I must admit he did what he promised until the checkpoints disappeared in 1992.'[9]

While the Dutch made some progress in northern Germany, Gallagher signed up Helmut Allie, from Miltenberg, Bavaria, to grow the business in Germany's Catholic south. Having previously distributed a German electric fence, the Ako, Allie knew the business. When invited to New Zealand to see the company, he declined, pointing out that he spoke no English and that 'he did not specialise in holidays'. He did have a son, Bernd, however, a tall, charismatic young business administration student who did specialise in holidays. He visited New Zealand for three months, January to March 1981, and was much impressed by what he saw.

Reflecting back on that visit today, Bernd Allie is struck particularly by how well Bill Gallagher motivated him, as a 23-year-old student, to become excited about selling Gallagher products to a large area of southern Germany.[10] Back home in Germany, the task wasn't simple. 'Most Germans, being conservative, assume that German technology is the best,' says Allie. 'So it was a real challenge to convince people that a New Zealand company could offer something better; at first no one could imagine such a thing was possible.' But they threw themselves into the task. Helmut visited dealers and field days tirelessly, while his young son concentrated on the public relations side and managed to have articles published in leading agricultural journals explaining the virtues of New Zealand-style pasture-based farming. By 1984 Allie Agratechnik had developed the south of West Germany into an important market for Gallaghers.

By contrast, Bill Gallagher had no trouble getting into France. Its regulations, he soon discovered, had a big hole in them, in that they mandated a standard that didn't exist. Having visited Limoges in 1975 and registered that France had by far the largest electric fence market in Europe, Gallagher was determined to dominate. But he hadn't reckoned on the wily French, who over the next few years provided some of the company's greatest dramas.

The company's first distributor, Count Louis du Nouvelle, a Limousin cattle breeder from Limoges who also had a cattle property in Australia, made only limited headway. Then Bill Gallagher was approached by Cipel, a division of General Electric (France). Its core business was battery manufacture, but according to the fashion of the times it had diversified downstream into products that used batteries, and was distributing the German-manufactured Horizont electric fence. Dissatisfied with the German machines, Cipel had commissioned a comprehensive survey of the industry in 1978 and found Gallagher was the only company to have a presence in most markets. Bill Gallagher met Cipel executives in Paris in November 1978 and found their approach fairly blunt: '[They] expressed the view that they were going into electric fence energisers, we seemed to have the best product and the most advanced, and they offered us the choice of a licensing agreement and royalties or they would develop their own without us. I was glad to be able to retort that I had just arrived in France from Holland where the Philips Corporation, which had considerable resources, had entered the field of electric fencing several years before. But in 1978 it was a criminal offence to sell a Philips electric fence energiser in Holland. I didn't say that Cipel couldn't do it, but pointed out that Philips had failed while our company, which had been in the electric fence business since 1938, had not.'[11]

Gallagher's counter-proposal was to give Cipel distributing rights for France and southern Europe. Within a few months it had sold a fair number of E12 and KM2 models. After long negotiations an agreement was signed in November 1979 whereby Gallaghers

ABOVE Much of Bill Gallagher's time was spent attending agricultural shows around the world. Here, in 1982, he is with Bernd and Martha Allie, Gallagher's German distributors.

would develop a new model specifically designed for the French market. Cipel paid development costs on tooling (around $100,000) in return for distribution rights. Colin Standing, the operations manager at Gallagher Electronics, led the team that developed what became the E8, which was marketed in France as the Ranch 90 and Ranch 45. It featured a modular design that could be serviced very easily and quickly.

The E8 proved a phenomenal success. In an 18-month period, through 1980 and early 1981, Cipel (then renamed Saft) took 38,760 of the E8s, as well nearly 4000 of the other models. Just over 40 per cent of all the energisers produced by Gallaghers in the year to June 1980 went to France. It was a gusher of extraordinary proportions, and very exciting for the firm at first. Dozens of new workers were employed at Hamilton, feverishly putting these together. Gallaghers picked up a Mobil Award for Exporting Success for its efforts. But, sadly, the French love affair fizzled out as quickly as it had erupted. Saft played hard-ball business. Within a few months of signing the agreement it had begun selling in Belgium, outside its area.

Then in 1981 Saft claimed it could manufacture the energisers more cheaply in France, and delivered Gallagher an ultimatum to meet this new low price or turn manufacturing over to it. It would pay Gallagher royalties instead. Not happy, but mollified at the thought of royalties, Gallagher acquiesced. That was until he discovered that Saft had taken an interest in the German company Horizont and had moved its manufacturing to its factory. Horizont's product was now coming off the same line as Gallaghers', and it didn't take too much imagination to see that his German competitor would soon make rapid technological strides.

It was the New Zealanders' turn to play hard-ball. Gallagher sued for damages, and when Saft lawyers flew to Hamilton in January 1984 to settle out of court he imposed a new contract on them. Saft could continue making Gallagher energisers, paying a royalty, but for the next five years it would also pay Gallagher royalties on all Horizont units sold in France. This restored some pride to the equation for Gallaghers, but at bottom what might have been the powerhouse of the European market produced comparatively lean returns. Through 1982 to 1985 Gallaghers tried three other distributors to sell the New Zealand-made product in France, but none of these made much progress. The fundamental issue was that French farmers showed little interest in permanent electric fencing, where Gallaghers had a clear advantage.

Meantime, Gallaghers' oldest export market, Australia, had caused a few headaches through the 1970s, particularly with the machinery business. In 1978 Bill Gallagher gained a few laughs at the Waikato Export Institute by saying that his firm had more bad debts in Australia than the rest of the world combined, which he put down to the inhabitants' 'natural dishonesty . . . you can still see the chain marks around their ankles'.

The typical Kiwi–Aussie banter had some substance in Gallagher's experience. In 1977, however, he found David Mullen, a thoroughly honest and promising young entrepreneur, and appointed his firm, Rural Sales and Marketing (RSM), as a sub-distributor in New South Wales. Compact and dynamic, and the same age as Bill, Mullen was born and raised in Sydney but, apart from a stint as a marketer with Colgate Palmolive, he had operated in the rural services sector. He and his wife Marg had formed RSM in 1973, borrowing $10,000 against their house. They operated from the third bedroom of their home in West Pymble and began selling Golden dog food for farm dogs and Permident ear tags for cattle.[12] By early 1977 they had built up the business so that they had a warehouse in Thornleigh, northwest Sydney, and three reps selling all manner of items, from Line 7 wet-weather gear imported from New Zealand to Bull Bags, a large balloon that could be put under a car and inflated using the exhaust to lift it out of a bog.

Mullen visited New Zealand for the Mystery Creek Fieldays in June 1976, looking for new products. He talked to Speedrite about its electric fences, but wanted to offer a more complete system. Gallaghers, it seemed to him, was primarily an agricultural machinery company, offering only three energisers and nothing else in the way of electric fencing. But it had a good reputation, and back home in Australia he learned that its agents, WH Billings, had put together the most comprehensive electric fencing system. Mullen rang up the general manager, Alan Hutchinson, and arranged to see him in Melbourne.

He recalls: 'Hutchinson was very much the old army colonel type, and his main focus was on steel. WH Billings, which manufactured

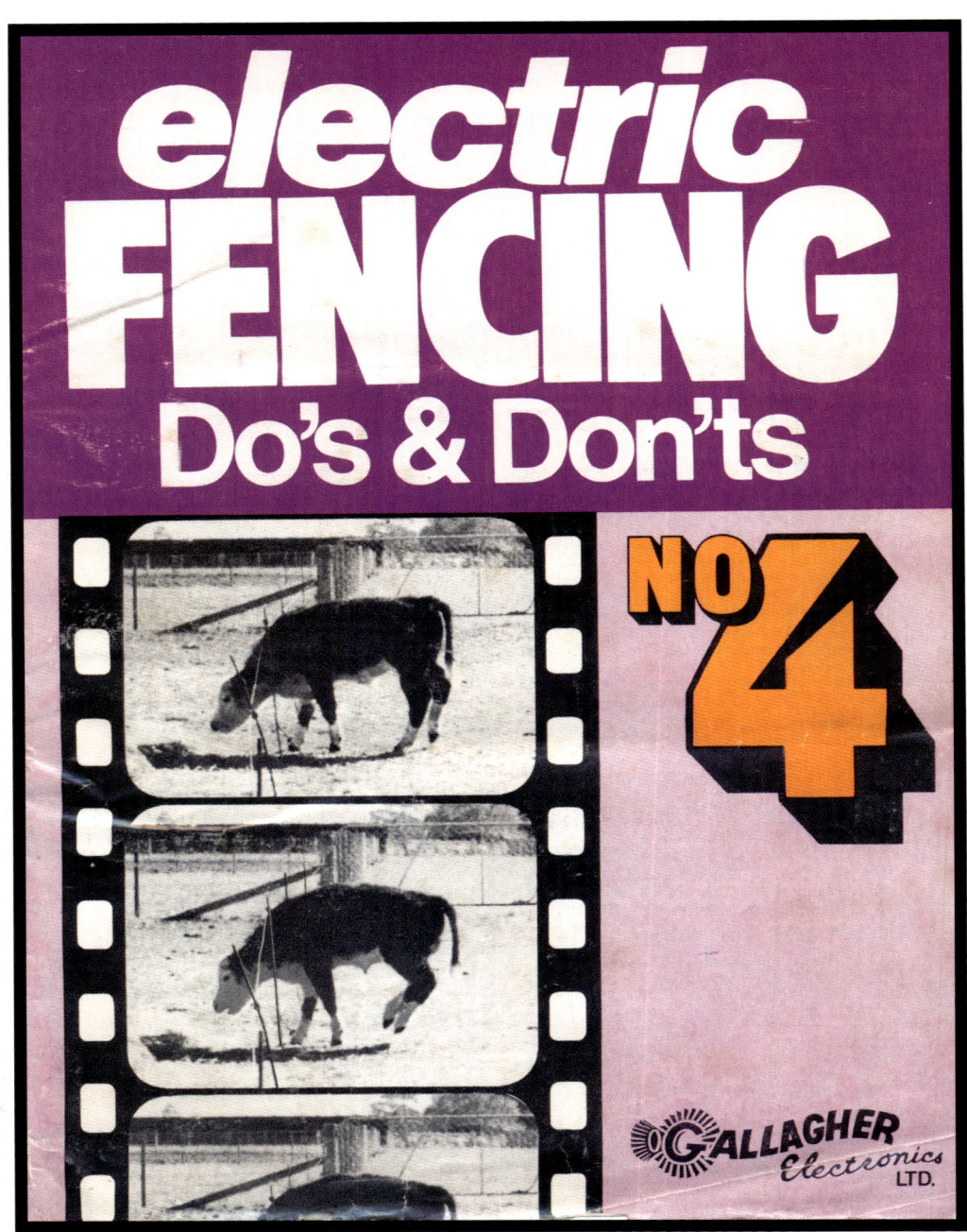

ABOVE Bill Gallagher was particularly fond of this graphic photographic evidence of the impact of his electric fence on a young steer. The images on the brochure were taken from a film by John McCutcheon, Melbourne.

electric fences, was a small, specialist company on the side, almost like a hobby. So I explained what I thought our marketing and distribution capabilities were and he said to me, "Well, we have a very small office in Sydney, which we want to close down because it's losing money. We'll give you the NSW and Queensland territories, if you like." I thought, beaut. To our great benefit, we arranged fortnightly supply deliveries from Billings and 60-day terms for payment, which is how we were able to finance rapid expansion. Also part of this package was education in permanent long-distance fencing, which was to become our "marketing point of difference".

'Billings arranged a trip with Bob Piesse, who invited us down to Victoria to learn the finer points of sheep, cattle and feral fencing. It was late February 1977, just after huge Western District fires that had destroyed a staggering amount of fencing. Bob pulls up at the side of the road where some contractors were putting in a conventional fence. And he walks over, doesn't introduce himself; looks at the end assembly, the strainer; walks down the line checking a few things, with four guys, including me, wandering along behind him.

'It was a bit awkward, and then I heard one of the contractors say to his mate, "Who's that guy? It's not Bob Piesse, is it?" I thought, wow, he's a legend. So we spent three days with Bob and it was absolutely enlightening. Bob was later awarded the Order of Australia for his contribution to Australian agriculture.'[13]

Mullen got stuck into the task and trained his men, having seen that the big opportunity lay in the larger farms west of the Dividing Range that had hardly been touched by the electric fencing market. And the key to winning that market was first to have a good, reliable energiser, but just as importantly to have an efficiently built fence. It was an exercise in farmer and retailer education. He began travelling about the field days in New South Wales, laying out his system on a canvas groundsheet beside the car in places with names like Coonabarabran. He strung the RSM sign between the door handles on the side of his car. He was a nobody compared with the men selling the Daken electric fence, an Aussie brand, who arrived in a 4x4, carting a sign-written six-wheel trailer. But sales quickly picked up. Bob Piesse turned up at one of the field days at Walcha, NSW, with piles of bolts, nuts and washers distributed around the seats of his station wagon and a pile of finished product in the footwell. Mullen was shocked to discover that he had been making line clamps for electric fences on the drive up: 'He proudly declared that he'd averaged two per mile, though he hastened to assure me that he had stopped reading as he drove quite some years ago.'

By 1980 RSM had eclipsed WH Billings entirely in terms of sales and Alan Hutchinson had tired of the business. He told Bill Gallagher he was selling, and Gallagher convinced Mullen to buy. Being short of capital, Mullen accepted some help from Gallagher in return for a 20 per cent stake in a new entity, Gallagher RSM Pty Ltd. The Mullens had 80 per cent of the distribution business in Australia and exclusive rights for the whole continent.

Initially, the new entity had to raise $80,000, which wasn't easy to find as most of the local banks weren't lending. Gallagher introduced Mullen to the BNZ in Melbourne, and to their surprise the manager readily agreed to lend the money. Mullen recalls, 'You could have knocked Bill and I off our seats; we went out that night and arrived at a restaurant on St Kilda Road, which was quite flash for what we were both used to, and we would have been the first people to sit down and last to get up, pissed as parrots. It was one of those memorable, mind-shattering times.'

Now consolidated under Mullen, the Australian business continued to grow rapidly. With typical Australian humour, Mullen commented that 'we succeed not necessarily because we are so clever, but fortunately for us our competition is not so smart'.[14] But Bill Gallagher could see that Mullen was very effective at running a sales team.

Thus, against the basic strategy of having independent distributors around the world, Gallaghers had in 1980 made its first investment in one of its international distributors. This arrangement brought some distinct advantages. The distributor, Mullen, enjoyed a large measure of confidence that the relationship was a long-term one in which he could invest with security. Gallaghers, meanwhile, had access to the business's accounts and therefore a much better understanding of the marketing business. In time, this new strategy would follow through to other markets.

Africa, meantime, had emerged as a surprisingly significant market. The impetus for this came from one man, Vaughan Jones. Born in South Africa, Jones had migrated to New Zealand in 1954 and successfully developed peat swamp land on Piako Road, Gordonton, just north of Hamilton. Argumentative and dynamic, Jones soon became bored with milking cows and divided his time between advising farmers on how to improve their productivity and inventing farm implements, such as spinner drain diggers and chisel ploughs. He was involved in the establishment of the Fieldays, first at Te Rapa Race Course in 1969, then from 1971 at Mystery Creek. He managed the operation for seven years, with his wife Auriel as secretary, until 1979, by which time he needed another challenge. Knowing the Gallaghers well, he called on Bill and was invited to look after Africa, Asia and the communist bloc for the group. Sales in those regions were close to zero.

In relatively short order, Jones decided the communist bloc was a waste of time. In Poland the only fences were around tennis courts. Men would each herd about 50 sheep all day with an Alsatian-type dog, and house them every night. Jones recalls, 'My host, the President of the Farmers' Union, took me to the restaurant with the shortest queue. After an hour we got in, and they apologised for having only mashed pumpkin and baked beans. I left a Gallagher B12 battery energiser with him with full explanations. A year later it was still in its box — because they could not buy a 12 volt battery. I found a farmer who wanted to try it, located a battery in a wrecked car, and erected a polywire fence. When I returned six months later, he was delighted. No cattle had got through it, but he still walked up and down the fence line with a long stick, because he had always done that with their low-powered units.'

Asia held better prospects, initially by using fences to hold back wildlife in tropical areas. Africa, however, was Jones's home turf. In 1979 the market was still in its infancy. Bill Gallagher senior had visited South Africa in 1974 and again in 1975, searching unsuccessfully for a distributor. Bill junior went in 1978 and appointed Maurice Williamson, who had a small business marketing the Poldenvale line of sheep-handling equipment. He was based in Pietermaritzburg, the capital of Natal, inland from Durban, in a grazing area. Jones started visiting him the following year, running field days and seminars, including one at the Weston

ABOVE 'The beige brigade', 1982. From left to right: Bill Gallagher, Vaughan Jones and John Gallagher.

Agricultural College that Jones had attended in 1946.

Working on the adage, 'If you want to sell ashtrays, you first have to teach people how to smoke', Jones approached the task of selling electric fences by teaching farmers controlled grazing. He would gather farmers, or better still agricultural college students who still had open minds, and talk to them about pasture management through strip-grazing and the cost savings that could be gained from high-power fencing systems. It worked, and the South African business flourished, so that for the year to March 1981 only the US, Australia, Britain, Holland and France (whose bubble had already burst) bought more. Bill Gallagher was mightily impressed, describing Jones's success there as 'phenomenal'.

Bill Gallagher immediately recognised that Jones understood the Dutch mentality that so permeated the South African market. His next assignment was to help him deal with the Dijkstras, who were always turbulent. Jones recalls: 'Typical farming areas in South Africa had about one third English, a third Dutch, and a third German. If you are weak there, you get run over. While in New Zealand, if you come on too strong you are seen as arrogant and to be avoided. So at first Bill was too soft on the Dijkstras, who were very firm, who spoke their mind and didn't back down. They were hard-working and devoted to supplying their relatives and friends, rather than all the potential Gallagher dealers in Holland.

'This was holding us back. Erik Dijkstra was concerned that their original dealers would not like losing their monopoly, so we devised a plan that gave the Dijkstras' dealers some time to adjust, while making it clear to them that competition was inevitable. If Gallagher didn't supply the other Dutch dealers, other New Zealand power-fencing companies always followed Gallagher into new markets and they would supply the competition.'[15]

In June 1981 Gallagher appointed Jones group marketing manager, with an open brief to work with distributors at home and abroad to spread the good word of New Zealand-style farm management, based as it was on electric fencing.

Settling down to the task, Jones's first insight was that there was still much more potential growth in the New Zealand market if the gospel of intensive grazing, using electric fences, was preached more energetically. Gallaghers had one salesman in New Zealand, Bill Fletcher, who had a gift for demonstrating and fixing farmers' fencing problems. But the bulk of the selling was through domestic distributors, Bell Booth Ltd and Joseph Nathan Ltd. Jones was convinced that such general-purpose agricultural distributors, who had so many other agencies to juggle, were 'useless' and just added another margin to farmers' costs. In March 1982 he persuaded Bill Gallagher to drop his New Zealand distributors in favour of establishing Gallaghers' own distribution network. From then the 700 domestic dealers were serviced by 11 Gallagher area managers, supplied out of depots in Palmerston North and Dunedin, with bulk warehousing in Hamilton. The change added considerably to Gallaghers' overhead costs, but it opened up the market substantially, achieving far greater sales.

Jones employed and trained mostly successful semi-retired farmers and sharemilkers, because they knew fencing and the benefits, and sent them off to beef and sheep farmers particularly to sell the message about increasing productivity through low-cost subdivision of paddocks. Jones was passionate: 'The farmer's main skill is growing and feeding pasture, which doesn't grow evenly through the year. Think of your lawn. In New Zealand's cool, wet winters it doesn't grow much, then in spring it's flush, in summer it dries off before you get a lift after autumn rains. At any time of the year the grass grows best if it's grazed for a short time, then left to grow, but not for too long. If left to grow rank, both the feed value and the dry matter yield decrease.

'So it's a constant juggling act of animals to achieve the optimum grazing pattern, and that changes throughout the year. So if a farm only has large paddocks, how can the farmer manage that grass without electric fencing? Dairy farmers in New Zealand had known this for a while and had mastered the art of rotational grazing, using low-powered electric fences to divide paddocks into much smaller segments. For a few years now, we'd had energisers powerful enough to extend the same benefits to sheep and beef farms, where containing large and aggressive bulls or sheep with their thick, woolly insulation required more power on the wire. But these farmers needed to have the benefits explained to them more energetically.'[16]

Jones's men fanned out across the countryside. Ernie Ranson was one. A practical joker, he delighted in initiating new salesmen

ABOVE Gallaghers created the brand name Insultimber for ironbark posts from Australia. The timber was self-insulating, saving the bother of putting insulators on each post to carry the electric fence wire.

ABOVE Insultimber was easier to sell than it was to produce; Gallagher and his partners spent a fortune on plant and equipment to cut the hardwood. Pictured here is their reciprocating gang-saw.

by rigging up chairs to give a jolt to the backside. Jones himself gave endless speeches to farmer groups and Ministry of Agriculture and Dairy Board offices, while churning out articles on pasture management for farming magazines, such as the *NZ Dairy Exporter*.[17] He even went so far as to encourage the Gallagher brothers in May 1984 to buy a 23 hectare piece of land surrounding the factory for a demonstration farm, which would showcase the benefits of rotational grazing to locals and international visitors alike. The publishers of the *Waikato Times*, Independent Newspapers Ltd, had bought the block, but had been told they couldn't build a printing press on the peat land. It created an opportunity for Gallaghers.

Internationally, Jones organised conferences where his stock speech to distributors was entitled 'Generating Demand for Gallagher'. Bill Gallagher says of Jones's impact: 'My philosophy was that if you've got reasonably honest, hard-working and intelligent salesmen and distributors, then their success came from motivation, and Vaughan was really good at that. He was very demanding of people, but he inspired them with the great mission of improving productivity for the benefit of the New Zealand economy, or Japan's, or Holland's.'

With this effort, sales in New Zealand kept pace with mushrooming international sales in the early 1980s, albeit with a greater emphasis on the many accessories that the company produced. The gathering importance of these accessories was recognised in September 1982 when Gallagher Plastics was formed to take over the assets of Specialised Plastics Ltd, a key supplier which had fallen into financial trouble. At the same time Gallaghers purchased Sun Plas Engineering Ltd, which made tools and dies for the plastic company. These materials were now too important to remain outside the group. Showing their usual flair for publicity, within a year Gallaghers received a Plastics Institute Export Award from Prime Minister Rob Muldoon for Gallagher Plastics' contribution to the power fencing system, which included the energiser packaging and modular plastic fence posts.[18]

The single most important accessory, however, made no use of plastic. It was a simple piece of wood. Bob Piesse had first alerted Bill Gallagher to the insulating properties of Australian

ABOVE Herbert Young (right), Gallagher's Peruvian distributor, demonstrates how an electric fence should be erected to two local farmers, late 1979.

hardwoods, which in the right conditions could do away with the need for separate insulators on fence posts for permanent electric fencing. As early as 1976 Gallaghers tried without success to patent the idea of using ironbark as an electrical insulator, as well as the idea of using a groove and hole to hold the wire. Gallaghers successfully trademarked the name Insultimber and had the posts on the market in New Zealand by 1977. Over the next few years the company fiddled around with different species of Australian hardwoods, before settling on the narrow-leaf ironbark that grew near Baradine, New South Wales. The product flew off the shelves; container-load after container-load came into New Zealand to provide the basis of cheap fencing at a time when marginal hill country was being broken in at an astonishing rate, propelled by Prime Minister Muldoon's generous farming subsidies. Because it was of such mixed quality, Bill Gallagher found it worth his while to fly over to Sydney and spend half a day sorting timber on the wharf, rejecting the bad stuff before it sailed to New Zealand.

Insultimber was easier to sell, however, than it was to produce. Its very hardness made it difficult to mill. Gallaghers started with a partnership investment in late 1978, which grew into a 50 per cent shareholding in Insultimber Australia Pty. By 1983 it had invested close to $2 million in a plant and Mullen had been drawn into the shareholding, but it was beset with constant problems. Still, it lent plenty of opportunities for fun. Kevin Marquand, one of the salesmen, remembered his colleague Jose Vedma made good use of Insultimber at National Fieldays. 'We'd bring out a new model energiser to show off and cunning old Jose would stand on an Insultimber platform and hang on to the wire to take the shock. He'd dare passers-by to do the same, but of course since they were standing on the ground they'd get the full whack.'[19]

Before long Bill Gallagher was travelling to Brazil to check out potential hardwoods there. Brazil itself promised a huge potential market for Gallagher electric fences, but excessive duties and tariffs made it commercially impossible. The rest of Latin America fluctuated as a market. Costa Rica opened up with a hiss and a roar in 1980, with $85,000 worth of goods being sold, more than for Ireland that year. But the snag came with trying to get paid. Bill Gallagher went there himself in May 1982 and managed to extract US$2400. In doing so, he marvelled at the range of exchange rates then operating:

20 colones to the dollar was the official rate; 48.6 was the market rate; but he noticed that his had been converted at 38.8.[20]

The rest of the money didn't come, but since Gallaghers had been given a mortgage over 15 hectares of land near San Jose as security for the shipment, it became a Costa Rican landowner. Around the same time the New Zealand property investor Bob Jones had been praising Costa Rica to the skies, since it didn't have an army, so Bill Gallagher tried to sell the land to him. Jones wasn't interested.

Chile was another good prospect early on. In the two years to March 1981 it performed well, but suddenly the orders dried up. Bill Gallagher flew over in November 1982 to try to kick-start a recovery and was mugged on the street for his troubles. Augusto Pinochet's authoritarian regime had evidently failed to stamp out petty crime. Gallagher had been to a nightclub on San Diego Street, Santiago, with Les Watson, a New Zealand friend he was travelling with. On the way out they were confronted by a couple of guys and a young woman wanting money. Not having learnt about such things, Bill indicated to them in universal terms that they should get lost. In retrospect, he was lucky to emerge with only a broken hand.

Colombia and Peru, meantime, produced the best revenues around 1983 and 1984, but were relatively small beer compared with the major markets. After a dinner meeting with his Mexican distributor in 1982, Gallagher lamented that 'beating the price down seems to be very much the way of life [here]'.[21]

Much of the business in far-flung regions elsewhere in the world concentrated on using electric fencing to separate wildlife from pastoral farms and agriculture. These efforts were celebrated in November 1983 at what Gallaghers dubbed the 'First World Elephant and Wildlife Seminar', held at the Hamilton headquarters. In Canada the company had worked with farmers and research groups to keep white-tail deer out of orchards in Nova Scotia and in the Rocky Mountains. It had also worked with honey producers in northern Alberta to separate black bears from the hives. This was no simple task.[22] Poul Dalgaard faced a similar challenge when he came across newspaper reports that polar bears were breaking into supply depots of the Sirius Sledge Patrol in the wilds of Greenland, eating vast quantities of condensed milk

TOP Spreading the message at an agricultural show in Arequipa, Argentina.

ABOVE Kenyan elephants learnt quickly about Gallagher PowerFences once they were installed around game parks.

and raisins and generally making a mess of the place. He contacted the Danish military and supplied them with battery-powered energisers, painted white, which worked very well.

Elephants were the primary adversary throughout Asia. The Malaysians were the first to approach Gallaghers for some assistance. Wild elephants were destroying palm-oil and rubber plantations. Between 1975 and 1980 crops worth hundreds of millions of Malaysian dollars had been destroyed. In response, landowners and the government had built log fences with barbed wire, costing M$20,000 a mile, in 1977. These hadn't worked. Then they had dug trenches costing M$5000 a mile and these hadn't worked. Elephants would simply stamp down on the sides and cave them in. In 1980, the Malaysians turned to Gallaghers and found that a two-wire fence protected the plantations very effectively. The company's distributor in Malaysia, Ling Chemist, built a good little business from this, which was consistently the biggest in Asia for Gallaghers during the early 1980s. By 1984 it had strung up 1500 kilometres of two-wire fence across the country.

Bill Gallagher enjoyed observing that 'anything with a nervous system' was containable with an electric fence. An elephant would typically investigate the wire with its trunk, a most sensitive part of its body, and wouldn't try again. But some animals were smarter and more determined than others. In Malaysia some elephants started swimming long distances in rivers to get around the fence, while others learnt to pull out the fence posts. In 1983 similar fences were installed successfully in Indonesia, although one elephant, formerly a trained animal, managed to crawl under the wire. That was easily fixed with a lower wire.[23]

African elephants, meanwhile, brought another level of aggression to the problem. One herd in Kenya found the energiser and trampled it into a flat piece of metal. India would naturally have provided a very good market for elephant fences, but highly restrictive import regulations, including duties and tariffs of over 100 per cent, made commerce very difficult during this period. In 1981 Gallaghers managed to get into Sri Lanka, where the main problem was that stray dogs would infuriate the elephants to such an extent that they would chase the dogs, sometimes through villages, with disastrous effect. But, again, the duties were prohibitive.

In 1982 the United States eclipsed Australia to become the company's single largest export market. But it was hard work. John Gallagher, Art Snell and Bob Piesse had toiled away with their experiments to prove the effectiveness of Gallagher fences against coyotes. They had their findings written up in an agricultural journal in May 1982. Henry Swayze made steady progress in the northeast, but most of the sales came from Snell Systems Ltd in Texas. However, Snell Systems didn't appear to be making any money from its efforts.

Art Snell, nevertheless, was persuasive and had drawn in some venture capitalists to help cover the costs of his development phase. They had paid a premium for shares in Snell Systems in 1980. Having seen the benefits of its investment in Australia, Gallaghers was keen to take a 20 per cent interest in Snell Systems by 1981, but Bill baulked at the asking price for shares in a company that continued to lose money. Eventually, in 1982, he settled for 10 per cent.

In Gallagher Group annual reviews the US market was routinely described as 'having enormous potential'. They struggled to get their arms around such a vast economy, however. Jones went through the country from time to time, like a dose of salts. Bill Gallagher, meantime, argued with Snell on a visit in May 1982 when he boasted of 10,000 dealers across the continent. Gallagher suggested that he needed to concentrate on motivating a few effective distributors 'instead of spreading it too widely'. 'Talk of large numbers of dealers and distributors is quite irrelevant,' he said, 'unless there is success.'[24] A gusher of French proportions in the US market would have sent the Gallagher Group into orbit, but it never quite arrived.

Perhaps it was the complacency that both Bill and John Gallagher had noticed in US agriculture, as it luxuriated in the cosy world of subsidies. This lessened the impact of the New Zealanders' message of using electric fencing to improve productivity. Perhaps it was the expense of Gallaghers' product. With the existing American product still selling at $40 — described by Gallaghers' technical people as $3 worth of parts in a biscuit tin — Gallaghers' models were selling at around $300. Originally, Gallaghers' controllers had sold for around $150, but Snell had persuaded Bill that if they were going to be four times the price of their competitors, they might as well be eight times the price so that they could make some money and spend it on marketing and development. This was nice in theory, but it provided something of a marketing challenge.

Meantime, it was a battle for New Zealanders just to be taken seriously. Bill was disheartened when one evening, sitting beside a professional engineer at a conference dinner, the man, who was obviously well-educated and knowledgeable, asked if he'd driven down from New Zealand. And despite the shared language, some ideas were lost in translation. Since it was in the business of selling grassland technology, Gallaghers sent some New Zealand grass seed to Texas. Labelling the contents simply 'grass seed', it soon discovered that this conveyed a different meaning in America, where grass was rolled into joints. Customs officials seized the goods and waited to see how the seed germinated before letting it through. Technical standards also provided a few hoops of fire. It wasn't possible to build one product, for example, that would meet both US and Canadian standards simultaneously, obliging Gallaghers to perform all sorts of convolutions and variations to gain approval.

Problems abounded also across the Atlantic. Fired up by the competition from Dan Cherrington, Les Dickinson had made good progress in the late 1970s in the UK market. Bill Gallagher admired his salesmanship. His style was not to put his foot in the door when selling, but his head. That way at least if they shut the door he could keep talking. At stalls he employed all sorts of tricks. He would rip a leaf from a pot plant, then attach the energiser to it so that a bolt of electricity would arc across. In the year to March 1982 he took more than $600,000 worth of product, equivalent to $2.2 million in 2012, making him Gallaghers' third-largest individual distributor. But then it all turned sour. Bill Gallagher started hearing whispers that Dickinson might start manufacturing energisers himself. Confirmation came in May 1983 when he travelled to Oakham and found that his distributor had been bragging at the local pub about how he was going to take over the market himself. Dickinson denied it for a while, but soon his own energisers were available and providing stiff opposition.

Scrambling to respond, and somewhat despondent about the problems he was having with distributors, Bill Gallagher decided to bring in-house the marketing of Gallaghers' products in the UK. The experiment with in-house marketing in New Zealand seemed to be going pretty well. Perhaps the British market had matured to the extent that the same could be attempted there? Gallagher

Engineering already had a subsidiary in England, Gallagher Agricultural Ltd in Warwickshire, which sold a modest number of Rotohoes and forage harvesters. So rather than find a new British distributor, Gallagher bought out Cherrington and combined its agriculture and electric fence marketing in a beefed-up Gallagher Agricultural Ltd. It wasn't at all easy. For the year to March 1984 the operation booked a heavy loss.

Ireland, by contrast, was on the up. The Gallagher name had instant cachet in its ancestral home. The first distributor, Edmund Brett, was a hotel-keeper from Mullinahone, County Tipperary. An entertaining character, he dabbled in all sorts of things, including bottled-gas distribution and undertaking. He was selling a few energisers by 1978, although it was hard to keep his attention and Bill Gallagher wanted more from such good farming lands.

Following the early success of his approach in the UK, he introduced some competition into the Irish market in 1979 by appointing two more distributors, Lucey & O'Connell in Cork and McGee of Ardee, north of Dublin. Neither of these lasted the distance. Bill Gallagher remembers PJ McGee as 'a great old guy', while his son Red was a rugby, racing and beer gentleman. Bill recalls, 'With Red we'd have a couple of pints for lunch, do some more business calls, then dinner with a few more pints, and after that we'd get down to some heavy drinking; I've never encountered anything like it.' McGee's went out of business a year or so later. After 1982, however, two entrepreneurial young men, John Lucey and Sam Nelson, established themselves in the south and north, respectively, tying their individual fates to the success of Gallaghers and growing the business.

John Lucey's story was not untypical. He recalls: 'My father, Jim, worked for Lucey & O'Connell as managing director. As a company that concentrated mostly on agricultural machinery, Gallaghers was only a minimal part of the business. Lucey & O'Connell closed in 1981. I was working with my father and loved the Gallagher product. So I left, taking Gallagher with me, and set up a new business that concentrated solely on Gallagher electric fencing. Everyone laughed. No one could make a living just out of electric fencing. I thought I'd give it a year — and I'm still doing it, trading as Gallagher Power Fencing Systems.

'New Zealand farming practice was so popular in Ireland as its farming had such a great reputation. We'd had Waikato fences for a while, but now Gallaghers' were twice the price and twice the output. Even back then innovation was central to Bill's designs. The modular system of the BEV II was a huge advantage and the first of its kind. If anything happened to it, it could be serviced and repaired in minutes, due to its innovative modular plug-and-play system. The farmer would say, "Oh my God, it's fixed." It was fabulous. All the others required soldering and lots of fluffing around. Our edge was that we knew what we were talking about: electric fencing was our speciality.

'We learnt how to put them up properly and taught Irish farmers how to do it. Ray Metcalf, a former Kiwi farmer then working for Gallaghers in Britain, would come across and our farmers would listen to him. They loved the Kiwi accent and respected him as a Kiwi farmer. Many more Gallagher New Zealand staff came to Ireland, teaching us and the farmers, year in year out. And very quickly we had an unreal impact on Irish farming through proper pasture management; we raised the bar and increased productivity. Funnily enough, while the farmers knew it was a Kiwi company, it wasn't long before a lot of Irish assumed Gallaghers was a local company. Bill still laughs about meeting an Irish lady in New Zealand who asked him if he was part of the Irish electric fencing company.'[25]

By 1985 little old Ireland was generating three-quarters of the revenue of its much larger neighbour, the United Kingdom. Countries rose and fell in their relative importance and in their demand for Gallagher products, but the overall trend between 1977 and 1984 was upwards. To handle a turnover of $20 million in the year to March 1984 (equivalent to $60 million in 2012 terms), the company had grown like topsy. Staff numbers had expanded from 50 to 275 as more people were piled on to keep pace with demand, housed in new buildings that crabbed outwards on the Kahikatea Drive site. Bill Gallagher describes the period as one of 'just having great fun going as fast as we could'. Supply officer Noel Hamilton describes it thus: 'When I arrived in 1977 the electric fencing side of the business was small, compared with the engineering side. There were two cars and if we took exports to Auckland you took a trailer and brought back a load of castings. But our exports started to boom with the assistance from the Muldoon government. We were taking orders, getting excited, shipping them out, winning

Export Awards, having parties and carrying on again. Not in an efficient way, as we discovered later when export incentives and agricultural subsidies were canned. However, the growth in export earning laid the foundation for our expansion. We were taking on the world and winning.'[26]

Amid the excitement, Gallaghers maintained a commitment to R&D, producing more powerful energisers every few years, along with an automatic remote monitoring system in 1979, which was complicated and took several years to perfect, and advances in solar-powered units. But the real emphasis remained on market growth and 'getting it out'.

Bill Gallagher senior still visited the complex. Noel Hamilton recalls an old gentleman coming into his office soon after he started work there, asking if he could have some of the old pallets that were lying out the back. He was helping out at the Assisi old people's home and wanted the pallets for firewood. Noel later discovered the old man was the company's founder. Bill senior attended board meetings and weighed in with advice from time to time, but the mantle had long since passed to his sons.

Of the brothers, Bill junior was the hungrier of the two to expand the business. He was prepared to spend on average 100 days a year overseas, scouring the earth for new markets and strengthening his relationships with key distributors. Erik Dijkstra was one who twice-yearly, at least, received the unique combination of 'reassurance and heat' from Bill Gallagher. 'In general, Bill has had a habit of maintaining long-lasting relationships. If you work with him, you sometimes wonder how that is possible. He's not without conflict. Like a marriage, no business relationship is always easy. And he managed to turn New Zealand's distance into a positive, by encouraging regular visits, inviting our whole family and treating us like family members. We'd go to Whangamata and out in his boat (only once, as it was such a frightening experience I wouldn't do it again). And then he'd visit us, more often than many of our Dutch suppliers. We found it very hard to understand how he could go on like that; he must have been impossible to live with. But that was Bill.'[27]

Back home, Bill was equally active. Aside from the day-today management of Gallaghers, in 1976 he became president of the Waikato Manufacturers' Association. This gave him a seat on the much heftier Auckland Manufacturers' Association, where he learnt a great deal from businessmen like Freddy Bruell, MD of Rex Industries and president of the Auckland association, Earl Richardson and Lincoln Laidlaw. Early on, the Waikato group had two companies go into receivership, and Gallagher recalls wading in to try to help them. Guided by wise old heads, he soon saw recurring patterns with companies in receivership: '. . . losing control over the numbers, slackness of the detail; going on an export trip and accepting "standard payment terms" when there was no such thing, so they didn't get paid; slack with their collectables, so they ran out of money; sloppy in their communications with distributors or export partners so that they had no follow-up minutes that set out what they agreed'.

The old hands taught Gallagher about 'pari passu' debentures, which he moved to in 1978. When the company had two banks with equal-standing debentures, the banks were covered in proportion to what they were owed; the practical effect for Gallaghers was that it became easier to borrow more with comparatively little paperwork. And in Australia, the BNZ had been there almost 100 years, with only three outlets, and had 'money sloshing over the scuppers' that it was only too happy to lend to the company.

The political environment at the Auckland Manufacturers' Association, however, was not what Bill Gallagher had expected: 'I was a blue boy from the provinces, who was all for free markets. I was used to competing openly, hated the barriers I was facing around the world, and could see the benefits of free trade wherever I went. You couldn't go to Argentina or India and not see that closed shops simply gave power and privilege to the few to screw the many.

'So it was a great shock to my young life to go to Auckland in 1976 to find that most of the manufacturers were Labour supporters, since they knew they could get a lot more out of the Labour Party, and ardent protectionists. But I went along with the export incentives happily, since they enabled us to grow fast and you could argue they compensated exporters for other distortions in the economy. And in hindsight we were too effective as lobbyists for the continued extension of export incentives, because ultimately it became unsustainable.'

TOP Bill busy pumping up his Irish distributor John Lucey.

During the early 1980s Bill Gallagher was appointed by the National government to several government advisory bodies, often at the instigation of Lance Adams-Schneider, now Minister of Trade & Industry as well as the local MP ('old Apple Cider', as Gallagher knew him). He joined the Industrial Property Advisory Council, which reviewed patent law and intellectual property protection, which was highly relevant to Gallagher. He sat on the Communication Advisory Council, which looked at the country's telephone networks, the post office, rail, broadcasting and electricity networks, and advised on future reform. The Manufacturing Development Council, which he joined in November 1980, advised on protection and export support. He also joined as a director the Import-Export Corporation, a government-owned company that exported wool and hides and dabbled in the commercial sector, usually unsuccessfully.

John Gallagher, meantime, had been involved in a number of committee roles in the 1970s, including being President of the New Zealand Underwater Association, and in the formation of the Waikato Promotion Society. He joined the Hamilton Chamber of Commerce in 1980 and began to raise the profile of the firm in that setting. He ran the Gallagher Group in Bill's frequent absences, and took a particular responsibility for personnel during these years. While Bill concentrated on growing the electric fence business internationally, John, who was happier to spend more time at home, gravitated to taking responsibility for Gallagher Engineering.

In hindsight this proved the short straw. The business kept ticking over, and enjoyed some little booms, such as supplying machinery for the kiwifruit industry, which, supported by tax breaks, was growing rapidly in the early 1980s. Until 1984 most New Zealand farmers had money in their pockets for capital items, such as Gallaghers' agricultural machinery, but competition was intense from large international rivals, such as Moller-Yamaha for the rotary hoe and forage harvesters. Gallagher Engineering still accounted for 18 per cent of the group's turnover in 1984, but its profitability was patchy and it had none of the dynamism of the electric fence business.

One of the key achievements of this period was Bill Gallagher's success in finding a handful of other energetic businessmen to help drive demand for the electric fences. Vaughan Jones at home, and the Dijkstras and David Mullen abroad, were the most prominent among them. But there were maybe a dozen others, such as Bengt Lunden, a meticulous Swede, who toiled away with Bill Gallagher's constant encouragement to build a business out of nothing.

As a result of all this, the Gallagher Group was clipping along tremendously by 1984, part of a field of perhaps a couple of dozen New Zealand manufacturers doing well internationally in the supportive environment of the time. Companies such as: Trigon Ltd, Hamilton-based plastic manufacturers; the Criterion Group, furniture manufacturers from Auckland; Fisher & Paykel Ltd, whiteware manufacturers; and Tait Electronics, CB-radio makers from Christchurch. Gallaghers held its head high among such a group of thrusters. In November 1983 the company won the Governor General's Award for Exporting; this was a special annual prize to a company that had previously won an export award and had continued to produce outstanding results for at least another five years.[28] It was a big deal for Gallaghers and the company celebrated by printing a supplement in the *Waikato Times* entitled 'Gallagher on top of the world'. This told the story of the company's progress, along with tales from far-flung markets, such as the deep teeth marks on plastic insulators that were silent testimony to the fury of disgruntled bears in Edmonton, Canada, as they were separated from their favourite beehives.

At a time of rising unemployment, Gallaghers was still taking on staff, with the full quota now reaching 264 souls. Its growing campus on Kahikatea Drive had a 'rip-roaring social club' and two canteens: one for the engineering workers and their boots, the other for the cleaner electronics workers. The office staff had morning tea in one and afternoon tea in the other. For many years an old Scottish lady with no teeth held sway at the engineering canteen. Janine Gallagher, who worked on the till during one holiday period, overheard someone comment when the old lady finally left, 'The least the Gallaghers could have done is bought the old bird a set of teeth,' but she was as good at gumming a sausage roll as anyone around the place.

In many ways Gallaghers' greatest achievement was the breadth of its international success. By 1984 the company was not reliant on any one market. Around 27 per cent of exports went to the US, 20 per cent to Australia, and 20 per cent to Europe, half of which went through Holland. The UK and Ireland took a further 10 per cent, and Scandinavia another 4 per cent. Africa, meantime, took 8 per cent, while Asia accounted for another 4 per cent (with the Malaysians being the most enthusiastic there). South America was the most difficult continent, producing less than 2 per cent of sales. Gallaghers hadn't yet achieved much penetration in either the Arab or the communist worlds, but beyond that the company had found footholds in most other regions of the globe, and strongholds in several regions. Political considerations were no barrier. Gallagher fences were sold in the UK, Argentina and the Falkland Islands while fighting was going on. They sold to the Israelis and the South Africans, and Bill Gallagher worked off two passports so as not to run into strife at the borders of countries inimical to those regimes.

Gallaghers was preaching the gospel of more efficient farming methods and making those methods possible; it was crashing down the gates of technical barriers to trade; it was becoming a national hero in its own land — and it was having fun in the process. Only one thing threatened to take the gloss off the celebrations in 1984: New Zealand appeared to be going down the gurgler. David Lange and the Labour Party he led came to power after the 14 July election in an atmosphere of crisis. The country was massively indebted and had been running large budget deficits since 1975. Market speculation about an imminent sizeable devaluation had led to a run on the currency that provoked a short constitutional crisis as the outgoing prime minister, Robert Muldoon, initially refused to accept advice from officials and requests from Lange for action.[29]

The crisis was averted, at considerable cost, but everyone knew that things would have to change. The structural government deficit would have to be addressed, threatening a painful period of adjustment domestically and the scaling back of the warm government support that Gallaghers had enjoyed for several years. The tide would be going out and, as the American investor Warren Buffett famously put it, the next few years would reveal who was swimming naked.

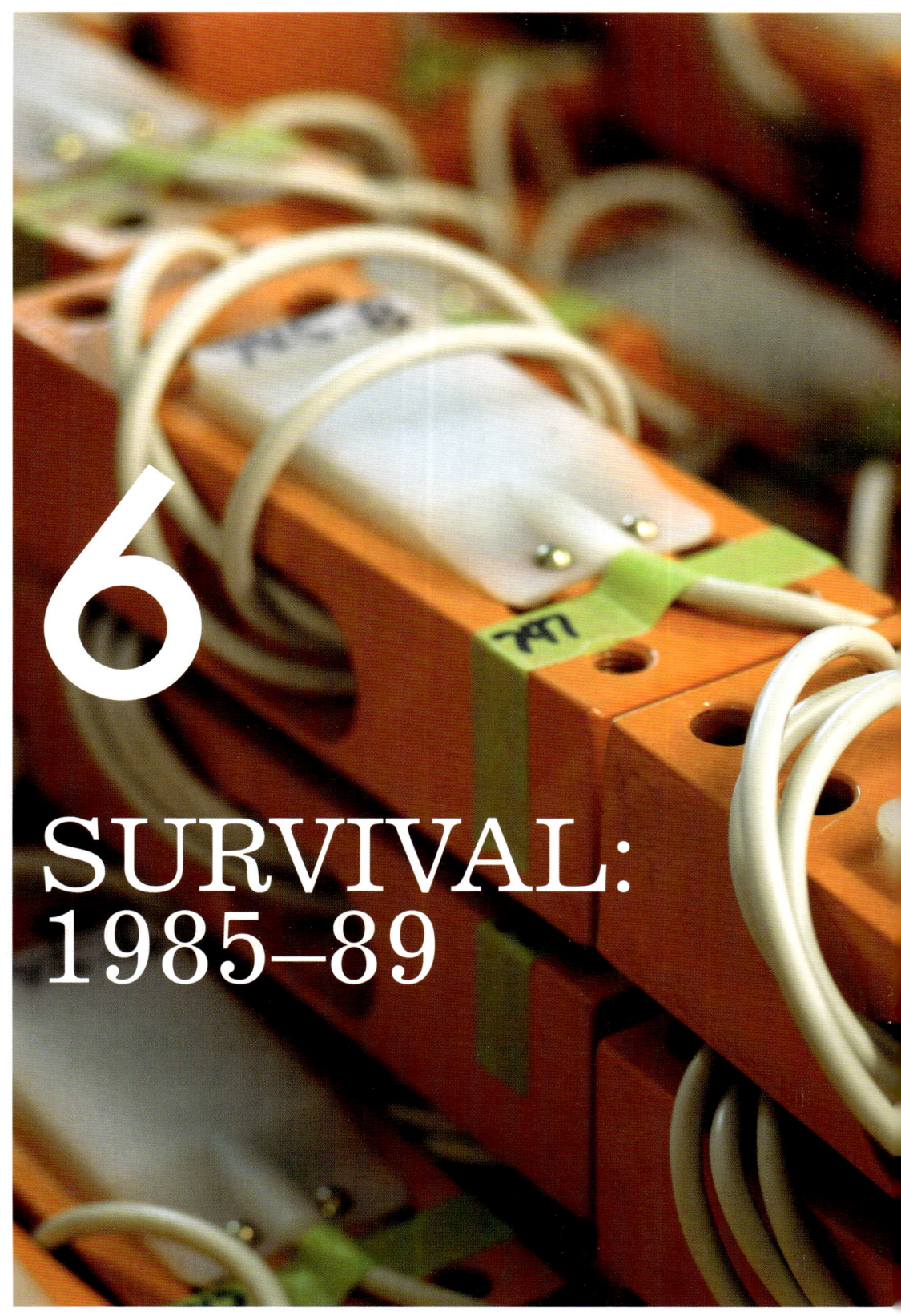

6

SURVIVAL: 1985–89

Chapter six

SURVIVAL: 1985–89

Treat people the way you'd like to be treated yourself, but don't ever expect it from others or you'll simply be disappointed.

— BILL GALLAGHER JNR

On a Monday morning, 2 February 1987, Jenny Gallagher was at home chatting on the phone to her mother-in-law. Her son Ian was at work, and two days earlier Bill had flown to Australia. The doorbell rang. Peering through the frosted glass she saw what she assumed to be a motorcycle courier holding a parcel. When she opened the door a helmeted man bearing a box with a bow on it said, 'Mrs Gallagher, I have a present for you.' He gave the back of the box a shove, and the barrel of a shotgun appeared out the front. 'You're being kidnapped.'

'Don't be so ridiculous,' Jenny recalls saying before he pushed his way inside. 'He put the phone back on the hook and told me, "Do what you're told and you won't get hurt." He ordered me to get my handbag while he left a note on the table. I was complaining, but the gun was real. He knew where my car was and instructed me to drive, with his gun in my ribs. Down the road past Gallaghers. He must have guessed I thought of stalling because he dug the shotgun into me saying, "Don't even think about it."

'From there we went out towards Raglan, down a side road towards the bush. Another guy was following us, and when we stopped he hauled me out, blindfolded and gagged me, bound my hands behind my back and spun me half a dozen times. We drove around for a while, then they spun me again and drove off again. Eventually we stopped and I was walked through the bush, beside a dirty little stream to a campsite. I sat in terror in a pup tent while one of them went off to make phone calls. Since Bill was overseas, I told them that John was the person they should talk to.'[1]

John Gallagher was in his office at 3pm when a man with a foreign accent came on the phone, saying, 'We've taken Jenny hostage.' Silence followed. Then the man continued, 'We want half a million dollars in small used notes.' After another long pause he added that he also wanted $500,000 worth of uncut diamonds. At that point John interjected. 'Where the hell do I get those? South Africa?' Australia, apparently, was the place. The man then told him not to go to the police, and that his family was being watched. Gallagher immediately contacted the police and tried to track down Jenny. When she failed to show at a 5pm arts society meeting she was supposed to be chairing, he realised it wasn't a hoax.[2]

No one could find Bill. He had been in Tasmania, then up to the company sawmill in Baradine, a remote part of New South Wales, looking at ironbark timber. This was the era before cellphones, and it took a full 24 hours to track him down, which raised a few suspicions at first — suspicions that mercifully were relieved when eventually a message found him and he started the long journey home as fast as he could. In practice, Bill's early absence proved handy, since it lent John an excuse to stall for time. He delayed through Tuesday while police technicians frantically started tracing the phone calls he'd received. Hoisting the Union Jack up the company flagpole was the signal that the Gallaghers were ready to negotiate. John demanded proof that Jenny was still alive. A few hours later he was instructed to retrieve a letter from Jenny that had been stowed in a rubbish bin by Lake Rotoroa.

Jenny, meantime, had spent two nights and a couple of days in a tent in the bush, blindfolded. Her initial fears were of big bush wetas falling on her face during the night and having to contemplate swallowing a large spider that was floating in her cup of tea. She had seen the spider from under her blindfold, but didn't want to let her captors know that she could see.[3] Far worse, however, was the anxiety that grew with each passing hour as the two men became increasingly agitated when their plans were frustrated and it became clear that the police were involved.

Rex Miller was the officer in charge of the operation, and he didn't stint on resources. Thirty-three of the 35 CIB officers in Hamilton were assigned to the case. Miller kept Bill hidden when he touched down in Auckland on the Tuesday evening, to enable John to maintain the stalling tactic that he was playing so well. Later the joke would be that it was lucky Bill hadn't been around at the start, since he surely wouldn't have taken the first call seriously, quipping something like: 'Fine, I'll pay the ransom, but only if you keep her.' The reality was deadly serious, and no one knew how the kidnappers would react to the pressure that by Wednesday morning was bearing down on everyone.

At 11.30 that morning the Telecom technicians secured a good trace on a phone call from the captors and isolated it to a telephone booth on the western side of the city. Fortunately some undercover officers were nearby, and they got there in time to see a man emerge from the phone booth. They followed him all over town, then a high-flying aircraft picked up the trail to bush near Te Pahu, 20 kilometres west of the city. Facing her third night of 'unrelenting terror' in the bush, Jenny waited in her tent, never quite sure if she was alone or not.

She recalls: 'The older guy was army trained and could move quietly. He'd scare me by suddenly saying something after I hadn't heard anything for a couple of hours. That afternoon he'd arrived back agitated and said they'd move positions, and I was made to walk blindfolded, wearing jandals and with my arms tied behind me. Constantly slipping over, I struggled along. We kept going up but clearly I was too slow. Eventually he stopped me, and made me lie down on a tarpaulin. Were they going to finish me off then and there? No, he wandered off somewhere.

'I was on the side of a bank and after a couple of hours of hearing nothing, I decided simply to relax and roll down the hill. Nothing happened; nobody grabbed me, so I got up and wriggled my hands free and started making my way down the hill. I could hear noises in the distance, dogs barking and cars. Two men in plain clothes who claimed to be police found me. I was so convinced that they were more people involved in the kidnapping that it took a few hours before I was sure that I was really free. Relief only really came when I saw my family again at John's place.'[4]

She had come out at 8pm on Wednesday. By then one of her captors, 24-year-old local Ronald Cree, was already in custody. An hour later the police captured the man who had planned the operation, Fred Orrell, an engineer from Manchester. Small-time crooks, they had been looking to make some quick money. For their efforts they received nine-year jail terms. This remains one of only a handful of kidnapping-for-ransom cases in New Zealand history.

Since it was the most dramatic thing to happen in the Waikato in many years, the local and national media gave it their full attention. The grateful Gallaghers thanked the local police by presenting a silver cup to be awarded annually for outstanding achievement.[5] But while Jenny was returned safe and sound, ultimately there was no happy ending. The soul-searching that followed laid bare the reality of Bill and Jenny Gallagher's marriage, which, in Bill's view, had been loveless for many years. Bill's true passions lay with the business; it had been all-consuming. Jenny left Bill at the end of the year, nine months after the kidnapping and a few weeks after their subdued twenty-fifth wedding anniversary celebrations.

They had responded to the trauma in different ways. Jenny struggled with memory loss and took a long time to find her feet again. Bill, unused to being in a position where he had no control, threw himself yet further into travelling and work. Meantime, the police investigation had revealed that John Gallagher's wife Glenice had been the initial target of the kidnappers, and that they had switched to Jenny only at the last minute because Glenice had two boys at home that morning. Deep emotions had been stirred throughout the family.

For the privately held company, the kidnapping and its aftermath had ramifications. In the early 1980s the brothers had bought their father out of most of the business; Bill Gallagher senior and Millie owned 8 per cent, while John and Bill had 46 per cent each. Then they had each put 15 per cent into trusts for their wives, so that Jenny walked away with a significant shareholding in the company. Although the transition was achieved with a minimum of rancour, and Jenny retained her interest in the company as the best place to invest her money, the change was awkward because it subtly shifted the balance of the shareholding and complicated what had been a simple arrangement. Fortunately, the relationship between Bill and John held firm. More than two decades later Jenny is still a shareholder, having her interests effectively represented on the board.

Such personal trauma and disruption was the last thing the Gallaghers needed in the late 1980s. Already they were beating against the strongest headwinds in the company's history.

In a few short years after July 1984 the New Zealand economic landscape had been transformed utterly. Manufacturing exporters like Gallaghers went from being treated like kings, cosseted and encouraged by a grateful government, to being left to fight their own way in a cruel world. The unwinding of import controls and the lowering of tariffs exposed once-profitable domestic strongholds to international competition. With the removal of interest rate and foreign exchange controls in late 1984 and early 1985, life for an exporter became a lot more complicated and uncertain; a year's profitability could be wiped out by a sharp rise in the New Zealand dollar or by a bungled foreign exchange contract. Many companies failed to make the adjustments necessary to endure this rapid transition, and fell by the wayside. Gallaghers survived, but it would be more than a decade before it again enjoyed the profitability that had been its happy lot during the final hurrah of the good times.

Few predicted such a turn of events when the Fourth Labour Government was elected at the 14 July 1984 election. It had been a snap election, called at short notice by National's leader Robert Muldoon, and this had allowed the Labour Party, led by David Lange, to be vague as to its economic intentions. The devaluation crisis that occurred immediately after the election and the bleak state of the government's books, with entrenched budget deficits and overseas debt approaching bankruptcy levels, made some adjustment inevitable. But when Bill Gallagher joined 30 other businesspeople and a host of union leaders, churchmen, farmers and social activists to attend a highly publicised Economic Summit in the parliamentary chamber in September 1984, he assumed that the now 20-year-old New Zealand tradition of encouraging exporters would retain its orthodoxy.

TOP With every year Gallaghers' stand at Fieldays got bigger. This marquee served as HQ in 1985.

In his speech to the summit, Gallagher attempted to explain how much of the firm's growth in the past 10 years, from 35 to nearly 300 employees, had rested on its ability to retain and reinvest its profits, as a result of export incentives.[6] If the company had paid tax on its profits, he estimated it would have grown much more slowly, so that in his estimation it would have been lucky to employ 100 people in 1984. Factoring in the PAYE taxation paid for the extra 200 employees they had in fact engaged, money saved by the state on benefits that may have been due if these people hadn't been employed, compared with company tax collected from a much smaller company, he calculated that the tax relief Gallaghers had received through export incentives had produced a tax benefit to New Zealand 'possibly 10 times greater than its direct cost'. This he thought a 'pretty good return on investment'. Rather than continue with the existing complicated incentives system, however, he argued simply that the government should tax only company profits that were distributed as dividends; any retained profits should be tax-free. In this way companies could grow. 'Don't let us eat the seed grain,' he implored the new government.

Trying to grapple with a massive budget deficit, however, the new Minister of Finance Roger Douglas was more interested in growing the tax base than in giving continued relief to exporters. In the November 1984 budget the government halted agricultural subsidies immediately and foreshadowed a swift end to export incentives as well. Gallagher recalls Laurie Stevens, head of the once-powerful Manufacturers' Federation, remarking that under Douglas he and the federation had never been so powerless; none of his arguments ever made a difference. But in reality the manufacturers did enjoy some success. As Gallagher puts it, 'all of us in the Export Institute squawked like hell' through early 1985; they were rewarded by having their export incentives phased out over five years rather than cut off immediately.

The Gallagher Group's golden run peaked in the 15 months to June 1985 (a change from a March to a June financial year had elongated the period). Aided by the 20 per cent devaluation of the New Zealand dollar in July 1984, export receipts were a bumper $14 million, but domestic demand was still strong, lifting total sales to $29.2 million. Adjusted for a 12-month period, sales of $23 million in 1985 represented a 15 per cent increase on 1984, which had been a great year for the company. Export incentives of more than $400,000 lifted annualised profits to $2.54 million ($6.3 million in 2012 terms).

Then it all went sour. Gallaghers was hit by a double whammy of collapsing domestic demand and a rising New Zealand dollar which wiped profits from its export efforts. On the home front, deprived of their agricultural subsidies, New Zealand farmers closed their chequebooks. The result was carnage in the rural service sector, with many agricultural machinery businesses going into liquidation. For Gallaghers, New Zealand electric fence sales tumbled from $7.2 million in 1985 to $4.7 million in 1986, despite the introduction of a widely acclaimed mini strip-grazer energiser; the agricultural machinery side (Gallagher Engineering) fell from $4.5 million to $2.5 million. Gallaghers was unable to reduce overheads fast enough in the engineering business to respond to such a drop, and Gallagher Engineering plunged deep into the red. In his chairman's review for the year, Bill Gallagher described the results as 'startling' and 'far from pleasing'.

Although the group had managed to increase export sales of electric fences to more than $14 million, its profits had been eaten away by violent movements in the exchange rate. Gallagher grumbled in his 1986 annual review that during the year the dollar had risen from being worth 68¢ to 88¢ Australian, a 30 per cent movement in the company's most important export market. 'No exporter has margins of this magnitude,' he said. Never having experienced anything like it — with a few minor exceptions, it was only in recent decades that the New Zealand dollar had only ever lost value in recent decades — they had little idea of hedging.

At bottom, Gallagher blamed government-led inflation, through government-sector pay rates and charges, which fuelled high interest rates, which in turn appeared to be lifting the dollar. He concluded that the company was left with three choices: (1) increase prices to retain profitability 'and lose the market'; (2) walk away from a market they had worked so hard to secure; or (3) incur losses and hope the exchange rate would come right. He noted with regret that Roger Douglas had promised that the 1984 devaluation would make up for the removal of subsidies; at that point the New Zealand dollar had been worth 59¢ Australian.

Meantime, domestic inflation ate into the company's competitiveness. Gallagher roared in a May 1986 speech: 'How can we compete with West Germany, which last year had inflation of 0.7 per cent, when in our economy nationwide wage increases over 15 per cent are allowed, because we do not have a free labour market, but are bound up in nineteenth-century union class-warfare thinking, held together by compulsory unionism.'[7] It was all very strange and bewildering: in theory New Zealand's relatively high inflation should have led to a weakening dollar, yet the reverse was happening and Gallaghers' exports were losing their competitiveness.

A couple of bad investments compounded Gallaghers' pain. The group's 1984–85 computer upgrade to a Data General MV 4000 machine proved a costly blunder. For every problem fixed in the software, six more were created. Worse, the roaring success of Insultimber, Gallaghers' trademarked Australian hardwood fence posts, led them to invest too heavily in their plant in Baradine, New South Wales, to mill the hardwood from the nearby Pilliga forest. The hardwood, not surprisingly, was very hard on machinery. The new plant came on-stream at the end of 1984 but had one problem after another, losing hundreds of thousands of dollars each year for several years. In David Mullen's recollection, it was 'a horror show'.

The upshot was that the group plunged into a trading loss for the year to June 1986. Thankfully, export incentives had only just begun their wind-down and these provided the group with $1 million. Even so, the final result, an after-tax profit of $350,000, represented a calamitous 86 per cent fall on the previous year's effort. In February 1987, a week after Jenny's kidnapping, chief financial officer Don Lindale gave a very gloomy report on trading results for the first five months of the 1986/87 financial year. He concluded that the company would be 'hard pressed' to make an operating profit for the year without urgent steps being taken.[8]

Nerves were strained in 1986 and early 1987, as the Gallaghers faced the certainty that export incentives would tail away to nothing over the next few years, the domestic market was likely to remain weak, and there was no end in sight to fluctuations in the currency. And indeed, the next three years were tough. Sales rose gradually from $24.4 million in the year to June 1986 to $28.8 million in the year to June 1989, but in real terms they were going backwards (in 2012 dollars, from $55 million in 1986 to $49 million in 1989). Profits were harder to come by and fluctuated between $900,000 and $2.2 million, reflecting currency shifts mainly. But at least they hadn't gone under. Gallagher says he never felt seriously worried, even in the worst of times in late 1986, because the company had a long track record of genuine operating profits and could easily sustain a couple of bad years. Some of his contemporaries who had never run an operating profit, whose profits had come entirely from export incentives, were the ones with good cause for nervousness.

Still, the game was undoubtedly tougher. For Gallaghers the big difference between 1986 and 1989 was that in the former year the company received $1 million in incentives, while in 1989 it paid $139,000 in tax. The cheques travelling between Inland Revenue and Gallaghers had irrevocably changed direction. Bill Gallagher grumbled in 1989 about this new and unpleasant experience:

> The exchange rate is reasonable [at the moment], inflation well down and now internationally competitive, interest rates are still too high and the added cost of fringe benefit taxes, land taxes and ever-increasing form filling are a concern. There should be compensation by government for the cost of being part of the Tax Gathering Service for Government. In any other commercial activity, a commission for the collection of tax or revenue would be paid.[9]

There was no chance of any commission, and in a relatively short space of time the company had to transition from the warm bath of generous taxpayer support for its efforts to the cold shower of standing or falling entirely on its own merits, while being plucked enthusiastically by the taxman.

When surveying the reasons for the Gallagher Group's survival and its continued profitability, albeit modest, it is clear that Gallagher Engineering was not one of them. That part of the business, which up until 1977 had been the core of the enterprise, was a casualty of the times, although it would take the Gallagher brothers a long time to accept the reality. Even in the good years of 1984 and 1985 Gallagher Engineering was not very profitable. The agricultural machinery lines didn't have scale; it was tricky to compete against large international companies when Gallaghers made only 150 machines a year.

In addition, stocks had not been well controlled, so that in 1986 Gallaghers possessed sufficient surplus forage harvester parts alone to build 400 machines. With farmers having locked up their chequebooks, there was no market for them.[10] Nor had Gallaghers innovated on this side of the business as much as it had with electric fencing. The old forage harvesters, post-hole diggers and rotary hoes had been good products in the 1960s, but by the mid-1980s, without radical improvement, they had come to the end of their life cycle.

To make matters worse, some international competitors, particularly the Spaniards, Italians and Australians, still retained subsidies of one sort or the other. There was no point grizzling, however, and in 1987, after two years of heavy losses, Gallagher Engineering designers worked closely with scientists from the Ministry of Agriculture and Fisheries and the DSIR to improve their products. But new models and a new management team failed to make an impact. Bill Gallagher drily noted in 1988, 'sadly the improvement anticipated has not come to fruition'.[11] Two more years of heavy losses in 1988 and 1989 prompted Gallaghers to scale down the operation significantly, reducing the product range and selling off surplus plant.

Bill Gallagher admits he didn't give the area sufficient attention. 'There's delegation and there's abdication. With delegation you monitor the situation and get involved if you have to make tough decisions. I abdicated the engineering side of it, leaving it entirely to John to run. I figured that my time devoted to electric fencing would produce 10 times the results than the same amount of time dedicated to agricultural machinery. And so I concentrated on fencing and neglected the engineering. But it came back to bite us, since over a period of five years it lost us more money than it had ever made. We should have got the axe into it much earlier.'

Too much emotion was bound up in Gallagher Engineering, however; the gears from the forage harvester provided the motif for Gallaghers' logo. The brothers found it difficult to make the rational decision to kill it off.

The Gallagher Group's continued survival rested squarely on the continued domestic and international success of the Gallagher electric fence. Back in 1983, Bill Gallagher had confidently recorded in his annual review: 'On the international scene we are only scratching the surface in many areas and expect to achieve considerable market penetration in the years ahead.'

Would that it had proved so simple. Global markets failed to open up like the waters of the Red Sea at his command. Perhaps it was because he was an engineer, but for whatever reason Gallagher was looking at the situation too rationally. Most of his speeches from the mid- to late 1980s included examples of the staggering inefficiency of the subsidised farming practices in most of the industrialised northern hemisphere. In 1984 he had visited a farm in Austria with only 12 cows, which with old equipment took an hour to milk. They were fed meal, and, despite a very high price for milk and much state support, the farmer was not well-off. In 1986 Gallagher talked to a dairy farmer in Vermont who was having trouble breaking even at $12.50 a kilogram of milk solids equivalent, and who wasn't going to survive because the price was about to fall to $10.50. This was at a time when most New Zealand farmers would be very profitable if they could achieve the equivalent of $2.50 a kilogram of milk solids.[12] The same year, Gallagher observed that in France the milk price was more than three times that achieved by New Zealand farmers, and yet with the high price of meal the French were barely profitable. Farm-gate beef prices in California were twice those in New Zealand, and again the Californians were struggling.

In those figures Bill Gallagher saw a massive opportunity. If northern hemisphere farmers could be shown the efficiency gains that could be found from low-input-cost farming practices and modern grassland management, as was practised in New Zealand, the world of agriculture could be transformed. Sure, not every landscape could grow grass like the Waikato, but most could produce a lot more than they did. And with the Gallagher electric fence, he had the essential tool to help them do it. Why wouldn't the world be interested?

Pretty early on, however, it became clear that the average northern hemisphere farmer, or at least the farming lobby groups that represented him, remained convinced that the primary solution to low farm profitability was more government support. Efficiency gains were not totally irrelevant, but were assumed to be a far less powerful agent for change than a good lobby.

For a while, like an old-time evangelist, Bill Gallagher preached that change was coming which would force all farmers to look at their practices; that the General Agreement on Tariffs and Trade (GATT) talks were leading to free trade in agriculture. He saw seismic economic shifts occurring, with socialist governments around the world abandoning the old orthodoxy of protecting producers at the expense of consumers, having realised finally that though they were less organised than most producer groups there were more consumers than producers. In 1987, after three years of radical economic reform at home led by Finance Minister Roger Douglas, Gallagher had clearly absorbed the message. Confidently he told a conference of his distributors in Europe that the best way to give the consumer the most economical product was to have a free market on his supplies, and to rely on market forces to make the best allocation of resources and ensure the survival of the most efficient producers.[13]

But the scales took a long time to fall from the eyes of the typical northern hemisphere farmer. In fact, 25 years later they still haven't. And as a result, Gallaghers struggled to achieve anything like New Zealand levels of electric fencing penetration — energisers per farm or per hectare farmed — in the big markets of North America and Europe. Undismayed, Bill Gallagher plugged on in the late 1980s, believing that ultimately it was in New Zealand's interests to promote lower-cost farming methods in Europe, since it would eventually make it easier for governments to lower subsidies, but he'd had to accept that the growth trajectories of his sales would not be as steep as once he had hoped. The golden goose that he thought he heard around the corner in 1983 stubbornly refused to appear.

Then there was the annoying problem of competition. After the first flush of business success in the late 1970s and early 1980s came the inevitable second phase, when the smartest competitors worldwide started copying Gallaghers' product. In some markets, notably the UK and France, where the primary competition had deep insight into Gallaghers' methods, the contest was strong.

Doggedly, Gallaghers sold greater volumes of product. But exchange rate fluctuations reduced the returns so that sales revenue increased more slowly. Even so, export sales for the electric fencing

ABOVE Sheep-control grazing with Insultimber, New Zealand.

business grew from $9.3 million in 1984 to $17.7 million in 1989, with most of the growth coming in 1985 and 1987. And while rampant domestic inflation in the earlier part of that period gobbled up most of those gains, the performance was sufficient to keep the little New Zealand company at the head of the international pack.

The key elements to that hard-fought ongoing success were continuing innovation, the strength of Gallaghers' relationships with its best marketers around the world, and the company's ownership structure, led by a principal who was committed to the task and was willing and able, along with the other family shareholders, to take a long-term view.

On innovation, being the first to sell high-powered, low-impedence energisers had established Gallaghers' reputation for innovation in the mid- to late 1970s. Gallagher never let that status slip. In late 1986, during the company's worst year, Bill Gallagher was fortified by reading Lee Iacocca's autobiography in which he told the story of salvaging a wobbly Chrysler Corporation.[14] Gallagher noted that even in the depth of his despair Iacocca had the insight to see that while investment in R&D focused on new models represented very significant day-to-day expenditure that did not help the company's weekly survival, without these new developments Chrysler had no long-term future.

It was no different in his business. Gallaghers needed to go on producing new models regularly to keep its nose ahead of the competition, and even in 1986, when profits were falling everywhere they turned, the company retained 12 full-time workers devoted to R&D. These men had developed 14 variations to the standard BEV II energiser to cope with the regulatory demands of various markets; they had also developed a new mini strip-grazer energiser that won prizes in 1985.

Other developments of this era included sophisticated fence voltage alarms to warn farmers of voltage drops caused by faults or excessive foliage, sealed cutout switches to keep out moisture and spider webs, better digital voltmeters which made it much easier to detect faults and measure the efficiency of earthing systems, light polywires with highly conductive metal strands, and geared reels and tumblewheels for the easier erection of long temporary fences.

And as time went by, Gallagher paid attention to protecting the company's intellectual property. This meant spending a lot to gain patents, and more defending them. Bill Gallagher, who by this time had passed several years on the Minister of Justice's Industrial Property Advisory Council reviewing New Zealand's patent copyright laws, outlined his philosophy on patents in a speech in October 1986:

> Patents are very much analogous to the action in a James Bond movie where you're out in front and you're throwing tacks and oil on the road for your followers to flounder into. There's nothing bullet-proof about them but it certainly slows down the timid . . . In our history we never conceived we would be so successful with high-powered electric fencing and patents were not taken very far around the world. We now have many followers into the first basic concepts. It's only with later developments and the more advanced models that we have patents of significance that some of our followers are now blundering into . . . When it comes to defending patents it is very much a matter of playing poker, whoever is prepared to put the most money on the table for legal actions is likely to succeed.[15]

Since there is no such thing as a world patent and taking out a patent in every country is prohibitively expensive (requiring 'more money than brains' in Gallagher's view), the company focused on the essential markets: the US and the UK; its home turf of Australia and New Zealand; Germany, and France. Then Gallagher's idea was to pick off the home of its strongest competition outside those big countries, which during this period was Denmark.

Defending past achievements only took the company so far. Gallagher also needed to extract more from his R&D investment. Thus far the 12-man R&D team comprised skilful technicians, most of whom had progressed from the factory floor. Colin Standing had been a skilful inventor but not a natural manager. His retirement provided the opportunity to increase the output of this division. In August 1987 Gallaghers hired John Walley, an electrical engineer who had been working in New Zealand for three years with Thorn-EMI's Kenwood appliances division. He had a background working for Rolls Royce and General Electric in the UK and promised much in lifting the productive capability of the organisation. His initial appointment was to head the R&D department. A confident Englishman, Walley didn't worry too much about hurting people's feelings. In the company's 1992 history he described the department he inherited as 'run down', 'gone to seed', and 'living on its past achievements'.[16]

A new set of eyes was useful, and Walley soon impressed the Gallaghers by solving a long-standing design issue in the US. Lightning strikes, so much more frequent in the American Midwest than in New Zealand, regularly fried energisers. Walley travelled to the States, studied the matter from first principles and correctly identified the problem. The most damaging lightning is positively charged and the unit's polarity was negative. By reversing its polarity to positive, the problem was reduced. Back home, Walley set about developing relationships with the technology department at the University of Waikato with a view to building the professional engineering capacity within the organisation.

Walley was also the man to take over from Bill Gallagher as the person primarily responsible for carrying on the fight to develop and maintain workable international standards for electric fence energisers. Since Gallagher's work on the CEE standard in the late 1970s and early 1980s, attention had shifted to the International Electric Commission (IEC), whose 61H Committee worked to develop standards for electrically operated farm appliances. Most countries would follow its lead. The secretariat of the committee was available and Gallagher pushed to have New Zealand Standards take it up. He was on the New Zealand Standards Council at the time. 'If New Zealand is going to make an international contribution,' he argued, 'electrically operated farm appliances was surely the most logical committee on which to concentrate.' They succeeded and New Zealand took on the secretariat. Meetings of the 61H Committee from the mid-1980s in Dublin, Tokyo, Rotorua and Frankfurt held threats and opportunities for Gallagher's business, but with strong input into the secretariat he was well positioned to guide the process so that the regulatory environment was not implacably hostile to continuous innovation.

In terms of relationships with distributors, this period bore out the wisdom of Bill Gallagher's earlier hunch about the benefits of using entrepreneurial, family-owned businesses with 'their own skin in the game' to drive growth in far-flung regions of the world. Gallaghers thrived in those places where Bill was able to carry on his preferred means of operation. He once told an interviewer:

> The real successes, the big successes, are the ones where we have the local entrepreneur and we are the backseat driver, where we own between 10 and 40 per cent, and the local guy runs it like us, but we can grow them from the backseat.[17]

By 'growing them from the backseat' he meant offering business advice and mentoring. Gallagher found, for example, that very few of his distributors knew how to organise finance well. Though they were great salespeople, they had not yet learnt how to sell their bankers on the value and future prospects of the business. In many cases, Gallagher could help.

If it went well, they achieved a unity of purpose, since the distributor was whole-heartedly committed to growing the business, while retaining sufficient autonomy to make the best of his local knowledge and adapt to changing local conditions.[18] Gallagher's ideal was for the distributor to devote a significant proportion of their business to his product alone, ideally more than 70 per cent. At that point their livelihood depended on Gallagher; they were truly mutually dependent. But since most dealers were naturally reluctant to expose themselves so thoroughly to one company, the arrangement only worked long-term if a relationship of trust developed.

In every market the circumstances and the dynamics were different. In Ireland, for example, Gallaghers had taken a minority stake in John Lucey's distribution business and a great relationship developed. John continued to be amazed that when he met Bill every six months or so, Bill always remembered the last thing they had spoken of at their previous meeting. The conversation would inevitably begin with, 'You said to me last time . . . , well I've been thinking about it, and this is what I reckon we should do.' Every few years Lucey would be invited to a conference in New Zealand, the experience of which, with its unique Maori welcome, had the power to weave a special bond with some suppliers.

Lucey gasped in horror as he witnessed his first hangi. He had missed the preliminary stages — the large hole being dug in the ground, the preheated rocks being rolled into it, the vegetables and meat placed over the rocks, then covered with a sheet and soil. Lucey arrived in time to see the ground being dug up. Then a white sheet was peeled from a steaming mass — whole cabbages that for a moment looked like heads. He thought he was witnessing the exhumation of the dead or the start of a cannibal feast.

Many friendships were fortified by late-night sessions at bars. Bill Gallagher's PA, Margaret Comer, frequently found herself in tricky situations during New Zealand conferences: dealing with three large Texan distributors who caused a ruckus in a Hamilton pub by chewing tobacco and spitting it on the floor; collecting visiting distributors from the lock-up in the early hours; haggling with hotel staff over the inclusion in a bill of a large 'miscellaneous' fee for one international distributor, which on investigation turned out to be for the services of a dog. It made the mind boggle. Some moments were more comical than stressful, however, such as when a shy new Indian dealer revealed, after he had had a bit to drink, that he knew the words to every Roy Orbison song and then bellowed 'Only the Lonely' in a thick Indian accent at 2am as he wandered down Hamilton's Victoria Street.

And always, Bill Gallagher showed enormous resilience. John Lucey recalls being the last to leave the bar with Bill and another Irish distributor, Ed Brett, early one morning midway through the 1987 distributor conference in Holland: 'By the time I staggered into the conference the following morning, Bill was just finishing his speech, looking like he'd been in bed at 9.30 the previous night with a cup of tea. He looked at me as if to say, "Mate, if you can't piss, get off the pot".'[19]

With Bill Gallagher there was always a little edge to the friendship. While he made a huge investment in time with his key partners, and welcomed them into his own home when they stayed in New Zealand, he sought to blend security and heat in his relationships with distributors, constantly adjusting the mix.

Gallagher offered to take a minority stake in Veldman & Dijkstra, the company's Dutch distributors, but they were reluctant to yield a shareholding. Gallagher scrawled in a report on another unsuccessful attempt to negotiate a purchase: 'Dooitze Dijkstra is pretty cocky, but perhaps it needs pointing out that they are a grand 11.2% of our business.' Eleven per cent isn't to be sneezed at, however, and they were expanding into other parts of Europe. Finally, in 1986 they let Gallaghers into a 10 per cent shareholding and a seat on the board. Erik Dijkstra saw that the New Zealanders' stake was 'an expression that they were more to each other than supplier and customer'. He says: 'The importance of Bill's loyalty to his customers shouldn't be underestimated. It gave you almost a guaranteed feeling, when investing in building the brand and expanding your company, that you did it with the certainty that you wouldn't have the agreement cancelled in three years over some disagreement.'[20]

And they had plenty of disagreements, the most vehement and long-running being the battle over royalties. Erik Dijkstra's recollection of the saga gives an indication of Gallagher's hunger: 'When we started to work with Gallaghers they didn't offer a complete system. I believed we had to offer the lot — posts, wires and everything else — so I gathered together the other material, including from some other New Zealand companies. Then in the mid-1980s Gallaghers came up with the idea that, because they were offering us exclusivity in our market, they deserved exclusivity back. The name of Gallagher is creating your business, so everything I sell, even accessories I bought in Holland, he wants a royalty for. I refused, he insisted, and every single visit for 15 years after that we'd fight over royalties.

'He's tenacious, he's aggressive and he's a great debater, fully exploiting the fact that English is a second language for us, which has us on the back foot. He will say "That wall is black," when it's obviously not, it's white, but he won't leave until we admit that it is black. He won't stop until he is right. And he has a memory like an elephant.'

Through the smoke of many battles, the Dijkstras and Gallaghers built powerful respect for each other. Bill Gallagher's street-fighting credentials were never clearer than in March 1988 when he sat down to their AGM nursing a couple of 'puncture wounds' from his stabbing a few days earlier in Amsterdam.

In Australia, David Mullen had done a great job in seizing

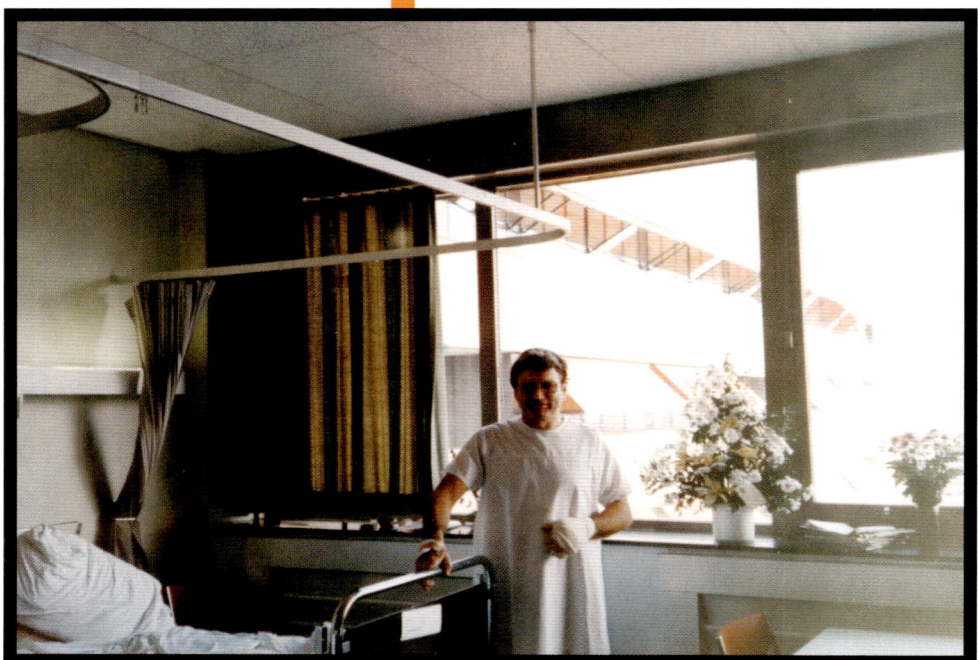

TOP Bill in a Dutch hospital, the morning after he was stabbed in March 1988.

market share for Gallaghers and growing revenues — sales for Gallagher RSM rose from $2 million in 1980 to nearly $10 million in 1988. In 1981 Gallaghers claimed 40 per cent of the Australian market, with its nearest rival, the Australian brand Daken, taking 35 per cent, followed by Speedrite, Waikato and Thunderbird, all with around 5 per cent. By 1987 Gallaghers dominated with 60 per cent; Daken languished with 18 per cent. Speedrite had clawed its way to 9 per cent. The key, Mullen says, was 'filling our territory managers up with knowledge. As they became experts on electric fencing they felt when they went on to the farm that they really were valued, somebody making a difference, and this gave them a real sense of job satisfaction. None of our rivals gave anything like such a service.'[21] Under Mullen and his effective sales manager, John Colless, the Australian market was taking more than a quarter of Gallaghers' exports.

Bill Gallagher was so impressed with Mullen that in 1984, when he and John resolved to bring some new blood onto the board of the Gallagher Group, they invited him on as an independent director. It was an indication of trust for Gallaghers to allow its biggest customer into the holy of holies, with access to all the group's figures.

Gallaghers' experience in the UK stood in contrast to its expansion in Holland and Australia. Having endured the disaster of his independent English distributor setting up as a manufacturing rival, Gallagher had set up a wholly owned subsidiary in England, the first for Gallaghers outside of New Zealand. It was proving a failed experiment. Gallagher listed off his mistakes in a 1984 speech: he had employed the wrong staff; employed too many staff; paid insufficient attention to set-up costs; 'lost a bit of control'.[22] He had moved reasonably quickly to tighten things up: 'It is a fact of life,' he observed, 'that you cannot afford in an international business . . . to carry people who believe that they have found the pot of gold at the foot of the rainbow.' And he extracted some lessons from the disaster, particularly the insight that professional bankers had long since worked out how to deal with poor reporting from distant outposts or recalcitrant debtors: to ask for information once or twice, and then, if it doesn't arrive, to turn off the money immediately.

Thereafter, Gallagher was much more demanding about the quality and timeliness of the information he expected. But even so, the wholly owned company, staffed by employees on the opposite

TOP The Dijkstras. From left to right: Meindert and Erik Dijkstra, an unknown friend, John Veldman and Dooitze Dijkstra.

side of the world to the owners, failed to show the dynamism of the family-operated distributors he had elsewhere. By 1989 the English market had been left behind by Mullen in Australia, Veldman & Dijkstra in Holland, and even by Helmut Allie in south Germany, in terms of revenues, while its overhead costs were enormous.

Yet the model that worked so well in Holland and Australia failed to produce dividends in the US. Art Snell's distribution business, which originally covered 28 states, had grown reasonably. In 1985 it was taking nearly $3 million worth of electric fencing product from Gallaghers, a figure only just eclipsed by both the Australian and the combined European market. But as a distribution business it had never been profitable. When the American started to run up a large debt to New Zealand by early 1987, Bill Gallagher began to lose patience. The Texan's style didn't help. Early in 1987 Gallagher visited Snell and reported: 'My evening with him was a long ear bashing. [Snell] paused a couple of times to ask a question on what he can do better but then didn't want to wait for an answer . . .'[23] Soon after, Gallagher and Snell went their separate ways, with Gallagher agreeing to buy Snell's share of the business (now 38 states of the US), effective from November 1987.

The evolving plan was to run Snell's old business from Hamilton. Mullen wasn't convinced that was such a good idea. Late one evening after a board meeting, as he and Gallagher were chewing over the issues, with a few beers, as was their wont, Mullen said: 'Jeez, Bill, you can't afford to have another England!' Quick as a flash, Gallagher shot back: 'Well, do you want a challenge?' Without giving it too much thought, Mullen decided he did, and so Gallagher sold him 51 per cent of Snell's old distribution business a few months later. They renamed the company Gallagher Power Fence Inc (GPF).

Mullen might have had cause to regret his decision in time. GPF was weak, with plenty of bad debts, stock that was outdated, and a mixed bunch of distributors. He installed Ian Morrison, a New Zealander, as president and they started tackling the problems. Mullen thought he could detect a change occurring in the distribution structure in the US, whereby the power of the long-line general product distributors was weakening so that it might be possible for GPF to have a group of sales reps selling direct to major retailers. He soon realised that he had got it wrong. Having bought a business turning over US$5.2 million a year in 1987, within 18 months they had a business turning over $3.5 million. In the 1989 year they lost nearly $500,000. It wasn't 'all giggle and laughter', as Mullen puts it; '... we'd created our own slump by frustrating many distributors through a radical change to our distribution strategy'.[24]

Fifteen years after Gallaghers' powerful energisers had been introduced to the market, only a minority of America's many conservative farmers had responded to its message of improving productivity through intensive grassland management. Still, Mullen was confident of turning things around eventually, and now, to a considerable extent, Gallaghers' future growth prospects depended on his marketing skills in the US and Australia.

Bill Gallagher's energy in scouring the earth for new markets continued to pay dividends, however. When he mentioned in speeches that they were making progress in Iceland, New Zealand audiences would invariably laugh. So what? But Bill would patiently point out that Icelanders have a million sheep, and on the island Gallaghers had no competition. Sales to Iceland may have only been $150,000 in 1989, but so long as he didn't sink too much time into it, it all added up. Harvesting 15 such small markets provided a significant revenue stream.

Outside the reasonably significant South African market, Africa included many places where Gallagher constantly had to fight the urge to spend a lot of time visiting distributors who would never amount to anything much. Tim Savory, for example, was a Zimbabwean farmer who sold Gallagher fences on the side. Wild buffalo often carried foot and mouth disease, so there was a job to do to keep them segregated from cattle, and Gallagher solar-powered models worked well. But the business seldom amounted to more than $50,000 a year and it was extremely challenging to extract any foreign exchange from Robert Mugabe's clutches.

The search for new export markets was made more urgent by the slack domestic market. Although it plunged from more than $7 million in 1985 to less than $5 million the following year, the New Zealand market for electric fencing equipment didn't continue down toward collapse like the market for rotary hoes and the other agricultural machinery that Gallagher Engineering had made. Electric fencing was counter-cyclical to a degree. In

ABOVE David and Marg Mullen.

tough times farmers thought twice about traditional fencing and were more open to conversion to electric fencing if it did the job more efficiently. But they still had to be persuaded, and the local competition had to be headed off.

Vaughan Jones had resigned as head of marketing in February 1985 to lead the local marketing effort of Alfa Laval, but the Gallaghers retained his input by inviting him onto the board of directors alongside Mullen. And he continued to make a contribution, with regular conference speeches and pep talks in which he carried on his domestic and international crusade to generate demand for Gallagher products by promoting intensive grazing practices made possible by modern electric fencing.[25] His address to a Gallagher area managers conference in 1988 was typical of his style, as he exhorted the salesmen to understand the mindset of New Zealand farmers, in order to captivate them and thereby drive demand for Gallaghers' products:

> Most New Zealand farmers are —
> - Individualists who are happy to work hard for their way of life, their family and for future security.
> - Optimists, who are always hoping for better seasons and better returns.
> - Many are wealthy businessmen who went without for what they have — so don't begrudge them their big cars and boats.
> - Boys with toys who like flashing lights.
> - Humans who make many decisions on hunches, likes and dislikes, and quite often buy on impulse.
> - People earning little net income but with a discretionary dollar.
> - People with strong loyalties who usually stick with the same brand of tractor, car, milking machine, religion and wife.
> - Farmers like all people are more easily influenced at a young age, so if we can convert young farmers to Gallagher at agricultural colleges, polytechnics, universities, young farmers' clubs, shows and other similar venues, we're more likely to have customers for life.[26]

TOP Gallaghers penetrated as far north as Iceland. Here Ragnar Eriikson inspects a high-plateau fence.

ABOVE The Gallagher electric fence protected Stonehenge from wandering stock.

Such insights and a big effort from the local marketing team, then led by Bill Grant, enabled the company to hold its ground in New Zealand. But the recovery was slow to assert itself. By 1989 New Zealand electric fence sales had ground their way back to $5.9 million, still well behind the 1985 figure, particularly after taking rampant inflation into account.

In those circumstances, the company seized any opportunities for publicity. In October 1987 a large sea elephant, which acquired the name of Humphrey, gave them a welcome break. The beast had come ashore at a farm at Opoutere on the Coromandel Peninsula and had taken to chasing the cows, smashing fences and generally causing mayhem. He was only brought to heel by a hastily erected Gallagher fence. After taking 7000 volts through his jowly snout he ceased to worry the cows, and Gallaghers made hay from the propaganda opportunity. Gallaghers' Mystery Creek exhibition that year featured a large fibreglass replica of Humphrey roaring behind a three-wire fence. Years later, during another Fieldays, when the real Humphrey had long since swum back to sea, his fibreglass double was seen floating in Hamilton's Garden Place fountain after a late-night escapade by some visiting Australian distributors.

Continued product innovation, good relationships with key international distributors and a continued drive for more exports all helped the Gallagher Group survive the rapid withdrawal of government support that coincided with a lean period for New Zealand agriculture, as well as a hostile environment in many of its major international markets. Again, Gallaghers' ownership structure was another important factor in the group's survival. Neither the company nor its shareholders were heavily indebted, and so they were able to ride out a few lean years, when dividends were poor, without a crisis. If the enterprise had been sold to new owners in a highly leveraged deal in 1985, it would in all probability have fallen over after a few years of modest profits during a period of double-digit interest rates.

There was never any prospect of Gallaghers being sold in 1985, however. The company's four owners — Bill and Jenny, John and Glenice — were all in it for the long haul. But the thought of forming a public company and floating some of the shares on the stock exchange did cross Bill's mind around 1985, when the share market was starting to lift and colossal fortunes were being made

ABOVE Humphrey the sea elephant separated from his adopted harem of cows by a PowerFence.

by a lucky few. He resisted the urge, helped by stern reminders from Vaughan Jones about other businessmen who had followed that path and subsequently lost control of their companies. Ossie James (once the owner of James Aviation), rural merchants AM Bisley & Co and Yates, the seed and gardening supplies company, sprang to mind. With a flood of new capital from public shareholders, the Gallaghers and their new board might have faced great temptation to spend the money on expensive acquisitions or badly thought through diversifications into industries and businesses about which they knew little. As it was, with a few minor exceptions, the Gallaghers stuck to their knitting and maintained a conservative approach to finance. And they were never limited by a lack of capital. In 1989 shareholders' funds represented 50 per cent of the group's total assets; they could always finance expansion if it made sense.

The biggest decision they faced in 1988 was whether or not to make a major investment in a new information technology system. Gallagher electric fences were the most expensive on the market wherever they were sold, but because of increased competition the prices they were achieving had not shifted much since the mid-1980s. The company had maintained its overall turnover only by increasing volumes substantially, which had required greater productivity from the workforce. After the shock of 1986, when the environment suddenly turned very hostile, relatively easy productivity gains had been made by reducing surplus staff and clamping down on the more exuberant spending habits.

Margaret Comer, who had started as personal assistant to Bill and John Gallagher in 1985, had quickly seen that things were a bit loose, particularly when Bill was overseas. John, she recalls, found it difficult to say no to the flood of requests for new cars and other benefits that came to his door the moment Bill hopped on a plane. The daughter of a police constable from Waihi, a mother of two and, prior to joining Gallaghers, the administrator of Waikato Hospital's Psychiatric Unit, Margaret was a self-confessed 'hard-headed old harridan'. She became Bill's 'eyes and ears' and took responsibility for putting together a company policy manual that put some structure and accountability around company cars and other perks. That caused a ruckus, but those changes were not as painful as the decisions Bill Gallagher had to make as he replaced some managers who had been perfectly adequate during the boom times but now needed to be replaced by professionals who were better equipped for the more demanding deregulated environment.

Phil Delany was one of the new appointments, joining the firm as purchasing and distribution manager in August 1987. In a short space of time he was causing mayhem among Gallaghers' long-term suppliers, whom he felt had been overcharging. To their shock he turned up and said, 'Give me that component at this price, or I'll get it somewhere else.'[27] Old drinking buddies and friends among the suppliers were instantly on the phone to Bill and John Gallagher to complain, but they quickly recognised that a new attitude was necessary.

Moreover, the task was much bigger than renegotiating a few supply agreements. Delany soon formed the view that in order to extract further productivity gains the company needed a new management system to coordinate the business's activities more efficiently. At that point Gallaghers operated two systems, one for production and one for accounts. Neither was particularly robust and the two didn't marry together well, making production planning difficult and sometimes chaotic.

Delany characterised the existing approach to production planning as the OSWO system: 'Oh shit, we're out'. Someone in the factory would realise they had run out of a component, and production would stop until one was found. In fact, the main problem with that approach was that it led to excessive hoarding of components, precisely to avoid the next OSWO moment. While the best Japanese manufacturers had developed the 'just-in-time' model for inventory, Gallaghers operated on the 'just-in-case' model. The result was that components worth hundreds of thousands of dollars, maybe several millions — nobody quite knew for sure — cluttered up the factory floor in case they might be required. When interest rates were around 22 per cent it was almost suicidal to have so much working capital tied up unproductively. Delany was impressed by US manufacturing guru Oliver Wight's philosophy and the Manufacturing Resource Planning (MRP II) system that he had developed with George Plossl. Noel Hamilton was also aware that Dunedin-based Mainland Products Ltd had used the MRP II system effectively for the production of Mainland cheese.

MRP II distilled insights from world-class manufacturing methods around the world to create an all-encompassing computer-based 'master production schedule' that drew on forecasts of demand from major customers to plan purchasing and production. It promised much greater sophistication in every aspect of the enterprise, from inventory management to bills of material, capacity planning and cost control. No other electric fence manufacturer around the world had anything nearly so sophisticated.

However, in 1987 it was thought that it might cost about $1 million for both the hardware and software to implement the system. Having burned through half that amount only a few years earlier on another computer system, the Gallaghers and their new board were nervous at the prospect. In fact, this would be Gallaghers' third computer system. The first, built for the company by Cambridge Computers in the 1970s, had an astonishing 50 megabytes of memory and was as big as a refrigerator. It was also 'murderously expensive' in Bill Gallagher's recollection, and he didn't trust its answers. They had managed to sell it when they upgraded to the second system. The second time they bought a standard package from a British firm and then changed it to suit the particular requirements of the Gallagher Group. This provided a feast for a steady stream of programmers from Auckland, or flown out from Britain, to fix the latest series of bugs. 'Every time they fixed one problem, five more emerged.'

In August 1987 Delany gained an enthusiastic supporter for his call for a new system when John Walley joined the firm. Together they built the case. By early 1988 Bill and John Gallagher were convinced. But since 1985 the brothers had brought in several independent directors, precisely to advise on such big decisions. Along with Vaughan Jones and David Mullen, the Gallaghers had recruited Bill McPhail, the chairman and managing director of local company Allflex Holdings, which sold ear-tags for livestock around the world, and Barry Paterson, a Hamilton barrister and company director.

The independents remained sceptical of MRP II and through the second half of 1988 debate raged over the proposal, with Walley apparently threatening to resign if the answer was no, since management would have been deprived of the tools necessary to do its work effectively.[28] The brinksmanship eventually paid off, and in late 1988 Bill Gallagher steered his board to a decision in favour of making the investment. The key insight this time, however, was not to try to create a unique system to suit Gallaghers' requirements; that way had led to disaster with the previous system. Instead Delany scoured the world for the combination of hardware and software that had worked best, and Gallaghers would change its operations where necessary to suit the hardware and software requirements. 'There was nothing sacred about the way we did things,' Gallagher recalls, 'so our philosophy was to rearrange our methods to fit a standard and proven package.'

The new hardware and software was installed over the Christmas break at the end of 1988, and over the next few months Walley led a team that would train staff to operate under the new system. It was a time of upheaval, culminating in a stocktake of everything in the warehouses over Anzac weekend, late April 1989.

The next few years would reveal whether the turmoil was worth it. But the intention was clear: continual and substantial improvements in efficiency and productivity were now priorities, alongside the old imperative of increasing export markets and turning out regular design innovations. In this regard, the Gallagher Group's experience was typical of what went on throughout the entire manufacturing sector in New Zealand in the late 1980s as government support and protection was stripped away. Gallagher squawked at many of the changes, but for the most part concentrated his energies on adjusting to the new realities. Those with genuinely good products and who were nimble survived; others went to the wall.

In 1988 the group celebrated its 50-year anniversary, based on a starting point of 1938, when Bill Gallagher senior first began making his electric fences. The brothers and their now elderly and frail father were justifiably proud of their achievements. The gathering of 460 men and women, including distributors from throughout the world who derived their living from this Hamilton-based company, was impressive. The group was slightly smaller in real terms than it had been at its peak in 1985, but with a turnover of $29 million in the year to June 1989 ($50 million in 2012 terms) the Gallagher Group was a solid medium-sized enterprise. There were fewer employees, down to 207 in 1989 from 264 in 1984, but they were more productive.

Back in 1986 the group had articulated its first corporate philosophy, which included the goal to 'Maintain and increase our world leadership in animal containment and applications such as pasture management'. And on that measure it remained successful. Its $2.2 million after-tax profit in June 1989 ($3.8 million today) was also below earlier peaks, but for the first time in more than a decade it was comprised entirely of genuine tax-paid profit, free of any government support. New professional managers were coming in, old rhythms and some relationships were being disrupted; it was a stressful time, but one when the company was alive and up for the challenge.

And while the old relaxed, backyard attitudes on the production floor were fast becoming part of history, the fun hadn't been extracted from the enterprise. Selling electric fences still created opportunities for giving friends and strangers a healthy zap. In 1989 Erik Dijkstra devised a publicity-raising competition with all the usual ingredients. He recalls: 'At exhibitions you always had people willing to grab the wires to show how tough they are. So when the latest model arrived we ran a competition at the show in which anyone who could hang on for 10 seconds received a bottle of whisky. And if you could hang on for a minute, you could take the energiser home. Since it cost 1000 guilders, then around NZ$1000, it was a decent prize. A thousand guilders for a minute's work. So we put up a sign saying, "We will employ you at rate of 60,000 guilders an hour for the easiest job in your life." Of course, this attracted enormous attention.

'We had 150 people trying their luck and most fell off after two shocks. But there was one guy in three days, a 22-year-old, who hung on magnificently. And when a journalist rang me afterwards to see if anyone won the prize I put him on to this guy. But when the journalist tried to talk to him, the boy's mother said, "No he can't come to the phone, he's in bed; he has been hanging on to an energiser for a minute and still hasn't recovered." In the end it took him about two weeks to come right.

'The journalist rang me back and said, "You lied, he didn't get 60,000 guilders an hour; it took him two weeks to earn that money!"'[29]

ABOVE A Gallagher conference in 1992, which brought together local senior management and distributors from around the world.

7

REGAINING MOMENTUM: 1989–95

Chapter seven

REGAINING MOMENTUM: 1989–95

Points of transition provide times of vulnerability in a family-owned business. And around 1989–90, big changes were happening to the lives of Gallaghers' principal shareholders and to the company.

First, Bill, the driving force of the company for the past two decades, had a new love interest. After his marriage to Jenny ended in December 1987, Bill spent a year or so in his late forties as a carefree bachelor, enjoying his spare time with a couple of diving friends, Murray Bindon and Bill Hay, two men who had found themselves in similar personal circumstances. Gallagher was at his happiest standing around the barbecue with a glass of wine at his bach on the beach at Whangamata, cooking freshly caught crayfish and maybe a dozen fat, juicy scallops in their shells. That would only be the starter. Mavis, the cook at Gallaghers' canteen, had cottoned on to Bill's needs and would present him once a week with two large cardboard boxes crammed with bacon and egg pies, casseroles and other assorted 'man food' that could be thrown into the microwave. The 'three musketeers', as the two Bills and Murray became known, selected merrily from Mavis's weekly bounty. Life was simple: each morning they would pull back the curtains to look

ABOVE Bill in his natural habitat: Whangamata.

at the ocean, declaring the conditions either PPC ('piss pot calm') or a 'two-bra day' (a term coined from an observation made by a buxom passenger during one particularly bumpy ride).

During this period Bill struck up a relationship with Judi Cochrane. Four years his junior, Judi came from a proud family. Her father's grandfather, Thomas Cochrane, came to New Zealand as a cabin boy, aged 12, jumped ship and as a young man set himself up as a landowner at Cochrane's Gap, Pollok, on the Awhitu Peninsula southwest of Auckland. Her maternal grandmother, Ada Brown, visited New Zealand from her home in London's Kensington as a child with her governess in 1886. She was photographed sitting on both the Pink and White Terraces earlier in the year they were obliterated in the Tarawera Eruption. She returned later and married Thomas Chapman, and together they owned several large farms in the North Island. Judi's parents, Frank and Ileen Cochrane, had a dairy farm at Tapapa, south of Tirau. Bill and Judi had known each other distantly for many years, because Judi had earlier married Trevor Graham, an engineering school contemporary of Bill's; Trevor and Bill had shared the same flat in Auckland for a year. Later, Trevor worked for Brian Perry Ltd, a civil engineering contractor based in Hamilton, and so the Gallaghers' and Grahams' social circles occasionally overlapped. Judi and Trevor had two children, Michelle and Chris.

Judi's marriage had been dissolved in 1979, then in August 1985 she suffered the tragedy of losing Michelle in a car accident. In her grief she resigned from her busy role as an executive assistant to Jim Barry at the machinery design company Barry Huber, and took up the less demanding position of executive secretary for Don Lindale, Gallaghers' chief financial officer. After nine months working downstairs at the Gallagher head office she was ready to resume her career and took up a post as a tutor in the Business Studies department at Waikato Polytech (now Wintech).

Judi and Bill's romance started on 11 April 1988 when they were invited to dinner at Don and Carol Lindale's home. There were 20 guests that night and they were the only ones single. Bill was 47, Judi 43. She remembers that the attraction was instant and powerful. Both of them, however, had been through difficult personal trials and they weren't in a rush. But by May 1989 they were ready. Seldom thereafter have they been separated. They married in February 1992.

What impact would all this have on Bill's business drive? After 20 years of intense activity he enjoyed a very comfortable financial base. Now, with the added joy of a new relationship, it was only natural that he might rethink his priorities. And indeed he did appear to be giving serious thought to entering a new phase of business life. In May 1989 he left New Zealand to begin his first three-week stint at Harvard Business School on the Owners and Presidents Management (OPM) Program. Bill had heard about the programme, which comprised several three-week sessions scattered over a period of three years, through a distant cousin, Bill Hall. Gallagher recalls: 'Bill Hall was a successful businessman who had run Hallmark, then Woolrest; he'd gone through the Harvard OPM programme and raved about it. And my philosophy has always been that once you'd stopped learning you were dead, and there were more than a few people walking round in that state, so I'd go on management courses every year, such as through the Institute of Directors. And of course, we faced plenty of challenges, not just as a company after several difficult years, but as a nation struggling to rebuild a weak economy. So it was interesting to get an international perspective.

'At Harvard I soon realised that I'd learn more from my fellow students than from the professors, because we spent our time working through three case studies a day on real businesses, trying to decide whether we'd put our money into each company. The reaction of these guys was fascinating; out of 60 in my group, 20 would be noisy, 20 were in the middle and the other 20 would not say boo.

'I started out at the noisy end of the middle group and finished at the quiet end. I thought I was tough, but quite a few of these men were super-aggressive. They wouldn't think twice about cutting a workforce in half. And on occasions I felt I could be dropped by a blow to the jaw during our debates.'

While Bill Gallagher's mind was churning with all the stimulation from Harvard, and with new love, his brother John was also veering off in a new direction. The more gentle and enigmatic half of the Gallagher brothers partnership, John had taken responsibility for the struggling Gallagher Engineering side of the business through the 1980s and had guided the group as a whole during Bill's regular absences overseas. But as the 1980s progressed John was increasingly drawn to community roles. He had been president of the Waikato Chamber of Commerce for five years, from 1981 until 1986, when Hamilton's mayor Ross Jansen encouraged him to stand for the Hamilton City Council. He was elected and spent his first term as chairman of the Planning and Development Committee, reviewing the city's district scheme. He became interested in tidying up the substantial, ad hoc collection of properties that the city had acquired over the years.

In his second term, from 1989, the now 50-year-old John Gallagher chaired Hamilton Properties Ltd, which managed the property portfolio, rationalised it and concentrated on gaining a return for the city. He was also elected in 1989 to the Waikato Regional Council; the following year he was elected to the University of Waikato Council. John says matter-of-factly, 'Over time I became more and more focused on the well-being of the community and in some exciting building projects for the City, and less focused on the day-to-day Gallagher business.'[1] Mayor Jansen retired in 1989, and fairly early in his second term on the council John started thinking about having his own tilt at the mayoralty at the 1992 election.

In August 1990, while the two brothers were contemplating new phases of their lives, their father died, aged 79, after a two-year illness. He had been active until the late 1980s, coming along to Gallagher Group board meetings, experimenting in the workshop and tending the gardens. He was widely admired and loved in the community, being known for his practical good works, such as making a hydraulic lift for the Assisi Home and Hospital. Despite his age, he had been seen repairing the roof on the First Presbyterian Church in Frankton, the centre of his and Millie's spiritual life. His slow exit naturally added depth to his sons' ruminations about their own rapidly passing lives and about what the next era should hold.

Into this mix walked the tall, slender figure of Neil Richardson. A Sydney-based business consultant with a postgraduate commerce degree from the University of New South Wales and a Doctor of Jurisprudence in international trust law from the University of South Illinois, he was fully conversant with the latest management ideas. He had been advising David Mullen in Australia since 1984, and came to Bill Gallagher's attention in 1987 when he negotiated Mullen's purchase of the majority stake in the US distribution business that Gallaghers had bought from Art Snell. One outside observer notes, 'Bill and Neil went into battle over the price and Bill didn't get his way.' The Australian made an impression, and, after Richardson had spent six months in 1988 at Nicholls University in New Orleans as a visiting marketing professor, Bill began to seek his advice.

In January 1989 Gallagher invited Richardson to chair a retreat for the group's senior management. The 40-year-old Richardson may have looked rather academic, with thick glasses and a pointed beard, but he had a very high level of self-confidence and didn't hesitate to highlight what he saw as shortcomings in the group's corporate, financial, manufacturing and marketing strategies. He zeroed in on Bill's desire to carry on as chairman and managing director, at the same time as being very active in the management of the group's many international distributors.

This, he ventured, was a recipe for ad hoc decision-making, poor communications, a failure to delegate authority, and a lack of clear and decisive management, primarily because of the inevitable long periods of Bill's absence on tours of distributors.[2] Many of Richardson's findings were strong meat, too strong for some around the table. But Bill seemed to enjoy the provocation.

It quickly became clear that there wasn't sufficient room around the place for both Neil Richardson and Vaughan Jones and his cohort on the board, who by and large were practical, no-nonsense businessmen who spoke a different language to the cerebral Richardson. Gallagher concluded that after three years of flat performance, the company needed an infusion of fresh ideas. Jones, Bill McPhail and Barry Paterson left the Gallagher board in March 1989. Richardson became a director in April. He cemented his role as Bill Gallagher's most trusted adviser soon after by helping Jenny and Bill conclude the settlement of their matrimonial split amicably, something that had eluded the local lawyers.

From the start, Richardson was an active director, paying close attention to the implementation of the MRP II project, led by John Walley. This was a difficult process, which unsettled many staff members and some customers, particularly those who had best manipulated the earlier, more casual and flexible arrangements. By March 1990 Bill Gallagher was sufficiently impressed with Richardson that he invited him to take up a full-time executive role in the company. After a little experimenting, they settled on a structure whereby Richardson became group managing director with responsibility for the day-to-day running of the company, while Bill was chairman and CEO. As a corporate structure it was somewhat unusual, since everyone in the firm ultimately reported to Richardson, who alone reported to Bill Gallagher, but Bill retained a direct involvement in international marketing and in particular the relationship with key distributors.

Gallagher had stepped back, but not entirely. He recalls: 'I had no clear idea how to structure it initially. Neil wanted to get his hands on the gearbox and I was happy to let him run the place. So, it was one-on-one, him reporting to me. And it's obviously important down the chain of command that any person has only one boss, so I tried not to influence directly the various managers who reported to Neil. But while there was a direct channel through Neil for direction downward, I always thought it essential that information came back up from all channels. You can't let all the information be filtered by one person. And that's partly why I found my trips so useful, since you'd get a report from a manager saying one thing about a particular market, but talking to distributors or customers on the ground you'd hear a completely different story.'

With his feet under the desk, Richardson applied what he described as a 'razor-sharp strategic focus' to the company. Within a short space of time many of the previous senior managers had been removed, with some predictable disruption. In 1991 the clean-out included John Gallagher, who formally stepped back from his semi-active role in the management of the company to concentrate fully on his local government interests. John remembers that he had been heading in that direction, but Neil 'gave me the final nudge'. He set up an office in the Hawkins Building, owned by his trust, in Tawa Street, to manage his personal investments. John continued to serve the region in a variety of roles, including Deputy Mayor of Hamilton City Council, Chancellor of the University of Waikato and chairman of the Waikato Chamber of Commerce. His efforts were recognised by the government in 2002 when he was made a Companion of the New Zealand Order of Merit (CNZM).

Meantime, Richardson recruited or promoted a new leadership team, prominent among this being Steve Hoffman. From an upbringing in rural Wairarapa, Hoffman began to learn his craft in rural business retailing and marketing during

14 years working for Dalgety, the nationwide stock and station company. This was followed by five years managing a rural Toyota dealership. He'd joined Gallaghers in 1989 as the national sales manager.

Having shuffled himself upstairs there was a sense that an era had ended for Bill Gallagher. Around this time, he received some well-deserved recognition for his efforts so far. In January 1990 he was awarded a Queen's Commemorative Medal for services to New Zealand, as part of the country's sesquicentennial celebrations. (He had already received an MBE in the Queen's Birthday Honours List in 1987.) Then in 1990 and 1991 he had the satisfaction of having the electric fence industry, which his company indisputably led, singled out for special praise by Michael E Porter, the Harvard Business School professor and author of *The Competitive Advantage of Nations*.[3]

At a time of great national anxiety about the lacklustre performance of the economy, even after Roger Douglas's radical reforms, Professor Porter had been brought to New Zealand to lead a research project that would identify industries in which the country enjoyed a genuine competitive advantage, and then to make proposals on how more such industries could be encouraged. At length, the Porter project concluded that the economy was in bad shape, with only a very few New Zealand companies having developed multiple sources of competitive advantage. To Porter's mind it was only in electric fencing, yacht building and a couple of aspects of software development that some New Zealand companies could claim to be world leaders.[4]

The electric fence industry, Porter concluded, was one of very few New Zealand industries based on exploiting created rather than natural advantages. It had benefited from having highly critical and demanding customers in its home market and fiercely competitive domestic rivalry among local firms. These conditions had provided the hot-house in which an internationally competitive industry had developed. In a country where cosy duopolies, industry associations or state-sanctioned monopolies (as in the case of most of the primary industries) were the order of the day, the electric fence industry was an island of unfettered free enterprise, where the leading New Zealand companies competed tooth-and-nail against each other in markets all around the world.[5]

Porter's admonition, 'If you don't have a competitive advantage, don't compete,' struck a chord with Gallagher, along with the observation that a sustainable competitive advantage was a set of 'unique, complementary activities which are hard to copy' and which enable the producer to claim a premium position. That was what Gallagher had always sought for his energisers and accessories. The goal was never to survive on cheap labour, government assistance or a favourable exchange rate, but instead to have products that were good enough to command premium prices on international markets, sustaining a good standard of living for its owners and its workers.

Porter's ideas reinforced one of the primary lessons Gallagher had taken from his time at Harvard Business School. One of the exercises there, a game called Conjugate, involved subjecting a series of businesses to a range of decisions about how much to invest in R&D, price and other inputs, and running it through a computer program that predicted the outcome of those decisions. Gallagher noticed that the expansionary style of business, with an 'abundance mentality', which spent heavily on R&D and sought high prices to recoup that investment, generated more wealth long-term than the 'miserable guys who concentrated on nothing other than driving the price down'.

So while Neil Richardson concentrated, initially at least, on the necessary but to Gallagher less than satisfying task of extracting more efficiency out of the business, Gallagher continued to concentrate on the aspect of the business he most enjoyed. That was 'going round the traps': travelling the world, cajoling and encouraging his key distributors into greater efforts to grow the market for his products, and looking for new opportunities in new countries.

In this lonely and tiring exercise, Bill Gallagher now at least had an enthusiastic partner, since Judi started joining him on his travels. It wasn't all champagne and caviar; some of their early ventures weren't particularly glamorous. In 1989 they visited Russia and China. In Russia their room had no shower and no plug for the bath, no soap and only threadbare towels. In their brutalist concrete hotel in Wuxi, China, they had a shower and soap, but that was the only concession to comfort. Soon afterwards Judi travelled to the Amazon with Bill, searching for a new raw material for Insultimber, since the supplies of Australian ironbark were no longer sufficient for the demand. They spent four days on an old boat travelling up tributaries looking for examples; the diesel fumes and heat in their

TOP The Gallagher board, 1989. Standing left to right: Gin Lim (company secretary), Don Lindale, Neil Richardson, David Mullen. Seated left to right: Bill Gallagher senior, Bill Gallagher junior, John Gallagher.

ABOVE Neil Richardson with his new national sales manager, Stephen Hoffman (right).

cabin below decks were so unbearable that they slept out under the stars at night. The next stop, at Lisbon, Portugal, sounded great until Judi realised they would be there a total of four hours, just long enough for Bill to scoot to a hotel room to meet a potential distributor before catching a plane to their next destination.

Getting lost on such adventures was not unusual. Judi found herself driving all around the world, searching for people whose contacts Bill had been given by New Zealand trade officials or who had written to him, while he read in the passenger's seat. In Finland one January they picked up a rental car and a map, then skidded their way for an hour and a half through ice to find a particular village. Being unable to find the address they had been given, they woke up a villager (hibernating at midday) only to be told that there was another village with the same name an hour's drive to the south; that was probably the one they wanted.

Judi soon proved a useful companion. Until that point Gallagher's practice had been to carry a Dictaphone and after each meeting, usually while driving or sitting at airports, he would conscientiously dictate minutes, ideas and letters that had to be sent out, working from a little notebook if necessary. Finally, after three weeks of meetings he would arrive back in Hamilton with bundles of tapes for his secretary Margaret Comer to plough through and transcribe. Eventually, Judi convinced him to buy a laptop, and she would type everything up as they went.

She recalls: 'Bill is incredibly organised and doesn't procrastinate. He deals with everything he has to resolve that day; even it means working in the hotel room until 1 or 2am to finish what has to be done, before a 6am pick-up the following morning. So neither of us would get much sleep, but it was very efficient. The process, however, was more enjoyable sitting on the plane, taking a sip of champagne every now and then, while his thoughts tumbled out quickly and I typed and edited them as we went along. Having a laptop saved a week at the Hamilton end, since Margaret could simply take the floppy disk and print everything out when we arrived. The next step was to find a laptop with a small built-in printer. Then he could sign letters and we'd find a fax that day; at that point things were really advancing.'[6]

It was an interesting time to be scouring the world. The global order was in flux. After the Berlin Wall fell in November 1989, East Germany immediately came into play as a potential market. For a couple of years, especially after July 1990 when the old East German mark could be exchanged for Deutschmarks one-for-one, there was a boom in the east before the former communist workers' savings ran out.

Latin America, long such a poor performer for Gallaghers because of its high duties and manifold economic problems, also seemed to be opening up to the world. Access to Argentina improved considerably around 1991, but after quite a good burst around 1992–93 progress tailed off. At a conference in Cancun, Mexico, surveying the scene in 1994, Gallagher lamented that in Argentina the landowners buy the fencing, but they have little to do with the farmers who actually work the land; there was a disconnect. The Gallagher message of lifting the land's productivity by modern strip-grazing methods fell on barren soil in a country that seemed hostile to new ideas. In Colombia the problem was even more basic. Electric fencing was seen as high-tech and therefore high-cost. It followed that if a person used it, they were seen as rich and were more likely to be kidnapped. This logic tended to dampen sales.

India also promised much in the early 1990s after Finance Minister Manmohan Singh started off down the path of deregulation and liberalisation in 1991, with much fanfare. Bill and Judi made their first serious visit to India in October 1992 when Vishnu Narain of Ibex, a manufacturer who had been trying to copy Gallagher energisers, said he wanted to become their distributor. Narain had come to the industry along a circuitous route. A microbiologist from Bangalore, he had worked in the brewing industry for Kingfisher beer, but he also had property in the northern part of the Western Ghats, where he grew Arabica coffee beans and spices. Worried about the plight of wild animals, he became interested in using fencing to separate wildlife from people, to reduce conflict over resources. He thought quality electric fencing, like Gallaghers, might do a better job than traditional fencing.

With Bill Gallagher's encouragement, he sold his plantation, returned to Bangalore and went into business selling energisers. In the next two years the Gallaghers visited Narain nine times and had high hopes for this massive market. Gallagher recalls a visit to Ooty, a township at the end of a switchback road high in the Western Ghats in southern India: 'There was a large wild elephant population there, and we'd heard that a German fellow was using our electric fence to keep them out. Sure enough, his place was like an oasis, full of lush vegetation, while everything else had been wrecked by elephants. So we held a seminar up there. And the first speaker was this German guy. He said that some of the old matriarchs were smart; they'd get a branch to knock the fence down, or they'd carefully wrap their trunk around the post, avoiding the wires, and pull it all over. So he had a double fence and ran wires down the posts as well and it worked great.

'The second speaker was a government man from the forestry department, an official. His statement was that electric fencing doesn't work; it's useless, the elephants go straight through it. At the end, I said, "I don't understand. Did you not hear the previous speaker who said it works fine? What sort of energiser are you using?" Well, he was using a local one. We had about a hundred local competitors making energisers in old plastic lunch-boxes that were hopeless. "Oh," I said, "that might be the trouble."'

A little further along his journey Gallagher gathered some positive reinforcement for his efforts when he met a cane farmer who had successfully used a Gallagher fence to keep wild pigs out of his crop. He was full of gratitude to the New Zealander for saving his livelihood.

Vishnu Narain saw great potential among small, marginal farmers who grew rain-fed crops once a year according to an ancient pattern, with the villagers collectively defending the crops from the wildlife. Some enterprising villagers knew they could produce three crops if they irrigated, but, with no one else helping to defend them from the wildlife, it was impossible. An electric fence, however, would make the impossible possible. Narain persuaded his brother, Krishna, to help him.

Soon Vishnu was riding all over the subcontinent on his little motorbike, with goods piled high and precariously, thousands of miles along pot-holed roads. He recalls: 'If I knew that the missionary phase of the business would last 15 years I might never have done it. It was very hard work, travelling everywhere from Bangalore and the south, right up to Jamnu in Kashmir, where we managed to sell a fence to keep the snow leopards out. We were

TOP Demonstrating the energiser to a nervous crowd in India.

ABOVE Vishnu Narain preaching the gospel in India.

ABOVE Bill and Judi Gallagher enjoying a mercifully cool day in India with Vishnu Narain, 1995.

carrying stuff on donkeys. And when I used my bike it was piled so high, when I stopped I had to prop it up against a tree. My abiding memory is lying by the side of the road one day, weeping. I'd run out of gas, had no money, I had endless problems with dodgy batteries, nowhere to stay — I couldn't take it anymore.'[7]

He soldiered on, but progress was painfully slow. By 1994 the duty on Gallaghers' product had tumbled from a calamitous 250 per cent to a still hopeless 120 per cent. And that was just one of the difficulties; import licences, letters of credit and Customs peculiarities all opened opportunities for obstructionism and bribery. After a huge effort and several tummy bugs, Gallagher quipped that if 20 million of India's 26 million public servants were sent home on full pay, the place would take off. In the year to June 1996 sales to the great subcontinent would still total only a miserable $42,989; even the humble Slovenians collectively took more.

India's trickiness was all the more galling to Gallagher because he had been devoting an increasing amount of his time to government policy and the cause of international free trade, and for a while he had felt that progress was being made. While he had taken to heart the logic of free trade, in the marketplace he continued to be confronted by barriers. With Neil Richardson on deck in Hamilton, Gallagher had accepted several ministerial appointments from the Jim Bolger-led National government that took office in late 1990. One of the first moves by John Falloon, the new Minister of Agriculture, had been to appoint a 12-man Agriculture Strategy Council. Gallagher was among the 12, and they focused on formulating a policy to make the most of New Zealand low-cost grassland farming.

The Minister of Trade, Philip Burdon, also invited Gallagher to join a committee to review New Zealand's Trade Development Board. While the Ministry of External Relations and Trade (MERT) favoured the board's disbandment, with its function folded into the ministry, most submissions to the committee wanted the separate trade board to remain. Gallagher, who happened to be the only exporter on the committee, produced a minority report supporting the retention of a separate, reorganised body. He won the argument and TradeNZ was established, with Gallagher later joining its board. He also joined a Manufacturing Advisory Group in 1991.

Meanwhile the Minister of Health, Simon Upton, had ushered through a series of radical reforms to the public health system, which over the decades had consumed an ever-larger slice of the nation's sparse funds. In 1992 Bill Gallagher accepted an invitation from chairman Ross Jansen to join the board of the new Midland Regional Health Authority. Under the restructured system, health authorities were set up to purchase services from primary providers and Crown Health Enterprises (the old hospitals in the main centres). Having strained every muscle in his own business over the past six or seven years to find efficiencies, in order to survive, Gallagher says he was 'profoundly shocked' by what he found in the health system.

He recalls: 'It was immediately apparent that the system lacked accountability and that most of the health professionals, though they did a wonderful job, had little appreciation of the value of money. Funds were simply available irrespective of performance or efficiency. The variation in performance just within our area, between hospitals in New Plymouth, Hamilton and Tauranga — what you got for your money — was incredible. So we reasonably thought at the outset that if we could at least get the levels of productivity that were achieved in the best places into all centres, we'd made great progress. This proved incredibly difficult.'

He learnt a similar lesson from being on the board of the Port of Tauranga when it was partially privatised. 'The productivity gains that were achieved at the port once basic private enterprise attitudes were introduced were incredible,' he says. 'The difference was night and day.'

Bill's increasing prominence as a flag-waver for economic reform made for an interesting dynamic in Hamilton. John Gallagher stood for more traditional conservative values, and came close to winning the Hamilton mayoralty in 1992. Though he missed out, he remained on the council. Meantime, their first cousin, Martin Gallagher, the son of Viv, had also been on the Hamilton City Council, but as a Labour Party man, coming from a teachers' union background. In the 1993 general election he won the parliamentary seat of Hamilton West for Labour. The Gallaghers were everywhere, occupying every political niche.

So while Bill Gallagher cast his net more broadly, the onus fell on his new managing director, Neil Richardson, to carry on the legwork of lifting the Gallagher Group's performance each year in order to stay ahead of the competition. After numerous bugs had been sorted out, and workers trained to input the correct codes for different parts and jobs, the MRP II system was proving its worth. With its ability to draw out projections of demand from large customers far more effectively, it sharply reduced inventory, thereby taking the pressure off requirements for working capital. The investment in the system was paid back within 18 months: partly from working capital savings, and partly from further increases in productivity as staff numbers bottomed out at 181 while output reached all-time highs. Sales per employee in 1992 were $200,000, up from $114,000 just four years earlier. In addition, once the MRP II system was operating effectively, accuracy was improved. Better forecasting of demand opened a whole new world of efficiencies. For instance, when it suited, they used the slowest ships they could find, to save on warehousing costs at either end.

Having a fresh set of eyes in the managing director's chair ultimately made it easier to resolve one of the company's long-standing problems: the fate of Gallagher Engineering. Having consistently lost money since 1985, it should have been closed earlier. But instead a series of efforts were made to breathe new life into the corpse, the last of which was a doomed venture in making safes. The efforts did not work.

Richardson was not at all surprised that John, and to a lesser extent Bill, had found it difficult to take the necessary step. He says: 'Gallagher Engineering was in many respects the sentimental core of the business. The idea of putting second-hand car differential gears into post-hole diggers, along with other such improvisations, reflected the nature of the company in New Zealand and had a whole lot of values around it. So it took a few years longer to close than what might have seemed rational.'[8]

Eventually, in 1991, the engineering business was sold to an Auckland company, Engineers for Industry. The Aucklanders struggled on producing some of the old Gallagher products for a few years. The sale had the effect of narrowing the focus of the Gallagher Group onto things related to electric fences, with the only exceptions being a few sidelines that used spare capacity in the tool-making and injection-moulding parts of the business. The most incongruous of these were the strangely successful Sunshine clothes pegs.

However, while the Gallaghers business narrowed in one sense, it was at the same time gaining new depth. As Gallagher Engineering closed, the group began seriously to peddle its electric fence technology to an entirely new set of customers. Having built its reputation by keeping four-legged animals in, or out, depending on the circumstances, Gallaghers now turned to the security market: using electric fences to contain or repel two-legged animals.

The potential to rig up farm electric fences around factories or yards for security purposes had always been obvious. Vaughan Jones found the practice widespread in South Africa in the late 1970s, when most farmers first wanted an alarmed electric fence installed around the farmhouse before extending it out to the paddocks. Gallaghers' first security job in New Zealand led to a celebrated court case. The Gallagher brothers' old diving friend John Pettit, a former policeman who owned a nursery in Otahuhu, had trouble with locals climbing over his fence at night, making a mess of his petunias and wrecking his equipment. In 1980 Bill Gallagher installed an MPE (medium-powered) energiser linked to a couple of wires around the top of Pettit's chain-link fence. It stopped the incursions immediately.

All was well for nine months, until one night in April 1981 when an internal alarm went off. Gallagher recounts the story: 'A police car arrived with two constables, one of whom goes to climb the fence to get inside. The other one points to the signs warning of an electric fence, but the first guy shrugs it off. "No worries." Of course, after he grabs the wire he does a standing jump of about 10 feet from the top of the fence, grazes his knee and feels nauseated. So Pettit gets a call from the local commander the next day telling him to turn that damn thing off. Pettit was stroppy — he was standing as the local Social Credit candidate against David Lange in the upcoming election — and he told the policeman to go to hell. Right, that was a challenge. So the only thing the police could find was a reference in the Crimes Act to a man-trap, some quaint English line about setting a device that causes injury or hurt.

'We went off to deposition hearings and the constable talks about his grazed knee and feelings of nausea; they also had someone from the Electricity Department who under cross-examination said the energiser complied with New Zealand Safety Standard 1525, and yes that the warning signs were the proscribed size. The only potential hiccup came when I stood up as an expert witness and explained to Judge Duncan that this was only a small energiser, putting out around 2 joules, whereas our best-selling farm energiser, the Super 60, put out 8 joules. I saw his eyes bulging; how far would he have jumped if he'd been hit by that? No, I reassured him, it's not proportional. And we got a good decision. The judge said there was no case to answer.'[9]

Pettit had his moment of glory in the papers the following day, having seen off the police charges.[10] However, Gallagher did not actively pursue the security market thereafter, preferring to stick to the company's agricultural knitting during the boom times of the early 1980s. The lean years of the later 1980s brought a reappraisal. A board paper in November 1987 noted that during the past three years the firm had had requests for basic security systems for farms, factories and compounds around car-yards and transport depots. To that point they had satisfied clients by using a mains battery unit and a fence voltage alarm. But the report continued: 'Requests for a more sophisticated system and purpose-built accessories have increased dramatically over the past year, so much so that a group of people had set up a business installing fencing and incorporating our security deterrent system.'[11] All indications were that Gallaghers' R&D team could produce a more sophisticated system that was compatible with widely used alarms. With this unique combination of deterrent and detection, Gallaghers felt its security offerings could develop into a 'potentially lucrative off-shoot business'.

By 1989 the system was working well, but their activities had drawn a query from the Chief Electrical Inspector at the Ministry of Energy, who questioned the legality of using electric fences for security. Was a fresh, and presumably higher, safety standard required for this different purpose? Bill Gallagher replied by referring to the Pettit case, bolstered by a legal opinion from leading Auckland law firm Russell McVeagh,[12] and the well-developed safety standards for energisers used on farms. He then made a counter-punching appeal to logic, telling the inspector that he strongly disagreed with the implication that a lower level of safety would be acceptable for agricultural fences.[13]

With the ministry off his back, in November 1989 Gallagher established a new company, Gallagher Security Fence Ltd, to market the security range in New Zealand. The plan was to test the idea in New Zealand before launching internationally a couple of years later. They quickly realised, however, that when it came to marketing there was no synergy at all between the security and animal containment industries. They were starting from scratch in the security market, introducing themselves to the key players, trying to break into a tight-knit industry with an entirely new concept. And, logic aside, some potential clients were nervous about the idea of electrocuting people. Bill Gallagher had always thought this squeamish response rather odd, since, as research had demonstrated, a very short pulse of electricity, though painful, left no permanent damage and was certainly far more humane than many of the security alternatives in use, such as razor wire, barbed wire or broken glass on top of walls.

Gallagher Security Fence Ltd picked up a few jobs through 1990 and early 1991, including projects to protect car-yards for Turners Auctions and sites for Telecom and Transpower. But just as quickly, cheap imitations started appearing in the marketplace; someone would attach an agricultural energiser to a fence that would more or less do the job. Gallaghers' men dismissed these as 'agricultural lash-ups', but their prevalence was a widespread nuisance at the lower end of the market. As a result, in its start-up phase Gallaghers' security business was subtracting rather than adding to the group's bottom line. After a couple of years of losses, in 1991 Richardson hired Steve Aldridge, an experienced marketer in the security industry, to drive the business.

Having taken to heart Michael Porter's message that if a company wants to be number one in the world then the best place to start is with the world's most demanding customers, Bill Gallagher was soon determined to test the security business in South Africa. That country's combination of a first-world economy and serious security problems had made it the crucible of the global security industry. In 1992 Gallaghers took a 50 per cent shareholding in the business owned by its existing agricultural distributor, Maurice Williamson, and renamed it Gallagher Powerfence SA Ltd. Aldridge spent six months in the republic building up the new business. On paper it was an exciting proposition, and Bill Gallagher readily predicted that the security business, both in New Zealand and internationally, would overtake Gallaghers' agricultural electric fencing within five years. The reality proved a harder grind, and the five years had to be constantly pushed out.

So while the group had stopped the bleeding from the loss-making engineering division by 1991/92, it was now pouring funds into marketing a new security concept to the world. In the medium term, at least, its prospects lay with maintaining Gallaghers' leadership position in the traditional animal containment industry for electric fences and extracting greater profitability from it. This was now Neil Richardson's primary responsibility, and he started talking about emulating McDonald's, the hamburger chain. McDonald's, he pointed out, was the best in hamburgers not necessarily because its products, the hamburgers, were the best in the world, but because its system — from supply chains, to marketing, to distribution, to management — was unmatched by its rivals.

So it had to be with Gallaghers. The product was only the starting point, the football as it were; it was what they did with it that would win the game. And that came down to constant innovation in extracting the best value from all facets of the business, which included R&D spending, the development of high-quality, low-cost manufacturing, marketing distribution, management systems, organisational design, training, purchasing, planning, and channel management.

Listening to one of Richardson's speeches, John Lucey, the company's Irish distributor, concluded that the Australian was a very professional person but he had no idea what he was talking about, 'with all these highfalutin' references to organisational design and hamburgers'.[14] Others, such as Erik Dijkstra, were impressed by the new dimension Richardson brought to the organisation. Dijkstra had long grumbled about Gallaghers' packaging. He recalls, 'Bill always used the Kiwi expression, "It does the job"; it didn't matter much what the box looked like, so long as the energiser "did the job".'[15]

The Dutchman thought the New Zealander could learn something from the Italian approach, where products were generally 'crap, but looked beautiful'. If Gallaghers packaged their quality products with a little more style, they could made real progress. Richardson was on the same wavelength. And while arguments with the Dutch over packaging would continue to rage, Richardson brought a new focus on drawing together an improved and standardised international Gallagher brand to replace the hotchpotch that had sprouted across countless markets over 20 years of rapid growth.

With Richardson at the helm the company's tone shifted subtly, but significantly, in a direction many observers describe as more 'professional'. It was not that the company was unprofessional under Bill Gallagher's direct leadership, but it carried a strong flavour of its freewheeling, fun-loving and at times chaotic and casual origins as a Waikato family company. One evening after the Fieldays in 1985, Bill and David Mullen, the chairman of the group and one of his directors, had too much to drink and fell into a hilarious egg fight in reception. Such antics were unthinkable with Richardson; he was no playful roustabout. And while Bill had his own highly disciplined systems for following up with distributors and dealing with clients, his business management had been predominantly intuitive in style, operating on what Jim Fletcher, the head of the industrial giant Fletcher Holdings for many decades, termed the 'old fliers' syndrome — the seat of the pants, the feel of the thing'.[16]

Richardson, by contrast, was coolly analytical and systems-orientated. All managers under him now produced written reports on a monthly basis; they worked to Key Performance Indicators; their training was formalised; and new ideas were subjected to formal business appraisals and interactive team discussions. And when it came to having firm discussions with some of the longer-serving distributors who needed to lift their performance, Richardson was better placed than Bill, who had been a drinking buddy, confidant, mentor and friend to some of them.

He also brought a new level of sophistication to the group's financial planning and reporting, including the concept of Economic Value Added (EVA), which was a tougher measure of progress. Having agreed on an appropriate rate of return for capital invested in the business, say 10 per cent, an arm of the business or an international joint venture was creating wealth if it generated better than 10 per cent; it was 'destroying wealth' if it fell below that level, even if it made a modest profit. This measure was consistently applied to the group's investments around the world and put the wind up more than a few partners. It could also be used as a sound measure for senior management remuneration. Performance pay could be linked to genuine wealth creation.

Richardson's first three years as managing director, to June 1993, were not easy. The domestic market fell into a trough again in 1991, with sales contracting by nearly a quarter and a major client falling into receivership, leaving Gallaghers with substantial bad debts. Bill Gallagher described it as one of the most difficult trading environments he had ever encountered.[17] Overall the group grew only modestly in three years — sales lifted from $31 million in 1990 to $37 million in 1993 ($49 million to $56 million in today's terms). Profitability had bounced around with currency fluctuations and was affected by the final losses and write-downs from Gallagher Engineering, but by 1993 was approaching $4 million. The taxman, however, now claimed a third of that.

Gallagher concluded that Richardson was making sufficient progress during an extended period of painful adjustment, and in July 1993 extended his contract for a further three years. Most significantly, he sold him a five per cent shareholding in the group. This was the first time anyone outside the family had held shares.[18]

By then the CEO and the MD had become great friends. That Richardson was a keen diver had helped. Neil and his wife Jan regularly made the weekend journey east to Whangamata, and business strategy was chewed over in the evenings, alongside crayfish and scallops. In 1993 the Gallaghers had built a new house on a beachfront section at Whangamata, which they named Casa D'Playa. A modest bungalow by the sea it was not; with seven bedrooms, and seven bathrooms to match, it stuck out at the southern end of the beach. Judi guided its design along with the architect, Peter Chibnall, including the gold-plated, dolphin-shaped taps in one bathroom that immediately became something of a Whangamata legend. The Richardsons had their regular room on the ground floor and it was a sunny arrangement.

While Bill Gallagher was happy with the efficiencies that had been gained since 1989, by 1993 he was impatient for genuine growth after such a long period of holding steady. When would all the hard work pay off? When would it start getting easier? Finding genuine growth was now the priority.

The security business, he was sure, would deliver, but not for some time yet. Growth could also come from the painstaking process of growing individual markets for the company's traditional animal containment products. On that score, the US was finally starting to deliver under David Mullen's guidance. Gallagher Power Fence Inc took more than $5 million worth of Gallagher products in 1993 and was about to grow a further 45 per cent in the year to June 1994. Following the nightmarish first few years after they had bought the company from Art Snell in 1987, when sales slumped and losses mounted, Mullen and his new president, Erwin Quinn, had managed to stabilise the ship. In the following years the business had grown strongly, to become the group's most important export market.

Quinn was a tall, immaculately presented, hard-working and experienced rural marketer, originally from Iowa, who knew the American psyche inside out. In 1990 Mullen had also taken over the struggling business of Henry Swayze, so that Gallagher Power Fence Inc was now the sole Gallagher distributor in the US. Mullen estimated that they had gained around 20 per cent of the market share in the States, dominating in the premium market. Steve Hoffman, Gallaghers' sales manager in New Zealand, never ceased to be amazed at their penetration: 'I've driven up to random farms in Missouri with Bill and Judi and asked the farmer if he had electric fencing and if so, what brand? And there'd inevitably be a Gallagher energiser there. This is 12,000 kilometres from home, up random driveways, and here is our product.'[19]

Another option to satisfy Gallagher's desire for growth was to go out and buy it, by purchasing a complementary business. And indeed one such business came into view during 1993. Franklin Machinery Ltd (FML) was a family-owned firm in Pukekohe, established in 1941 in similar circumstances to Gallagher Engineering. The founder, Jack Richards, had been a sharemilker with a desire to be his own boss. He had begun installing milking machines and selling water pumps. Around 1945 he developed the first power-lifting rig in New Zealand for bore servicing, having cannibalised an old Austin Seven for its motor. Richards then progressed to manufacturing simple metal products — harrows, steel calf and cow bales, and pig troughs — from a dirt-floor factory on Pukekohe's King Street.

Soon after his son John joined the business as a 15-year-old in 1950, he was set to work cutting 100 tons of $^3/_8$ inch square steel rods into fence standards. Since safety gloves were too expensive, the boy was given a roll of insulation tape to wrap around his hands for protection. In 1957 a Matamata manufacturer of farm gates who had been selling through a stock and station chain decided to go direct to farmers; the stock and station company need a new supplier and Richards was invited to fill the void.

In the early 1960s FML had been the first in New Zealand to manufacture zinc electroplated gates. The demand for these rust-proof gates was strong and the company grew, overcoming many difficulties, not the least of which was having to get around the cartel that controlled zinc imports to New Zealand through government-granted licences. Richards tapped black market supplies of zinc until he won the contract to take all the scrap battery cases and trimmings from Union Carbide Batteries, extracting the zinc he needed. He also tracked down someone in Australia who was prepared to teach him the art of hot-dip galvanising, which was a much more efficient process.

At its peak during the rural boom of the early 1980s, FML was producing 24,000 hot-dipped gates a year, together with another 20,000 gates on contract for a Hamilton rival. It had also built expertise in gate hardware, particularly the hinges, which were comparatively high-value products, and in producing the Kiwitah, a galvanised steel fence post.

By the early 1990s the strength of the company lay in its unique gate products, particularly the hinges, where it possessed several registered designs and many patents, all of which it defended vigorously from any infringing rivals. The company was dominant in the New Zealand market, with its hardware on 90 per cent of New Zealand farms, and its exports were growing.[20] In 1992 David Mullen took up the distribution rights for Franklin Machinery in Australia, and it was soon obvious that the products were highly complementary with Gallaghers'.

Mullen encouraged Steve Hoffman to talk to FML about distributing its gates in New Zealand. FML had a team of six people selling its gates and hardware, from Kaitaia to Bluff, while Hoffman had a team of eight calling on the same people. In the spring of 1993 he met Don Wilcox, FML's general manager, and Ian Richards, John's son, who was now production manager, and thrashed out an agreement for Gallaghers to take the distribution rights in New Zealand. They simply added Franklin Machinery products to the Gallagher catalogue.

Within a few months, Bill Gallagher spied a larger opportunity. The closer they came to FML, the more they were convinced that the Pukekohe operation could be greatly improved if it was given the same treatment that Gallaghers' operations had received since 1989. It was nothing like the old Gallagher Engineering, which produced 150 complicated rotary hoes a year; FML manufactured high volumes of relatively simple pieces at its purpose-built factory at the end of Subway Road, Pukekohe. It would lend itself well to the computer scheduling and mass-production techniques that Gallaghers now managed effectively using the MRP II system. John Richards, arguably the most dynamic of the family, had now retired from the company and was spending most of his time in Queensland. FML was fat and juicy — a good business that was in need of fresh leadership.

With a turnover of around $6 million it wasn't huge, but its business would strengthen the New Zealand sales operation and a takeover or merger would provide Gallagher Group with experience in integrating another company within its wider operating and management structure. Over the Christmas break of 1993–94, Bill Gallagher and Neil Richardson hammered out a deal with John Richards in which Gallaghers would take a 55 per cent stake in FML and assume responsibility for all operations.

The deal took effect on 1 February 1994, and several senior Gallagher managers spent the first half of the year travelling regularly to Pukekohe applying Gallaghers' MRP II systems to the Franklin Machinery operations. Margaret Comer, who had grown with the company since 1985 and was now head of Gallaghers' corporate services, commuted daily as she led the complete overhaul of FML's human resources. She also became a director of FML. In essence, most of the management overheads were stripped out of the Pukekohe operation, leaving a tidy manufacturing unit, while work practices were brought into line with the disciplines established at Gallaghers.

This was all successfully achieved and Franklin Machinery soon began to sing as a business unit within the Gallagher Group, although its inclusion was not without drama. The factory workforce included a strong gang component. At the end of the first year the Pukekohe staff were bussed south to Hamilton for the Gallagher end-of-year party; chaos ensued as the evening progressed, and the experiment was not repeated.

The financial year to June 1995 was the first to include the full contribution from Franklin Machinery, and, together with booming international sales for Gallaghers' animal containment systems and the first flickering of progress in the security market in the UK, it all started to come together nicely for the Gallagher Group. Sales for the group reached $52 million ($75 million in today's terms), by a clear margin the largest in the history of the group, even after taking inflation into account. Profits were nudging $8 million before tax, again a company record. The company had done what the country had needed it to do: it had survived the transition from government support to standing on its own two feet, and it was now doing well.

Particularly pleasing was the broad base to the good result. In animal containment, Peru had burst from nowhere to become almost a million-dollar market; sales in Mexico had doubled to nearly $500,000; after nine years working with other companies, Bernd Allie had rejoined his father Helmut in southern Germany and together they had grown their business into a significant operation that was now taking $2.5 million worth of product annually from Gallaghers; Veldman & Dijkstra were up a further 30 per cent to nearly $5 million; the Danes had more than doubled their demand to more than $1.2 million. While recession in Australia had seen that market go sideways through the early 1990s, the US continued to 'grow like the Watsons', in David Mullen's description.

In the UK security market they had picked up some interesting jobs, most notably for the electricity supplier National Grid. In 1994 its directors had a two-fold problem. The first part of the problem was that thieves were breaking into substations and stripping out the earthing copper, and this threatened the system. But secondly, being thieves, they failed to pay much attention to 'closing the gate behind them'. National Grid directors were worried that children might wander through the great holes left in the perimeter, to be killed by the 220,000 volt main lines. An electric perimeter fence seemed like a good solution, but there were still some doubts about its legality in Britain.

Gallagher recalls, 'Fortunately, the lawyer to whom they turned for an opinion was a country solicitor who had been brought up with Gallagher electric fences on farms. He contacted us and we sent him the judgment from the Pettit case.' The solicitor gave security electric fencing the all-clear and over the next year or so Gallagher

ABOVE Safeguarding the National Grid in the United Kingdom.

PowerFences were installed at around 200 sites throughout Britain.

British Gas was the next big client. It had sterile zones and double conventional fences around its compressor stations, with microwave beams to detect any interference. But the system was plagued by false alarms, set off by rabbits, autumn leaves and just about anything else, with the result that the rapid response unit was losing interest in responding rapidly. Gallagher Power Fences were installed and, to the delight of British Gas's management, there were virtually no false alarms and security around its stations was transformed.

Success with National Grid and British Gas was a relief because elsewhere the security market was proving a nightmare. Gallaghers had not yet cracked the South African market, although the company was better placed now that the new GM, Birger Kirsten, had relocated the company from the agricultural region of Pietermaritzburg to Jet Park, Johannesburg, which was far better for the security market.

Prospects in less developed markets were equally bleak. Bill Gallagher's report after a trip to Calcutta in February 1995 was typical. He had been talking to Union Carbide about putting fences around their estates and had met with disbelief when quoting US$50 per metre. Barbed-wire fences could be erected for US$3.30 a metre, but the main competition came from cheap security guards, who worked for US$1 day. A team of 24 men patrolling the boundary in shifts of six, 24 hours a day, cost only $6000 a year. Meanwhile, the duty on Gallaghers' system would be 98 per cent. For the time being, progress would come only from rich countries, and then only slowly.

By now the years of investment in R&D during the lean times — $1.2 million in 1992, $1.4 million in 1993 — were expected to pay dividends. The company now had more than 100 patents. John Walley had built up a substantial team of young graduates, which included 11 electrical and four mechanical engineers by 1995. And since 1993 they had been equipped with the latest Pro Engineer CAD programs. The result of their efforts would be the next generation of energisers, dubbed the SmartPower system.

With an LCD screen that gave information on energy output and voltage, which greatly expanded the options for alarms, SmartPower would bring much more technology to the electric fence. It could register an increased load on the fence from long grass and feed more power into the system. It also included a remote control, which would save long walks in the rain and cold to turn a fence off or on. The new offering would be many times more expensive than the competition's 'dumb boxes that ticked', but Gallagher and his team were confident that once farmers began using it and saw its advantages word would spread and SmartPower would drive a new growth phase for the company.

Gallaghers was also investing in capital equipment. In 1995 the company purchased its first 'pick and place' machine for attaching miniature components to circuit boards. Workers still hand-constructed many components of the energiser and other products, but surface mount technology would be applied from here on in to the most fiddly bits, with gains in reliability as important as the productivity gains. Air conditioning and anti-static vinyl flooring were also introduced in 1995 to create a less dusty environment, which again was essential to improving reliability.

The good performance in 1995 and good prospects thereafter were particularly pleasing for Gallaghers, since they held the promise that the group could continue to contribute directly to the community from which it had grown. In the late 1980s, during the company's and the country's leanest times, the Gallaghers had emerged as significant philanthropists in Hamilton. The origins of their largesse stretched back to 1984 when the Gallagher Charitable Trust was formed to own the large block of land surrounding the Gallagher factories, which had been bought from Independent Newspapers Ltd. Over time, as some of the land was subdivided, the trust's assets had grown so that it became a sustainable charitable entity. Its first major project was to give $500,000 over five years from 1988 as an endowment for Sport Waikato, a regional sports trust that had been founded a couple of years earlier to promote sport and healthy lifestyles in the region. By 1990 the Gallaghers were also supporting the Hamilton Rescue Helicopter and the Waikato Medical Research Foundation.

John Gallagher's council activities led them naturally to take a leadership role in fundraising efforts for civic assets. In June 1994 he joined the Hamilton Leisure Pool Trust to raise $3 million for a new community pool. John says he and Bill had the philosophy that they wouldn't ask others for money unless they could put their

ABOVE Gallagher security, Kenya, 1996.

hand on their heart and say that they had already put in money themselves. So the Gallagher Charitable Trust made a significant early contribution, which got the ball rolling, and as a result they received naming rights for what became the Gallagher Aquatic Centre when it opened in 1997. Margaret Comer, who handled the details of these sponsorships, says that the contribution made directly to the community was for her a big part of the satisfaction of working for the Gallagher Group. 'When considering a proposal we asked would our staff be proud to be associated with the sponsorship, and when the name started to appear on things like the Gallagher Aquatic Centre everyone was proud. It gave them a lift in so many ways, right down to the thumbs-up our salesmen would get climbing out of their Gallagher-branded car at the petrol station. Bill's and John's generosity led to a warm feeling for the company in the community, and that was a real positive for the group.'[21]

And while community spirit helped bind staff to the group, the Gallaghers had long appreciated that a clear financial stake in the company's fortunes was also important. Bill Gallagher senior had started the tradition, and even during the struggle of the late 1980s his sons had been in the habit of devoting a figure equivalent to around 12 to 20 per cent of tax-paid profits to an annual bonus for staff. Bill Gallagher recalls: 'During the tough times, with the upheaval of new systems and new people, morale was sometimes strained and I was looking for ways to lift commitment throughout the company. Over the years, I'd seen the difference between sons of farmers and sons of coal miners; the farmer's son would pick up a bolt on the ground, while the coal miner's son would kick it out of sight. It reflected the mind-set of the self-employed. So the goal with profit sharing was to give them some sense of ownership in the company's performance, to get them to nudge their fellow workers if they were doing something wasteful. When they'd say, "Oi, that's my bonus you're wasting," I knew I had achieved my goal.'

By 1995 the group was in a strong financial position. It had near zero debt, it had paid off its stake in Franklin Machinery Ltd within two years; it could, if it wanted, pursue more growth through more acquisitions in New Zealand and around the world.

Life was good for Bill Gallagher; he was busy maintaining

international relationships for his company, active in the cause of trade and political reform; and with Richardson worrying about the day-to-day concerns of the company, he had time for the odd diving adventure. Murray Bindon ('Bindo'), Bill Hay and several others joined him and Judi every couple of years for an excursion. The Solomon Islands came first, where Bill taught Judi to dive. This was followed in 1994 by Truk Lagoon in the islands of Micronesia. The Japanese merchant fleet had used the lagoon as a replenishment station for provisioning its army in Singapore, but the Americans had trapped them in their hole in February 1944 and in a brutal 48 hours had sunk 60 ships and 275 aeroplanes, most of which remain at an easy diving depth.

As Bill and Judi explored the ghost fleet of Truk Lagoon, having as many as five dives in one day, Bill had the satisfaction of knowing that 50 years after that bitter struggle, the protagonists were now both enthusiastic buyers of his electric fences. The 'Yanks' provided the group's largest single export market, while the Japanese now ranked eighth, snapping at Ireland's heels.

Gallaghers remained a private company, but now that Neil Richardson had a shareholding it was no longer simply a family company. The big question now was how that new dynamic would play out. Would the visions nursed in the breasts of Richardson and Bill Gallagher, in particular, remain in sync?

8
STALLING: 1996–99

Chapter eight

STALLING: 1996–99

The operation was a great success . . . but the patient died.

— A FAVOURITE BILL GALLAGHER EXPRESSION

From the outside, Bill Gallagher and his company seemed on top of the world in 1996. With Judi and Margaret Comer, Bill flew to Dallas, Texas, in June to receive the Excellence in Communication Leadership Award (Excel) from the International Association of Business Communicators (IABC) at their annual conference. It was quite a big deal. He had been nominated by Jillian de Beer of the IABC's New Zealand chapter, and was the first person from the southern hemisphere to receive the award. He joined august company: Jean Pierre Garner of SmithKline Beecham Pharmaceuticals and John Young, CEO of Hewlett Packard, had been recent winners.

Gallagher told the conference in Texas: 'We are really in the business of influencing the future, by changing the world's agriculture practices across languages and social barriers, to unsubsidised agriculture.' His message was that using modern power fencing New Zealand farmers were able to be internationally competitive without subsidies, and there was no reason why farmers throughout the rest of the world couldn't follow their example. On leadership, he added, 'A leader must have two ears and one mouth and use them in that proportion.' His style was to coach his staff to find their way to the right answer: 'No one has sole rights to being right, including me. I learnt long ago that if you are going to make all the decisions around the place you have to keep making all the decisions. You don't get much bigger and you finish up with a team of yes men — a one-man-band, which is quite different to establishing an organisation where you are asking people to think and make decisions.'[1]

It must have been gratifying for Gallagher that the politicians in New Zealand took a momentary break from their election year warfare to pass a Notice of Motion through Parliament congratulating him on the achievement. A couple of months later, he was one of four New Zealand business leaders invited to accompany Prime Minister Jim Bolger on a trade mission to South Africa, where they met President Nelson Mandela and Archbishop Desmond Tutu. The party went to a New Zealand versus South Africa rugby test match in Cape Town, sweeping through the crowds to the stadium accompanied by outriders and sirens. Now that was the way to get to a rugby game, Gallagher thought.

Back home, however, things were going rather less swimmingly. After a couple of good years of growth and profitability for the Gallagher Group in 1994 and 1995, the upward trend stalled in the year to June 1996. Revenues fell 7 per cent to $48 million and the after-tax profit dropped 40 per cent. Gallaghers had manufactured more product than ever before, including the new SmartPower energisers, but sales flagged because of a drop-off in international demand, because of growing competition in key markets, and because the SmartPower energisers had a lot of teething problems. With hindsight, Gallagher acknowledges that the testing procedures they had in place for new products were not sufficiently thorough.

Worse, the pressure of events laid bare an increasingly wide divergence of view between Bill Gallagher and his managing director Neil Richardson on what should be done. Through 1996 their relationship, which had promised so much, deteriorated to the extent that Richardson left in December. The months surrounding Richardson's departure would prove the most difficult period in Gallagher's 40 years at the helm of the company.

What went wrong? At one level the two men disagreed over

business strategy. One of the key areas of contention was how best to market Gallaghers' products, especially in the all-important European market. Richardson was convinced that the old arrangement of a dozen or so mainly small distributors scattered across the continent, which had been the key to the growth of the market in its early days, had now reached its use-by date, particularly since Europe was rapidly moving toward genuine economic union with no borders and one currency. In Veldman & Dijkstra they had one very competent and professional distributor, but many of the others were small, family operations each with their own warehouses (21 in all) and set-ups that, in Richardson's view, lacked the technical and promotional skills to bring the relatively complex new SmartPower system successfully to market.

Richardson was excited at the potential efficiency gains of having one warehousing and distribution system for the whole of Europe, guided by one powerful sales and marketing organisation that could develop the skills and resources to market new products effectively. Veldman & Dijkstra would be key to this. In November 1996 he proposed forming Gallagher Europe as a joint venture between the Gallagher Group, Veldman & Dijkstra and other potential investors to assume control of all European sales and marketing. Down the line, he saw the possibility of floating Gallagher Europe on a European stock market as an agricultural marketing and distribution business.[2]

Bill Gallagher was not convinced by this argument. He had built his business by developing long-term relationships of reciprocal dependency with distributors all around the world and saw the network he had created as a real competitive advantage. The key to it, in his view, was having a reputation for loyalty to his distributors, even to the point of helping them out when they were in serious trouble. That way the best distributors would feel sufficiently confident to devote 70 per cent or more of their business to Gallagher products, which tied their fate to his fate. And so he was prepared to accept mediocre performance in, say, Sweden and Portugal, if that was the price to pay for maintaining a reputation in the market for standing by his distributors. This was the key to having two distributors in Ireland who devoted virtually their entire business to selling Gallagher products and who did the job very effectively.

'I see my competitors going around chopping off heads,' Gallagher told an inquiring academic a few years later.[3] And the result he had seen was that none of his competitors' distributors or dealers trusted them sufficiently to devote themselves fully to the task. As one of his distributors put it, 'When the MD of one of Bill's primary New Zealand competitors came to see you and said "it's a lovely day," you went outside to take a look, just to be sure; with Bill you could trust what he said.' Gallagher's preferred approach, over the long term, was to shift the emphasis toward the good distributors and away from poorly performing ones, without creating a ruckus.

Gallagher and Richardson also disagreed over where to find future growth. Richardson saw limited scope for rapid growth in a business focused largely on electric fencing. The company had swallowed Franklin Machinery Ltd comfortably and, in his view, should continue to grow by making more acquisitions that took the group into new areas. He told an American business professor who put together a case study on Gallaghers that he saw a future where Gallaghers' core business would expand alongside the acquisition of new businesses and the development of new products, with the idea of becoming 'a micro cluster for packaged electronics'.[4]

While he had gone along with Richardson's broad strategy through 1994 and into 1995, by early February 1996 Bill Gallagher had come to the opposite view. He now opposed growth by acquisition as an active strategy, preferring to grow the business generically through its existing animal containment and security businesses, and by acquiring new businesses only on an opportunistic basis and only if they were highly complementary to Gallaghers' existing business.

A couple of recent studies by business academics had influenced his thinking. One was the work of Canadian management thinker Henry Mintzberg, who had published articles in the *Harvard Business Review* leading to his 1994 book, *The Rise and Fall of Strategic Planning*.[5] Mintzberg made the point that nobody can predict major discontinuities, such as oil shocks and financial crunches, nor can anyone predict the moves made by competitors that can turn an industry on its head. He argued that while the trend of big businesses had been to bind themselves up in ever more complicated five-year plans, the best companies had been reactionary; companies that were sufficiently nimble to adapt to a rapidly changing environment. Mintzberg's writing lent academic weight to Bill Gallagher's instincts. Gallagher explains it this way: 'I've always been a bit contemptuous of serious planning. It's worth having a day a year thinking about where you're going, but 100-page strategic plans can be a waste of time. You can have the best strategic plan, but if your competitor does something or the market changes you have to respond. And if you can't hold your basic strategy in your head, it is too complicated.'

'Gallaghers' entire international marketing system, which was the core of the company's success, had been developed opportunistically: having a contact from somewhere, going past the next month and dropping in, finding a distributor that was interested, giving him a patch and if he's successful helping him grow. That, it seemed to me, was far better than determining a rigid course from Hamilton then going out and finding an unwilling partner, which nine times out of ten doesn't work out.'

In September 1995 Gallagher joined his old Harvard classmates for their annual reunion, which as usual included a presentation from a leading business thinker. This time the reunion was in Berlin and the speaker was Hermann Simon, a German marketing scholar and consultant.

Simon's work condensed the wisdom of what he described as the 'hidden champions', the 'world's best unknown companies'.[6] The examples he used were Germany's famed Mittelstand, the small and mid-sized companies that generally weren't household names but often dominated their respective niches globally. The chainsaw-maker Stihl was one of the higher-profile examples. Running through Simon's 10 points on the typical characteristics of these companies, Gallagher had been amazed to find so many described the Gallagher Group. Among them:

- The 'hidden champions' strive for world market leadership — and nothing else. They consistently pursue the goal to become No. 1 in the world in their markets/segments and once they have reached this position they defend it vehemently.
- In defining their markets narrowly [the 'hidden champions'] observe both customers' needs and technology. They are highly focused and deep rather than broad. They concentrate on their

core competencies and target groups and avoid distractions or diversification.
- The 'hidden champions' are very close to their customers . . . Their strategies are value, not price, driven. Customer loyalty receives high attention.
- The 'hidden champions' are highly innovative in both product and process.
- The 'hidden champions' rely on their own strengths. They mistrust strategic alliances and outsource less than other companies. They see the foundation of their competitive superiority in things which only they can do.
- The 'hidden champions' have idiosyncratic corporate cultures associated with excellent employee identification and motivation.
- The leaders of 'hidden champions' live their leadership. Their leadership is authoritarian in the principles and flexible in details. The average tenure of the CEO is 30 to 40 years.[7]

Again, Simon reinforced Gallagher's instincts, fortifying them against the arguments of his managing director. 'Narrow the speciality and take it wide' became his motto; growth by acquisition into diverse industries was out. Simon's examples also fortified Gallagher's determination to produce premium products for premium markets. Richardson was arguing that they should aim for the mass market, for more than a 50 per cent market share in a wider geographical range, including the United States. This required yielding some, or maybe all, of the price premium.

Lurking in the background to the desire to grow rapidly by buying companies and getting into new products, and integral to Richardson's plan for Gallagher Europe was the notion of floating parts or all of the Gallagher Group as a public company on stock exchanges. A fresh infusion of capital would fund faster growth. Neither John nor Bill Gallagher was keen on this. John had seen too many families lose control of their businesses in short order. The Firths, Bisleys and Winstones sprang to mind.

Bill had been more open to the idea at various times, but was now highly sceptical about its benefits. 'I'd sooner own half of x,' he says, 'than a quarter of $2x$ along with all the arguments and complications that come with public companies.' And the more he saw of how his business's profitability fluctuated with the vagaries of New Zealand's exchange rate, the more perils he saw in exposing himself to market opinion. 'We could float on the exchange and then have a couple of bad years due to a high New Zealand dollar, the market could cane us, and suddenly our market capitalisation could slump to dangerous levels and we'd have to worry about hostile takeovers.' At bottom, he preferred working for himself than for a bunch of analysts or money managers.

A tension therefore developed between the natural desire of a manager to grow the business as quickly as possible, so as to be in command of a billion-dollar business, and the equally natural desires of cautious family shareholders who are happy to see their asset grow more modestly, appreciating the greater security that caution provides. Such a tension was scarcely unusual for private companies that had reached a certain threshold. There were good arguments in support of both directions.

In the end, Gallagher and Richardson were unable to resolve their differences. The fact that they had become such good friends early on added an emotional element to the equation. Bill's daughter Janine, who watched from the sidelines, got to the core with her observation: 'When you get to Dad's height in business you don't come up against people who roll over; you come up against strong characters with strong differences of opinion and no one backs down.'[8]

Richardson, who in 1995 had been appointed chairman of AgResearch, the country's largest Crown Research Institute, was not lacking in confidence. He was determined, and convinced that the future of the company lay in the balance. But as one wit commented, 'Neil was impressive, intelligent and a trusted adviser of Bill; he was also a lawyer, an academic and an Australian.'

Richardson's problem was that he couldn't convince Bill Gallagher to agree with his prescription. But it was his response to the impasse that led to the breach. Bruce Munro, an Auckland businessman who joined the Gallagher board immediately after Richardson's departure, surveyed the aftermath and concluded it reflected one of the core challenges facing the company: 'Bill had total power and mana within the company. He was chairman, CEO, a dominant shareholder and he knew the business inside out, down to the most minute detail. Therefore it was very difficult for his staff ever to win an argument with him. He was simply too strong. So, ironically, his own strength could become a weakness in the company. Because some competent people, having failed to debate issues successfully, would try to go around him, which would lead to distrust and their departure. And Richardson was a classic example. Because he couldn't carry Bill with his arguments, he went out and did some things on his own, without putting them openly on the table. Anything to avoid having the hassle of fighting with Bill. Some of them may have been the right thing to do, but in Bill's mind that wasn't the point. It seemed to me that it led to mistrust.'[9]

After a sharp deterioration in their relationship over the 1995/96 New Year break, Bill Gallagher brought Richardson in for a 'Come to Jesus' meeting at his home in February. Bill's notes of the meeting show that he grumbled about Richardson practising 'the mushroom style of management' (keeping him in the dark and feeding him dung) and, despite clear direction from him and the board on the question of European marketing, deliberately going around and defying his will. To make matters worse, he noted, Richardson displayed what Bill felt was TDC ('thinly disguised contempt'). Gallagher made it clear that he intended to be totally involved in the company for the next 10 years and that they could work together or go their separate ways.

An apparent truce followed, but this fell apart on 1 November 1996 at a management strategy session at the Brooklands retreat centre at Waingaro, north of Hamilton. There Richardson argued that carrying on as a Hamilton-based company, focused on electric fencing only, and marketing through an ad hoc mixture of group-controlled subsidiaries and local distributors, would lead to a static business with declining capability and the likelihood of losing some of its key independent distributors. Instead, he said the clear and unanimous recommendation of management was to move to regionally based business, with the head office still in Hamilton but with strong new companies like Gallagher Europe, possibly floated on the stock exchange, growing the business internationally.[10]

Then Richardson laid it on thick: his presentation declared

'Personal desires must give way to the best-interests of the business and all its stakeholders.' He concluded by describing the choices facing the company as being:

- A static business with a short-term limited view, declining capability and the potential for mis-alignment between executive and non-executive shareholders.

OR
- A growth business, with a long-term vision, encompassing all stakeholders.

- Desires and reactions as the driver of business decisions.

OR
- Wealth creation through a coherent business strategy and effective risk management, supported by appropriate structures and decision processes.

Isolated, with all the senior management with the exception of Margaret Comer supporting Richardson's general thrust, Gallagher interpreted the presentation as 'an assassination attempt'. He felt that the message was clear and brutal: get out of the way so management can do the right thing for the company and its 'stakeholders'.

When Judi picked up Bill at the end of the conference he was, she says, 'white, angry, hurt, feeling betrayed and having never experienced anything like it in his life'. His supporters within the firm had moved on over several years, and he now felt 'entrapped and encircled'. He faced a choice: he could yield to the pressure from Richardson, and ultimately he and John would risk losing control of the company if it was floated and new shareholders came in; or he could remove Richardson and retake the reins of the company.

A few days later he and Judi pulled together a crisis meeting of old friends and advisers — Steve Saunders, an industrial psychologist who had worked with Gallaghers, profiling senior management and prospective sales staff; Jerry Rickman, his accountant; John Weir, his lawyer; Peter Taylor, a Wellington business adviser who had been the facilitator at the Brooklands retreat; Margaret Comer; and his brother John. Ultimately, provided Bill and John Gallagher retained their nerve and their determination, there would be no contest given their overwhelming domination of the shareholding. As Saunders observes, 'Neil came to a gunfight armed with a knife.' But did they still have the self-belief?

Bill Gallagher admits they were shaken. After months of relentless struggle he was fatigued and his resistance was faltering, but in the final analysis he was in no mood to give in. Richardson had always said he would resign if he felt that Bill lost confidence in him. Gallagher made it clear that that time had come, and so Richardson left in December 1996. An amicable settlement was soon reached to sell his five per cent shareholding back to the company, and Richardson has since remained in Hamilton. A few years later the National government appointed him chair of the Foundation for Research, Science and Technology, and he would become involved in several high-tech start-up companies.

At the same time, David Mullen, who was very busy with his businesses in the US and Australia, and unhappy with the level of politics developing within the group, also left the Gallagher board. This was another blow for Bill Gallagher. Reeling from the loss of both Richardson and Mullen, he announced that he would be 'taking a more detailed involvement with the business than in the recent past' and appointed Richardson's chief ally in the business, John Walley, as business development manager.[11] Walley had been a strong supporter of Richardson's arguments but said he accepted Gallagher's decision.

In February 1997 the Gallaghers invited Bruce Munro and Rob Booth to join the board. Booth was their long-lost first cousin, the son of Bill Gallagher senior's younger sister Violet, who had been adopted out as an infant. He had been raised by a prosperous farming couple from the East Coast and had emerged a freewheeling entrepreneur. Takapuna-based Munro was a professional director with plenty of experience in business recovery. He was chair of the New Zealand Wool Board, an appointment that had grown out of work he had carried out for a South Island woollen-mill operator, Alliance Textiles.

Munro had been introduced to Gallagher by Steve Saunders, who felt his friend Bill could use the advice and support of a strong independent director. Munro recalls that he told Gallagher he had two conditions when working with family companies: no nepotism, and while he didn't expect the owner and CEO always to take his advice, if his advice was seldom taken it would be clear he wasn't needed.[12]

A few months later, in August, the board was strengthened further by the arrival of Rick Christie, an experienced businessman with an oil background who had been CEO of TradeNZ, the government's trade development agency, between 1990 and 1996. As a TradeNZ director Bill Gallagher held Christie in high regard.

Meanwhile, there was no let-up in the pressure on the business. The year to June 1997 was again difficult. Sales were flat at $48 million, and the pre-tax profit had halved again from the previous year's poor result to $2.5 million. A strong exchange rate wasn't helping, but the distributor network had also been unsettled by the speculation that had surrounded Richardson's plans.

While Gallaghers' people were distracted, big changes were occurring in the camp of one of their strongest competitors. The Palmerston North-based Speedrite had become an annoying opponent in certain markets around the world, especially in Australia — so much so that Gallagher had considered buying the company. The problem was that he suspected that Speedrite's owner, Dave Healy, would rather chew off his arm than sell to his bitter Hamilton rival. 'I'd sued most of our competitors over the years for patent infringements,' Gallagher concedes, 'for a bit of legal sport, with the result that I tended to be the centre of the dart board amongst the competition.'

One day he had discussed the problem with Des Scott, the managing director of Tru-Test, a manufacturer of precision proportional-flow milk meters and weigh-scales for stock. A privately held company founded in 1963 by a frustrated King Country dairy farmer, John Hartstone, Tru-Test had grown to become an international leader in its niche. Its success had parallelled Gallaghers'. And since they weren't in competition, Gallagher and Scott were fairly open with each other. Showing Scott around his factory one day, Gallagher proposed a cunning manoeuvre whereby Tru-Test bought Speedrite and then flicked it on to the Gallagher Group. Nothing came of the idea, but a few weeks later, in September 1996, while working through his morning bowl of porridge, Gallagher was shocked to read in the newspaper that Tru-Test had bought Speedrite as part of a broader strategy to strengthen its export base with a complementary product.[13] Thereafter Gallagher nursed a grievance against Scott in his breast that one day would demand satisfaction. In the short term, Tru-Test's acquisition was of strategic concern since it potentially strengthened an already dangerous foe.

Competition was equally fierce in the European market. Gallaghers stayed ahead of the game with continuous innovation, but constantly had to defend its intellectual property. Gallaghers' polywire was a typical example. The early polywire had 15 or 21 strands of polyethylene run through with threads of copper to provide conductivity. The problem with copper polywire, however, was that the thread would break if it was flexed too much, rendering the fence useless. So stainless steel was used, but this had high resistance. Manufacturers experimented with different metals and methods, but the general consensus was that mixing metals was a bad idea, since it led quickly to corrosion.

However, Gallaghers' R&D department struck a successful combination with polywire that had nine strands of metal through it, three of copper and six stainless steel. This worked well and stayed conductive. They patented it and took it to market, but in short order, by 1998, half a dozen manufacturers, mostly European, were infringing the patent. Gallagher fired off 'cease and desist' letters and, when that didn't work, sued the biggest. This display of aggression worked, with the rival company offering to settle literally on the steps of the Federal Patent Court of Germany in Munich, offering some payment, legal costs and a royalty for future use.

Meantime, by the winter of 1997 Gallagher had come to reconsider elevating John Walley. Gallagher's view was that Walley's strengths remained best suited to his earlier, and significant, R&D role. His relations with Walley soured after July 1997, when Gallagher appointed Rob Booth to an executive role in the company, with clear instructions that if he fell under a bus Booth was to be acting CEO and chairman.

The sudden manoeuvre was prompted by a diving expedition to Bikini Atoll with John Gallagher, his son Keith and Bill's son Ian. Driving to the airport, the thought occurred to Bill Gallagher that they may not come back — many things could go wrong in such a remote and radioactive spot where the dives were up to 55 metres deep — and if so, Walley was the next highest-ranking executive and would take over running the company. Since Gallagher no longer found that prospect acceptable, Booth was drafted in at short notice. It was a clinical way of registering a vote of no confidence in Walley, and thereafter things began to unravel entirely. At the end of the year Walley wrote a pessimistic review of strategy between 1991 and 1997, which concluded that little scope remained for further cost savings in the organisation, while restating Richardson's critique of the company's marketing strategy.[14] He left the company in January 1998.

Also during 1997 Steve Aldridge, the general manager of Gallaghers' fledgling security business, resigned. He had been with the company since 1991 and left to further his own career with Gallagher's best wishes. But the result was that Gallagher had lost around half of his top tier of management and a key director in little more than year.

The company was showing signs that it might go the way of many family businesses, stumbling at the point of transition from family to professional management. Now Rob Booth was the deputy CEO. A man with a passion for flash cars, he soon convinced Bill that Gallaghers should sponsor his son Andrew to race in the Formula Palmer Audi circuit in the UK. There was something approaching a commercial rationale for the investment, since the people involved in both the agricultural and security markets tended to have an interest in motorsport, but it was marginal at best. Costs quickly ballooned far in excess of Booth's predictions.

While Booth was not a natural fit at Gallaghers, he did have the virtue of being someone Gallagher felt he could trust. Bill Gallagher says now: 'Rob was a great help to me in that time, when the going was rough. In fact, he lived with us for about six months. The difficulties with Richardson and Walley had taken a real mental toll; my confidence had been shaken, my decision-making wasn't always good and I was quite depressed. I was overweight, wasn't feeling well, and Rob was upbeat, enthusiastic and he wasn't interested in playing mind-games.'

ABOVE Gallaghers' connection with motor racing was brief but colourful. The driver is Andy Booth.

All the changes, the dramatic exits and sudden arrivals, together with the intrigue that dragged on for the best part of two years, had been very destabilising for the group. Yet the fundamentals of the business remained sound. Market surveys in 1998 showed that Gallaghers had 65 per cent of the energiser market in New Zealand, and internationally the early problems with SmartPower energisers had been overcome and sales were picking up. The remote control that came with SmartPower proved very popular and was extended to the full range of Gallagher energisers. In the year to June 1998 a decline in the New Zealand dollar helped the company to lift sales to $56 million and after-tax profits to $4.2 million. The foray into gates and their hardware with Franklin Machinery Ltd had been successful, so that in February 1998 Gallaghers bought the rest of the shares to own the business outright.

Bruce Munro was dispatched to Holland to act in what was almost an arbitration role between Bill Gallagher and the Dijkstras, in a bid to resolve several contentious issues about European marketing. The result of many meetings was something of a compromise. Veldman & Dijkstra wasn't given the entire European market or folded into a new company that would be floated on the stock exchange as Richardson had envisaged, but Munro did conclude that it was the best in the region.

In September 1998 Gallagher and Veldman & Dijkstra signed a joint venture to form Gallagher Europe. This new entity merged V&D's activities in North Germany, the Netherlands, Belgium and France with Gallaghers' fully owned subsidiary in the UK. It would also provide promotional, logistical and warehousing services to smaller European distributors. The ownership was 54 per cent Veldman & Dijkstra interests and 42 per cent Gallagher Group, with the remaining shares in a trust for the staff. Munro became chairman. It was hoped the introduction of the Dijkstras' marketing skill would rekindle the British market, which had struggled for 15 years.

At home in New Zealand Gallagher was drawn into a showdown with the unions on site. Arguments began over his desire to introduce random drug testing at the factory. He later told radio journalist Kim Hill, 'Well . . . with 300 people we have a few people who do get involved with happy weed. We're running presses and a plastic moulding shop, tool making, you know, quite dangerous machinery . . . having people on the job who are partly doped out of their mind is not acceptable.'[15] But the Engineering, Printing and Manufacturing Union went out on a limb to resist any such testing, saying it attacked the dignity of workers.[16] Gallagher concluded that the unionists had 'their feet firmly in the air' on the issue.

The broader issue, however, was Gallagher's desire to shift the workforce from a rigid collective agreement, the essential elements of which had been in place for decades, onto individual contracts. These would fatally undermine the power of the union, and it resisted stoutly. When Margaret Comer announced the shift to individual contracts, the union called a stopwork meeting. As a member of the Engineers' Union of 25 years standing, Gallagher turned up and sat down in the front row. A tense discussion followed, in which he was invited to leave. 'No way,' he said. 'I'm a member and I'm just here to listen.' At the conclusion of the union meeting he convened a staff meeting in which he corrected several falsehoods.

That was too much for the union, and Gallagher was summoned to Wellington for a disciplinary hearing — a kangaroo court in his opinion — where he was expelled for not acting in the best interests of the union. The national secretary of the Engineers' Union, Andrew Little, later grumbled that Gallagher was trying to play both sides and had an obvious conflict of interest: 'He knew the level of influence he commanded in what was a generally unskilled company. It was more than paternalistic, he was telling people what was good for them.'[17]

Bill Gallagher enjoyed a good argument, and his tongue-in-cheek style was captured live on National Radio in January 1999 when he explained his attitude to penal rates to interviewer Kim Hill:

> *Gallagher*: I say after you've done 40 hours you should be paid at a discount, not the same rate, and certainly not time and a half.
> *Hill*: Why, why?
> *Gallagher*: Because you're not worth as much after 40 hours.
> *Hill*: But that . . . though . . .
> *Gallagher*: You know, the real world is you get paid with your work.
> *Hill*: Yeah, but hang on, Bill. My hours, after I've worked 40 hours a week, that forty-first hour is worth a great deal to me, it may be worth less to you.

ABOVE The Gallagher Group board, 1999. Standing left to right: Bruce Munro and Rob Booth. Seated left to right: John Gallagher, Bill Gallagher and Rick Christie.

Gallagher: Well, it's worth less to the employer.
Hill: That's the point of negotiation, isn't it?
Gallagher: Yeah, but it's worth less to the employer.
Hill: Yeah, but that's your problem. If you want me to give you one of my worthless hours, then I'm going to say to you that I need that hour more than you do, you're going to have to pay me more for it.
Gallagher: No trouble, we just bring in temporary workers, and that's what we used to do.
Hill: [laughs]
Gallagher: You've got the choice. You're working 40 hours and off you go and we'll bring in some temporaries, and that's just how we used to run it. Not very good. [laughs]
Hill: I think that you just explained why you fell out with the union, though, haven't you?
Gallagher: [laughs] Yes.[18]

But Gallagher had his way. Within a short space of time all bar one of the company's 300-odd workers had moved to individual contracts, and thereafter the company could increase production quite substantially at short notice without incurring transaction costs or bringing in temporary production staff. When the overtime rate was dropped, the standard hourly rate increased to make the pay the same for an average week of around 42.5 hours.

Gallagher's greatest excitement at the time of his Radio New Zealand interview in January 1999 was the progress that was finally being made by the company's US security subsidiary selling electric fences for prisons. In general, security had taken much longer to gain momentum than planned. Gallagher Security USA had been launched in Chicago in 1995 to sell the product directly to clients, but it had failed to fire, not least because it ran into interference from the city's chief engineer who did not want to know about electric fences and effectively locked the city against the New Zealand invaders.

Gallaghers' manager there, Bob Gilmour, had reported somewhat feebly to the board in April 1997: 'It may sound like a broken record but calendar year 1997 will be the year of Gallagher Security (USA) Inc! We are breaking through the resistance to buy our product.'

Rumours of a breakthrough proved premature, and the US security business booked another ghastly loss in the year to March 1998. Surveying the scene in Chicago, Gallagher confided in his board in December 1997, 'the degree of politics in this issue is immense'. Al Capone was mentioned. But then a change in strategy that saw them selling security fencing through dealers, rather than directly, finally began to pay dividends. Contacts were made in the prison industry. In May 1998 Gallagher attended a mock riot in a disused state prison in West Virginia, where they trialled the Gallagher Security PowerFence. The results were good and orders began to flow. Sales quadrupled to $420,000 in the year to March 1999, and the company finally had some momentum.

The strongest market for security remained the UK, however, and Gallagher Security Europe continued to perform well there. Elsewhere, South Africa had enjoyed a boost after Gallagher's trip there as part of the New Zealand government trade mission in 1997, when he was accompanied by Mike Foley, his new South African manager. But the deals made on that trip tapered off again until a Black Empowerment Partner was found for the business. Ubambo, a company owned by black South Africans with good connections to the African National Congress, took 49 per cent of Gallagher Power Fence (SA) Ltd in April 1999 and the way was open to compete more effectively for government contracts. It was the only way to do business in the new South Africa. In other markets, as ever, growth depended on the quality of the local distributors: Veldman & Dijkstra had made some progress in Holland; the distributors in Colombia, by contrast, managed only $1014 worth of sales despite the ample scope of the market.

Just as they had with electric fences for agricultural use, Gallaghers led the industry in working to develop a code of practice for the installation and safe operation of electric security fences, though early experiences in New Zealand persuaded Bill Gallagher to change his approach. He realised in hindsight that by organising industry consultation, in partnership with the Ministry of Energy, to develop a New Zealand Code of Practice his main achievement had been to wake up his agricultural competitors to the opportunities in the security industry. So when it came to the UK they produced the Gallagher Code of Practice, which avoided stirring up the competition, and this was soon recognised by the UK Health and Safety officials as the gold standard.

It was this new and very demanding part of the business that most energised Gallagher through the many trying months as he, Munro and Booth set about rebuilding the senior management strength of the group after its period of upheaval. The core of the management now consisted of Booth, Margaret Comer and Steve Hoffman, the international sales manager. From the board Munro was particularly active, drilling down to gain a full understanding of the business. His search highlighted many gaps in the quality of information being produced by the firm's MRP system, which was now nearly a decade old. In exasperation, he told the board in March 1998, 'We still don't know which are our really profitable lines.'[19]

This was basic knowledge that any manufacturing company needed in order to make rational decisions. Munro was impressed by Steve Tucker, a young accountant who then reported to the company secretary; he seemed to be the only person in the business who understood the cost structure and would eventually produce the answers for which Munro was looking. Tucker would be put in charge of the next project to upgrade the manufacturing operating system.

Externally, David Mullen continued to be a major figure in the wider Gallagher family. The US and Australian markets, for which he remained the distributor, took nearly 40 per cent of Gallaghers' exports, $12 million in 1998. In terms of generating fresh demand for Gallaghers' products, the US was most important. Between 1990 and 1998, sales to Gallagher Power Fence Inc increased from $3 million to $8.6 million, with Mullen and Quinn painstakingly and methodically growing the business against the grain of a market that remained deeply suspicious of 'foreigners'.

As Mullen describes it: 'The whole strategic plan was to take a territory, which consisted of one, two or three states, and build it up till it was above break-even with one territory manager, and then we'd gamble on splitting the territory in two and putting a second guy on. Usually we found we were breaking even on both territories within a year.'[20]

Every now and then they encountered a colossal job, such as one in the late 1990s on a property adjoining the Red River in Texas. Some farmers from Mexico had bought a 3200 hectare property with no internal fencing and wanted it divided up into paddocks for sheep, as well as a new external fence to keep out the coyotes. Mullen remembers delivering two containers of Insultimber, three semi-trailer-loads of wire and eight of Gallaghers' biggest energisers. Their most successful product, however, was the S17, a solar-powered energiser that was well-priced and portable and could drive a temporary 1.6 km long fence. Even after an initial problem with water getting behind the solar panel, Gallagher Power Fence sold 11,000 of these energisers in their first year.

The distributing businesses themselves had also grown significantly. Gallagher Australia (80 per cent Mullen, 20 per cent Gallagher Group) was turning over A$12.6 million in 1999 and throwing off steady profits, while Gallagher Power Fence (60 per cent Mullen, 40 per cent Gallagher) turned over US$14 million in 1999 and was also profitable. As well as selling Gallagher equipment, both of Mullen's businesses sold some complementary products, such as Spring Tight Deer Fencing and Miraco water troughs in the US, with Franklin gate hardware and Ruddweigh Livestock Scales in Australia. Depending on the exchange rates, the combined revenues of those two businesses weren't that far off the Gallagher Group itself.

After a short period of despondency, it became clear that his differences with Richardson and Walley had only served to increase Bill Gallagher's determination in business. Turning 58 in January 1999, he was at a stage of life when his father had already devoted the best part of two decades to his boat and was in the process of passing the baton of his small business to his sons. Bill, by contrast, was more actively involved than he had been since 1989.

It was an exciting time; the widespread adoption of email by 1998 was revolutionising the operation of an international business. He had now dropped his involvement in the Regional Health Authority and several other outside board appointments. Steve Saunders, who watched him closely through this period, concluded: 'Bill Gallagher has pretty good EQ and a very high IQ, but he also has a bloody amazing AQ (Adversity Quotient), which expressed itself in mental toughness.'[21] Another staff member made a similar point differently: 'If the neighbour's dog left a turd on his lawn, rather than throw something at it, he thinks about what he can do with it.'

Gallagher would continue to tell anyone handy that he was in business 'for fun and profit; and that it isn't great if I have to settle for just one or the other'. After the promise of 1995, when the company had at last overcome the transition from operating in the subsidised and protected environment of the early 1980s to the challenges of high taxation, strong international competition and a wildly fluctuating currency, it was immensely frustrating that the company had once more gone sideways for four years.

Yet, with the boundless optimism that so often characterises entrepreneurs, Gallagher remained convinced that the sunny uplands of success in both security and agriculture lay just around the corner. His enthusiasm for the challenge had the power to carry people along with him — from a worker on the assembly line in Hamilton, after a word of encouragement during one of his wanders through the plant, to a struggling distributor in a foreign land who was given a pep talk over dinner.

The primary question in early 1999, however, was whether Bill Gallagher would be alive long enough to see those sunny uplands. He had been blessed with enormous energy, but his eating habits had finally caught up with him. Judi had been shocked when she had first observed his lifestyle 10 years earlier: 'He'd come home on a Tuesday night having been flying all over the place and eaten on the plane, then he'd go to Rotary and eat another dinner, before we'd go out for a third. Typically, he'd have no breakfast, but he'd inhale a hot pie for morning tea. He loved anything fried. We'd go out for lunch and I'd have a salad that came with chips; he'd order a double hamburger with fries and then he'd eat mine as well.'[22]

With his diving and a good metabolism, he had remained in tolerably good shape during the 1980s, but he had had a scare in 1990. One chilly night out walking after a hearty meal of herrings in Copenhagen he had complained to Judi about pains in his chest. It hadn't amounted to much, but once they had returned home he was found to have had a very small heart attack.

Considering himself healthy, Bill had carried on much the same way in the 1990s. By 1999 he was 20 kilograms overweight and Judi had persuaded him to go for short jogs. One Saturday morning in January she found him looking sombre as he returned to their beach house at Whangamata after one such run. He was having trouble breathing, feeling heavy and looking grey. A visit to a cardiologist the next day revealed six blockages of more than 90 per cent in his heart arteries and he was admitted straight to hospital. A major heart attack had been imminent, but as it was he had done a lot of damage.

Since the blockages were not easy to fix with stents, complicated bypass surgery looked inevitable. Judi recalls: 'Bill was in a bad way, particularly as he was told that he probably shouldn't dive again. His world was collapsing. I asked the cardiologist whether a radical change in diet could get him back on track, and he dismissed the idea: "Diet doesn't work because people won't follow it." Well, that just made me more determined. I'd heard of the Pritikin diet that had been developed by a guy in California, and seven days after his near miss we arrived at the Pritikin Clinic in Santa Monica Beach. For a month we stayed there, with Bill living on beans, vegetables and oatmeal for breakfast.

'Six weeks later, without any medication, his cholesterol was almost normal, his blood pressure was down, and he'd lost 20 kilograms. But it was very difficult; he was very difficult. We'd be out for dinner and he'd be playing up to the crowd, imploring me with a plaintive look on his face and I would sometimes have to take his plate away. People looked at me as if I was a dragon, but I wanted him to live.'[23]

Taking the long-term view, few doubt that Judi's firm enforcement saved Bill. He remained on a strict Pritikin diet for a year then settled on something close to it thereafter. And he began a steady exercise regime on a newly installed home gym. More than a decade later, past 70, he remains in fighting good health.

During the early months of 1999, however, the new diet provided plenty of material for gallows humour. Gallagher had a series of lines: 'This diet may not make me live longer, it's just going to feel like it'; 'I've done the crime, now I have to do the time'; 'This diet is easily understood: if it tastes good it will be bad for you, and if it tastes bad it will be good for you'.

Judi's determination reached stratospheric levels. When the flight attendants on the Concorde failed to deliver Bill's special diet as requested she calmly reached into her handbag and whipped out a can of beans for them to heat for him. A minute later she silently fished a can-opener out of her handbag as well, after the hostess had shamefacedly confessed that they couldn't find one. Meantime, the relentless supply of beans had a predictable effect on his metabolism; during the critical first months staff members learnt not to follow him down the stairs, and hesitated to accompany him in the lift.

9
A NEW DIRECTION: 1999–2001

Chapter nine

A NEW DIRECTION: 1999–2001

OK, now that the dog has caught the bus, what is he going to do with it?

— A FAVOURITE BILL GALLAGHER EXPRESSION, HEARD, FOR EXAMPLE, BY MURRAY BINDON WHEN GALLAGHER HAD DISMANTLED A BROKEN-DOWN BOAT ENGINE AND LAID THE PARTS ON THE DECK ON A BUMPY DAY

Bill Gallagher was at the Pritikin Clinic in Santa Monica, paying a lot of money to eat poor man's food, when he received an extraordinary email from John Williams, the owner of Production Engineering Company (PEC). It contained PEC's financial information in full detail. Nothing was concealed. The message was simple: Are you interested in investing in my company?

Gallagher had known Williams for more than 25 years, since 1973, when PEC had entered the electric fencing market. For a short time the company offered Gallaghers fierce competition with its Grassfence energiser. When Gallagher corralled the domestic manufacturers to form a standards committee, he and Williams spent some time together and developed a mutual respect. Gallagher rated Williams, who was three years older, an 'intelligent and gentlemanly businessman'; Williams meantime had been amazed that Gallagher had freely shared with him and their other New Zealand competitors information about international standards and the industry overseas that he had so laboriously and expensively gained from his own efforts.[1] When he had quizzed Gallagher on his altruism, Bill simply replied that he wanted New Zealand companies to lead the field, and if he had to have competition he'd rather it came from home than from elsewhere.

A decade later, in September 1984, Gallagher and Williams had both been invited to the Labour government's Economic Summit as representatives of industry. In his speech to the conference, Williams laid out some hard truths that had been forgotten in an economy distorted for decades by government intervention. 'Everyone must understand,' he said, 'that permanent new jobs are created only when our products are made more cheaply, made better and marketed more effectively than those of our overseas competitors.'[2]

Thereafter the two men had watched each other from afar. PEC was based in the small town of Marton, deep in the countryside between Palmerston North and Whanganui. By 1999 it had grown into a substantial business, employing around 300 staff with a turnover of $55 million. The company had three primary businesses: electronic petrol pumps; retail point-of-sale systems for service stations; and access security control systems. The petrol pumps dominated the market in New Zealand and did well in Australia; the service station EFTPOS systems also dominated the domestic market and were selling with varying degrees of success throughout the southern hemisphere; while Cardax, the access control system, had some truly impressive international clients, such as the London Underground. Good as it was, however, the company was seriously short of cash.

Chewing his beans in Santa Monica, Gallagher thought, 'Heck, we could do something with this.' Manufacturing petrol pumps didn't interest him, neither did EFTPOS systems for service stations, but a sophisticated access control system would be highly complementary to Gallaghers' perimeter fence security business. Nobody in the world offered a system that combined access control with perimeter security. They could create a unique product. He knew immediately that he would make an offer.

PEC's history had many similarities to Gallaghers'. The company was founded in 1939 by John Williams's father, Reg, a fitter by trade who had worked during the 1930s for Pallo Engineering, a Wellington manufacturer of petrol pumps and washing machines.[3] According to John Williams, as war with Germany approached, the company's Estonian-born owner, Karl Pallo, came under suspicion and government officials asked Williams's father to report regularly on Pallo's activities. The Estonian quickly realised what Reg

Williams was up to and sacked him. The unemployed Williams was soon after invited by government officials to quote for a munitions contract to supply 20,000 two-inch smoke bombs for the army to use for field practice.

Having been awarded the contract, Williams persuaded his father-in-law, Charlie Haddock, who owned the Club Hotel in Marton, to help fund his new company. Williams called it Production Engineering, and Haddock both bought a vacant factory and funded the equipment required to produce smoke bombs.[4] Further war contracts followed, and soon PEC was employing 90 people 24 hours each day making parts for Bren gun carriers, bomb striker pins, foot pumps and striker discs for hand grenades. After the war the workforce shrank, but Williams still found work for 30 staff making 24,000 rice ploughs for China on contract to the United Nations Relief and Rehabilitation Administration (UNRRA).

Unexpectedly, the orders for rice ploughs dried up in November 1947 and Reg Williams cast about for new ways to employ his workers. Having had experience repairing petrol pumps and other oil-industry products before the war, he did the rounds of the oil company head offices in Wellington asking if there was anything they needed. When he found that they desperately needed a reliable gear-oil pump for mechanics to use when filling gearboxes, he spent the summer holidays designing and testing his own pump, which he dubbed the PO60 gear-oil pump. Williams was rewarded with an order from Shell for £5000 worth of product, equivalent to around $350,000 in today's terms.

With that under his belt he grew the business rapidly, as he designed various pumps and valves for the oil industry, while turning his hand to any other contract that came his way. Soon he had his own foundry and was melting down six old Vickers Vincent aircraft that had outlived their usefulness to the Royal New Zealand Air Force up the road at the Ohakea air base. The scrap metal was used to make road signs. Meanwhile there were plenty of boys keen to join young John Williams after school to play real war games in the Vickers Vincents as they lay waiting for the furnace at the back of the foundry, still with the pilot's seat, joystick and most of the instrumentation intact.

In 1950 Sir Percy Mills, later Lord Mills and a Cabinet minister in Harold Macmillan's government, visited New Zealand as managing director of the Avery Group. He was looking for a New Zealand agent for the Avery-Hardoll range of bulk meters and self-sealing couplings for aircraft refuelling. The local oil companies all directed him to Reg Williams, and an important relationship was formed. By 1955 PEC had begun manufacturing petrol pumps, using Avery-Hardoll components. Success followed their every move, and by 1960 PEC was the major supplier of petrol pumps in New Zealand.

By then Williams's only son, John, had completed engineering and science degrees from the University of Canterbury, before working as a designer for Avery-Hardoll in Britain for two and a half years. He returned to Marton in 1963 to help his father deliver PEC's largest order to date: 300 Supermix Blend Pumps for BP. These pumps handled both Super and Regular petrol, as well as three different blends of the two. Fresh from the UK, John Williams introduced rudimentary production control to the Marton factory and put systems in place for costing. Two years later, in 1965, the 60-year-old Reg Williams handed the business over to his son. John recalled: 'Reg said, "I see some challenge in you and you're good at looking after production and dealing with bank managers and production control and costing and pricing. I will continue to design any new products in the tool room. If you want to ask me questions you're very welcome to do so. If you don't like the answers you get, then you don't have to accept my answers." I was only 28.'[5]

And so the driven, business-orientated son took over as the father shuffled off to the workshop, where he was happiest designing and making prototypes of innovative products. It was almost a replay of the Gallagher story.

As the 1960s drew to a close, John Williams was nervous about his company's dependence on the oil industry and began looking for new angles to the business. The new technology of solid state electronics interested him, and so he began talking to Ray Crutcher, a sales rep for Fairchild, one of the major US electronic component suppliers. Crutcher was immediately impressed with PEC's ability to measure fluids very accurately, and saw that if they could marry that expertise with solid state electronics there was an opportunity to make real progress.

Crutcher introduced Williams to two electronics experts, Kevin

Low, who was working at the DSIR's radiation laboratory, and Rob Wilkinson from the Post Office's communications division. Between them they designed the EL10, a system that enabled all-night radio operators for taxi cooperatives to accept prepayment for fuel and then direct taxi drivers, and members of the public, to serve themselves at a designated petrol pump.

Next, they produced the 'Multicoin' petrol pump controller, which accepted 50- and 20-cent coins. This, Williams proudly recalls, saved many motorists who would otherwise have been stranded in remote locations late at night. The 'M System' that followed in 1971 introduced optional self-service to New Zealand motorists. This was the first product that could tell the person at the till how much the customer owed. These sold well, until the first oil shock of 1973 put the industry into hibernation for a couple of years.

A foray into electric fences kept the business ticking over during the lean times, but it was in 1974, at the height of the oil slump, that Williams made one of his boldest investment decisions. Kevin Low had joined PEC and was sure that the latest microprocessor technology would revolutionise the world. He convinced Williams to spend $30,000 ($350,000 in today's terms) to buy one of Intel's earliest Microprocessor Development Systems, serial number 50, complete with its paper tape reader.

They set out to develop the world's first microprocessor-based petrol pump and pump controller, and succeeded in 1977 with the EMPEC pump and the MICRO-M pump controller. PEC claimed that its EMPEC 80 pumps were the first in the world to use LCD display technology. These sold so well in Australia that PEC established a sales office in Sydney and an agent network throughout the continent.

With export incentives added to the mix, the company was doing very well. They also had another winner in the 'Retron 80', an electronic petrol pump register to show the value of the petrol pumped, which could replace the traditional Veeder Root mechanical register, with its rotating volume and price drums. All around the world the mechanical drums were struggling to cope with the rapid rise in fuel prices caused by the second oil shock in 1979. (The drum recording the price was having to spin much faster than the drum recording the volume in litres, placing increased load on the gearboxes. More than a few had blown up.) Such was the international demand for their electronic pump registers that Williams contracted Fisher & Paykel, a larger New Zealand manufacturing firm, to build and market the Retron 80 worldwide, which it did successfully.

Why was this little New Zealand firm so innovative? Williams concludes that it rested on the combination of having young men like himself and Kevin Low experimenting, and their location in a small market that was open to innovation. By contrast, in the vast northern hemisphere markets the oil companies had made such large investments in old technology that they found it difficult to abandon them.

The next breakthrough came in 1985 when, at the Shell service station in Remuera, the southern hemisphere's first EFT transaction was placed from a PEC 'Autoserve'. The Autoserve terminal enabled motorists to purchase petrol 24 hours a day using a credit or debit card. It was a little ahead of its time and didn't really take off, other than for trucks, but the technology was reconfigured the following year to create an integrated point-of-sale (POS) terminal in the sales room — EFPEC. This terminal was effectively a smart cash register, able to automatically process petrol sales along with chips and chocolate from the sales room, including sales using bank cards.

This was leading technology, made possible by New Zealand's advanced and innovative EFT system. The jump on the competition enabled PEC in 1989 to beat IBM and other international competitors to supply 400 EFPEC terminals to Caltex in Australia. That year PEC exported products worth $8.4 million, mainly to Australia. Exports were 60 per cent of turnover. At that point, PEC was investing 13.5 per cent of its sales revenue in R&D, helped along by various government schemes.

Rather than continue with incremental improvement of its EFPEC terminals, Williams's team resolved to create a revolutionary point-of-sale terminal named 8850. This product incorporated an imported motherboard used in laptop computers, rather than one designed by PEC. This decision meant that the 8850's motherboard capability was continually upgraded as laptops improved, without the need to undertake costly in-house motherboard redesigns. By the early 1990s this new system was ready and Williams was convinced he had a world-beater.

The world's largest oil industry product distributors, however, told him that PEC had to prove itself as a viable supplier in a major market region before the 8850 could be launched internationally.

Brendon Deere, who had masterminded the expansion of PEC's retail automation division, selected the southern hemisphere as the region. Outside Australasia they focused initially on Shell and Caltex.

Some stunning success followed in South Africa, and by 1995 they had won a high percentage of the point-of-sale market for Shell and Caltex's top-end service stations in the southern hemisphere. Shell in Argentina and Australia didn't play ball, nor Caltex in New Zealand, but everywhere else in the region and also in parts of South East Asia they locked in the business. Export sales reached $19 million in 1994.

None of this was easy, however. Staff numbers exploded from around 100 in the late 1980s to 250 in the mid-1990s as the company struggled to cope with endless requests from distributors for customisation of the product in each of the 25 countries in which it was selling. John Williams later concluded that they only managed because of the practical nature of New Zealanders: '[New Zealand] is a classless society, so our hardware and software designers are quite prepared to go around the world and talk to the service station proprietor. You wouldn't get an American software designer going down and getting his hands dirty talking to a service man, that would be below his monetary class. But we're a smaller group of people and we like listening and we are prepared to listen to other people and all their good ideas get incorporated into our new products.'[6]

Meantime, while the retail terminals went through several stages of evolution, and while PEC continued to produce new generations of petrol pumps, using Tatsuno components from Japan in preference to Avery-Hardoll's product from 1982, Williams had developed a third stream to the business. In the early 1980s, as the company could see electronic funds transfer was the way of the future, it wanted to learn more about reading magnetic stripe cards, such as credit cards. Williams became aware that the technology was being used to control access to buildings. The systems available on the market, however, were fiendishly expensive: $400 for a door reader and about $12,500 for a central processing unit out the back.

Williams's team at PEC launched into the access business as a way to learn about magnetic stripe cards. And using their knowledge of microprocessors, they quickly devised a way to put intelligence into the door reader itself, doing away with the need for a central processing unit. The readers, marketed as Cardax, sold for just $1500. Over time, however, as systems grew, it became unworkable having to re-programme every door each time one of the customers' staff members left. PEC developed a Commander that looked after 50 door units; then it produced a Unix-based Cardax Command Centre that could look after 50 Commanders. Cardax's Command Centre simply ran on a PC, which by the mid- to late 1980s was relatively inexpensive. This gave Cardax a major advantage over its big competitors, such as Honeywell, whose systems required an expensive mini-computer to control a similar number of access points.

Cardax's first major customer, in 1982, was Databank in Wellington, a company formed by a consortium of banks to process banking transactions. Workers would have to swipe their card and type in a PIN number, giving a high level of security. But the key relationship was formed with Telecom New Zealand in 1987, when PEC was contracted to create a system that controlled access to Telecom's centres in Hamilton, Palmerston North and Christchurch, and their dedicated control rooms.

Over the next few years Telecom's needs expanded, particularly at the start of 1990 when the combination of the country's 150th anniversary celebrations and the Commonwealth Games generated a perceived security risk. Planners worried that disgruntled individuals might disrupt key elements of the nation's infrastructure. At the same time, massive restructuring and downsizing at Telecom since its corporatisation in 1987 meant that it had lost control of the old key system for securing sites.

In responding to Telecom's requirements, the Cardax team, led by Graham Dawson, developed a unique system that allowed Telecom to control sites from North Cape to Bluff. Once they had worked out how to do it for Telecom, the system was transferable to other large sites with many buildings, such as universities.

In the late 1980s they had already had some success with Australian universities, starting with a single building at the University of New South Wales. They were able to grow and expand their coverage across campuses as their capability increased, pioneered by their work for Telecom. In Australia Cardax soon secured important sites such as the Tidbinbilla Deep Space Tracking

Station outside Canberra and the nuclear reactor at Lucas Heights.

Flush with early success in Australia, Cardax opened a new front in the UK in 1989. It established a small office in London to enable the company to assess how the Cardax range measured up against the leading US security products that dominated the market at the time. The breakthrough clients were Citibank at Canary Wharf in London, the law firm Allen & Overy, and the London International Financial Fund and Futures Exchange. These prestigious clients led to PEC's surprisingly deep penetration of the access control market in the City. In April 1993 Cardax won a high-profile contract to install access control systems for the London Underground.[7] PEC also secured the Portsmouth site for Matra Marconi Space.

Further international expansion followed opportunistically. In Thailand, for example, Williams had a connection with the Yip In Tsoi group because its managing director, Thienchai Lailert, had studied 30 years earlier at a New Zealand university under the Colombo Plan scheme. He had stayed at Williams's home in Marton during the holidays and they had kept in touch. When Williams looked for a Thai agent for Cardax in 1992, he contacted Yip In Tsoi. Their first site was a Dow Chemical plant in Bangkok.

Through the rest of the decade Cardax built on these foundations and began to pick up clients as diverse as Moscow Television, Warsaw Airport, Radio Holland in Singapore, Telekom Malaysia, the Jakarta Stock Exchange, the Korean satellite earth station, a large number of waterfront towers in Hong Kong, the Chinese Construction Bank in Beijing, most of the major banks in South Africa and several buildings for the Cape Town City Council. Graham Dawson, the general manager of Cardax, remembers how tough it had been in the early 1990s to sell their products internationally. 'New Zealanders were thought to be good only for sheep and dairy, and so we were constantly having to break new ground and do the impossible.' It became a little easier, he remembers, after Team New Zealand won yachting's America's Cup in 1995. 'Suddenly people realised that really good technology could come out of New Zealand; our image shifted subtly and we certainly noticed a difference selling Cardax. It was a little easier.'[8]

By the late 1990s, then, PEC appeared to be a very successful company that had stood the test of time. As a New Zealand technology-based exporter it knew it had to be 'world class' to survive, and that it needed to be a global player with a decent revenue stream in order to support an ongoing R&D effort. PEC and Williams had received as many export awards as the Gallagher Group.[9] PEC, alongside the Gallagher Group and eight other companies, had been identified in 1998 by an academic research group as being among New Zealand's finest businesses, and used as a case study to understand 'how New Zealand's leading firms became world-class competitors'.[10] It stirred the imagination that an outfit from Marton could provide high-tech access control to the London Stock Exchange and be the leading provider of retail automation systems to oil firms in the southern hemisphere. The romantic tale had become a staple of magazine features and ministerial speeches.[11]

But, as is so often the case in business, the reality was a lot more tenuous and nerve-wracking. PEC was turning over around $55 million worldwide, but its business was heavily dependent on its retail automation systems; they accounted for around 55 per cent of PEC's turnover and most of its profit. Petrol pumps generated around 8 per cent of the revenue and were generally only breaking even in the late 1990s, while Cardax provided the other 35 per cent of revenue and most of the glamour for the company. But, as Williams concedes, 'Cardax never made any money; profits were always "round the corner" or about to kick in next year.'[12]

So, much depended on retail automation, but Williams was becoming increasingly nervous about disturbing trends that he saw in the international oil industry. One oil company had recently called for tenders to supply its entire petrol pump requirements in all South East Asian countries and Australasia. Only a handful of big multinationals could satisfy the requirements of the demanding contract. The oil industry seemed to be regionalising. Williams was 'dead scared' this regime could soon be applied to the retail automation market, threatening PEC's core business.

His response was two-fold. In 1997, he redoubled efforts to develop what he believed would again be world-leading products. In retail automation, a new generation of systems called MAX would replace the 8850 system. Carrying the same logic over to access control, PEC began work on a new generation of products there, which they would call Cardax FT. Secondly, Williams planned to secure agreements with large multinational organisations that he hoped would be best placed to market and support these products in an environment where scale was becoming increasingly important. By late 1998 PEC was well advanced in negotiating a worldwide retail automation agreement with Unisys and was making some progress on a potential deal with Johnson Controls for Cardax.

John Williams bet the shop on a new burst of growth, delivered by ground-breaking new products and improved marketing systems. In 1998 he had a big vision: 'Too many New Zealanders only expect our yachties and our rugby players to be the best. They find it unbelievable that they can be "up to the best in the world" in developing and manufacturing new technologies.'[13] The primary difficulty in realising his vision to be the best in the world, however, was the substantial R&D costs that had to be borne for an extended period before the next generation of products could be brought to market. By the second half of 1998 it was obvious to Williams that PEC needed to raise extra funds. Until then he had kept PEC private and had funded growth by retained profits. Now he engaged Credit Suisse First Boston to raise $10 million on the venture capital market in return for a 25 to 30 per cent shareholding in PEC.

His timing was unfortunate. New Zealand's already thin venture capital market was being buffeted by the sharp Asian financial crisis. By Christmas 1998 there were no takers, but two companies indicated they were prepared to buy the company outright: the Advantage Group, a publicly listed investment company with an EFTPOS business, and the Gallagher Group. A full sale of the company wasn't what Williams had in mind, but he eventually conceded that he had few other options. 'In the end,' he says, 'I concluded that selling was the best way to protect the future employment of at least the majority of PEC's staff members; it needed someone who had the money to keep going on the R&D.'[14]

Looking at the situation coolly from the outside, Bill Gallagher was more matter-of-fact in his assessment: 'The plan to raise money on the market in October 1998 had failed, but the real problem was that some of Williams's staff had already spent half the new money; money that they now hadn't raised. Meantime, the company was losing cash generally as it was nowhere near recouping its huge ongoing investment in R&D. And it was in "Death Valley" in two of its three businesses, Cardax and Retail Automation. They were trying to sell their existing product, but at the same time marketing staff were talking about the new product coming down the track.

Yet the new generation wasn't ready. So they were killing sales of the old one, without having the new one to sell.'

Bruce Munro advised Gallagher that if he waited six months he would get the business from the receiver for nothing, but instead Gallagher and Rob Booth held intensive discussions with Williams through April 1999. The problem was that Williams was determined to keep PEC's three businesses together, as they had always been in Marton. Gallagher was only really interested in Cardax. The Advantage Group, on the other hand, wanted only the retail automation business, since it fitted well with its EFTPOS offerings.

Steve Tucker remembers travelling to Auckland to meet the Advantage men with Bill Gallagher: a couple of Waikato 'hicks' visiting the 'e-boys'. 'We arrived and all the Porsches were parked up outside. There was a team of lawyers there and all the young guys from Advantage in flash suits. It was typical Auckland culture. We were by ourselves. A lady came round offering tea or coffee. Bill asks for a peppermint tea. No, she didn't have that. "No worries," says Bill, and he whips out a tea bag from his suit pocket.'[15]

The upshot of their discussions was that the Gallagher Group would buy PEC from Williams, who then retired, and immediately on-sell the retail automation side of the business to Advantage.

He may have been a hick, but Gallagher managed to arrange it so that PEC, in its entirety, cost him around $21 million, while Advantage had committed to take one division for $15 million. The deal was signed on 31 May 1999 and announced the following day.[16] Williams later lamented Gallagher's swift footwork, saying he'd made a 'lower price' sale to Gallaghers 'as a quid pro quo for the buyer agreeing to retain his ethos and management style'.[17] But with the company in serious trouble, its survival depended on finding a solution that actually worked.

And while it sounded great to have obtained two out of three of PEC's businesses effectively for $6 million, Gallagher was taking on the problematic rump. Advantage took 120 staff, 60 per cent of the revenue and most of the profits; Gallaghers was left with 149 staff, 40 per cent of the revenue and very little profit. Cardax needed further substantial investment before its long-promised profits would eventually arrive.

At the time, Advantage was a stock market darling. Since the second half of 1998, when the entrepreneur Eric Watson had bought shares cheaply and installed a young lieutenant, Evan Christian, as chairman, its share price had risen 350 per cent.[18] Many of the people working at Advantage had become instant millionaires.

The Advantage Group's progress thereafter was somewhat chequered. The PEC purchase was just one of many for the group in 1999 as its share price swelled during the e-commerce boom that was followed by the technology crash in mid-2000. Having fallen victim to the crash, the company's shares were approaching 'penny dreadful' status by 2001, but it kept operating and changed its name to Provenco in March 2003. Williams's plans for worldwide distribution through Unisys fell through.

Gallagher, meanwhile, was cock-a-hoop. Having approached the security market from the farm upwards, taking electric fences from the paddock to industrial zones, he had now acquired a genuinely high-tech company that could add much sophistication to his products. In September 1999 he predicted that Cardax would double in size in three years and reach world leadership in six years.[19]

If only it were so simple. Disentangling PEC's three businesses and their R&D operations, while trying to make sense of their financial systems to gain some insight into what elements were profitable, was a major exercise. And Cardax's problems were not going to be fixed quickly. Kahl Betham, one of Cardax's software engineers, recalls the first thing Gallagher said when he came to PEC's offices in Marton as the new owner of the company: 'Our most important task is to sell what's available today (SWAT) — guys, we're on SWAT, don't sell vapour wear; we need to keep working on the next generation and dreaming up new products, but none of that is a substitute for selling the products we have on the market right now.'[20] Both tasks, selling existing product and bringing Cardax FT to the market, proved more difficult than expected.

Nor had Gallagher bargained on the culture clash that soon began. Many of the PEC workers were naturally wary of the new owners from the north. A swift deal had seen the old company split asunder, with half of it going to a bunch of Aucklanders, and the rest owned by electric fence manufacturers from provincial rival Waikato. The agricultural types at Gallaghers knew virtually nothing about software; how could they possibly understand the Cardax business?

At first the Cardax team was reassured that it would remain in the Manawatu for the present, but within a few months, in March 2000, Gallagher announced they were relocating to Hamilton.[21] Some key personnel decided not to go. Some weren't given the option. The arrival of Margaret Comer in Marton came to be dreaded, as a fresh layer of redundancies would inevitably be announced.

Things sometimes descended into farce. In one of his first PowerPoint presentations to Cardax, Bill Gallagher thought he'd be clever by slowly changing the Cardax logo from yellow to orange over the course of the presentation. However, as Steve Bell recalls, 'he was using a crappy old projector and so nobody in the audience saw this subtle piece of humour'. So Bill pointed it out, with a grin on his face, to general rolling of eyes. Up in Hamilton, meanwhile, not everyone was impressed with the new arrivals. The old Gallagher hands soon nicknamed one of the more talented, and highly paid, Cardax men 'Fig jam' (F*** I'm Good, Just Ask Me).

It was more than just two tribes — one highly educated and theoretical, the other more down-to-earth and agricultural — eyeing each other sceptically. Over the years PEC and the Gallagher Group had evolved very different styles of management. In some ways, PEC resembled a public service atmosphere. There were pay bands, for example, based to a large degree on time served. Gallaghers had no such bands. Gallagher managers used Key Performance Indicators to evaluate performance and paid accordingly.

At PEC, a wide range of benefits, allowances and perks had accumulated over the years. Comer came down and swept most of those away, and not surprisingly she wasn't popular. She recalls arriving one day to find a witch's broom in her car park. Another time, she discovered everyone in the building was wearing a black t-shirt. To her credit, however, she drew on more than a decade's experience in human resources at Gallaghers and Franklin Machinery to manage the transition at PEC without having one personal grievance claim brought against the company. Most recognised things had to change. At the same time, the Gallagher Group provided a more structured working environment. Parts of the old PEC empire had a freewheeling atmosphere. There was a house in the nearby university town of Palmerston North where, according to Comer, 'software guys wandered in and out whenever they wanted, with very little oversight or accountability'.

The staff were shifted to Hamilton and a very different style of operation, where certain behaviours and standards were expected. Staff were encouraged to think for themselves and had open access to the boss, but there was a tight management team, a clear chain of command, clear timelines and accountability, and a healthy Waikato scepticism toward anything that might be termed 'touchy-feely'.

In the end, Bill Gallagher didn't feed the illusion that his company was a democracy, where things happened if the majority wanted it so. He would listen and communicate the best he could, but ultimately responsibility and decision-making rested with him, and he was accountable for it. His favourite line, always delivered with a grin, was: 'You may live in a democracy, you don't work in one.'

Merging these two very different styles of management was difficult. Wayne O'Halloran was hired soon after the purchase to run Cardax's operations and watched the shake-down occur: 'Some hard calls had to be made, some people left, and as far as I was concerned everyone involved was treated fairly and openly, but the key to settling things down lay in convincing the PEC guys, who felt passionate about their product, that the passion remained, even though we had a different way of operating.'[22]

And while the Cardax people had to adapt to the Hamilton environment and a new way of doing things, their arrival fundamentally altered the Gallagher Group. Margaret Comer considers it the biggest single change in the company's history: 'We were agricultural and advanced for what we did, but now we were developing sophisticated access control systems, and we had teams of software developers, totally different birds to what we'd had before. And it's been good for the company; it's lifted our R&D, raised the quality of the people we've employed, generated a better balance from graduates to more mature workers.'[23]

Amid all the tumult, bruised egos, ruffled feathers and displaced would-be prima donnas, it was clear that once things settled down the general sophistication of the Gallagher Group would be lifted to a new level, with direct benefit not just to the security side of the business but also to the agricultural side.

The inclusion of PEC also prompted Bill Gallagher to expand his board of directors to draw in broader experience. Through the Institute of Directors he found Paul Hargreaves and Richard Janes. Hargreaves had started out as an accountant in Christchurch before co-founding Computer Bureau Ltd in 1965. CBL (later named DataCom) provided shared-use computer services to a group of client companies. He was CEO through the 1980s and early 1990s as DataCom rose to become one of the country's leading IT companies, and remained a director in 2000. Since 1994 he had been chief executive of the Crown Research Institute NIWA (the National Institute of Water and Atmospheric Research Ltd).

Janes, a chemical engineer turned company director, had chaired the Wools of New Zealand board and held many other directorships in agricultural industries. He brought a particular expertise in trademark branding to the table. Meantime, Gallagher director Rick Christie stood down after an investment company of which he was a board member invested in a company competing against Gallaghers.

The expanded board had plenty to worry about with Cardax during its first couple of years within the Gallagher Group. Cardax FT, the next-generation product, was not a few months away from launch as Gallagher had initially hoped. But the company was fortunate in persuading Shell Australia to give it the large job of providing access control for its new head office in Melbourne as its beta test site for the Cardax FT system — providing the opportunity to test the system in a real-life situation before its release to the market.

Ultimately the controller in Melbourne would govern Cardax systems on sites all across Australia. Cardax's general manager Graham Dawson recognised that it was unique opportunity for them to test all of FT's new features 'with a fully understanding client who realises that they are at the leading edge' of the new technology.[24] Installation began in December 1999.

As it turned out, the client needed to be understanding. Dawson concedes they took on the task 'a bit early', prompted by the client's concerns about an anticipated Y2K problem. With the FT system, the controller was designed to plug into the standard IP infrastructure and computer network, using internet-based access controllers protected by encrypted links. This was a significant advance on earlier systems and on anything their rivals offered, but lots of things could go wrong. Steve Bell, the development manager for Cardax, recalls: 'It was an extremely stressful time for everyone. In some ways it was a textbook case of how not to release software; we put it in and struggled to get it to work. At the start, it was a major triumph for us if our server stayed up without crashing immediately. Then after a while we got it to run for a week, which was awesome. We had the whole R&D team working on resolving the issues and supporting the guys on the ground in Melbourne. By the winter, we'd reached the point where it would last a month, but we were still finding bugs and struggling to persuade all the features to work. So it was a major challenge to be thrown into the deep end and to come out alive with the customer still liking us. We managed that and, for all the anxiety, the Shell head office experience significantly sped up the development of the product, because under the stress of a real-life, large and complex system we learnt a lot of lessons fast.'[25]

It didn't seem fast to Bill Gallagher. Initial projections had Cardax FT ready for general release early in 2000. This was revised to September 2000, but it was not until April 2001 that the team felt it had sufficiently stabilised Shell's head office and that the Cardax FT version 1 could be launched generally. In its relocation of designers to Hamilton the company had lost a few key team members, which had slowed things down further. Cardax first displayed FT at the Security Tech Expo in Sydney at the end of March 2001, before taking it to another trade show in Birmingham, England, in May. Version 1, however, only had basic access control and alarm monitoring. It wasn't until Cardax FT version 2 was released in October that year that the whole system became widely available.

In the meantime, through 1999, 2000 and most of 2001, the Cardax business stumbled along in 'Death Valley', with the promise of a fancy new system coming down the track making it difficult to sell existing products. The rapid relocation of manufacturing from Marton to Hamilton spawned a few production and quality problems, compounding the pressure. Management reported 'disappointing results' and sales woefully missed target. In the year to June 2000 Cardax managed sales of just over $10 million and lost $2.6 million before tax; in the following year sales had fallen to $8.9 million and the loss was $1.5 million. Stressful indeed. And all the way through, the huge complexity of the FT system and its problems drew heavily on the group's R&D resources and senior management time. The Gallagher Group was making a major investment in this new business; Bill Gallagher ruefully noted in the 2001 annual report that while the security side of the business 'continues to display vast potential . . . to date we have little to show for our efforts'.

The primary driver in buying PEC was to marry Cardax's access control technology with Gallagher's perimeter fencing technology to create a unique product. However, that was clearly going to take a while. Once FT was up and running well, the next phase would be to incorporate the perimeter fencing. As it was, the two lines of the security business had different distributors in Australia and Holland and only a partially overlapping market. And while the perimeter fencing business was not growing in the leaps and bounds for which Gallagher had hoped, at least it was profitable in most countries. Birger Kirsten, a South African, was in charge of the PowerFence business, and his regional offices and contractors were now making good progress on British infrastructure projects and prisons in South Africa and Australia.

The toughest job lay in convincing nervous officials that electric fencing was safe for people with devices like pacemakers. Charles Tomas, a government purchaser in South Australia, started using Gallagher PowerFence for prisons there in 1999 and recalls 'quite a rigmarole' to win over prison officers and officialdom. 'No one wanted to be the first to use electric fencing,' he says, 'but once we had a reference site up and working well, we were away.'[26]

Ironically, however, he had been won over to PowerFence by its greater reliability in detecting intrusions without excessive false alarms. Existing systems, by contrast, tended to generate endless false alarms and entailed high maintenance costs. That the PowerFence also provided a few thousand volts of deterrent was almost a secondary consideration.

To Bill Gallagher's fury, however, New Zealand's Corrections Department wasn't interested in the product. He grizzled in one interview in 2001: 'They're too busy chasing escaped criminals to look at new technology . . . It's hard to be a disciple in your own country.'[27]

Still, the security business made for some exciting projects. Veldman & Dijkstra's security wing won the job of installing an electric security fence around the site used for the trial of the two Libyans accused of the bombing of Pan Am Flight 103 over Lockerbie in 1988. The circumstances were unusual since the trial, which began in May 2000, took place in a specially convened Scottish court, located at a disused United States Air Force base near Utrecht, in the Netherlands. Security was tight, and it was real coup to have a Gallagher PowerFence system entrusted with the task of providing one line of defence. When Bill and Judi Gallagher were shown around the installation in early 2001, the usually trigger-happy CEO was slightly miffed that he wasn't allowed to take photos of his company's masterly work.

Adding to the mix of excitement, expectation, frustration and downright agitation during these first two years after the acquisition of PEC, the Gallagher team had resolved on another great overhaul of its IT and manufacturing operations system. The impetus for the upgrade had come well before the PEC purchase. In 1998 Bill Gallagher, Bruce Munro and Rob Booth took stock of the company's operational performance and concluded it needed to go up another notch. Steve Tucker was put in charge of an operations strategy that had four drivers: to be sufficiently flexible to handle the peaks and troughs of demand efficiently; to be more responsive to customers; to manufacture at the lowest cost; but also to lift quality standards.[28] Tucker says they knew they were pretty good in each of those areas, but also that they were not 'world class' in any of them.

It was now coming up to 10 years since the company had installed the MRP II system, and according to its reckoning Gallaghers had reached class B by the standards of its creator, Oliver Wight. To go to the next level required another gear change. The smart money was now on Enterprise Resource Planning (ERP) packages, which introduced new software systems that drilled down further into the manufacturing process to achieve additional efficiencies.

In 1999 Gallaghers settled on using SAP software and invested around $2 million in a programme to implement the new system through 2000. The software only took them so far; the real investment came in spending the time to analyse exactly where the snagging points were and in understanding the processes and patterns of demand coming from the handful of vital customers, such as Veldman

& Dijkstra, so that these were met in the most efficient manner.

As usual, the transition was fraught with difficulties. The implementation of SAP coincided with the transfer of Cardax manufacturing to the Hamilton site. The circuit boards were made at Gallaghers' main plant, and the access cards were manufactured next door at Gallagher Plastics. At the same time, a worldwide shortage of electronic components created headaches on the supply side. Then, on the demand side, good global agricultural conditions and successful Gallagher marketing led to a spike in demand for its energisers and electric fence accessories. The result by February 2000, as Booth reported, was that 'operations are stressed to say the least'. By May the company simply wasn't able to keep up with supply. Gallagher lamented to his board, 'This is our four-year cycle, and the third cycle in my memory of being unable to supply.' However, he reminded everyone that the object of the SAP implementation was to try to break this cycle by improving the company's ability to predict a sudden surge in demand and to be prepared for it.

With customers around the world howling for Gallaghers product, the workforce swelled to 415 and production ran 24 hours a day until the crisis passed. And in time the ERP package paid good dividends. The most striking figure was the reduction in the work-in-progress at the factory from around 8000 units at any one point in time to around 800. This came from very careful juggling of batch sizes for various components. Steve Tucker describes their thinking: 'Previously we'd worked out the most efficient minimum batch sizes for each component and had stuck to it. But as a result, we were making 500 of one component, for example, and only 20 of the next component in the line. This meant that the other 480 of the first component went into stock. Why were we doing that?

'It may have been most efficient for each component, but overall it was highly inefficient. So we worked hard to align the minimum batch sizes to be as consistent as possible through the production process. It's not always practical. There are still examples, like in plastic injection moulding, where we might make a run of 1000 but only use 200. It's just physically not economical to change the die. But overall we've been able to greatly reduce the number of components in the system at any one time.'[29]

The same thinking also enabled the company to substantially reduce the manufacturing throughput time for each product. This

ABOVE The Gallagher TSI combines a computer, weigh scale and animal performance software to enable farmers to measure individual animal and herd performance easily.

had a major secondary benefit in improving its ability to detect quality problems in real time. As Tucker describes it: 'Our old style of work-centre management meant that quality issues weren't identified in real time because it was typically a week, if not more, before some components reached the next work centre, where a problem might be identified, such as a scratch in the plastic. In the meantime, hundreds more of the same component could have been produced with the same flaw. With the new system, by contrast, we'd only have made 10 or so in one work centre before they were passed straight away to the next one. So we now had the ability to pick up quality issues in real time.'[30]

So, as well as reducing work-in-progress, and thus working capital tied up in stock, and reducing the percentage of product rejected by picking up quality problems earlier on, the revamp of the group's operating process produced a 40 per cent reduction in product design time, a 75 per cent reduction in manufacturing lead time, and a 50 per cent increase in delivery speed over the course of two years.[31]

Such dividends, however, were all in the future in mid-2000, when Cardax was losing money and Gallaghers' factory couldn't keep up with supply on the agricultural side. Raising the stakes further, meantime, was the decision to build a new five-storey headquarters for the company in front of the factory. The influx of white-collar workers from Cardax meant there wasn't sufficient office space to go around, and besides, the group's existing two levels of offices at the front end of the old engineering factory, which had been built in the 1970s, were inadequate even before Cardax's people were taken into account.

Judi Gallagher, who had a strong design background, worked closely with architect Peter Chibnall on both the exterior and interior plans and layout of the building. With its curving black-glass front facing State Highway 1, bisected by a five-storey-high atrium that later on was capped by a giant Gallagher logo, the new headquarters made a very clear statement: this was a serious and successful international business. A new cafeteria, named Jo's after the famed horse that had inspired Bill Gallagher senior's first tinkering with electric fences, occupied the western side of the ground floor and opened onto a courtyard.

Bill Gallagher junior's office and the boardroom were on the third floor, with half of the top floor reserved for open-plan function rooms for conferences and presentations. Rising forcefully as it did above the surrounding low-lying factories, the new offices from the third floor up offered wonderful views over Hamilton to the north and out across distant farms to the massive volcanic formation of Mt Pirongia to the south.

The building was completed in April 2001 and formally opened by the Governor-General, Dame Silvia Cartwright, on 15 June, amid great celebrations. It received a New Zealand Institute of Architects award and transformed working conditions for those housed within it, but as Bill Gallagher noted in his next board report, 'now we're settled in we have to keep our sales up to stand the extra cost'.

Fortunately, the traditional agricultural side of the business was doing very well, helped by a sinking New Zealand dollar which increased margins on exports. The electric fencing business alone produced $47 million in sales and nearly $6 million in profit after tax in the year to June 2000, rising to $53 million in sales the following year with profits slightly reduced, but still strong. The Australian and US markets, in particular, were booming. Between them they took nearly 45 per cent of Gallaghers' agricultural exports. Meantime, Franklin Machinery, the maker of gates and hinges, was humming along, with record sales of nearly $10 million in the year to June 2001 and profits over $2 million. This humble business in Pukekohe was easily eclipsing Cardax.

On the farming side, Gallaghers' business continued to evolve and expand along a logical path. From being a manufacturer of electric fence energisers, Gallaghers had steadily extended its range of related accessories through the 1970s and 1980s. In the 1990s it had added gates and their associated hardware, and had described itself as leaders in the 'animal containment' business.

By the late 1990s Bill Gallagher could see that the industry was moving slowly but surely in the direction of electronic identification of animals, so that the productivity of individual animals could be better measured, and regulators, and ultimately customers, could gain greater assurance about the origins of the meat, wool or dairy products on the market. If Gallaghers was going to chase the value in the industry and grow, one obvious direction was to expand its offering to encompass 'animal management', rather than simply containment.

A good starting point was weigh-scales for stock. Regular measurement of an animal's weight provides a powerful tool for identifying the productive and eliminating the unproductive. For Gallagher, who was in a hurry, it was simplest and fastest to buy an existing business, and in 1998 he had settled on an Australian firm, the International Scale Company, which made Ruddweigh Scales. David Mullen had been Ruddweigh's distributor in Australia for several years and the product had combined well with Gallagher fencing.

Following the successful formula used with Franklin Machinery, in the winter of 1999 Gallagher bought 50 per cent of the company from its founders, Bruce and Sally Thompson, with a view to taking the rest a little later on, assuming all went well. The plan was that Ruddweigh Scales would provide extra cashflow to help Gallaghers develop its own technology in electronic identification readers. There were obvious potential synergies between this new electronic bent to the agricultural business and the access control technology that Gallaghers had acquired with Cardax.

Meantime, the Gallagher Group had received an unexpected bonus from its purchase of PEC in 1999. It had uncovered a little goldmine in the petrol pump business that John Williams appeared to have regarded as a dying branch of his empire, a mechanical hangover from earlier times. Bill Gallagher recalls: 'Amongst the background papers for the PEC purchase there was a 12-page treatise from the advisers on how to close down the petrol pumps business quietly. I looked at numbers and they'd allocated $1.25 million in overheads to petrol pumps. Hell, I thought, what's wrong with $250k? They had all sorts of people: a pay clerk who no longer did the pay, a travel agent on the staff, a system improvement manager who I didn't think could tell me how much his improvements had saved and even a gym instructor.

'Naturally enough, the core staff were nervous and asked me about their future. I said simply we need to get cost out of the business and out of the product. If we can make it profitable, your future is good, if not then you'll have to find something else to do. So your future is in your hands, and boy did they respond. Little things

ABOVE A BP fuel pump, the surprisingly successful product Gallagher gained from its purchase of PEC Ltd.

like the phone bill dropped $40k, the power bill shed $30k, and in a set of pumps that cost $15k to produce, they found $2500 savings and the pumps worked better. And in all this they were guided by Tony Dobbs, a long-serving PEC employee, who we installed as general manager. Within six months we had a profitable business. Within two years it was very profitable.'

It soon became Bill Gallagher's favourite joke when doing the rounds with Cardax customers, one that Steve Bell heard on countless occasions: 'Oh, I bought PEC for Cardax and it is losing me money, but lo and behold the petrol pump business, which was supposed to be a dog, is going gangbusters.' Whether the joke was designed to engender sympathy in the minds of Cardax customers or something else, Bell could never quite divine.

There was no doubt, however, that the petrol pumps' surprising profitability helped offset Cardax's losses. For the year to June 2001 Dobbs was pleased to report sales of $12 million and a net profit before tax of $1.3 million, which was 420 per cent up on budget. 'Morale and the work ethic are extremely good,' he reported.

All in all, the two new divisions from PEC — Cardax and the petrol pumps — had added around $20 million to the group's turnover, which along with organic growth in Gallaghers' existing businesses lifted the group's sales from $54 million prior to the purchase in 1999 to $83 million in 2000 and $95 million in the year to June 2001. Profitability had not lifted much, but once Cardax came right future prospects looked bright indeed.

In 2001, at yet another time of great national angst, when the gloss had come off New Zealand's reforms, Helen Clark's Labour government had alienated much of the business community, external migration was rising and the New Zealand dollar was falling like a stone, the Gallagher Group once more emerged like a shining star amid general gloom. It was fast approaching the status of a $100 million company and remained a world leader in its core industry.

Ten years after his first visit to New Zealand, Harvard professor Michael Porter was invited back to New Zealand for *Catching the Knowledge Wave*, a conference jointly sponsored by the government and the University of Auckland. His prognosis was somewhat pessimistic: Nothing much had changed, so that New Zealand

ABOVE Gallaghers Deputy CEO, Steve Tucker.

was still generating relatively few globally competitive businesses. The country's relative lack of private sector R&D was a constant complaint.[32]

The Gallagher Group, which now employed around 60 in its R&D department, spending $5 million annually, remained an outlier, building on New Zealand's international reputation for good grassland technology.[33] The Gallagher story was now a staple in books celebrating New Zealand entrepreneurship, such as *No 8 Wire: The Best of Kiwi Ingenuity* and *World Famous in New Zealand: How New Zealand's Leading Firms Became World-Class Competitors*.[34]

By 2001 the Gallagher Group had put the upheaval of Neil Richardson's and John Walley's exits well behind it. And while the company was still going through a period of transition as it absorbed three new businesses in Cardax, PEC Fuel Pumps and Ruddweigh Scales, it was regaining a measure of stability. Rob Booth, who was a transitional figure, stood down from his executive role in the firm after a bout of illness in the winter of 2001, although he remained a director. Bill Gallagher was once more fully engaged with the business. From the board level, Bruce Munro contributed substantially with strategic advice and a continuing active role in shepherding the evolution of Gallaghers' sometimes fractious but always highly productive partnership with its Dutch distributors Veldman & Dijkstra.

In Hamilton, 32-year-old Steve Tucker's emergence as the leading executive below Bill Gallagher had been recognised by his appointment as an executive director in 2000, in addition to his role as group operations manager. He would soon be packed off to the Darden School of Business at the University of Virginia for further management training. Compared with the mercurial and at times flashy Booth, Tucker was relatively quiet and down to earth, but he commanded the respect of his team, was straightforward in his dealings and knew how to run an operation profitably.

Steve Hoffman in animal management systems marketing, Birger Kirsten in perimeter security and Margaret Comer in corporate services were all now long-serving executives. Comer's role was broad: 'Bill,' she once memorably remarked, 'is like this huge jet going through the place and I'm cleaning up bits behind him.'[35] Meantime, Gallagher had found a good chief financial officer in Geoff Copstick. With Tony Dobbs succeeding in the petrol pump business, the main area of continuing instability was leadership of the Cardax division.

Having turned 60 in January 2001 Bill Gallagher was once more fighting fit and full of enthusiasm, particularly for the challenge of building a world-beating security business, but also to increase the company's strength in the wider field of animal management. Tucker observed a man with a renewed sense of purpose: 'The most striking characteristic of Bill is that he is incredibly enthusiastic and 110 per cent committed to the task. And linked to that is the fact he has an exceptionally enquiring mind. It never ceases to amaze me how much stuff he's really interested in, whether it be global warming or the economic prospects in Azerbaijan, as well as everything related to the business — productivity, tariffs, taxes, opportunities, people, politics, policies, technical matters, engineering matters, electronic developments, anything that comes along. And he can talk insightfully on all those topics, which makes working for him an immense challenge and a pleasure.'[36]

Judi, meantime, ensured that he was taking fewer risks with his health, but he wasn't easing up on his diving. And his role as travelling salesman for the firm continued to have its hazards. Thomas Friederichs, the manager of Gallagher Security (USA) Inc, Gallaghers' perimeter fencing business in the US, recalls a couple of incidents that weren't that atypical: 'On one of his Florida visits Bill was keen to spend a day out diving at the Bahamas. Judi grabbed me before we left: "Thomas, he's not to dive alone." Of course, the moment we get out there the weather's getting rough and he's off the boat diving on his own. And a few of us are sitting on the boat as the minutes go by, drinking our beer and getting increasingly nervous. After 45 minutes I'm not far off having a heart attack, imagining the stories in the newspapers, "NZ entrepreneur missing . . . diving alone . . . irresponsible hosts . . .", when he pops up quite a ways away. He'd wanted to look at a wreck that he'd seen.

'On another visit, Judi and Bill happened to be in Florida on the fourth of July. We invited them to our usual redneck celebration consisting of a horde of illegal fireworks in a field across the road and plenty of beef and beer. Midway through, one of the bigger rockets tipped over after it had been lit and just about took Bill's head off. He was sitting down having a glass of wine and just happened to lean over to get something in the instant that this mortar flew by horizontally. Judi was not happy.'[37]

RIGHT Margaret Comer, who rose through the business as it grew, starting as Bill Gallagher's PA. She is now director of the company's corporate services.

10

THE ROAD TO BUCKINGHAM PALACE: 2002–06

Chapter ten

THE ROAD TO BUCKINGHAM PALACE: 2002–06

Bill sees opportunities that no one else even thinks about. He gets enthused, and we have to get enthused as well. Sometimes the idea won't come together, other times it will, but there's always a steady flow of entrepreneurial ideas. And then when he's got something between his teeth, he doesn't let go. Be it at your peril to ignore the dog with his bone.

— WAYNE O'HALLORAN, OPERATIONS MANAGER, GALLAGHER SECURITY

In September 2004 a fathers' rights activist, Jason Hatch, seized a split-second opportunity during a tour of Buckingham Palace to scale a couple of walls and clamber onto a balcony where, dressed as Batman, he unfurled a 'Fathers 4 Justice' banner. The 32-year-old painter and decorator from Cheltenham had lost access to his children several years earlier and *Batman* was the last film he had seen with his son. Since then he had been protesting from various high-profile vantage points, pathetically dressed as the superhero of both their dreams. 'I may not be able to see my kids,' he told reporters, 'but they can see me.'[1]

Whatever sympathy his desperation might have aroused, his success in breaching the palace's defences was a security fiasco. Sir John Stevens, the Metropolitan Police Commissioner, said that Hatch was 18 seconds away from being shot, and that it was 'unacceptable' for officers to have to decide instantly whether an intruder was a protester or a terrorist. Scrambling, amid numerous investigations, for an effective, non-lethal means of preventing further such embarrassment, the Royal Household turned to Allen Fencing, one of Gallaghers' channel partners in the UK (firms that were the 'channel' to market). Within a few weeks a Gallagher electric fence had been welded into place at a number of vulnerable points.

A London police source was quoted as saying, 'The installation of the fence is the strongest measure yet taken to protect against intruders. It will administer a shock to anyone who touches it, temporarily disabling them and giving police time to make an arrest.'[2] Although the police didn't mention names or quantify the shock, back in Hamilton Gallagher jubilantly pointed out that the Queen was being protected by his company's energiser.[3] If the Caped Crusader tried again, he'd get a thrill from the 8000 volts. Holy smoke, Batman!

The Gallagher PowerFence had come a long way since the first formal efforts to build a perimeter security business 15 years earlier. Gallaghers had succeeded in establishing both the industry and itself as global leaders, entrusted with the most difficult jobs. The call-up at Buckingham Palace had followed years of painstaking work in the UK. As well as protecting the many installations of National Grid and British Gas, waterworks and telecommunications sites had become standard fare for Gallagher PowerFences.

The horrific terrorist attacks in New York and Washington DC on September 11, 2001, had raised security levels around the world, and Gallaghers was well placed to benefit from increased security requirements around vital pieces of infrastructure. The change was not instantaneous, but the opportunities gathered through 2002, particularly in the US after Gallaghers' subsidiary there gained GSA status, a preferred supplier grade for US government buyers. Now on the inside track, Gallaghers won several large US Navy orders and other US government jobs to put perimeter fencing around highly sensitive sites, the details of which unfortunately cannot be released.

Frustratingly, however, just as the US PowerFence business was finally starting to generate some operating profits after years of business development, the company found itself embroiled in a lengthy and expensive court case against a former employee. Meantime, another US staff member departed after it was discovered that the company credit card had been used to pay for plastic surgery. There was some debate as to whether the results should be regarded as company assets, but the reality wasn't funny. It was never easy trying to run businesses scattered all around the world from a central point in Hamilton, New Zealand.

Such distractions aside, Gallaghers' security business was finally progressing in the US. Thomas Friederichs had taken over management of Gallagher Security (USA) Inc in May 2005. He knew that his ultimate boss was a great enthusiast for this relatively small, but growing, part of the Gallagher empire. After years of selling electric fences to farmers, it was not surprising that Bill Gallagher found it thrilling for his company to have an active role on the fringes of the 'war on terror'. He joined Friederichs whenever the opportunity arose, and in so doing displayed the qualities that in most instances ensured a loyal following among Gallagher staff around the world.

Friederichs recalls: 'Bill and I did a military show at the highly secured Quantico Marine Corps base in Virginia. You have to be invited to present a product there, so it was quite an opportunity. It was easiest for us to drive from Orlando, pulling a big trailer. And Bill comes with me in the truck on this long drive. He's the only guy I know who can doze off in the car and then when he wakes up pick up the conversation right where we left off. Coming off the base one day, I realised I had a problem with the trailer. Quick as a flash, he's out and under the trailer figuring out what the problem is. It's about 110 degrees, with high humidity and Bill's wearing a suit. But no matter. He loves his work and he rolls up his sleeves. You can't help working hard for a guy like that.'[4]

Gallagher Security (USA) Inc had its office in Sanford, Florida, around 50 kilometres north of Orlando. It was also responsible for the perimeter security fencing business in the Caribbean and South America. Friederichs spent a lot of time down in Panama, keeping watch over a large project there to secure a series of control and repeater towers in remote and relatively inaccessible spots along the length of the canal. For years these had been regularly plundered for copper, solar panels and anything else of value, and the PowerFence for the first time successfully deterred the bandits. Conditions were not great in Panama, but they were worse in Curaçao, in the Dutch Antilles, where one of Gallaghers'

ABOVE A corner of Buckingham Palace showing the Gallaghers electric fence installed after a man dressed as Batman made his way through the palace's defences.

channel partners erected perimeter fencing around a prison full of women who had been used as drug mules by Colombian traffickers.

In each country Gallaghers' footprint was a little different. Over nearly 30 years a structure had built up around the agricultural fencing business. On the security side of Gallaghers' business, PowerFence distributors and channel partners had sprouted here and there throughout the 1990s. Then with the purchase of PEC in 1999, Gallaghers inherited a network of small regional offices that dealt with a number of independent channel partners for Cardax. Many of the Cardax partners weren't interested in perimeter fencing, and likewise many of the PowerFence distributors had no expertise or entrée into the world of software and access control. As Bill Gallagher puts it: 'While Cardax's and PowerFence's end customers were often the same, the dealers and channel partners were quite different. The fencing business was dominated by what the British called "hairy armed fence builders", for whom software and programming was a bit of a mystery. Whereas the access control guys are technos — good at software and at configuring systems. But get them to build a fence and the strainer posts fall out. So, it wasn't necessarily a natural fit.'

Some, however, saw the opportunity to integrate the products. One of the earliest integrators was the AES Group of Thailand, led by Henny Beeber. An experienced and successful Cardax distributor, Beeber was awarded a contract in 2002 to install an electric fence system around the perimeter of the Bank of Thailand Note Printing Facility in Bangkok. He used the Gallagher Trophy Electric Fence System and integrated the perimeter fencing with Kalatel CCTV equipment, so that the bank could use CCTV to watch any intruders detected trying to penetrate the electric fence perimeter.

Having completed the first job so well, AES was chosen by the Bank of Thailand to be its preferred supplier and more projects kept rolling in. Commencing in 2003, AES was given the task of installing Cardax security systems for the bank's Cash Centres located in 10 provinces around Thailand, its new ink plant and its note printing facility just outside of Bangkok. For these and subsequent projects, the access control systems were integrated with CCTV, alarm sensors, perimeter protection, and additional PowerFence at the new note printing centre. And so the business grew and grew within Thailand, Cambodia and Laos, establishing Gallagher

Security Systems as a key player in the regional security market.

Bill Gallagher and Beeber had clicked immediately. An outspoken Jewish New Yorker, who had been schooled at Cornell University and spent time in the early 1980s working on the Moroccan air defence system, Beeber had settled in Bangkok in 1988, initially to upgrade the Royal Thai air defence system. He had formed a partnership in 1992 with Yip In Tsoi and had been selling Cardax product ever since. Soon after Gallaghers took over the Cardax business, Bill and Judi visited Bangkok. Beeber recalls, 'Bill and I instantly bonded because we realised we were both avid divers. We went out to dinner and he's an interesting guy: he's technical, business-savvy, well-spoken, sociable and gregarious. That combination makes him one of a kind.'[5] From the Gallaghers' perspective, their life and their business had just become more interesting for having met the American expatriate and heard his stories.

Gallagher Security grew on the back of efforts like those of Beeber all around the world. Ruswin Locksmith & Security was a small operation in Townsville, Queensland, that began using Gallaghers' PowerFence systems for perimeter security and graduated to Cardax over the years. As Ruswin's business expanded to Papua New Guinea and Indonesia, Gallaghers' products travelled with it, breaking down barriers as it entered each market.

Ruswin's man in Indonesia, Stuart Neal, remembers dealing with the owners of a major gold and copper mine on the island of Sumbawa in 2004. The site was very remote and relied on a communications tower on the top of a nearby hill that could be accessed easily only by helicopter. But local crooks kept finding a way up the hill to extract all the valuables from the site, at great cost and inconvenience to the owners. The simple solution, Neal told them, was a PowerFence. 'Oh no,' the mine manager said, 'an electric fence would be culturally insensitive; the Indonesians don't like them.'[6]

Two more break-ins later, however, Neal's phone rang: 'Get that freakin' fence here, now!' In short order they had it up, and before long an alarm came through that someone was interfering with the fence. The operators were able to pan the CCTV camera down to watch the invaders try to get through. One was zapped and they all raced off. Meantime, the camera operator captured a still photograph of their faces, and by the time they had made it down the hill the local police were waiting to arrest them. Over the years, other Gallagher products were added to the Sumbawa mining operation, including a Cardax access control system covering more than 500 doors.

On the Cardax side of the security business, Cardax FT's greatest test came in India in the early 2000s. In 2001 Reliance Industries, the subcontinent's petrochemicals, communications, power and textiles behemoth, resolved to install the Cardax access control system at its new Dhirubhai Ambani Knowledge Centre. This was a 56 hectare technology park, named after Reliance's founder and located on the Thane-Belapur Road, Koparkhairane, in Navi Mumbai. Some 15,000 men and women would soon work there, primarily for Reliance's communications division.

Winning the contract was hard enough. Ian Meadows, then a technical account manager for Cardax, remembers that the company had come to the attention of Reliance in the mid-1990s. A worker from Cardax's first channel partner in India, IPSS, had shifted to a role within the Reliance conglomerate and had helped open the door for some smaller jobs.[7] Reliance then introduced Cardax's New Zealand staff to Digital Alarm Technologies (DATS), which took over from IPSS as Cardax's Indian channel partner, and it was through DATS that Cardax began a long and arduous competitive process for the Knowledge Centre. Graham Dawson describes the Reliance men as 'the hardest negotiators I've ever come across'. After a year and a half working with them on the technical side of the brief, Dawson recalls, 'they then brought in the commercial guys and it was shocking. We had to be prepared to walk away.'[8] Eventually Dawson and his colleagues defeated a rival Israeli firm for the job and work on installation began in 2003.

That's when their real problems began. Each of the campus's 15,000 employees had an access card, and with a 24-hour command centre and much movement to, from and within the site, the Cardax system had to cope with up to 150,000 events a day. As Meadows admits, 'the paint was still a bit wet on the FT system and the massive demand on the controller kept busting it'. But they had been given the job, not simply because technically Cardax had the best chance of managing the huge volumes, but also because the Reliance managers wanted a company that would not walk away when the inevitable problems arose. They had been burnt in the past by multinationals that had completed massive jobs, taken their money and disappeared.

Meadows and other technical support people spent months shuffling between Hamilton and Mumbai until all the bugs were fixed. He now observes, 'The system has worked perfectly ever since, laying the foundation of a good relationship with both arms of Reliance.' The project also assisted the development of Cardax FT. Solving the problems generated in Mumbai helped make the product much more robust. And being able to list such a high-profile contract as Reliance Industries in its history provided a real boost to Cardax and Gallaghers generally in India. In 2003 PowerFence was installed in Parliament House in New Delhi and the Indian Space Research Organisation had a Gallagher PowerFence erected around its perimeter.

Closer to home, the Australian market was going well for Cardax. The universities were a stronghold, and in 2000 the Tertiary Education Gallagher Users Group (TEGUG) was established to hold biannual meetings to network, discuss issues and share solutions. This proved a masterstroke. The big universities who were already Cardax customers talked to their peers, and in short order Cardax was being used in 31 out of the 33 major tertiary institutions across Australia. Bill Gallagher attended some of the early meetings and quickly saw their worth: 'In the early days these used to be quite fractious. Some guy would start sounding off about why he couldn't do something, that Cardax was missing some important functions. And we soon learnt to shut our mouths, because inevitably some other guy would stand up and say, "Well we're doing it with the same system you've got, and this is how." So it was an excellent way to gather robust feedback from our customers, even though in many instances the problems corrected themselves.'

Strong defence relationships between New Zealand and Australia helped Cardax gain opportunities in the high-security end of the market. In 2004 Cardax FT was modified to meet Australian type 1 classification, the highest level, so that it could be sold to its military and sensitive government sites, mainly for intruder alarms. The result, Cardax Ultra Sec, extended the levels of encryption already available in Cardax FT to new levels, and was designed to protect against a technical attack. Over the following years, it was rolled out to numerous sites, including the Lucas Heights nuclear reactor in New South Wales.

The strength of the Gallaghers offering was the sophisticated and flexible command centre that had been developed for Cardax. It was capable of incorporating not only perimeter fencing but a host of other related products. Charles Tomas, a purchasing official for South Australian prisons and other government facilities, was one customer who had quickly registered Cardax's unique value proposition.

Tomas recalls: 'The biggest benefit we saw was that Cardax provided an open platform. Traditionally, you had been a captive client group; you would buy product A, that could only be serviced by A, and you were charged a premium for it, and because it was all proprietary you either had to use A for any changes or upgrades or be faced with the enormous cost of throwing the whole lot out and starting again. Cardax really shook up the market because it had multiple partners, which meant you could have several firms tendering for installation, maintenance and upgrades. As a government purchaser I was seriously interested in that.

'More than that, the Cardax software had open architecture with the ability to integrate third-party products. Again, unlike some of the traditional proprietary providers which locked all of these up, with Cardax you could search for the most competitive provider of each different aspect. A prison might have between six and eight major subsystems — CCTV, biometrics, sophisticated intercoms systems, access control, perimeter, x-ray machines, etc. Having competition potentially at each level made a big difference to the overall price. And with the Cardax Command Centre drawing together all these strands you ended up with a more coherent system. Previously you'd have to have a dozen computers on the main desk. Cardax was able to interface these into one platform solution without costing a fortune. It is the glue that holds the other parts together.'[9]

But, as ever, the product was only part of the story. For Tomas, the values that lay behind the Gallagher products were equally important as he transitioned from being a client within the South Australian public service to setting himself up as a private consultant advising a range of government and private sector clients on specialist products. He observes: 'Having dealt with a lot of businesses, I found that many are not based around integrity. Whereas that is clearly important to Cardax and the Gallagher Group. They're interested in seeing their channel partners succeeding and in building long-term relationships. As an outsider looking in, the first thing you notice is the number of long-serving staff, people in Australia like Steve Simpson and Kel Bartley. There's obvious job satisfaction there and that gives you confidence. There's a sense that they're leaving a legacy in the stuff they sell you. And, right at the top, Bill's the guy you can ring up and talk to. He'll give you his home phone number, which is a clear differentiator from the other big security businesses around town. I'm not a huge customer, but Bill has come and stayed at our home for three days. He was down on his hands and knees playing with my three-year-old son and his train set, really getting to know him. That's what makes him who he is; this acute business sense combined with a real commitment to relationship-building.'[10]

But, as we've seen, Bill Gallagher is not all warm and cuddly. By 2003, after four years of ownership and heavy investment, Cardax still hadn't returned a profit. Turnover for security — both perimeter security and Cardax — had fallen two years running to little more than $16 million. In those circumstances, Gallagher was more than capable of some tough talking. General managers of Cardax who did not produce the goods were replaced. Gallagher kept up the pressure until the mind-set was right.

Steve Bell, one of the old hands from PEC, watched the slow transition: 'In the PEC era we built up infrastructure and people without growing the sales. John Williams's stated goal in life was to have a great place for his staff to work in. We soon came to appreciate the more realistic attitude of Bill Gallagher, which was "Make sure your sales are there before you grow", and the primary goal was to make enough money to have a stable place in which to work. Only then can it really be enjoyable. We also had to get rid of some of the gold plating we had on Cardax, some of the overly idealistic design concepts. And that's where we needed the practicality of Bill. We had to be able to get product on the market at the right price while still developing the biggest possible bang for the customer.'[11]

Kahl Betham, now in the position of strategic business executive, describes the same transition as being from 'over-engineered cool things that were too expensive and too late' to products that the market wanted now.[12] An important shift came with the addition of business analysts to the R&D group in 2002. Their job was to talk to customers, to understand their needs completely, and to have products created that met those needs. So around 2003, Cardax added the ability to monitor burglar alarms to its access control systems, working in partnership with Chubb. Once that was in place revenues began to expand substantially.

After four years of painful losses between 2000 and 2003, the security division scrambled to its first modest profit in 2004. Bill Gallagher told his board that their efforts had finally been rewarded, but everyone was conscious of the scale of the challenge they faced in extending those green shoots into a profitable global market position in security. The experience made Gallagher all the more conscious of the value New Zealand's reputation for farm technology had brought to its animal management business. Gallaghers' brand had benefited from that international reputation and, indeed, had added to it. But there was no such New Zealand reputation in the security business, no such wind at their backs.

Also in contrast to Gallaghers' agricultural business, where to some extent the industry flew under the radar of the biggest conglomerates, in security it faced some of the biggest and richest companies in the world: GE Security, Siemens, Honeywell, Chubb. These companies had immensely powerful relationships and market position. Gallaghers had to counter that strength by being more responsive and nimble. At the other end of the scale, Gallaghers' channel partners in every market battled against the myriad small security firms who would bid low for projects, usually by mistake, because they had miscalculated the costs. Such firms would come and go, but meanwhile, as they did in every contracting industry, they made it difficult for everyone.

With its higher level of sophistication, Gallaghers' reputation in the market rested to an extent on the quality of its installers. And while the company had developed a rigorous certification process, mistakes were inevitable. Gallaghers could provide the best system in the world, but if the installer had skimped on the power supply, it could be difficult. Bill Gallagher groans when thinking of some examples: 'A little bit of trouble goes a long way.'

The broader task had been made more challenging by the instability at the top of Cardax's management and the structural disjunction between the perimeter fencing and Cardax businesses within the Gallagher Group. Birger Kirsten continued to manage the perimeter fencing business worldwide, while Cardax had a succession of general managers after 1999, each struggling with the beast and none of them working particularly effectively with Kirsten. Each of the key markets had its own special flavour. In Australia, perimeter fencing was run by David Mullen's Gallagher Australia Pty, while Cardax was managed separately from New Zealand. In the UK, PowerFence had been based in Canley, near Coventry, alongside Gallaghers' animal management business. Cardax's office had been at Luton since 1991. Both businesses were relocated to Nuneaton around 2002, but two general managers, one for each business, were retained. These two men didn't see eye-to-eye, and so both businesses struggled for several years.

Progress was made in 2004 when Bill Gallagher formed Gallagher Security Management Services (GSMS), a new division in the Gallagher Group that encompassed both Cardax and perimeter security. Now Gallaghers' two security arms would be forced to wave in unison, with the vision of offering building and facility managers around the world a unique range of security options. Kirsten led the new division initially, but in 2005 Bill Gallagher took the general manager role to bring some stability to that part of the business. He appointed Curtis Edgecombe sales manager.

With the combination of Gallagher and Edgecombe, the revolving chair at the top of Gallaghers' security business finally came to a stop. The new man won Bill Gallagher's confidence and grew into the role. Edgecombe, who had moved to Hamilton from Auckland as a youngster, had a management degree from the University of Waikato and had worked with a private engineering firm in Hamilton. Immediately prior to joining Gallaghers, he had spent three years in Singapore looking after a division of Downer Engineering. Now as sales manager of GSMS he was responsible for a division that turned over nearly $25 million (around a fifth of the group's revenue). Most of its business was offshore, and much improvement was expected. Together with Wayne O'Halloran, who had joined Gallaghers a couple of years earlier from the dairy industry and now led the operations for GSMS, Edgecombe's task was to form a cohesive group that could make the most of its technically good products.

Like any good manager, Edgecombe enjoyed good timing. An extensive R&D effort on the perimeter fencing side was finally

BELOW Curtis Edgecombe.

bearing fruit. Gallaghers' PowerFence had Trophy 6 controllers from January 2001. Six months later these were superseded by the Trophy 48, which could run 48 zones and had its own software package that could measure the voltage and sense if vegetation was growing around the fence.

But while these energisers could be plugged into a Cardax FT controller, they were not fully integrated. Basically, the Cardax controller could turn the perimeter fence on and off, but not much else. In July 2006 the situation was transformed by the arrival of Trophy FT which, as Bill Gallagher puts it, 'took us from the Model T to a Rolls Royce in one step'. It brought all the features of Cardax FT to perimeter fencing — encryption, multiple time zones, multiple holidays, alarm escalations and the rest — and it could be plugged seamlessly into the Cardax FT controller as part of a wider system, encompassing access control, perimeter fencing, CCTV and anything else that was necessary, across multiple sites if need be.

Edgecombe knew he was onto a winner: 'We were one of the first in the world to put perimeter fences through high-level software and were unique in merging access control and perimeter fencing so seamlessly. And since we'd designed our own hardware and software, they worked together well. The result was more elegant and robust than anything produced by the majority of our competitors, who bought hardware in and developed software to work on it. I'd inherited Cardax FT that had been the launching pad to give us credibility in the global access control business, and which had been performing well for four years or so, and now with Trophy FT as well, we had a great opportunity to compete strongly, especially in highly regulated sectors.'[13]

By early 2006, then, Gallaghers' security business looked to be on the cusp of genuine growth. Its channel partners were generating exciting jobs all around the world, and the division was no longer losing money. But Bill Gallagher still would not have wanted to rely on it for the company's meat and drink. Fortunately, Gallaghers' traditional business continued to perform very well.

For as long as Steve Hoffman, the international sales manager for Animal Management Systems (AMS), had worked for the company, he had heard predictions that the security side of the business would soon overtake agriculture. This assertion had provided all the motivation he needed to prove it wrong every year, as Animal Management's sales continued to grow and leave the security boys well behind. Gallagher AMS boomed in 2002, producing the best operating profit to that point for the firm. Just when they seemed on top of the world, however, Hoffman and the Gallagher team found themselves under a short burst of intense fire from local competitors Tru-Test.

Having launched into direct competition with Gallaghers in the late 1990s by buying the Stafix and Speedrite electric fence brands, Tru-Test had raised the stakes further in 2001 by purchasing PEL, another well-known New Zealand brand. Under its managing director Des Scott, Tru-Test raised $10 million on capital markets for further expansion and recruited prominent Auckland businessmen Don Turkington, Mike Smith and Robin Congreve to its board.

In October 2001 Scott boasted that the company's revenues had swollen from $12.3 million a decade earlier to $107 million; its aim was to be a billion-dollar company. There was talk of an imminent IPO (initial public offering).[14] The company seemed to be following a strategy of rapid expansion through acquisition and, at first glance, it appeared to be working. Having swallowed PEL and several other businesses, Tru-Test was streaking past the Gallagher Group's revenues, which in 2001 stood at $95 million.

While not yet a serious threat internationally, Tru-Test was becoming genuinely annoying in New Zealand and Australia. It moved aggressively to lock up major distributors by offering generous, possibly even loss-leading, rebates in return for exclusive supply. Hoffman was shocked in August 2003 when one of Gallaghers' long-term dealers, Williams & Kettle, accepted the deal and shut Gallaghers out of its stores. Advising the Gallagher board of this 'very disturbing trend', Hoffman noted that Williams & Kettle was the third major Australasian retailer to accept Tru-Test's arrangements, following Wrightson and Elders.[15]

Gallaghers and Tru-Test were now locked in a fierce, sometimes desperate race for market share. Hoffman retaliated by securing exclusive supply to the Farmlands chain in New Zealand, but Gallaghers' chief financial officer Geoff Copstick was moved to sound a warning to the board: 'While so much executive team time is directed at Cardax the rest of the business risks slipping out of focus. We have seen that the Gallagher Group's historic profits are very much in Tru-Test's focus. We are vulnerable. Without drastic cost reduction or a quantum increase in revenue this year we will be struggling.'[16] Then, in another blow, Gallaghers' German distributor Allie Agratechnik defected to Tru-Test in 2003, after 23 years in the stable.

The Allies had been selling Tru-Test's weigh-scales since the 1980s and so had a long relationship with the company, but more importantly they felt encircled by the territorial expansion of Gallagher Europe under the Dijkstras and concluded they had better prospects for growth with the rival firm, with no restrictions on territory.[17] This jeopardised nearly $2 million worth of Gallagher sales in southern Germany and, worse, threatened to extend the fierce Australasian competition to the key market of continental Europe.

Bill Gallagher could take some comfort, however, from indications that the wheels were falling off Tru-Test's go-cart as it raced toward billion-dollar agribusiness status. Some institutional investors that had bought into the unlisted company in 2001 for more than $3 a share, on the expectation of a later IPO and continued growth, were grumbling by December 2003 when the value of the shares had fallen and growth had stalled. Irritation focused on Tru-Test's purchase of BrainZ Instruments Ltd, a high-risk, high-tech company in the medical field. The BrainZ investment rapidly turned sour. Tru-Test's AGM, held just before Christmas 2003, was untidy as one institutional investor successfully forced the chairman Robin Congreve to resign, while Shareholders' Association chair Bruce Sheppard strutted around wearing a milking apron and long gloves, vowing to 'clean up the board' that presided over 'either a pigsty or milking parlour'.[18]

Sensing a good opportunity, Gallagher swooped in early March 2004, securing 13 per cent of Tru-Test's shares from disgruntled investors for a mere $1.20 a share, a 'fire-sale price' in the words of *Rural News*.[19] By May Gallaghers had lifted its stake to nearly 15 per cent. It then applied to the Commerce Commission for permission to launch a takeover bid for Tru-Test outright. Des Scott and the Tru-Test board resisted stoutly, arguing that a takeover would lead to Gallaghers' domination of the New Zealand electric fence industry. Gallagher countered by pointing out that New Zealand had no barriers to international competition and that his bid was in the best

ABOVE Gallaghers' message to the Brazilians. Relax — you're surrounded by great security.

interests of Tru-Test shareholders and customers. He also criticised Tru-Test directors for spending considerable company funds defending against his bid. To mollify the Commerce Commission, Gallagher offered to sell the PEL electric fence brand if successful with the takeover. This wasn't sufficient and Gallaghers' request was turned down flat, on the grounds that it would lead to undue concentration of power in the domestic market.[20]

Three months later Gallagher launched a second bid, this time telling the Commerce Commission that if successful it would divest the Stafix brand, which held greater market share than PEL in New Zealand. To maintain pressure on the Tru-Test board, he circulated a letter to Tru-Test shareholders before the upcoming AGM in which he described the company's performance as 'pitiful'. Once more, however, in February 2005, the Commerce Commission refused permission; his plans were thwarted. It wasn't all bad news, however. At the end of 2005, Gallaghers sold most of its Tru-Test shareholding, achieving $1.75 a share, a healthy profit on the original investment. Meantime, it had successfully distracted its rival.

Gallagher observes: 'Des Scott and the Tru-Test guys spent 18 months fighting us off and took their eye off the ball.' Operationally, Tru-Test fell off the pace and its growth plans were thrown into reverse. It lost $1.7 million in the year to August 2005 and a further $2.2 million the following year, while its revenues were becalmed at $98 million in 2005 and $102 million in 2006, well back on earlier in the decade.[21]

The Gallagher Group, by contrast, had made good progress in the early 2000s, despite facing the same difficult trading conditions as Tru-Test. The rapidly appreciating New Zealand dollar around 2004 and 2005, and a devastating drought in Australia, trimmed back profitability for both businesses. But through it all Gallaghers kept growing strongly. By 2006 Gallaghers' turnover had reached $121 million, having nearly doubled in the first six years of the century. With profits after tax approaching $12 million, Gallaghers had shown itself profitable even in the most adverse currency conditions.

The ingredients of Gallaghers' steady and continuing success were much the same as ever. The maintenance of good, long-term relationships with key distributors — such as

David Mullen in Australia and the US, the Dijkstras in Europe — continued to work well in the core animal management business. In the States, Mullen had shifted Gallagher Power Fence Inc's base from San Antonio, Texas, to North Kansas City, Missouri, in 2003. 'San Anton', as it was affectionately known, had been Art Snell's home turf, but it didn't make great sense as a hub for a growing business that now reached all parts of the US, with its largest potential market of grass-growing farmers in the belt between Oklahoma and Montana.

As the business had grown under Mullen's leadership in the 1990s, warehouses had been added in Cincinnati and near Portland, but this was unwieldy. Looking for a good single central site, the company took the advice of freight servicing company UPS and settled on Kansas City, which lies within the central core of the US, within four days' trucking range of the entire country. At first, in 1999, Mullen and Erwin Quinn found a warehouse in Kansas City that was within a limestone cave, just off the Missouri River. Miners had worked out the limestone, leaving caves 25 metres wide, reaching kilometres underground. Mullen recalls that the cave provided cheap warehousing, where the temperature changed barely two degrees all year round, but it was claustrophobic. Some of the staff 'could hack it', others couldn't. In 2003 Mullen consolidated all the US warehousing at a new, above-ground site in North Kansas City.

Meantime, the market continued to grow well. By 2005 Mullen's business in the US was turning over US$18.6 million, while Gallagher Australia did A$22 million, much of this business driving demand for goods manufactured by the Gallagher Group in Hamilton.

Continued innovation enabled the brand to maintain its premium position in the market. In 2006 Gallaghers launched 28 new products into markets around the world, including the MX7500, the world's most powerful energiser. The new PowerPlus range included battery models with energy saving on light loads. There were also new products designed for horses and goats, and new bungee cords for gates. And while it was true that Cardax soaked up a lot of the R&D spend, sometimes to the irritation of the folks in Animal Management Systems, most recognised the boost the company had been given by the arrival of the Cardax people from Marton. As Bruce Munro observes: 'The Cardax team had operated at a different level of sophistication to fencing. They were used to

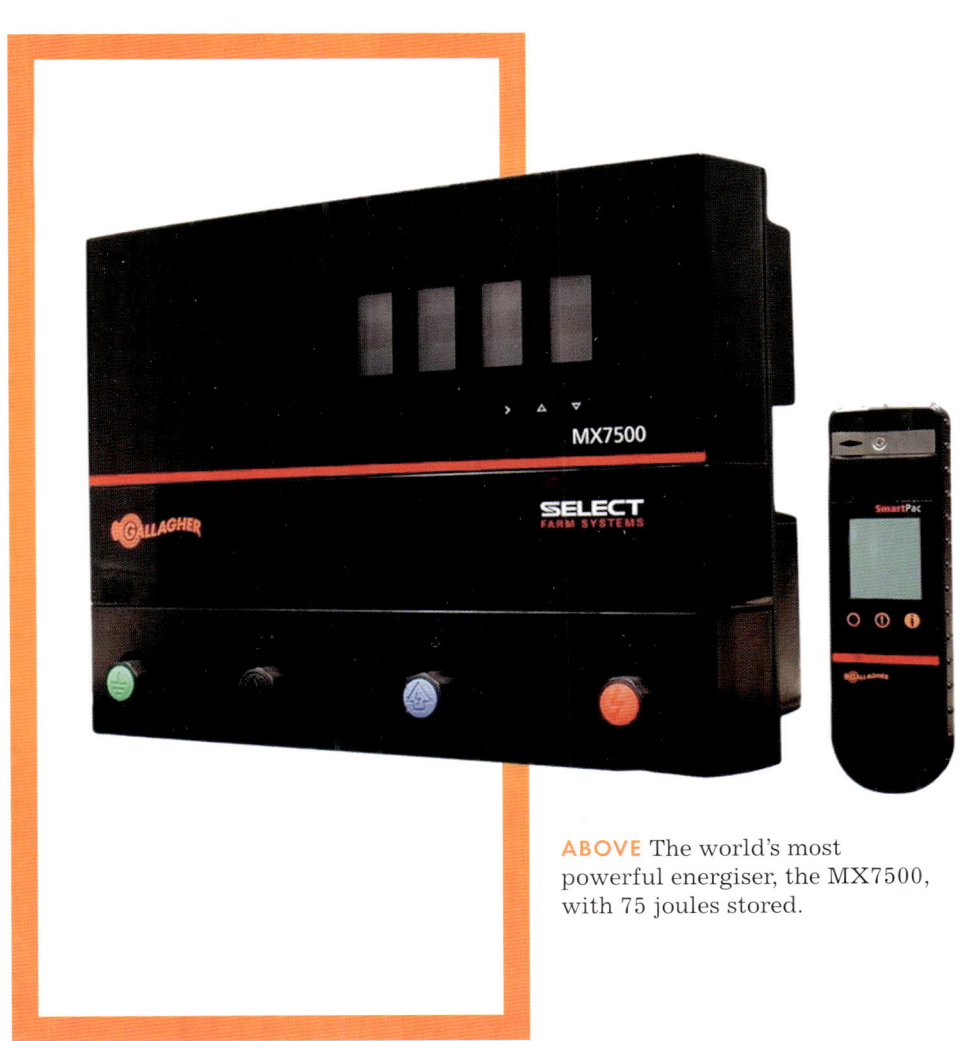

ABOVE The world's most powerful energiser, the MX7500, with 75 joules stored.

operating in territory where obsolescence could happen overnight, and where international competition from huge firms was deadly serious — so it was a totally different league to the electric fencing market. New ideas, expertise and levels of professionalism in R&D were successfully dragged through to the benefit of the Gallaghers' traditional business.'[22]

Gallaghers' expansion into the markets for gates, hinges and weigh-scales had generated a large part of the growth in the animal management sector. In the 2000s weigh-scales and electronic identification (EID) products were featuring more prominently in Gallaghers' suite. Gallaghers Select Farm Systems, launched in 2004, combined electronic weigh-scales with electronic tag readers. Now farmers could easily gather information about the weight gain of their animals over time, in electronic form automatically uploaded to the screen. That said, as David Mullen recalls, when half the farmer customers had not yet used a computer, it was a time-consuming business for Gallagher reps to teach retailers and end-users how to operate this new tool. In time, however, its utility for guiding breeding programmes would become obvious.

Government regulations about traceability of cattle also promised a further engine of growth to this side of the business. Motivated partly by a desire to manage potential outbreaks of diseases such as BSE and foot and mouth, Australia had made EID of cattle compulsory in all states in 2003; Canada followed in 2005. Other countries, including New Zealand, were expected to do the same. Having positioned itself well in another growing market, Gallaghers purchased the remaining 50 per cent of Ruddweigh Scales from its original Australian owners in 2005 and transferred the manufacturing to Hamilton.

Operationally, Gallaghers' Hamilton factories had bedded in the gains from the overhaul of manufacturing, warehousing, delivery and ordering systems since the early 2000s. As Steve Tucker recalls, it was big investment to install the ERP computer system in 1999–2000, but by 2006 the group had doubled in size and complexity, juggling dozens of businesses operating in a large number of jurisdictions, with fluctuating currencies and the challenges of managing employees, distributors and partners remotely. 'The investment,' Tucker says, 'paid real dividends as we were able to manage substantial growth successfully.' And so the group was able to manufacture competitively and profitably, even when the New Zealand dollar swung against it.

That said, in 2005, when the New Zealand dollar was at historically high levels against the US dollar, steps were taken to source some product (insulators and some gate hardware) from China and to outsource some software development to India. Bill Gallagher now observes that while the initiatives were easy to justify on paper, in practice they both proved difficult to manage: 'By global standards we haven't got huge production runs and we soon learnt that if you want to keep in-house control over quality in relatively small production runs it is much simpler to continue production at home.' So most outsourcing proved a short-term experiment.

Perhaps the biggest difference between the growth paths of the Gallagher Group and Tru-Test in the mid-2000s reflected the quality of their acquisitions. In the mid-1990s Bill Gallagher had consciously rejected a growth-by-acquisition strategy. He was worried that if the company became obsessed with growth at any cost, in pursuit of some random billion-dollar figure, it would inevitably make bad decisions over its acquisitions. The temptation would be to grab any likely company that came along and to pay too much, in one's eagerness to find growth. Instead, Gallagher's acquisitions had been opportunistic and cautious: if something good came along at the right price, he would take it; if not, so be it.

This approach spared the company major disasters. Ruddweigh Scales had been a relatively small investment that became a modest contributor in a strategically important part of the industry; Franklin Gates had been a modest investment that grew into a reliable contributor to the group; Cardax became a more significant investment over time, although it was as yet only a modest contributor. But the best acquisition of all remained PEC Fuel Pumps. This little company, still based in Marton, continued to go from strength to strength in the mid-2000s, more than making up for Cardax's slow rise to profitability.

The rapid turnaround in PEC Fuel Pumps, led by Tony Dobbs, in the years after Gallaghers' 1999 purchase of the business hadn't been a fluke. The company continued to perform well in the mid-2000s. And because some of the parts for the petrol pumps were

ABOVE Another animal management innovation, the EID Sheep Auto Drafter makes reading electronic identification ear tags and weighing and drafting large numbers of sheep safer, quicker and quieter.

imported in yen and the pumps were sold either locally or in Australia, a high New Zealand dollar was generally good news for the business. This provided a natural hedge for the group against a rising dollar, which traditionally hurt other parts of the business.

When profits from Animal Management Systems subsided as the New Zealand dollar rose in 2004 and 2005, the booming fuel pump business provided a sizeable slice of the group's profitability. In 2006 the former ugly duckling of the PEC empire provided 40 per cent of the Gallagher Group's after-tax profits. Revenues had surged from $12 million in 2001 to $31 million in 2006 (roughly three-quarters Australia, one-quarter New Zealand). Dobbs's efforts were helped by unprecedented demand for fuel pumps in New Zealand and Australia during the mid-2000s. In the month of March 2004, for example, the Marton factory produced 136 pumps, a record for the company; but records were regularly being broken.

The company's positive culture was a less tangible, but equally important reason for Gallaghers' continued success. After a few rocky years in the late 1990s the group had regained its balance under Bill Gallagher's leadership, and even as his sixty-fifth birthday approached in January 2006 his enthusiasm for the business continued to inspire a cohesive management team and the wider workforce, which had swollen to 658. As the head of the company, a major shareholder and an enthusiastic evangelist for its products, Gallagher continued to drive and personify the company's culture.

Just what that culture was, that 'unique feel of the place', is quite difficult to define. Steve Hoffman tried to express it: 'It's something incredibly flexible and generous at one level; flexible in that he will sometimes sign off a proposal for a reasonably significant investment on my recommendation, without formal business plans, because he has faith in me and my judgement. Generous in his time and his hospitality. And yet at another level, it's incredibly tight, such as around the correct protocol of how to deal with customers and each other. There are standards and ways of doing things — openly and transparently — that are absolute.'[23]

Like most successful leaders, Gallagher led by example. Steve Tucker was perhaps the one most closely exposed to this phenomenon. He observes: 'You've got to have your wits about you when working with Bill. His work ethic is outstanding; he's usually the last person to leave the offices in the evening. He travels like a machine;

you can't watch a movie on the plane if you're sitting next to him because he'll be working away. So it's his style that drives the culture in the organisation, right down to the little things. Emails must be responded to that day; he does it, and he expects everyone else to follow his lead. That's how you have a culture of responsiveness. If for some reason I haven't answered a query from some far-flung part of the organisation and he's been copied in, I just know he'll be in my office wondering what's going on. And if he comes out of a meeting with an idea, he picks up the phone and deals with it. That's another part of the general culture: you get on with stuff, make decisions and don't procrastinate.

'Hospitality is the other hallmark. He and Judi are awesome hosts. When you travel a lot you realise what a difference it makes if someone takes the trouble to arrange a nice dinner or to do something special. And Bill has embedded that approach in the company; you build good long-term relationships by going the extra mile when hosting people. But above all, he practises what he preaches. He's not the kind of guy who gives orders on his way out the door to spend the weekend on his luxury cruiser.'[24]

Not everyone who took a job in the Gallagher Group understood or successfully navigated their way through the company's modus operandi. Those who misinterpreted the friendly, relaxed, family atmosphere for an invitation to lassitude and inertia soon found themselves unwelcome. And those who came from highly political organisations, where game-playing between rivals on the senior management team was an expected part of doing business, either had to change their approach or find a new job.

But those who did grasp the essentials of the Gallagher way have tended to stay. Statistically, the saying goes that if you stay at Gallagher for five years, there's a 65 per cent chance you'll stay for life. The reality is not quite as strong as that, but it's not far off. And by the mid-2000s the senior management team had a look of stability around it. Tucker, Comer and Hoffman now had long careers with the company. Geoff Copstick had been chief financial officer for more than five years. Working alongside them were a significant group of people who had long-term aspirations. Kahl Betham put his finger on the attitude: 'The company's willingness to promote from within and grow people is very important. They've taken risks on me, developed me, and it's a company-wide approach. It's why people stay, because they can see a progression, they can follow the career of Steve Tucker from being a member of the finance team to deputy CEO, and they're part of a company that wants to win globally against the big guys.'25

At the top of the structure, Gallagher and Steve Tucker had worked out a good relationship. Tucker assumed broad responsibility for the daily operations of the company, the supply chain, R&D, IT and the Animal Management side of the business. Curtis Edgecombe, as general manager of Gallagher Security Management Systems, Margaret Comer with Corporate Services, and Tony Dobbs, managing director of PEC Fuel Pumps, continued to report directly to Bill Gallagher.

The complications flowing from having a shareholder outside the family in the 1990s had rather spoilt the prospects of the next generation of senior managers for gaining a stake in the company; the experience had reinforced the Gallaghers' instinct that life was much simpler if ownership was kept within the family. The only change to the shareholding has been a transfer of five per cent of the shares from Bill to Judi Gallagher. However, the staff bonus system continued to give everyone in the company a strong personal stake in its success — the key to the system being, in Bill Gallagher's estimation, that it is not a right or entitlement, but a gratuity at the discretion of the directors and shareholders.

Nor is the bonus a set percentage of pay given to everyone, but a genuine reward to those who have worked hard and created value, the absence of which sends a powerful message to those who have coasted along or failed to achieve results. And since the total sum available for distribution depended on the profitability of the group, it added an edge to the natural rivalry between different parts of the business. Life wasn't comfortable around bonus time for the highly paid software developers on the security side of the business when their division was losing money and thus depriving the folks at Animal Management and PEC Fuel Pumps of some of their hard-earned booty.

ith all parts of the business now in good hands, Gallagher steadily handed more responsibility over to his managers, leaving himself free to focus on the parts

of the business that he found most exciting. As ever, that included a lot of travel into exotic markets to find new entrepreneurs and new opportunities to grow the business, particularly in the security field, which continued to fascinate him. There were few places more interesting for that business than the Middle East.

Gallagher became aware of Bilal Chehime in 2002, when he kept getting phone calls from Dubai in which this man complained about various Cardax distributors who were meant to be servicing the region. Chehime, a Lebanese businessman who had spent a decade in Canada before returning to the Middle East in 1998 to set up a security business in Dubai with some partners, had come across Cardax at an exhibition in Birmingham in 2001. He liked it and started marketing the product around the Middle East, alongside the CCTV and other security products that formed his business. But he didn't get on well with the Cardax personnel in the UK who had oversight of the Middle East. Chehime preferred to work direct.

He recalls: 'I rang up Bill Gallagher and told him his men weren't capable of understanding the nature and structure of business in the Middle East and that he should come and see us and see the opportunities here. And that's what he did. I told him who we are, how we think, how the market works, that we like Cardax and have potential projects but we want to deal direct with the factory, not go through some useless middleman. And Bill was extremely flexible, modest, experienced and very generous; he was also open-minded, with a very long vision, and he evaluated us in the proper way. He really found value in me.'[26]

Having made a connection, Bill sent Graham Dawson up to Dubai on regular visits to help Chehime grow the market. They travelled around the major exhibitions and targeted the leading security consultants throughout the region, and soon had Cardax installed on some big sites, including Fujairah International Airport in the United Arab Emirates.

In 2006 Chehime decided to set up a new business on his own in Lebanon, his homeland. He visited Gallagher in Hamilton and explained his dream of establishing Cardax Middle East as a partnership between them. Gallagher recalls: 'I saw in Bilal a real opportunity. He's a very active sales guy, while his number two man, Sharbil Khalil, is a super details man. When you put the two together you have a really good combination. And so when Bilal

ABOVE Dubai Security Show, 2009. From left to right: Hassan Chehime, Ian Meadows, Bilal Chehime, Bill Gallagher, Sharbil Khalil, Karl Philbin and Imad Chehime.

ABOVE Judi, Nabia and Bilal Chehime and Bill in Lebanon, 2009.

moved to Lebanon we became partners, in the same way that we did with our electric fencing distributors in the 1980s. We took a 20 per cent stake and he fronts as our Middle East office, which works well in that environment. It has our name on the company, which comforts our customers and doesn't give the impression of just being another middleman for them to try to get around.'

And so, 35 years after his earliest forays into new international markets, Bill Gallagher was still in his element: on the hoof in far-flung places finding a new horse to ride, an interesting new friend to visit, a family with stories of struggle from the hard lands of the Beqaa Valley to prosperity in a new business frontier. And in turn, his new partner knows that the New Zealander is no fly-by-nighter. 'Bill gives us the spirit,' Chehime says; 'I am with you, he tells me, don't worry, my babies. I'll help when things get rough.'[27]

11
THE RELENTLESS DRIVE FOR INNOVATION: 2006 AND BEYOND

Chapter eleven

THE RELENTLESS DRIVE FOR INNOVATION: 2006 AND BEYOND

Life is like a dog-sled team . . . If you're not the lead dog, the scenery never changes.

— ONE OF BILL GALLAGHER'S FAVOURITE QUOTES, FROM
THE WIT AND WISDOM OF LEWIS GRIZZARD

The legendary American investor Warren Buffett often observed that wealth is hard to accumulate and easy to lose.[1] The same can be said of market leadership in any business. The reality is that most businesses don't keep their competitive edge over an extended period. Most of the Kiwi export manufacturing companies that were prospering when Gallagher leapt to prominence in the late 1970s have disappeared, some because of bad luck, others because of bungling, complacency, arrogance or fatigue at the top. Of the dozens of electric fence manufacturers in New Zealand operating when Gallaghers began its invasion of foreign markets, only two — Gallaghers and Tru-Test — remained alive in the late 2000s.

That Gallaghers has survived and continued to grow reflects, above all, a determination by its owners to carry on, concentrating on what the company does well, while cautiously adding new elements to the mix as opportunities arise. It was important that this was done in a manner that challenged and stretched the organisation but was never of a magnitude to imperil the company if it didn't work out.

And the formula for success remained remarkably consistent over several decades. In electric fencing and ultimately animal management, it entailed investing sufficiently in R&D to generate innovative products that could command a premium in the marketplace. Manufacturing excellence was Gallaghers' strength, honed steadily over the years with each successive upgrade in operating systems. Since the early 1980s Gallaghers had also undertaken the distribution and marketing of its products in New Zealand and in one or two international markets, with most success on its home turf. But overall most of the demand for its products was driven by entrepreneurial distribution and marketing companies, partly or wholly owned and operated by local marketing specialists.

Bill Gallagher's special skill had been to inspire and motivate those distributors, and while there had been plenty of failures over the years, a few key long-term relationships continued to produce results over an extended period; David Mullen's businesses in Australia and US and the Dijkstras' in Europe were the most significant of these, but there were many others, including John Lucey in Ireland, Ian Hendrie in Canada, and Surge Miyawaki in Japan.

But nothing lasts forever, and in the late 2000s changing circumstances led to a fundamental rethink of Gallaghers' distributing and marketing arrangements for Animal Management Systems, with the result that by 2010 the Gallagher Group had taken direct control of the major markets of North America and Australia. Together with New Zealand, these markets now account for around 80 per cent of Animal Management's sales. This represents one of the most significant transformations in the history of the company; senior executives within the Gallagher Group now carry the primary responsibility for driving future growth. The role traditionally played by entrepreneurial partners will continue elsewhere, particularly in non-English-speaking markets and most notably in Europe, but in terms of the overall shape of the group the balance has shifted.

The changes reflect the outcome of one of the longest-running debates within the Gallagher Group. Since the 1990s a number of managers, including Neil Richardson and Steve Hoffman, had been arguing that it was time to take over some of the international distributors. They believed that by controlling wholly owned subsidiaries in the key markets the company would enjoy greater coherency, as well as consistency of brand and presentation, and would be free of the constant arguments with independent distributors about pricing and where the profits should lie.

Respectable management theories and examples from countless

ABOVE Bill in Japan in 2004 with Yutaka Miyawaki, Gallagher's longest serving distributor.

multinational corporations could be found to back this as a sound strategy. Bill Gallagher had remained unconvinced, pointing to the consistently poor performance in the UK, the group's one wholly owned subsidiary in the Animal Management division. Entrepreneurs with their own 'skin in the game' had been the wellsprings of his growth in the past, and loyalty to his distributors remained his credo.

The turning point came in 2006 when Ian Hendrie, Gallaghers' long-serving Canadian distributor, wanted to retire. Ian and his wife Jane had started with Gallaghers in 1979 and built a strong business, Gallagher Power Fencing System (Canada), with its offices and warehouse at Owen Sound, 200 kilometres north of Toronto. Consistently they generated the fourth highest export receipts in the Animal Management business, after the US, Australia and Europe. The Gallagher Group owned 20 per cent of the company to the Hendries' 80 per cent. Hoffman argued strongly that the group should buy out the rest of the company.

He recalls: 'We were entering a new phase in the business when the early entrepreneurs were reaching an age in life that they wanted to exit, and because of our mutually exclusive business relationship, in reality there was only one logical buyer of the business: us. Meanwhile there was an enormous consolidation going on worldwide of electric fence competitors and we were getting squeezed. So to take direct control of distribution made sense, and after much persuasion we convinced Bill to purchase Canada.'[2]

With Canada in the bag in May 2006 and no immediate disasters, eyes turned to the much more important US market, which David Mullen had controlled since 1987 (owning 60 per cent to the Gallagher Group's 40 per cent). This was Gallaghers' biggest export market by far, and from his home base in Sydney Mullen had motivated a team over the years to run a successful business from its headquarters in Kansas City. Gallagher USA had 48 employees by 2007. Erwin Quinn had been president since the early 1990s. 'Six foot two, always immaculate and with quite a presence about him,' Mullen says, 'Erwin couldn't sleep past 5am, so started working early and had an incredible, contagious work ethic; he was an effective "do-as-I-do" leader.' At the same time John Lewin, the national sales manager for a decade, was 'technically proficient and also very capable of explaining the important elements simply so that the territory managers could get their heads around them'.[3]

Gallagher USA's turnover had grown steadily throughout the decade from US$16 million in 2000 to US $23 million in 2008 and it had been consistently profitable. Mullen estimated that Gallagher held 20 per cent of the electric fence market in the US, and continued to dominate the premium end. This was a great effort in a market that has never been easy. Bill Gallagher observes: 'Controlled grazing is still not really practised in the US. You'll go on a farm in Missouri where they can grow grass most of the year and they'll have an energiser putting 5 joules of energy onto the fence, but out of 300 acres he'll have only seven paddocks, leaving beef cattle in one paddock for several weeks at a time. If they operated 100 paddocks using strip grazing they'd grow beef faster and more of it.

'But most farmers are not interested in increasing productivity; most of their profits still come from subsidies. I talked to one farmer, an Amish guy, with this sort of set-up, and he just laughed when I suggested he change to a New Zealand style of farming. Moving cattle around would be too much work. Clearly he hadn't heard of opening the gate and letting them walk through. So it has been a great disappointment. Meantime, the Amish farmer was operating a M800 energiser, only about eight years old, with the carton still neatly sitting beside it.'

So the business had never grown to 50 times the size of New Zealand's turnover, as it might have if the company had achieved similar levels of penetration, but it was still significant nonetheless. And traditional farmers now comprised barely 50 per cent of the turnover in the US. Much of the fencing now went to hobby or lifestyle farmers, who kept a few animals, especially horses. Pasture management didn't concern them; it was all about keeping their pets safely and effectively contained.

The business in the US wasn't broken, so it would be a big call for Gallagher to change arrangements. Mullen, who was nearing retirement himself, was open to discussions. He had in mind passing his Australian business on to his son Richard, but was content to spare him the rigours of a life spent flying between Sydney and the US in order to operate both businesses.

Gallagher Group director Bruce Munro was enthusiastic about

the purchase, having long promoted the benefits of the group 'controlling the chain', from the factory to the customer: 'In the late 1990s the group didn't have the resources to buy out the big distributors, nor did it have the people-capability to run those international organisations. So it was better to leave the existing distributors in place. Nor would I recommend buying Europe completely, because we don't have the ability to succeed in a multi-lingual, highly bureaucratic area. We'd bugger it up for sure. But where English is spoken, by the late 2000s it was highly desirable to gain full control. For a start it would end the fighting over transfer pricing and the level of market support, so we could make the profits where it made most economic sense.

'But there was also a strategic drive. Being responsible for distribution brings us closer to the market-face in key areas outside New Zealand. It would also force us to face up to improving management beyond our shores. To be a world player we need to understand the real market situation first-hand, rather than rely on second-hand feedback from distributors.'[4]

Thus the debates raged for a while until early 2008, when a deal was reached between the Gallagher Group and David Mullen's company for the group to purchase Gallagher USA outright. The Canadian and US operations were then combined into Gallagher North America.

The next logical step was for the Gallagher Group to purchase Gallagher Australia (owned 80 per cent by David Mullen, 20 per cent by the Gallagher Group). Again, this was a big decision, since Mullen's Australian business was working well, turning over A$27 million in 2008, up from A$14 million in 2000, and consistently profitable. Mullen had been in business nearly 30 years and had established the Gallagher name in Australia. Gallaghers' general manager in Australia, Malcolm Linn, summarises the Mullen approach: 'David was a very driven man, extremely well-organised, very demanding of his people, and not ungenerous. He created a well-disciplined rural sales organisation. And he was quite conservative in terms of understanding clearly the marketplace he was playing in and not venturing outside it. So he augmented the Gallagher suite with products that fitted, things like electric stock prodders, a range of manufactured gate-fitting products and fencing accessories. And since Gallaghers' products helped farmers increase their productivity through pasture management, he recognised early on that it was logical also to measure how that productivity is being captured through weigh-scales, electronic ear tags and attaching data. So that was our space.

'But he also recognised that in order to educate farmers to use new products, he needed a lot of support and service through good local managers, which required high margins. Over a long period with this consistent approach he built arguably the best-serviced agricultural brand in Australia and succeeded in a market that rewards loyalty. Several of his salesmen have served more than 20 years and are well respected in their regions. Gallagher has an icon brand in the rural sector that in many ways is inter-generational. I often say to our resellers and farmers, we're less interested in selling you an energiser today than in ensuring your son buys one. That captures what Gallagher is about.'[5]

Having had a lean patch around 2000 when reinvigorated competition had seen Gallaghers' share of the electric fencing market slide below 50 per cent for a while, Mullen had again lifted it toward 60 per cent by the late 2000s.

However, the arguments in favour of taking direct control of distribution in North America all applied to Australia. In addition, Mullen also retained the perimeter security fencing (PowerFence) business in Australia, while the Gallagher Group controlled the Cardax access control business in Australia directly. In the US both PowerFence and Cardax had always been kept separate from Animal Management. The Australian security arrangement was far from perfect; it complicated and slowed down the seamless integration of Gallaghers' security offerings in that market. Moreover, much wider strategic changes were in the wind.

In 2007 New Zealand Trade & Enterprise, a government agency, sponsored a 'Better by Design' review of the Gallagher Group, which went through every aspect of the business and made a series of recommendations. One area of interest to the reviewers was marketing and branding, where they argued that the group should strive to create a global technology brand around its strengths of innovation, service, quality and integrity. As it was, the group operated three main brands — Gallagher, Cardax and PowerFence. One big idea was to drop the Cardax and PowerFence brands in favour of a single,

ABOVE Animal management systems for horses are big business.

umbrella Gallagher brand. It would involve a major rebranding exercise, much analysis and great costs . . . but instinctively Bill Gallagher was drawn to the notion that a unified Gallagher brand in the security area would be the last step in integrating the Cardax and PowerFence sides of the business into a unified security offering.

The situation was complicated, however, in Australia, where Gallagher Australia Pty, 80 per cent owned by David Mullen, controlled the Gallagher brand for electric fencing. An additional factor was that Gallaghers' 30-year relationship with David Mullen was not quite as close as it once had been. It had drifted from being a special relationship in the 1980s and early 1990s, when Mullen was a director of the Gallagher Group and an integral part of the team, to something less. Little niggles had accumulated over the years, patience had worn thin.

And while Mullen's efforts in the US and Australia had provided a good stream of dividends for the group and had underpinned growth for Gallaghers' Animal Management section, on many strategic issues there was a contest of wills. The simplest and tidiest solution was for the Gallagher Group to buy Gallagher Australia outright. After some negotiation this was effected in July 2010. David Mullen's son Richard has remained working for the firm, and is now national sales manager.

With the North American and Australian distribution for Animal Management folded into the tent, the balance of the Gallagher Group had shifted decisively from a manufacturing company that undertook some distribution and marketing of its goods in its domestic market to something broader, where distribution and marketing became core activities. It had been building over a decade, since the acquisition of PEC in 1999 which had catapulted the Gallagher Group into distribution and marketing on the security side internationally.

Now, in 2010, the group was directly responsible for marketing most of its output. The fortunes of the group would depend as much on its newly acquired skill as an international marketer as on its long-demonstrated strengths in R&D, design and manufacturing. In the marketing lingo of the day, the group had evolved into a 'global technology company with expertise in the design and development of security, animal management and fuel pump systems', and one that offered 'end-to-end design, manufacturing and marketing of products and solutions'. It was the start of a new era.

The job had expanded, but the old imperatives of the business remained. On the Animal Management side the trends of the early 2000s continued through the decade: continued innovation in the products, steady expansion into electronic identification of animals, and the never-ending search for improvements in business systems to lift quality and reduce costs. On innovation, Gallaghers completed development of the Smart TSI (Touch Screen Indicator) data collector and weigh-scale head, which was far ahead of anything else on the market in terms of functionality and usability and won the Innovation Centre Award at the 2008 Mystery Creek Fieldays.

Weigh-scales and chip readers have made the measurement of growth in livestock easy, and Gallaghers' team has devoted much R&D into making its systems as user-friendly and simple to use as possible. The extension of mandatory electronic tagging for livestock, however, has been slower than expected in most countries. Gallaghers prepared to capitalise on growth to come, and in the meantime took on the marketing challenge of persuading conservative farmers to see intensive, electronic animal management as a way to improve productivity, rather than a cost to be avoided or postponed as long as possible.

In all manufacturing the object is to maximise volume in order to lower costs per unit. In electric fencing, Bill Gallagher carried on trying to win permission to take over domestic rival Tru-Test. Their combined volumes would offer considerable efficiencies, helping both businesses compete internationally. The New Zealand Commerce Commission remained rigidly focused on domestic competition and implacably opposed to Gallaghers' proposals. Gallagher was more successful with gates, acquiring Greyson Gates of Putaruru and consolidating manufacturing operations at the Franklin Gates site in Pukekohe. This sideline business has grown into one of some substance, producing revenues of around $10 million a year. Gate hardware — hinges, latches and gudgeons mainly — remained an important element of the gates business, despite being susceptible to competition from China, depending on the exchange rate.

The next quantitative leap in operating systems, following the introduction of the MRP II system around 1989 and a SAP-based system in 2000, came with Lean Manufacturing, introduced in 2010. Also known as Toyota Production System, Lean Manufacturing began with a lengthy analysis of every aspect of operations, with a focus on 'continually challenging waste and performing tasks in a consistent and identical manner'. It extended to having videos made of people at their work-stations to figure out how far they were having to reach for each part, and designing a process whereby everything they needed was easily within reach. Like a supermarket shelf, each container of parts was replenished just in time.

This process yielded another round of significant efficiencies. In the plastic moulding department, for example, where tools are built for each moulding, then torn down once the run is complete, the time taken to tear down 90 per cent of the tools was reduced by 50 per cent. Similarly, the changeover times for the Surface Mount Technology machines were reduced from two hours to 20 minutes or less. Performance scoreboards, mounted on screens on the factory floor, measured real-time progress on the floor, while a New Products Introduction bench allowed new products to be fully built outside the normal factory assembly line so that any glitches could be resolved by the R&D team without impacting on the full factory.

The Lean process also led to significant improvements in shipping times by eliminating any activity that added nothing to the essential task of getting the product from the assembly line to market. And the numbers coming from the Hamilton factory were not insubstantial. In the calendar year 2010, 333 containers were sent by sea, carrying more than 2 million kilograms of product, while a further 130,000 kilograms of product was air-freighted in 419 consignments. Where air freight made sense, average delivery times were reduced to 1.2 days to Australia and two days to the US. These sorts of efficiencies opened up whole new levels of savings.

Wayne O'Halloran recalls: 'The pattern for the Aussie market had always been to make it here, ship it to Australia and distribute it from there. Then we had a few staff issues in Australia and we thought, why not courier it? So we closed down the Australian distribution business and all its administration, and brought the whole lot back here. All the orders come through our SAP system and we have a daily delivery to Australia; orders are out of the factory by 4pm and, in the eastern states, they generally reach our channel partners for start of business the next morning. We found we could deliver faster out of New Zealand to most Aussie customers than you could get an across-city courier to deliver within Sydney.'[6]

ABOVE 'A beautiful piece of security fencing', to Bill Gallagher's eyes at least, at work for an Indiana Department of Corrections facility, United States.

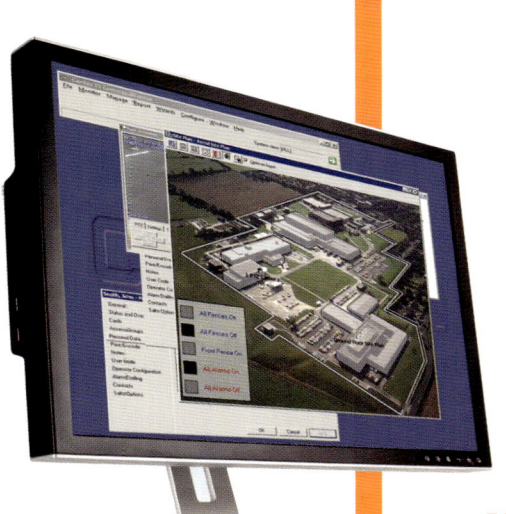

TOP The SmartTSI system allows farmers to control their electric fencing from home.

BOTTOM Cardax software enabled many aspects of security to be monitored from one screen, a major advance on comparative systems.

Big improvements in productivity, innovative new products, steady extension into new and related fields and seamless control of the chain from manufacturing through to distribution and marketing in most of the big markets have allowed Gallaghers' Animal Management business to more than hold its own in a challenging environment. Actual revenue figures for this side of the business have swollen from $67 million in 2006 to just over $100 million in 2011. A significant part of the increase has come from acquiring the rest of the distribution businesses in Australia and North America, but the steady expansion of the underlying business remains an achievement in tough economic times.

The improvements brought about by the Lean Manufacturing operations naturally applied as much to Gallagher Security as they did to Gallagher Animal Management. In 2005, six years after the PEC acquisition, security had been struggling when Curtis Edgecombe was appointed sales manager, after four general managers in quick succession. Revenue was down to $21 million in the year to March 2006, having shown no real improvement in five years.

Within that big picture, fortunes varied. The Cardax business in Australia was going very well, more than quadrupling in size in five years and generating nearly half the division's revenue. New Zealand was less than half the size of Australia, but also growing respectably. Everywhere else was in trouble. Over the next three years, to March 2009, with Edgecombe and Bill Gallagher working intensively on the fledgling division, it finally found some momentum. Revenues doubled to $42 million in the year to March 2009. The global financial crisis fouled up projections of continued growth for the next year, but more modest growth returned in 2011.

Gallagher Security's traditional strengths were Cardax in Australia and PowerFence in the UK. Everything continued to go well in the first area, with Gallagher enjoying many long-term relationships 'across the ditch'. La Trobe University in Melbourne is one such example. Cardax was installed on six doors in the Eastern Lecture Theatre in 1998. Since then the product has spread throughout the university's 330 hectares, so that it now controls 1012 doors across 60 buildings on several campuses. A series of upgrades to the latest

Gallagher Command Centre means that well beyond merely opening and closing doors, the system provides a full audit trail of events, a flexible tool for handling temporary staff or approval for a student to gain access to a certain area for a limited time, and a host of other features that have been discovered following the experiences of the other 30 or so universities operating the system in Australia.

The system interfaces with several third-party systems the university has installed over the years, including a Digital Video Recording system. And Gallaghers' UltraSec intruder alarm is being used to secure an area where 'high consequence substances' are stored. Designed to defeat a highly sophisticated electronic attack, this system includes high levels of data encryption and monitored communications to meet standards required by the Australian Radiation Protection and Nuclear Safety Agency.

As the old Cardax and PowerFence businesses were merged in Australia under the Gallagher name, Gallagher and Edgecombe looked for ways to extract more value from the system. The challenge was to shift perceptions of security, so that rather than being viewed simply as another cost to be minimised it was recognised as an essential part of a company's management systems to minimise risks and improve productivity. This would only ever be a partial shift, because there will always be customers who are interested only in securing their businesses at the lowest cost. And Gallagher had a good message to sell here. An example often used was Cadbury Australia's site in Ringwood, Melbourne, where Cadbury took very seriously its duty of care to ensure there was no contamination of its product. Gallagher installed 4 kilometres of fence around the site's perimeter, divided into 12 zones. The result for Cadbury was a saving of around $1 million a year in manpower, since patrols were no longer required.

At the other end of the scale, Gallaghers' desire to place its product at the heart of business systems resonated best with companies working in highly regulated industries. This aspect of the business began when one customer — Christchurch Airport — wanted to use its access control card to ensure that only people whose training was up to date could operate air-bridges. Having swiped his or her card the operator would be able to extend the bridge if everything was up to date. If their annual training was due within a month they would receive a message; if it was overdue the bridge wouldn't move. It was a simple idea, but one that had not previously been applied to the product.

Mining was another area where a host of applications presented themselves. Cardax had first been installed at the copper mine at Mount Isa in 1990. In 2003 the mine was bought by Xstrata, a Swiss conglomerate. As one of the deepest mines in the world, reaching 1800 metres below the surface, health and safety would always be a paramount business concern. Through the 2000s Cardax's technology was used for more and more applications. The old manual tag boards were replaced by Cardax's electronic recorders to provide the all-important information of who was in the mine at any one time, and to ensure everyone was in a safe depot before blasting began.

The Command Centre interfaced with CCTV to monitor the whereabouts of underground staff within the mine at any time. Then the Cardax system integrated with the HR systems, usually SAP or Oracle, to link with training and competency: this person was able to access that area at a certain time; that person had an up-to-date licence to operate this piece of machinery. In a huge organisation with thousands of workers, this brought significant gains for assurance and risk control, with the key being the ability of Gallaghers' Windows-based software to interface with other systems, so that data could be imported to the Cardax system easily and effectively.

Bill and Judi Gallagher visited the mine in 2009, a visit that provided Bill with a vivid story to tell other customers or channel partners as he travelled round the world. After a one-hour safety briefing, they had been driven into an elevator in an air-conditioned ute, in which they sank 1 kilometre into the earth. From there they drove the next 800 metres down a 6 metre wide tunnel on a 7 degree slope, deeper and deeper. When they finally opened the doors it was as if they were in an oven, around 45 degrees Celsius.

But the important message he would tell was how, over the years, the company had migrated from dealing only with the security manager of the mine to having discussions with the business security people, the HR people, and managers in charge of operational efficiency, stability, regulatory compliance and insurance. With each step they took up the chain, to managers with ever-larger budgets at their disposal, Gallagher increased the perceived value of its system to the mine. And some of the gains for the client were unexpected,

ABOVE Mike Foley and Bill Gallagher in a gold mine in South Africa, 2008.

such as the more than $1 million a month saved by the mine when access cards were introduced for contractors. A quick reconciliation of hours billed versus the electronic record of when contractors were on site revealed regular over-billing.

The resources boom in Australia in the late 2000s helped increase demand for Gallagher Security products, so that revenues in that country alone swelled past $20 million in 2011. Frustratingly, Gallaghers' attempts to generate similar volumes of work in Brazil, another great mining economy, have so far been held back by high import taxes. Supposedly designed to protect the local market, to Bill Gallagher's way of thinking these simply disadvantage their consumers.

Gallagher Security's other traditional cornerstone market, perimeter fencing in the UK, had been through a rockier decade. From being the biggest market for Gallaghers' products in 2001, disjointed leadership on the ground and a few failed bids for big projects had seen its revenues fall precipitously to barely $2 million in 2006, well short of breaking even. Edgecombe replaced two general managers, one for Cardax, one for PowerFence, with one new general manager for both sides of the business. David Bentley, then in his midthirties, took on the role. He had been with Gallaghers since 1991, when barely out of university he began fixing broken energisers in the Canley warehouse. Having worked his way through the ranks in each department, gaining a good understanding of both the technical and marketing side of the business, he galvanised the team back into action. Growth resumed and by 2010 Gallagher Security in the UK and Ireland was approaching $10 million in revenues.

Bentley, aided by periodic visitations from Bill Gallagher, focused on strengthening the network of fencing contractors, security firms and consultants who used or recommended Gallagher products in the marketplace. Having put perimeter fencing around a lot of utility sites in the 1990s, Gallaghers' team found itself in the happy position of having to supply contractors with equipment to upgrade the security on those sites to higher specifications required for sites of Critical National Infrastructure. Electric fences 4.6 metres high, often linked with access control, CCTV and other elements, continue to spring up around gas terminals, power stations and oil refineries, all to protect these valuable sites from the predations of terrorists.

Terrorism remains an equal threat in the US, but the American dream still proved elusive for Gallagher Security. The progress Gallaghers had made at the start of the 2000s in perimeter fencing was reversed in the middle of the decade as local competitors with greater access to government jobs elbowed them aside. Their GSA (preferred supplier) status lapsed, increasing the challenge further. Meantime, several attempts were made to establish a presence in the access control market, initially with little progress being made. Two of the international leaders in the field, GE and Honeywell, with whom Gallagher competed successfully abroad, dominated at home. Bill Gallagher notes wryly that he has experienced fewer barriers in China than in the US security industry: 'It's highly regulated, the marketplace is very pro-US manufacturers, especially after the Buy America Act, and local firms have the inside running on most government contracts.'

Gallagher Security revenues in the US withered away almost to nothing in the year to March 2007, putting a lot of pressure on Thomas Friederichs, Gallagher Security's head. As he says: 'It is a costly place to do business. If you want to be taken seriously you have to do the trade shows, of which there are many, and you can't just turn up, you need to have a big booth there as well. So it's costly. But as Bill Gallagher regularly pointed out to us, we need to make the money to justify the cost; he's not interested in working for nothing.'[7]

Bill Gallagher's patience was tried, but he wasn't about to give up on the largest market in the world. Curtis Edgecombe weighed in with the argument that for too long they had 'nickled and dimed it' in the US, and to succeed they would have to invest seriously to develop a base. The company also needed to shift away from its earlier approach in which Gallagher USA had acted as the installation contractor itself, which may have made sense initially but offered little scope for expansion. Instead, it should adopt the more usual Gallagher model, where it acted as a pure distributor with a focus on developing a network of channel partners. Edgecombe won his case, but unfortunately the extra resources went in from 2007 just as the global financial crisis was about to hit.

By 2011, however, the rewards from its efforts were beginning to flow and the team did have a few exemplar jobs to which they could refer. The Birmingham Water Works Board in Alabama was one of the first water utilities in the US to raise its security to meet the new anti-terrorism requirements ordered by the US Environmental Protection Agency (EPA). The perimeter fence would deter or detect any intruders across six separate facilities, but as Terry Oden, the Works Board security director, said, the deciding factor for going with the New Zealand firm was the ability of the Gallagher Trophy FT Command Centre to integrate with its existing security and access control system.[8]

Gallagher now has four or five channel partners bidding for prison work in seven states; in the three years to 2011 they picked up 33 prisons, mainly for perimeter fencing, and momentum was gathering. A relationship was also formed in 2011 with Anixter, a Fortune 500 company based in Illinois that supplies communications, security and IT infrastructure products to companies around the world. Anixter now preferred to use Gallaghers' access control system. 'Given the scale of the opportunities in the US,' Edgecombe says, 'if we get it right we could transform the security business in five years.'

As Bill Gallagher has noted, gaining access to the Chinese market was in many ways easier than in the US, although it could scarcely be considered a cakewalk. The market grew in fits and starts during the 2000s. The first Trophy FT PowerFence system was installed in China in May 2010 to secure the 1.2 kilometre perimeter of the Government Research and Development Centre for Fighter Aircraft in Anhui Province. Cardax also made early progress with the massive project to provide the access control and central management system for the Guangzhou Baiyun International Airport. The system was integrated with CCTV, while the cards, which were used by 20,000 employees, were linked with lighting and the HR system. At last count, readers controlled access to 108 boarding gates.

In 2010 Peter Francis, Gallagher Security regional manager, Asia Pacific, visited China on two New Zealand Trade & Enterprise trade missions. Having made many new contacts, he signed an exclusive distributor partnership with Chinese firm Joosee Smart Technologies at the end of the year. This led to a new level of activity, with Gallagher perimeter security systems being installed across China around electrical substations, military sites and hydro-power stations, as well as manufacturing and residential zones.

Elsewhere in the broader Asia region, Certis CISCO, a major

security provider headquartered in Singapore, vied with AES, Henny Beeber's firm in Bangkok, to be the leading regional supplier of Gallagher equipment. In 2009 Certis installed an access control and security system for the City of Dreams in Macau, a massive gaming resort that spread over four towers. The Cardax system had to cope with more than 1000 doors and 80 elevators, as well as integrating with the alarm systems, building management systems, HR databases and video surveillance systems.

In Thailand, Beeber continued to nurture his relationship with the Bank of Thailand. Its second note printing plant, which was opened in October 2007 in Phutthamonthon, featured a fully integrated access control and perimeter security system around its entire border including a 1.8 kilometre, 4.5 metre high Gallagher PowerFence protecting the note printing facility's most sensitive area. Beeber explains that the Gallagher system was chosen because of its 'very high levels of data encryption and flexibility to integrate with other systems such as CCTV, IP intercom, crash barriers, vault vibration sensors, building management and HR systems'. The net, however, spread far and wide from Bangkok. AES installed Gallagher gear at the Phnom Penh and Siem Reap Airports in Cambodia, while, teaming with one of its sub-distributors, AES installed a Gallagher PowerFence for the new Bank of Myanmar in Nay Pyi Taw — the strange new capital city created on a green-field site in the jungle for one of the world's most obscure regimes.

Further west, the Indian market finally started to produce fruit for Gallaghers and its partner Ibex in the second half of the 2000s. The agricultural market had proved dispiriting, since every little village manufacturing shop produced its own cheap versions of energisers. Bill Gallagher describes them as 'lunch-boxes that tick', and worries about the many risks taken around insulation and safety, but most of them worked sufficiently well to make life difficult for Gallagher out in the countryside.

Around 2000, Vishnu Narain entered the perimeter security field with the first major job for the aeronautical industry in Bangalore. He gained an opportunity through a personal contact, but it was sufficient to introduce the concept to a sceptical country. Again, Narain soon faced stiff competition from 'agricultural lash-ups', improvised efforts to connect an agricultural energiser to a wire fence, which were very cheap and worked in a fashion but offered

ABOVE Margaret Comer organised a seventieth anniversary ribbon for Gallaghers' head office building in 2008.

TOP Ravi and Prima Narain, Gallagher Security, Malaysia.

RIGHT Gallagher access control systems are in place in countless workplaces in New Zealand and around the world, including the author's office.

none of the features that Gallaghers could provide.

Bill Gallagher had long talked of the necessity to distinguish between a need and a market. India had plenty of need for his products, but there hadn't been the ready money available to pay for them, and thus to generate a market. The context was changing rapidly through the 2000s, however. A major breakthrough came in 2010 when Ibex Gallagher won the contract to install a 10 kilometre fence around India's largest automobile manufacturing site, the new Tata Motors plant in Gujarat province to manufacture the Nano. This wasn't an electric fence; the Tata executives preferred to use a taut wire fence that could use Gallaghers' technology to measure any mechanical disturbance to it. Divided into 105 zones, the taut wire fence was integrated with a digital video system by the Cardax FT platform. This was not the first project completed for Tata, perhaps the greatest of all of the great Indian conglomerates — Gallagher perimeter fencing had secured four power grids for its subsidiary Tisco — but it was the biggest.

With such projects and such clients in the bag, Gallagher finally had some momentum in the subcontinent. Dozens of prisons, as well as commercial sites, soon followed. With Ibex having made good progress with perimeter security, Bill Gallagher had granted it the distributing rights to Cardax as well in 2002. No one would say India is an easy market, but with rapid growth in many sectors and plenty of security problems, a country that has held such promise for Gallaghers for so long is now expected to deliver.

Further west again, Bilal Chehime continued to drive demand for Gallagher products in the Middle East. In 2008 the Cardax access control system and Command Centre were chosen for installation in the new Etihad Towers complex in Abu Dhabi — five shimmering towers with more than 1300 doors and dozens of lifts to control. Having shifted his headquarters from Dubai to Lebanon in 2006, Chehime felt sufficiently confident to return to Dubai and set up a satellite office there in 2011. He battled his way through the usual difficulties of business in tightly controlled economies. With a channel partner wanting to bid for work at the Dubai airport, Chehime discovered that New Zealand was not approved as a country of origin for such work. Australia was, however. Bill Gallagher's swift reply was that they were an Australasian company, and it was decided to put that on the label. However, New Zealand was soon approved as a supplier, with the help of New Zealand Trade & Enterprise.

In Turkey Gallagher Security's channel partner is Pronet, an Istanbul security company started in 1995 by three young entrepreneurs. Bill and Judi Gallagher have travelled several times to Istanbul to meet Ari Dinar and Alp Saul, descendants of Jews who escaped persecution in Spain and settled in Turkey in 1690, and to learn about the complexities of Turkish economic life. But the thing that has impressed Gallagher most is Saul's commercial energy, which has seen the company's equipment, mainly access control and Command Centre, installed for five trading banks, three telecoms (including 700 door-readers across 20 buildings for Vodafone) and the Topkapi Palace in Istanbul. The jewels and ancient manuscripts collected by the Ottoman sultans are now protected by Gallaghers.

The result of all this activity in far-flung regions was that the Asia, Middle East and the Africa divisions were generating nearly a quarter of Gallagher Security's export revenues through the late 2000s, keeping pace with the overall growth of the group.

In each area, whether it be the happy hunting ground of Australia, the bad lands of the US or the frontier environment of Iraq, Gallagher Security's constant battle is against the 'big boys' on one hand, the handful of leading multinational brands, and the 'cheap jacks' on the other, local versions of electric fences and access control systems that continually spring up, often with no great respect for international standards or patent laws.

In most circumstances Gallagher Security doesn't attempt to compete with the 'cheap jacks', but instead focuses its attention on succeeding against the large internationals. Positioning itself as the largest of the independents, Gallagher wins major projects by having more innovative products and being more flexible and responsive to the wishes of the customer. As Bill Gallagher is wont to say, 'With the big boys it's how it comes out of the box or nothing; with us, we're prepared to meet special requirements. Oh, we'll charge them for it, but at least it will do what they want.'

The primary marketing task of Gallagher and his team is to win over major security firms and consultants to using Gallagher

ABOVE Aerial view of the Gallagher compound on Kahikatea Road, Hamilton, 2009.

systems, or to recommend them. When Bill Gallagher declares 'We've got him dyed orange,' in reference to the company's ruling colour, they have achieved their goal. But the dye, no matter how bright, soon washes out if Gallagher products lose their innovative edge or if the specials don't work.

In a 2011 interview Gallagher identified his security division's ability to leverage the competencies and resources from within the whole Gallagher Group as a key ingredient in its success: 'Our in-house resources for tool making, plastics and electronics manufacturing and logistics mean that production can be controlled end-to-end, from concept design to manufacturing. The benefits of this include quality control, rapid development and deployment to manufacture, and the ability to produce economic short runs as well as large production capability. All of this is centrally managed on our Hamilton site.'[9]

Gallaghers can only be more flexible and responsive than its larger competitors because it doesn't have to rejig contracts and relationships with half a dozen internationally dispersed suppliers to produce something slightly different, if that is what is required.

On innovation, the group's commitment to R&D has, if anything, expanded in recent times. In 2011, around 105 of Gallagher's 600-odd New Zealand employees were working in the R&D section, with a budget of more than $14 million (around 8 per cent of the group's revenues). In 2006 the budget was around $5 million. At bottom, the R&D division develops the new products and the improvements to its existing products to justify the company's premium position. An inflection point came during the global financial crisis when, like every other firm, Gallaghers' senior managers batted around the idea that some form of retrenchment was required.

Steve Tucker recalls discussing the issue with Bill Gallagher: 'During the crunch, when multinationals were arbitrarily laying off hundreds or thousands of workers as revenues fell, we faced the same pressure. But with Bill and John Gallagher we've been able to escape the tyranny of the short-term focus that plagues publicly listed companies. Bill would rather make $2 million less this year and carry on with R&D in the expectation that there will be a greater payback in the future because we've continued to lay the foundation for the next round of innovative products, while many of our competitors have stopped spending. Indeed the retrenchment amongst our competitors is a real opportunity to spend and prepare a new generation of products ready for the next upward cycle in the industry.'[10]

R&D on its own, however, is no business miracle. As Curtis Edgecombe reminds his team regularly, 'Creating technology for technology's sake gets us nowhere; it's about creating technology that solves business problems.' Customers are generally reluctant to pay a premium for development costs and will push back at every opportunity. Bill Gallagher has a ready response: 'Our R&D people don't work for nothing — aren't they unreasonable?' That either wins a laugh or a shrug of the shoulders, but it's only the quality of the product and its usefulness that ends the argument.

And so by 2011 the R&D department had progressed access control software up to Version 6.10, which made standard the ability to warn cardholders when a particular competency was about to expire, along with a host of other options laid out on the Command Centre screens, right down to little things such as being able to shut down a building's heating and lighting when no one is in the building. Version 7 was nearing launch, set to take the product to a new level whereby the Command Centre would be able to integrate all the disparate security systems in a site into one simple interface on a single screen — CCTV screens, alarm systems, fire systems, perimeter fencing, access control and anything else can be monitored and controlled from a single screen. This had been done before by other companies, but only at great cost and usually only with their own proprietary model of CCTV, fence or alarm. In addition, Gallaghers' system works on a touch screen. Its promise is a substantially cheaper and more flexible solution that can potentially work with anything that's in place.

Much of the R&D spend is focused on the never-ending task of updating Gallagher software to work with each successive upgrade of other systems with which they are integrated. This is the curse of a fast-moving industry. Biometrics, for example, is rapidly becoming a favoured means of identifying people allowed access to a site. The South African market is one of the early adopters. MTN, a South African telecom company, for example, has abandoned traditional swipe cards, which were often lost or used as a spoon for eating or other such tasks, in favour of fingerprint readers.

Such readers have had a chequered past, with many early versions not working well, but Gallagher has partnered with one of the best, the French company Sagem Biometrics. A lifetime devoted to manual labour without gloves can sometimes make fingerprint reading difficult; facial recognition software or iris scanners may prove the best option. Gallaghers' R&D team has written the software required for its system to integrate with the leading providers of each device.

Less fancy perhaps than software design, but also important to the quality of the overall offering, is the meticulous work of making small improvements to the design of accessories, of which there are many for the fences. Much depends on the shape of a nut or a link, its ability to maintain pressure, its corrosion resistance, the extent of the torque range for maintaining a viable connection (will it work if some 'hairy-armed fencer' over-tightens it?) and its ease of installation.

All these things are worried over endlessly, as is the aesthetic appeal of the resulting parts. And over the years, the R&D department has developed interfaces to third-party products, such as the Insens disturbance sensor, which was designed in South Africa to deal with sites prone to excessive false alarms from vibration sensors. This small metal device, which is mounted on a vertical fence post, can sense if the entire fence is being pushed over and will sound an alarm.

Continuous, steady improvement is a given for any successful technology company, and Gallaghers has not been unique in that regard. The main change in the late 2000s has been the final achievement of the original goal of the PEC purchase in 1999, where the Cardax and PowerFence strands of the security business have been fully integrated. Structurally this has been achieved by resolving ownership separations, such as in the Australian market, and legacy management rivalries, such as in the UK subsidiaries. In terms of the product, each iteration of the Command Centre has deepened the integration between the perimeter and access control systems, as well as widening the net to other third-party systems.

The culminating act of integration has been a major rebranding exercise, long in gestation but finally introduced to the international markets in 2011. This retired the Cardax and PowerFence brands in favour of a unified Gallagher offering. Deputy CEO Steve Tucker, who led the exercise, says that despite their best efforts over the years the gaps between the company's various divisions had become too wide, with the PowerFence and Cardax divide only the most obvious among many. This had led to 'silo mentalities' within the organisation that proved stubbornly difficult to counter.

Now that complications caused by different distribution and ownership models in its biggest English-speaking markets had been resolved, there was an opportunity to break down those silos. Over the years a plethora of sub-brands had sprouted, from SmartPower and SmartFence to PowerPlus and Trophy FT. These were diluting the impact of the group's limited marketing and sponsorship spending. If big security customers in New Zealand thought of themselves as only Cardax customers, millions spent by the group to sponsor a project under the name of Gallagher weren't much use. In the marketplace, too, the group's various brands and sub-brands were leading to confusion.

Far better, then, to eliminate all the sub-brands in the animal management and security spheres and to present the company and its products to the world simply as Gallagher. More than that, the exercise, which coincided with Gallagher taking over full distribution of its products in the key markets of Australia and the US, provided the opportunity to think deeply about the company and its values. The result, after around 18 months of analysis, was the expressed desire 'to create New Zealand's first true global technology brand'.[13] That would inspire the team, especially in Hamilton.

In terms of the value proposition for customers, the exercise had Tucker and his team thinking not just about what they offered — the best electric fence or access control system — but also why they offered it and how. Answering the question of why, they concluded that they wanted to 'redefine what's possible for their customers'. Whether it be using an access control system to interface with HR systems to manage health and safety requirements in mines, or temporary electric fences to significantly improve the productivity of land, Gallaghers would provide a solution that could take the customer's business in a direction they might not previously have thought possible.

As to the 'how', they alighted on the phrase 'brilliant simplicity'. Tucker explained: 'Brilliant means the practical genius in the blood of our staff, the ability to make category-creating products, that people look at and say, "Wow." Simplicity means products that are simple to work with and that people like to use. For instance, when a customer picks up one of our products, and taps on, say, our touch screen indicators, people would say, "I should have thought of it, it's brilliant. And it's so easy to use."'[11]

There are plenty of examples to which Gallagher could refer that demonstrate this approach, including the Command Centre Version 7 that corrals all the elements of security into one easy-to-control screen, and the SmartFence, a portable fencing system with a built-in reel, posts and wires, containing everything a farmer needs to set up temporary fences quickly and simply.

Richard Janes, a Gallagher Group director, took an interest in the rebranding exercise and how the 'brilliant simplicity' approach feeds through to marketing: 'The brand position is products that are technologically advanced, but something you can "plug and play", that looks like it is something that you can use easily.' This flowed on to packaging and branding that was consistent and simple, which demystified the features of the product and showed the benefits. The SmartFence was a case in point. The meaning of the title wasn't as clear as it could have been. Henceforth it would be known as the Gallagher Instant Fence.

Retiring such well-known brands as Cardax and PowerFence was, as Tucker admits, 'gutsy', but long term he and Bill Gallagher concluded that a strong, clear and consistent Gallagher brand, reinforced by clearly articulated values, would provide a rallying point for the group as it emerged as a unified manufacturing and marketing organisation in most of its key international markets. Significantly, the original Gallagher colours, orange and black, and its logo, were retained. Some argued that the logo with its cogs from the forage harvester were unsuited to a modern global technology company, but Tucker defended it on the grounds that it tied in with the company's values of pioneering innovation and reinforced the idea that Gallagher had stood the test of time.

This heritage value that comes with the Gallagher brand continues to be reinforced immeasurably by the presence of Sir William Gallagher, still at the helm of the company that his father founded in 1938. Inevitably, with this visible and active head of the company out in the market regularly, demonstrating his personal commitment to the business and its products, the company and its brand will remain linked with the personality of its leader and the values he represents.

In New Zealand, which still accounts for around a quarter of the group's revenue, the Gallagher name carries all sorts of emotions with it, including pride in a New Zealand company that has consistently competed globally in areas requiring technical innovation, mixed with an awareness of the contribution made to the local community.

But the power of the personality attached to the Gallagher brands extends well beyond New Zealand's shores. Malcolm Linn, the general manager in Australia, sums it up well: 'Everyone says Bill is passionate, because he is. But he's more than that; he's very committed to understanding as much as he possibly can about the business. He can engage very quickly in a relevant conversation about what we do as Gallagher employees. That's a real strength, because it gives people reassurance and a sense of empowerment because you can quickly share a vision with the owner, meaningfully. And when the leader exudes excitement and energy about the products, it is contagious. You're not just selling any old product, you're selling something special. And, of course, customers pick up on it as well.'[12]

And so as the company prepares to celebrate its seventy-fifth anniversary in 2013 as a global company with hundreds of people employed around the world, a strong professional management team, and a well-established reputation in animal management, security and fuel pumps, it has developed a life of its own that could carry on with or without the active participation of its owners, the Gallagher family. But for the time being it enjoys its peculiar character and an extra edge as it continues to be led by Sir William Gallagher, a Kiwi business legend who, in his early seventies, retains the same hunger that he and his brother John showed when they took the reins up from their father 40 years ago.

That status as a Kiwi business legend, confirmed by a knighthood on New Year's Eve 2010 (which followed a CNZM in 1998), rests in part on the achievements of the company, having survived and prospered for so long as a manufacturing exporter and employer, and having built and maintained a globally recognised brand. Sadly, such achievements have been relatively rare. But Sir William has also exhibited the traits so beloved of New Zealanders in their leaders, in particular the blend of toughness in business and humility in everyday life. His toughness is not doubted by anyone

ABOVE The Gallagher board. From left to right: Steve Tucker, John Gallagher, Margaret Comer (board secretary), Sir William Gallagher, Bruce Munro, Richard Janes, Geoff Copstick and Simon Graafhuis (chief financial officer).

who has had to negotiate a deal with him. Nor did he hesitate to take on the unions when they strayed beyond what he considered the bounds of reasonable behaviour. He had no trouble 'laying down the law' when required.

On the other hand, it's less usual for the boss to eat in the cafeteria every day that he's in the building, alongside the cleaners, warehouse men and senior managers. Similarly, in the summer at Whangamata, where he has a pretty nice boat, he'll be seen waiting in line at the petrol station for his sticky bun and gas wearing old shorts and a towelling hat, engaging in light-hearted banter with anyone and everyone. In a country that despises anyone with a stuffed shirt, Sir William Gallagher fits the local ideal.

It is also less usual in New Zealand for the owner of a successful business to keep going over an extended period, let alone more than 50 years. The more typical pattern is to establish a successful business, build it to the point that the owner's material needs are catered for, then sell it to a multinational. The Gallaghers have grown their business and persevered for years to build up the security side in a hostile environment. They have turned down buy-out offers that have come their way over the years, partly out of patriotism, but, for Sir William in particular, because no amount of money would replace the joys of doing business.

Many have described him as singly focused on business. This was brought home forcibly to his daughter Janine in 2007 when Bill finally had to have that heart bypass operation. She saw him the night of the operation and thought he looked terrible. But when she returned on the third day she found him sitting on his bed in a t-shirt and boxer shorts, with a drip in his arm, conducting a business meeting with four guys wearing suits: 'I could see the sparkle back in his eyes, the old drive was back, and it's obvious he needs the business as much as the business needs him.'

Some 40 years after Bill and John Gallagher launched their father's small business into the global exporting game, Bill is still out there, now travelling as Sir William with Lady Judi at his side. Still talking to people, growing the business, looking for new opportunities. The main difference now is that there's a big operation back home, guided by Steve Tucker and a team that is committed to redefining what's possible in animal management, security and fuel pumps.

POSTSCRIPT

Life is about learning; when you stop learning, you die.

— TOM CLANCY

Strangely, there are quite a few people walking around in this condition.

— BILL GALLAGHER CARRIES ON THE THOUGHT

In December 2012 Sir William and Lady Judi Gallagher finally moved into their new house on Hamilton's Pembroke Street, overlooking Lake Rotoroa and, through the trees, the Gallagher factory. Its construction had been a long-running affair, starting in 2007 when they began extending their existing house, where Bill had lived since 1981. The old house stood at the upper end of a sloping section, and the plan had been to build an entertaining area dug into the lower end of the section, with an indoor pool, bowling alley and a vast space for big crowds. Generous hospitality has always been an essential element of Bill Gallagher's style of doing business — why not do something extraordinary? Judi took on the task of designing the new complex.

Having dug a great hole in the hillside and sunk many concrete piles around the edges — sufficient, it appeared to a casual bystander, to provide the foundation for a medium-sized skyscraper — the Gallaghers discovered that the old house, which was supposed to sit on top, was of good materials but very light and distorted. This provided Judi with the opportunity to work on a much greater canvas, and she set about replacing the wooden house with a steel and wood construction. Planning laws meant the shape of the house

ABOVE Sir William Gallagher receiving his knighthood from the Governor General, Sir Anand Satyanand.

was restricted largely to what had been there before, but Judi transformed it into a chateau with countless intricate features, such as turrets, spires, statues and fountains, fleur-de-lys castings on the ridgelines and concrete-plaster lions on the keystones above some of the windows.

As the years passed and concrete beams of a size typically used for the construction of motorway bridges were dropped into place in the middle of a tightly packed residential hillside, the project naturally became a source of interest to many Hamiltonians. It wasn't necessarily the greatest spectacle the city had seen since the Gallaghers launched the *Hamutana* in 1958, but it wasn't far off, and people were naturally curious about what exactly was going on. Bill's standard response to the inevitable question as to when it would be finished was to say, 'We're moving in after Christmas . . . but we're not sure which one yet.'

The shell was more or less watertight by January 2011, in time for Judi to host a function inside to celebrate Bill's knighthood. She dressed the concrete walls with black curtains, and the celebrations culminated in a huge fireworks display, launched from barges on the lake.

Lady Judi's influence on Bill's life has been noticeable. As Steve Saunders observes: 'Bill by nature is quite ascetic. He's quite happy with simple things. For a long time he drove a Citroën; nice but not very expensive. The most expensive thing he had was a Rolex watch, which he bought when he was drunk one day. Judi brought much greater enthusiasm for celebrating and demonstrating success, which overall has been helpful. Bill had been a bit too understated.'[1]

The Gallaghers' home now stands out — white, gleaming, a miniature fairy-tale castle on the hill — not completely over the top, but not understated either. It is the home of a couple who have achieved a few things and are not afraid to have a little fun.

The other striking thing about the house, in terms of the Gallagher story, is its location: barely two kilometres from the home of Bill's childhood and the original Gallagher workshop. The current Gallagher headquarters and factories are even closer, as is Hamilton's CBD. Aside from a few years as an infant and at university, Bill Gallagher has passed his entire 71 years living and working within a radius of a couple of kilometres of his current home. True, he has probably spent a fifth to a quarter of his adult

ABOVE Glenice, John, Lady Judi and Sir William Gallagher.

life travelling to all points of the globe in search of new customers for his goods, and he has devoted his professional life to building a genuinely international company, but through it all he has remained anchored to his home town.

Indeed, the wider Gallagher clan are staunch Hamiltonians. Bill's daughter Janine and son Ian live within easy striking distance. Janine, with two children, Chanelle and Brandon, is engaged at the time of writing to Nick. Ian lives beside the Narrows, a beautiful section of the Waikato river, with his wife Debi and their three children, Charlotte, Danny and Logan. Debi, a girl from Sussex, England, started her working life with Gallagher UK in 1994 as a company artist and product manager. Ian now works in Gallagher's training division.

In 2012 Sir William Gallagher adopted Judi's son Chris, whose father had died and to whom he'd been a father figure for 20 years. Chris lives on a farm at Te Kowhai and has four children: Demi, Conner, Peyton and Tyus. At the time of writing he is engaged to Claire, who has four children, Jaime, Kayleigh, Luke and Sam. John and Glenice Gallagher's two sons, Tony and Keith, also live nearby. Tony is engaged to Jodi and they have a baby, Sam; Jodi also has a daughter, Mikayla. Keith, who works at Gallaghers in the R&D Department, is married to Judi. They have two children, Joshua and Catherine.

And while the reach of the Gallagher Group extends further into global markets each year, its owners — Sir William and Lady Judi, John and Glenice Gallagher and Jenny Gallagher — have been loyal to the city that gave them their start. Not just in the sense of retaining the bulk of the company's workforce and manufacturing facilities in Hamilton, but also in terms of supporting good causes throughout the region.

Over the 70-odd years the Gallaghers have been in business, Hamilton has grown from a rural services township with fewer than 30,000 souls to become the nation's fourth largest city, with a population of 200,000–350,000, depending on how far the count extends into the surrounding hinterland. It is a city on the rise. Even so, the trajectory of the Gallagher Group's growth has far outstripped that of the city in recent decades, and

ABOVE Lady Judi and Sir William Gallagher in their new home, still under construction, July 2012.

so the firm's relative prominence has grown with each passing year.

This is partly a reflection of the fact that the Gallagher Group is one of the city's largest private employers. It has bucked the trend of manufacturing decline to remain one of the last locally owned companies of real substance. But more importantly, the Gallaghers have continued to stand out as leading benefactors, with the result that the Gallagher logo seems to be everywhere.

Rob Hamill, a New Zealand rower and winner of the inaugural Atlantic Rowing Race with Phil Stubbs in 1997, is one who has had a long association with the Gallaghers. In 2002, as part of a group trying to organise a rowing race on the Waikato River, where the University of Waikato team would take on Cambridge University, Hamill approached the Gallaghers. He recalls that Bill Gallagher and Margaret Comer saw value in the event and provided seed funding for the inaugural race. It was a success, and last year the Gallagher Great Race celebrated its tenth anniversary as a highlight on the local calendar.

A few years after their initial meeting, listening to Bill Gallagher speak at a conference, Hamill was struck by a comment Bill made about his father: 'Bill said, "Father told us we should care about our fellow man," and that he and his brother John had taken that instruction to heart and saw themselves continuing a legacy begun by their father to support great community initiatives.'[2] That support, Hamill soon realised, wasn't open-ended. 'Bill made the comment to me once, that if people took their support for granted, or didn't do what they said they would do, they'd be knocked off the list pretty quickly.' Similarly with Margaret Comer, the conduit between the company and many of the groups it supports, Hamill observes that she is 'hugely supportive' of projects, but 'equally insistent that progress has to be made . . . [and] won't put up with any nonsense'.[3]

When the Waikato Rugby Union was looking for outside interests to help get a new stadium project over the line, Gallaghers came on board as one of the three key sponsors. Graham Bowen, who joined the union board in 2002, the year the stadium was opened, has worked closely with Bill Gallagher and Margaret Comer ever since. His comments are typical of those who have dealt with the Gallaghers: 'Every time we've found ourselves struggling, the Gallagher Group have been outstanding at helping us bridge the gaps. But just as

TOP Sir William diving in Mozambique with a fish he named Fred.

ABOVE Margaret Comer with her husband Bob and the Waikato rugby team, sponsored by Gallaghers.

ABOVE Gallaghers' sponsorship of Wintec's student commons led to it being called the Gallagher Hub.

importantly, they've also used their own leverage to appeal to other business leaders to help and assist. So their leadership role has been critical to us. And Bill leads from the front. He'll come to most games, talking to everyone, and any time we hold a function or an auction or a dinner, he'll always be there. And he'll be the first with his hand up at the auction, bidding high to set a benchmark for others to follow.

'Then when it comes to sponsorship, I deal with a lot of business leaders. He would be one of the best people to deal with. He will give you a definite indication first time you meet as to whether a proposal has legs. You're not left wondering. And the good thing is, that he has the authority to make it happen. You know that you'll get a straight answer, and he's never gone back on his word.'[4]

The Gallagher logo now appears all around the rugby fields, on the stands, on the players' shorts, even on the grass for the big matches.

Sponsorship of rugby has a commercial rationale, in terms of building the Gallagher brand among an audience that uses its products. Other sponsorships, such as the money invested for the naming rights of the student commons at Wintec, now the 'Gallagher Hub', probably don't stack up as a purely commercial sponsorship for the company, but they form a hybrid between sponsorship and philanthropy. After his appointment as Wintec's chief executive in 2003, Mark Flowers quickly appreciated the extent of Gallaghers' commitment to community affairs, 'not just in terms of sponsorship', he says, 'but also having someone senior turning up at any regional discussions, Chambers of Commerce meetings and any city gathering'.[5]

Flowers had a couple of things in mind when he approached Gallaghers for naming rights for the Hub: 'The money was nice, but just as important was the endorsement by Gallaghers that the sponsorship implied.' In return, the company gained a good profile in one of the country's largest institutes of technology.

The Gallaghers, in the meantime, have an equally generous philanthropic relationship with the University of Waikato. The Gallagher Academy of Performing Arts is just one outcome of that enduring relationship. In March 2008 the university recognised the brothers' contribution by awarding Bill and John Gallagher each an honorary doctorate.

The Gallaghers' sponsorship of Hospice Waikato is more philanthropic than commercial in nature, though equally dear to the hearts

BELOW At Government House, Wellington, for Sir William's investiture. From left: Ian, Lady Judi, Sir William, Janine and Chris.

of all involved. Margaret Comer had been a long-time board member of the hospice. When the board resolved to launch a major fundraising campaign in order to build new facilities in early 2007, it had the good sense to ask Bill Gallagher to be its patron. Richard Small, then chair of the board, recalls: 'Once we had Gallaghers on as our lead sponsor, everything fell into place.' As the largest sponsors, the Gallaghers took the naming rights for the new facilities which opened in March 2010. The Gallagher Family Hospice provides essential care and support for people with a life-limiting illness and their families and friends, free of charge. It receives around 70 per cent of its ongoing funding from the District Health Board and fundraises for the rest. So Gallaghers' involvement is substantial and continuous.

Many more such stories could be told, but the point is made. The Gallagher Group led by Sir William Gallagher, has made and continues to make a powerful contribution wherever it sets its mind to it. Its primary purpose as an international company is to provide customers around the world with good products that they are happy to pay for, because — whether it's a farm made more productive by electric fencing or a mine made safer by sophisticated access control systems — their businesses are improved.

In addition to that, Gallaghers has always been conscious of its role in broadening New Zealand's economic base by successfully exporting technologically advanced manufactured goods. When times have been hard, it hasn't been tempted to give up or sell out, being convinced that it could continue to succeed from New Zealand. And finally, the Gallaghers themselves have enjoyed the rewards of their efforts, and a large part of that enjoyment has been the opportunity to give a lot back to Hamilton and the Waikato, the community from which they sprang.

ABOVE Bill Gallagher with the framed awards won by his father. The awards are: an MBE for services to the community; Fairfax Media NZ Business Hall of Fame laureate 2012; Rotary International Paul Harris Fellow; and Waikato Business Person of the Year 1998.

Endnotes

Note: All quotes from Bill Gallagher are from interviews with the author, unless otherwise stated.

Introduction: 'For fun and profit' — the Gallagher Story
1. Paul Goldsmith (PG) interview with Erik Dijkstra, February 2011.
2. G Crocombe, M Enright & M Porter, *Upgrading New Zealand's Competitive Advantage*, Oxford University Press, New York, 1991, p. 127.
3. H Simon, *Hidden Champions: Lessons from the World's Best Unknown Companies*, Harvard, Boston, 1996; also 'Lessons from Germany's Midsize Giants', *Harvard Business Review*, March-April 1992.

Chapter 1. Inheritance
1. See M Villette & C Vuillermot, *From Predators to Icons: Exposing the Myth of the Business Hero*, Cornell University Press, Ithaca, NY, 2009.
2. *From Ireland to New Zealand: Eight Generations after Thomas Gallagher and Bridget Comerford*, compiled by Alison Honeyfield, Evagean Publishing, 2009.
3. Ibid., p. 51.
4. Ibid., p. 154.
5. Ibid. p. 156.
6. James Gallagher probate 1920, Archives New Zealand, BBAE, 1569, Box 469, 14256.
7. See G Hubbard (ed.), *Taking on the World: The Gallagher Story*, Gallagher Group, Hamilton, 1992, p. 138ff; also Archives New Zealand, Akl, BBAE, 4985, Box 194 D51/1932.
8. *From Ireland*, p. 170.
9. Hubbard, p. 2.
10. *Hawke's Bay Herald*, 5 December 1889.
11. Records of Prime Manufacturing Co, Milwaukee, Mil MSS 109, and *Milwaukee Milk Producer*, August 1936; the *Daily Illinois* of 30 July 1936 reported on the rural electrification administration testing an electric fence near Washington, a single wire carrying a charge of electricity; 'cows learn fast'.
12. *From Ireland*, p. 170; Hubbard, p. 1.
13. *From Ireland*, p. 182; listed in the *New Zealand Gazette*.
14. Hubbard, p. 2.
15. *Evening Post*, 2 November 1938.
16. P Goldsmith, *We Won, You Lost, Eat That: A Political History of Tax in New Zealand Since 1840*, David Ling, Auckland, 2008, p. 189.
17. NM Taylor, *The Home Front*, Vol. 2, Department of Internal Affairs, Wellington, 1986, p. 752.
18. Hubbard, p. 4.
19. 63 Seddon Road was later renumbered 85.
20. Hubbard, p. 5.
21. Family members give the date of Henry's return as 1947, although *From Ireland*, p.117, records that he arrived in 1949.
22. NZ Patent no. 99929.
23. PG interview with Molly Gallagher, February 2011.
24. Hubbard, p. 28.
25. For further details, see Goldsmith, *We Won, You Lost, Eat That*.
26. Vogal was incorporated on 20 August 1954.
27. D Ausubel, *The Fern and the Tiki*, 1965, quoted in J Belich, *Paradise Reforged: A History of the New Zealanders, 1880–2000*, Penguin, Auckland, 2002, p. 353.
28. Hubbard, p. 27.
29. Ibid., p. 11.
30. *Waikato Times*, 15 December 1951.

Chapter 2. Young Bill Gallagher: 1941–62
1. PG interview with May Gallagher, October 2011.
2. PG interview with Molly Gallagher, October 2010.
3. Ibid.
4. PG interview with John Gallagher, August 2011.
5. *Dominion*, around 8 January 1955.
6. *From Ireland*, p. 182.
7. LF Herreshoff, *The Compleat Cruiser: The Art, Practice and Enjoyment of Boating*, Sheridan House, NY, 1956.
8. *Waikato Times*, 15 September 1958.
9. PG interview with John Young, January 2011.
10. PG interview with Jenny Gallagher, March 2011.
11. J Bassett, *Prospero's Island: A History of the School of Engineering at the University of Auckland*, 2003, provides additional background.
12. *New Zealand Herald*, 2 April 1962.
13. PG interview with Jenny Gallagher, March 2011.

Chapter 3. Resourceful Young Men: 1962–70
1. *From Ireland to New Zealand*, p. 180.
2. *Waikato Times*, 13 June 1962; *New Zealand Farmer*, 5 July 1962.

3   PG interview with D Phillips, February 2011.
4   NZ Patent no 133264.
5   D Coy, *The Foremans*, Hamilton, 2009, p. 28.
6   Hubbard, p. 43.
7   Precision Electronics Ltd was incorporated on 24 February 1966.
8   *Vanity Fair*, February 2011.
9   The quote comes from William Johnson Cory, a tutor at Eton: 'Nor need you regret the hours you spend on much that is forgotten, for the shadow of lost knowledge at least protects you from many illusions.'
10 *Hamutana* log, November 1961.
11 Hubbard, p. 40.
12 EV Sale, *Kelly: The Adventurous Life of Kelly Tarlton*, Heinemann Reed, Auckland, 1988, p. 46.
13 J Pettit, *Treasure Below: The Adventures of a New Zealand Treasure Hunter*, Halcyon Press, Auckland, 2008.
14 Arthur C Clarke, *The Treasure of the Great Reef*, Harper and Row, London, 1964, p. 15.
15 M Lipyeat & L Wright, *Delving Deeper: Half a Century of Cave Discovery in New Zealand*, Hazard, Christchurch, 2003, p. 77. Cold Water Creek was written up in an early edition of *Dive* magazine.
16 Sale, p. 66.
17 *Hamutana* log, 27 January 1968.
18 'Divers face eruption and bombs', *New Zealand Herald*, 30 January 1968, and *New Zealand Herald*, 31 January 1968.
19 Pettit, p. 73; *Bay of Plenty Times*, 3 July 1968.
20 Sale, p. 94; see also C Ingram, P Wheatley, L Diggle, E Diggle & K Gordon, *New Zealand Shipwrecks: Over 200 Years of Disasters at Sea*, 8th edn, Hodder Moa, Auckland, 2007.
21 MF Allen & K Scadden, *The General Grant's Gold: Shipwreck and Greed in the Southern Ocean*, Exisle, Auckland, 2009, p. 173.
22 Pettit, p. 73.
23 Ibid , p. 75.
24 Pettit, p. 93; S Locker-Lampson, *Throw Me the Wreck Johnny: Memories of Kelly Tarlton*, Halcyon Press, Auckland, 1996, p. 75.
25 Locker-Lampson, p. 51.
26 Sale, p. 99.
27 Ibid., p. 103.
28 Allen & Scadden, p. 134.
29 Pettit, p. 81.
30 *From Ireland*, p. 177.

Chapter 4. Playing Doubles: 1971–77
1   Gallagher Electronics' sales were $797,000 and net profit $61,000, compared with Gallagher Engineering's $1.67 million sales and $137,000 profits.
2   P Dixon to Bill Gallagher, 19 December 1974.
3   Bob Piesse to Bill Gallagher, 9 January 1968; Gallagher to Piesse, 27 February 1968.
4   Gallagher to Piesse, 21 August 1970; Piesse to Gallagher, 25 August 1970.
5   See Goldsmith, p. 262, for depreciation rates.
6   ICW2680 15 record 57/9/260, Archives New Zealand.
7   Bill Gallagher speech to Waikato Export Institute 15 October 1986, and speech 7 April 1984.
8   PG interview with Janine Gallagher, March 2011.
9   Hubbard, p. 53; *Waikato Times*, 28 August 1971.
10 AATJ w 3566 7428 923, Archives New Zealand.
11 John Gallagher to Les Dickinson, 18 September 1974.
12 PG interview with Jenny Gallagher, March 2011.
13 PG interview with John Gallagher, August 2011.
14 Ibid.
15 *Evening Post*, 3 September 1977.
16 Dan Cherrington to Bill Gallagher, 12 November 1975.

Chapter 5. The Electric Fences Take Over: 1977–85
1   PG interview with Erik Dijkstra, February 2011.
2   'The future for New Zealand's agricultural-associated products in international markets and trade', Dan Watkins Lecture, 27 August 1984; published in *New Zealand Agricultural Science*, August 1984.
3   C Campbell-Hunt et al., *World Famous in New Zealand: How New Zealand's Leading Firms Became World-Class Competitors*, Auckland University Press, 2001, pp. 35, 185.
4   Bill Gallagher, 'Main elements in developing export sales', speech to the Export Institute of New Zealand. Auckland Division, 31 May 1978.
5   PG interview with Erik Dijkstra, February 2011.
6   Ibid.
7   Ibid.
8   PG interview with Poul Dalgaard, September 2011.
9   PG interview with Erik Dijkstra, February 2011.

10 PG interview with Bernd Allie, August 2011.
11 Bill Gallagher interview, *Newelectronics*, February 1982.
12 PG interview with David Mullen, August 2011.
13 Ibid.
14 Ibid.
15 PG interview with Vaughan Jones, October 2010.
16 Ibid.
17 See, for example, *NZ Dairy Exporter*, 15 July 1982; for background on the history of New Zealand pasture management, see: PW Smallfield, *The Grasslands Revolution in New Zealand*, Hodder & Stoughton, Auckland, 1970; BH Levy, *Grasslands of New Zealand*, Government Printer, Wellington, 1970; NZ Agritech, *New Zealand's Agricultural Excellence*, Auckland, 2002.
18 *Waikato Times*, 7 December 1983.
19 PG interview with Kevin Marquand, December 2010.
20 Bill Gallagher trip report, May 1982.
21 Ibid.
22 Papers presented at the First World Elephant and Wildlife Seminar, Gallagher Group, 22 November 1983.
23 Gallagher, Second World Wildlife Power Fencing Seminar, Dubbo, NSW, November 1985.
24 Bill Gallagher, trip report, May 1982.
25 PG interview with John Lucey, November 2010.
26 PG interview with Noel Hamilton, October 2010.
27 PG interview with Erik Dijkstra, January 2011.
28 The award was presented on 3 November 1983; *Auckland Star*, 7 December 1983. See *Evening Post*, 3 September 1977 for a report on the earlier export award.
29 See M Bassett, *Working with David. Inside the Lange Cabinet*, Hodder Moa, Auckland, 2008, p. 101ff, for details.

Chapter 6. Survival: 1985–89

1 PG interview with Jenny Gallagher, March 2011.
2 *Waikato Times*, 5 February 1987.
3 Ibid., 13 March 1987.
4 PG interview with Jenny Gallagher, March 2011.
5 *Dominion*, 14 March 1987; *NZ Woman's Weekly*, 27 April 1987.
6 Economic Summit proceedings, Vol. 1, p. 181.
7 Bill Gallagher speech, 'Waikato vision for the 1990s', 2 May 1986.
8 Don Lindale, February 1987 review, Gallagher Group board papers.
9 Gallagher Group annual report, 1989.
10 Hubbard, p. 88.
11 Gallagher Group annual report, 1988.
12 Bill Gallagher speech, 'Utilising R&D for maximum advantage', 15 October 1986.
13 Bill Gallagher speech, November 1987, Groningen.
14 L Iacocca with W Novak, *Iacocca: An Autobiography*, Random House, New York, 1984; Bill Gallagher speech, 15 October 1986.
15 Bill Gallagher speech, 15 October 1986.
16 Hubbard, p. 94.
17 Campbell-Hunt et al., p. 116.
18 Ibid., p. 117.
19 PG interview with John Lucey, November 2010.
20 PG interview with Erik Dijkstra, January 2011.
21 PG interview with David Mullen, August 2011.
22 Bill Gallagher speech, 7 April 1984.
23 Bill Gallagher trip report, USA 1987.
24 GPF annual reports; PG interview with David Mullen, August 2011.
25 See V Jones, '50 Years of Power Fencing', *Proceedings of the NZ Grassland Association*, Vol. 49, 1988, pp. 145–9.
26 V Jones, 'The Farmer', Gallagher Area Managers Conference, February 1988.
27 Hubbard, p. 92.
28 Ibid., p. 95.
29 PG interview with Erik Dijkstra, January 2011.

Chapter 7. Regaining Momentum: 1989–95

1 PG interview with John Gallagher, August 2011.
2 Minutes of Senior Management Conference, Okoroire Hotel, 28 January 1989.
3 ME Porter, *The Competitive Advantage of Nations*, Harvard, Boston, 1990.
4 Crocombe et al., p. 127.
5 Ibid., pp. 85, 122.
6 PG interview with Lady Judi Gallagher, October 2011.
7 PG interview with Vishnu Narain, September 2011.
8 PG interview with Neil Richardson, February 2011.
9 Reserved decision of Judge PJ Duncan, District Court of Otahuhu, 10 March 1982 (case heard 27 October 1981).
10 *New Zealand Herald*, 28 October 1981; *Dominion*, 28 October 1981.
11 Dave Wilson, 'Report on Proposed Gallagher Security System', 11 November 1987; this was probably Electric Security Fencing Ltd, set up in 1986.

12 Opinion from RL Towner, Russell McVeagh, 9 February 1989.
13 Bill Gallagher to P Morfee, Chief Electrical Inspector, Ministry of Energy, 10 February 1989; a working party on the standard was set up under Morfee, and the standard drafted in November 1990, issued on 29 November 1990 and approved by the Minister of Energy on 22 January 1991.
14 PG interview with John Lucey, November 2010.
15 PG interview with Erik Dijkstra, February 2011.
16 P Goldsmith, *Fletchers: A Centennial History of Fletcher Building*, David Ling, Auckland, 2010, p. 137.
17 Annual report, 1991.
18 Leaving Bill with 35 per cent, Jenny 10 per cent, John 35 per cent, Glenice 15 per cent and Richardson 5 per cent.
19 PG interview with Steve Hoffman, November 2010.
20 See *Waikato Times*, 2 February 1994, for background.
21 PG interview with Margaret Comer, November 2010.

Chapter 8. Stalling: 1996–99
1 *National Mutual* (the magazine of IABC), 26 June 1996; *Sunday Star-Times*, 14 July 1996; *New Zealand Herald*, 15 April 1996.
2 Neil Richardson, 'GGL strategy to 2001 and 2010', 1 November 1996; PG interview with Neil Richardson, February 2011.
3 Campbell-Hunt et al., p. 117.
4 Gallagher Case Study, A Beckenstein of Darden Graduate Business School, University of Virginia, and TD Cullwick, Ernst & Young, New Zealand, draft, February 1996, p. 12.
5 H Mintzberg, *The Rise and Fall of Strategic Planning*, Free Press, New York, 1994.
6 Simon, *Hidden Champions*; see also 'Lessons from Germany's Midsize Giants', *Harvard Business Review*, March-April 1992.
7 Simon.
8 PG interview with Janine Gallagher, February 2011.
9 PG interview with Bruce Munro, November 2010.
10 Neil Richardson presentation, 'The GGL strategy to 2001 and 2010', 1 November 1996.
11 Bill Gallagher, letter to distributors, 29 January 1997.
12 PG interview with Bruce Munro, November 2010.
13 *New Zealand Farmer*, 19 September 1996; *New Zealand Business*, October 1996.
14 John Walley, 'Review of Strategy, 1991–97'.
15 'Saturday Morning with Kim Hill', National Radio, 22 January 1999.
16 Restated in *The Metal*, April 1999.
17 *Unlimited*, 2001.
18 'Saturday Morning with Kim Hill', 22 January 1999.
19 Minutes, GGL board reports, March 1998.
20 PG interview with David Mullen, August 2011.
21 PG interview with Steve Saunders, December 2010.
22 PG interview with Lady Judi Gallagher, October 2011.
23 Ibid.

Chapter 9. A New Direction: 1999–2001
1 PG interview with John Williams, April 2011.
2 Proceedings of Economic Summit, p. 232.
3 H McDonnell, 'Pallo, Karl — Biography', *Dictionary of New Zealand Biography, Te Ara: The Encyclopedia of New Zealand*, updated 1 September 2010.
4 J Williams, 'PEC (NZ) Ltd — 1939 to 1999: A Brief History of PEC's Achievements Prepared for Marton's 125 Year Celebrations'.
5 Colin Campbell-Hunt interview with John Williams, December 1998.
6 Ibid.
7 *Wanganui Chronicle*, 28 April 1993.
8 PG interview with Graham Dawson, July 2011.
9 PEC's awards included the Air New Zealand Award for Overall Excellence in Exporting, 1994.
10 Campbell-Hunt et al., p172.
11 See, for example, *Management Magazine*, March 1995 and April 1998.
12 PG interview with John Williams, April 2011.
13 Colin Campbell-Hunt interview with John Williams, December 1998.
14 PG interview with John Williams, April 2011.
15 *NZ Infotech Weekly*, 13 December 1999.
16 PG interview with Steve Tucker, November 2010.
17 See *Dominion* and *Evening Standard*, 2 June 1999.
18 Campbell-Hunt et al., p. 172.
19 Annual report, 1999.
20 PG interview with Kahl Betham, November 2010.
21 *Waikato Times*, 6 March 2000.
22 PG interview with Wayne O'Halloran, November 2010.

23 PG interview with Margaret Comer, November 2010.
24 September 1999 board report.
25 PG interview with Steve Bell, May 2011.
26 PG interview with Charles Tomas, March 2011.
27 *Unlimited*, 2001.
28 Campbell-Hunt et al., p. 70.
29 PG interview with Steve Tucker, November 2010.
30 Ibid.
31 Campbell-Hunt et al., p. 77.
32 Michael E Porter speech, 'New Zealand competitiveness: The next agenda', 3 August 2001.
33 *Unlimited*, 1 June 2001.
34 J Bridges & D Downs, *No 8 Wire: The Best of Kiwi Ingenuity*, Hodder Moa Beckett, Auckland, 2000.
35 *Unlimited*, 2001.
36 PG interview with Steve Tucker, November 2010.
37 PG interview with Thomas Friederichs, March 2011.

Chapter 10. The Road to Buckingham Palace: 2002–2006

1 *Sunday Times* (UK), 19 December 2004.
2 *Evening Standard* (UK), 8 October 2004.
3 *New Zealand Herald*, 12 October 2004.
4 PG interview with Thomas Friederichs, March 2011.
5 PG interview with Henny Beeber, March 2011.
6 PG interview with Stuart Neal, March 2011.
7 PG interview with Ian Meadows, August 2011.
8 PG interview with Graham Dawson, April 2011.
9 PG interview with Charles Tomas, March 2011.
10 Ibid.
11 PG interview with Steve Bell, June 2011.
12 PG interview with Kahl Betham, November 2010.
13 PG interview with Curtis Edgecombe, November 2010.
14 *Sunday Star-Times*, 21 October 2001.
15 Hoffman, board report, September 2003.
16 Copstick report, board papers, September 2003.
17 PG interview with Bernd Allie, August 2011.
18 *Dominion Post*, 24 December 2003.
19 *Rural News*, 16 March 2004.
20 *Independent*, 25 August 2004; *Dominion Post*, 27 August 2004.
21 *Dominion Post*, 8 November 2007; revenue figures from Tru-Test annual reports (the company had dropped out of wire in 2004, which reduced sales).
22 PG interview with Bruce Munro, November 2011.
23 PG interview with Steve Tucker, November 2010.
24 Ibid.
25 PG interview with Kahl Betham, November 2010.
26 PG interview with Bilal Chehime, March 2011.
27 Ibid.

Chapter 11. The Relentless Drive for Innovation: 2006 and Beyond

1 A Schroeder, *The Snowball: Warren Buffett and the Business of Life*, Bloomsbury, London, 2008, p. 132.
2 PG interview with Steve Hoffman, November 2010.
3 PG interview with David Mullen, August 2011.
4 PG interview with Bruce Munro, November 2011.
5 PG interview with Malcolm Linn, May 2011.
6 PG interview with Wayne O'Halloran, November 2010.
7 PG interview with Thomas Friederichs, March 2011.
8 Terry Oden quoted from a Gallagher case study, 'Birmingham Water Works Board'.
9 *NZ Security*, January 2011.
10 PG interview with Steve Tucker, November 2010.
11 See Harvard Business School case study, R Deshpande & K Chi-Ho Wong, 'Rebranding Gallagher'.
12 Quoted in the Harvard Business school case study.
13 PG interview with Malcolm Linn, May 2011.

Postscript

1 PG interview with Steve Saunders, December 2010.
2 PG interview with Rob Hamill, June 2012.
3 Ibid.
4 PG interview with Graham Bowen, May 2012.
5 PG interview with Mark Flowers, May 2012.

Acknowledgements

This book would not have been possible without the cooperation and assistance of Sir William Gallagher, his wife Lady Judi, and Margaret Comer. My first acknowledgement is to them. I'm indebted, of course, to many others. In particular I'd like to thank: Bernd Allie, Henny Beeber, Steve Bell, David Bentley, Kahl Betham, Murray Bindon, Graham Bowen, Colin Campbell-Hunt, Bilal Chehime, Bob Comer, Poul Dalgaard, Graham Dawson, Erik Dijkstra, Curtis Edgecombe, Mark Flowers, Thomas Friederichs, Chris Gallagher, Ian and Debi Gallagher, Janine Gallagher, Jenny Gallagher, John and Glenice Gallagher, May Gallagher, Molly Gallagher, Katie Giles, Bruce and Di Goldsworthy, Simon Graafhuis, Rob Hamill, Noel Hamilton, Paul Hargreaves, Bill Hay, Stephen Hoffman, Richard Janes, Vaughan Jones, Malcolm Linn, John Lucey, Kevin Marquand, Ian Meadows, David and Marg Mullen, Bruce Munro, Vishnu Narain, Stuart Neal, Wayne O'Halloran, John Pettit, Doug Phillips, Neil Richardson, Steve Saunders, Richard Small, Charles Tomas, Steve Tucker, John Williams and John Young. Particular thanks also to Mike Moore for his foreword and to Nicola Legat and Kimberley Davis at Random House for their great effort.

Index

Abraham & Williams 41
Adams-Schneider, Lance 81, 189
Advantage Group 304, 305–306
AES Group 330, 378
AgResearch 274
AKO electric fence 90
Aldridge, Steve 252–253, 280

Alex Harvey Industries (AHI) 98
Alfa Laval 220
Allflex Holdings 226
Allie Agratechnik 162, 341
Allie, Bernd 23, 161–162, *163*, 259
Allie, Helmut 161–162, 217, 259
Allie, Martha *163*
Allison, Jock 11
AM Bisley and Co 89, 96, 224, 273
Anixter 377
Arc-Rite electric fence 90
Ausubel, David 52–55

Barrier Fence Company 91
Barry Huber 234
Barry, Jim 234
Bartley, Kel 335
Beckett, Charlie 56
Beckett, Isaac 73
Beeber, Henny 330, 331, 378
Bell Booth Ltd 172
Bell, Steve 307, 309–310, 319, 335
Bentley, Dave 16, 375
Betham, Kahl 306, 335, 350
BEV II energiser 25, 123, 130, 141, 149, 154, 185, 208
Bindon, Murray 232, 265, 294
Bolger, Jim 247, 269
Booth, Andrew 280, *281*
Booth, Rob 277, 279, 280, *284*, 287, 385, 312, 313, 321
Bowen, Graham 400
BrainZ Instruments 341
Brett, Ed 212
Brett, Edmund 184
Brian Perry Ltd 234
British Gas 261, 327
Brown electric fence 90
Brown, Ada 234
Bruell, Freddy 187
Bryant, Jim 73
Buffett, Warren 28, 99, 191
Bunyan, Doug 117
Burdon, Philip 247

Calcott, John 110, 111
Cardax 14, 29, 295, 301–302, 303, 304, 305, 306–307, 308, 309–310, 311, 313, 315, 316, 317, 319, 321, 330, 331, 332, 333, 334, 335, 336–337, 339, 340, 344, 347, 352, 364, 366,
371, 372, 373, 375, 377, 378, 381, 386, 387, 388
Casares, Vincent 136
Casares, Vincent junior 136
Certis CISCO 378
Chehime, Bilal 16, 352–355, *353*, *354*, 381
Chehime, Hassan *353*
Chehime, Imad *353*
Chehime, Nabia *353*
Cherrington, Dan 135, 136, 140–141, 183, 184
Cherrington, John 135
Chibnall, Peter 255, 315
Christian, Evan 306
Christie, Herb 42
Christie, Rick 278, *284*, 309
Cipel 162, 164 — *see also* Saft
Clark, (Sir) Tom 70
Clark, Helen 319
Clark, Mary (Dot) 70
Clarke, Arthur C 12, 106
Clements, Peter *110*, 111
Clow family 36–37
Clow, George 38
Clow, Sarah — *see* Gallagher, Sarah
Clow, Viv 78
Cochrane, Frank 234
Cochrane, Ileen 234
Cochrane, Judi — *see* Gallagher, Lady Judi
Cochrane, Thomas 234
Colonial Ammunitions Company (CAC) 46, 51
Comer, Margaret 16, 25, 212, 224, 242, 258, 264, 268, 276, 283, 287, 307–308, 321, *323*, 350, 351, 379, *390*, 400, *401*, 405
Congreve, Robin 340, 341
Cook, Norm 79
Copstick, Geoff 321, 340, 350, *390*
Cords, Wolfgang 161
Cornet, Fred 99
Cree, Ronald 197
Criterion Group 190
Crittal Engineering 89
Crutcher, Ray 297

Dalgaard, Poul 136, *137*, 157, 178–181
Dalgety 239
Dawson, Graham 301, 302, 309, 332, 352
Day, Les (Akki) 68
de Beer, Jillian 268
Dearling, John *110*, 111, 116
Deere, Brendon 300
Delany, Phil 225, 226–227

Dickinson, Les 134, 135, 136, 183
Digital Alarm Technologies (DATS) 332
Dijkstra, Dooitze 148–150, 213, 216 — *see also* Veldman & Dijkstra
Dijkstra, Erik 11, 19–21, 148–150, 154–155, 156–157, 158, 161, 171, 186, 190, *216*, 228, 253 — *see also* Veldman & Dijkstra
Dijkstra, Meindert 149, *216* — *see also* Veldman & Dijkstra
Dinar, Ari 383
Dissanayake, Gamini 11, 12
diving, scuba 12, 65, 70–71, 76–77, 78, 81, 101, 102, 104–116, 265, 279, *401*
Doak, Wade 78, 106, 107
Dobbs, Tony 319, 321, 347, 349, 351
Douglas, Roger 200, 201, 206, 239
Downer Engineering 337
du Nouvelle, Count Louis 162
Dudek, Jim 141

Edgecombe, Curtis 25, 337, *338*, 351, 371, 372, 375, 376, 385
Elder Smith Goldsborough Mort (Elders) 99, 100, 124, 340
elephants, control of *158*, *180*, *181*, 244
Elingamite 106, 108
Elpa Services 136
Engineers for Industry 249
Eriikson, Ragnar *221*

Falloon, John 247
Farmlands 340
Firth Concrete 89, 273
Fisher & Paykel 190, 298–299
Fletcher Holdings 254
Fletcher, Bill 172
Fletcher, Jim 254
Flowers, Mark 403
FML — *see* Franklin Machinery Ltd
Foley, Mike 286, *374*
Foreman, Mortie 92
Francis, Peter 377
Franklin Machinery Ltd (FML) 256–259, 264, 271, 282, 288, 307, 316, 317, 347, 367
Freer, Warren 129
Friederichs, Thomas 322, 328, 376

Galco Products (Galco Engineeering) 52, 69

Gallagher Academy of Performing Arts 403
Gallagher Agricultural Ltd 184
Gallagher, Alfred J 36, 37, 70
Gallagher, Alfred William (Bill senior) 13, 17, 18, 19, 34, 37–41, 42–52, 54, 55, 56, 63–67, 69, 71–74, 73, 76, 77, 79, 85, 88–89, 91, 92–93, 94, 96, 98, 100, 101, 102, 105, 111, 116–117, 122, 130, *131*, 134, *137*, 143, 169, 186, 197, 227, 236, *241*, 264, 277, 288, 315, 391, 400
Gallagher Animal Management Systems 25, 339–340, 344, 349, 351, 359, 361, 364, 366, 367, 371
Gallagher Aquatic Centre 264
Gallagher Australia 288, 337, 344, 363, 366
Gallagher Charitable Trust 262, 264
Gallagher, Chris 234, 398
Gallagher, Edna 65, *79*
Gallagher Electronics 121, 122, 144, 151, 152, 164
Gallagher Engineering 32, 92, 101, 121, 151, 152, 183–184, 189, 201, 203, 204, 218, 235, 249, 250, 256, 258
Gallagher Europe 270, 273, 275
Gallagher, George 36
Gallagher, Glenice 138, 197, 222, *397*
Gallagher Group 11, 17, 18, 23, 26, 27, 30, 121, 133, 132, 189, 200, 203, 205, 222, 223, 227, 236, 248, 258, 259, 264, 269, 270, 272, 273, 279, 288, 303, 304, 307, 308, 309, 310, 319, 321, 334, 337, 340, 341, 343, 344, 347, 349, 350, 359, 361, 362, 363, 364, 366, 384, 388, 398–400
Gallagher, Henry 38, 43, 48, 52, 56, 61, 69, 88, 122
Gallagher Hub, Wintec *402*, 403
Gallagher, Ian 107, 130, 194, 279, 398
Gallagher, James 36
Gallagher, Janine 107, 108, 117, 130, 143, 190, 274, 391, 398, *404*
Gallagher, Jenny (née Geddes) 83, 84, 85, 101, 105, 108, 135, 143, 194–197, 198, 202, 222, 232, 237
Gallagher, John 13, 18, 21, 28, 42, 60, 61, 62, 63, 67–68, 70–71, 72, 74, 76, 79, 82–83, 89, 93, 94, 96, 99, 100, 101, 105, 106, 108, *110*, 111, 114, 117, 121, 122, 133, 136–140, 141, *142*, 143,

170, 175, 182, 189, 195, 196, 197, 198, 204, 222, 224, 225, 235–236, 238, *241*, 248, 249, 262, 264, 273, 276–277, 279, *284*, 384, *390*, *397*, 403
Gallagher, Keith 279, 398
Gallagher, Lady Judi (née Cochrane) 12, 16, 234, 240–242, 243, *246*, 255, 256, 265, 268, 276, 289–291, 312, 315, 322, 331, 350, 351, *354*, 373, 382, 391, 394, 396, *397*, 398, *399*, *404*
Gallagher, Martin 248
Gallagher, May 42, 46, 62, 67, 70, 78, *79*, 89
Gallagher, Millie (née Murray) 38, 42, 43, 46, 63, 65, 74, 78, *79*, 105, 134, 197, 236
Gallagher, Molly 51, 52, 61, 62
Gallagher North America 363
Gallagher, Olive 60, 65, *79*
Gallagher Plastics 175, 313
Gallagher Power Fence (SA) Ltd 286
Gallagher Power Fence Inc 217, 256, 287–288, 344
Gallagher Power Fencing System Canada 361
Gallagher Power Fencing Systems 184
Gallagher PowerFence 14, 15, 16, 223, 261, 311, 312, 330, 331, 333, 337, 339, 364, 366, 372, 375, 378, 386, 387, 388
Gallagher Powerfence SA Ltd 252, 311
Gallagher RSM 168
Gallagher, Sarah 37, 38, 70
Gallagher Security 25, 371, 375–376, 377, 382, 384
Gallagher Security Europe 286
Gallagher Security Fence Ltd 252
Gallagher Security Management Systems (GSMS) 337
Gallagher Security USA 285–286, 322, 328, 361–362, 363, 376
Gallagher, Sir William (Bill junior) 10–13, 14–16, 18, 19, 21–22, 23, 25, 26, 27, 28–30, *31*, 34, 36, 42, 46, 60–63, *64*, 65, 67, 68, 69, 70–71, 72, 74, 76–77, 78, 79, 81, 82, 84–85, 89, 90, 91, 92, 93, 94–96, 98, 99, 100, 101–102, *103*, 104, 105, 106, 107, 108, 109, *110*, 111, 114–116, 117, 120, 121, 122, 124, 126, 127, *128*, 129, 130, 133, 134–136, 141–143, *142*, 144–145, 148, 150, 151, 152, 153, 154, 155, 156, 157, 159, 161, 162, *163*, 165, 168,

169, *170*, 171, 172, 175, 177, 178, 181, 182, 183, 184, 185, 186–187, *188*, 189, 190, 191, 194, 195, 196, 197, 198, 200, 201–202, 203, 204, 205, 206, 208, 209, 210, 211, 212, 213, *214*, 217, 222, 224, 225, 226, 227, 232, *233*, 234–235, 236, 237, 238, 239, 240, *241*, 242, 243–244, *246*, 247, 248, 249, 250, 251, 252–253, 254, 255, 256, 258, 259–261, 262, 264–265, 268–269, 270–271, 272, 273–275, 276–277, 278–280, 282–285, *284*, 286–287, 288–290, 304, 305, 306, 307, 308, 309, 310, 312, 315, 316–319, 321, 322, 323, 326, 327, 328, 330, 331, 333, 335, 336, 337, 339, 341, 343, 347, 349, 351–352, *353*, *354*, 355, 358, 359, 360, 361, 362, 366, 367, 371, 373, *374*, 375, 376, 377, 378, 381, 382, 384, 385, 388–389, *390*, 391, 394, *395*, 396, *397*, 398, *399*, 400, 403, *404*, 405, *406*
Gallagher SmartFence *24*
Gallagher, Thomas 34–36
Gallagher, Tony 398
Gallagher Underwater Supplies 81, 82, 102
Gallagher, Violet 277
Gallagher, Vivian (Viv) 43, 48, 51, 52, 61, 62, 67, 69, 85, 88, 89, 94, 122, 248
Gallaghers Select Farm Systems 346
Geddes, Jenny — *see* Gallagher, Jenny
Geddes, Rene 83
Geddes, Sam 83
General Electric 29, 162
General Grant 108, 111, 116
Gera, Norm 52, *73*
Gilbert, Darcy 105
Gilmour, Bob 285
Graafhuis, Simon *390*
Graham, Michelle 234
Graham, Trevor 81, 234
Grant, Bill 222
Greyson Gates 367

Haddock, Charlie 296
Hall, Bill 235
Hamill, Rob 400
Hamilton, Noel 185, 186, 225
Hamutana 72, 74–76, *75*, 77–78, *79*, *80*, 81, 82, 83–84, 85, 88, 99, 102, 105, 107, 108, *110*, 111, 114, 116, 117, 134, 396
Hargreaves, Paul 309
Hartstone, John 279

Harvard Business School 28, 235, 239, 272, 319
Hay, Bill 232, 265
Healy, Dave 279
Henderson, Brian 68, 81
Hendrie, Ian 359, 361
Hendrie, Jane 361
Hickey, Ben 150
Hill, Kim 282, 283–284
Hoffman, Steve 25, 238–239, 241, 256, 257, 287, 339, 340, 349, 350, 359
Holyoake, Keith 127
Honeywell 29, 301, 336, 376
Hocker & Co 90
Hough, Horace 56, 65, 69, 73
Huizinga, MH 154, 155
Humphrey the sea elephant 222, 223
Hurn, John 134
Hutchinson, Alan 165–166, 168

Iacocca, Lee 208
Ibex 27, 243, 381
Insultimber 173, 174, 177, 202, 207, 240, 288
International Scale Company 317
IPSS 332

James Aviation 224
James, Ossie 100, 224
Janes, Richard 309, 388, *390*
Jansen, Ross 236, 248
Jayawardene, JR 11
Jeffries, Roy 38
Jones, Auriel 169
Jones, Bob 178
Jones, Vaughan 23, 100, 169–171, *170*, 172, 182, 189, 220, 224, 226, 237, 250
Joosje Smart Technologies 377
Joseph Nathan Ltd 172

Kahikatea Drive factory 121, 130–133, *132*, 141, 143, 190, 315–316, *379*, *383*
Kemp, Dick 69
Khalil, Sharbil 352, *353*
Kirsten, Birger 310, 321, 337
Kneebone, John 100
Koltec 149

Laidlaw, Lincoln 187
Laison, Henry 109
Lange, David 191, 198, 250
Leaf, Eddie 55
Lean Manufacturing 367–368, 371
Lewin, John 361_362
Lim, Gin *241*
Lindale, Carol 234
Lindale, Don 202, 234, *241*
Linn, Malcolm 363, 389

Little, Andrew 283
Llewellyn, Don 100
Locke, John *110*, 111
Low, Kevin 297–298, 299
Lucey & O'Connell 184
Lucey, Jim 184
Lucey, John 23, 184–185, *188*, 211–212, 253, 359
Lunden, Bengt 190
Lundex 159

Major, John 51
Manaia 102
Marine Services 102
Marquand, Kevin 177
Martynstein, Cedric 12
McDonald's 253
McGee of Ardee 184
McGee, PJ 184
McGee, Red 184
McPhail, Bill 226, 237
McQuillan, Pat 141
Meadows, Ian 332, 333, *353*
Metcalf, Ray 185
Miller, Rex 195
Mitzberg, Henry 271–272
Miyawaki, Yutkaka 360
Moller-Yamaha 189
Moore, Mike 11
Morrison, Ian 217
Moss, Vince 130, 133
MRP II system 225–226, 237, 249, 258, 287, 312, 367
Muldoon, Robert 175, 177, 185, 191, 198
Mullan & Noy 68, 89
Mullen, David 23, 165–167, 177, 202, 213–215, 218, *219*, 220, 226, 236, *241*, 254, 256, 259, 277, 287–288, 337, 344, 346, 358, 361, 362, 363–364, 366
Mullen, Marg 165, *219*
Mullen, Richard 362, 366
Munro, Bruce 274, 277, 282, 284, 287, 305, 312, 321, 344–346, 362–363, *390*
Murray, Millie — *see* Gallagher, Millie
Mystery Creek Fieldays 100–101, 124, *128*, 129, 165, 169, 177, *199*, 222, 254, 367

Narain, Krishna 244
Narain, Ravi 380
Narain, Vishnu 15, 16, 243–247, *245*, *246*, 378
Narian, Prima 380
Nash, Walter 42
National Grid 15, 259–261, *260*, 327
Neal, Stuart 331
Nelson, Sam 184
New Zealand Trade & Enterprise 364, 377, 383

Norman W Hutchinson & Sons 126

O'Brien, Bill 43, 46
O'Halloran, Wayne 308, 326, 337, 368
Oden, Terry 377
Orange Field Days 99, 100, 126
Orrell, Fred 197

Packer, Aussie 93
Page, Evelyn 98
Page, Jack 98–99
Pallo Engineering 295
Pallo, Karl 295
Paterson, Barry 226, 237
PEC (Production Engineering Company) 14, 18, 29, 294–300, 301, 302–303, 304, 305, 306, 307–308, 309, 310, 312, 317, 318, 319, 321, 335, 347, 349, 351, 366, 386
PEL — *see* Precision Electronics Ltd (PEL)
Pettit, John 109, *110*, 111, 112, 250–251, 259
Philbin, Karl *353*
Philips Corporation 162
Phillips, Doug 90–92
Piesse, Bob 126–127, 140, 167, 168, 175, 182
Plastic Products Ltd 92, 98
Poole, Jack 71
Porter, Michael E 28, 239–240, 252, 319–321
Precision Electronics Ltd (PEL) 96, 98, 340, 343
Production Engineering Company — *see* PEC
Pronet 383
Provenco 306

Quinn, Erwin 256, 287, 344, 361

Ranson, Ernie 172–175
Reid, Alan 63
Reliance Industries 332, 333
Reynolds, Ralph 79, 102, *103*, 104, 105
Richards, Ian 247
Richards, Jack 256
Richards, John 256–257, 258
Richardson, Earl 187
Richardson, Jan 255
Richardson, Neil 23–25, 236–238, 240, *241*, 247, 248, 249, 252, 253–254, 255, 258, 265, 269–270, 271, 273–276, 277, 280, 282, 288, 321, 340, 351, 359
Rickman, Jerry 276
Roose Shipping Company 78, 89
RSM — *see* Rural Sales and Marketing

Ruddweigh Scales 288, 317, 321, 346, 347
Rural Sales and Marketing (RSM) 165, 167, 168 — see also Gallagher RSM
Russell McVeagh 251
Ruswin Locksmith & Security 331
Rutland Electrics 134, 136

Saft 164 — see also Cipel
Saul, Alp 383
Saunders, Steve 276, 277, 288, 396
Savage, Ralph 141
Savory, Tim 218
Scherer, Len *110*, 111
Schneider 29
Scott, Des 279, 280, 340, 341, 343
Seddon Park 53, *54*, 55–56, 60, 63, 63–67, *66*, 71–72, 73, 74
Shaw, Bob 73
Sheppard, Bruce 341
Siemens 29, 336
Simon, Hermann 28, 272–273
Simpson, Steve 335
Singh, Manmohan 243
Slark, Tony 109
Small, Richard 405
SmartPower energiser 261–262, 269, 270, 282
Smith, Bill 73
Smith, Eddie 141
Smith, Mike 340
Snell, Art 138, 139, 140, 141, 182, 217, 236, 256, 344
Snowden, KM 74
Southcombe, Stan 93
Specialised Plastics Ltd 175
Speedrite electric fence 42, 90, 278–279, 340
Standing, Colin 141, 209
Standing, Colin 164
Stevens, Laurie 200
Stihl 272
Sun Plas Engineering Ltd 175
Sunshine clothes pegs 249
Surge Miyawaki Co Ltd 23, 136, 359
Swayze, Henry 138, 256
Swayze, Henry 182
Taboo 55

Tait Electronics 190
Tapper Construction 89
Tarawera 114
Tarlton, Kelly 78, 106, 107, 109, *110*, 111, 112, 116
Taylor, Peter 276
Telecom 252, 301
Thompson, Bruce 317
Thompson, Sally 317
Thorn-EMI 210
Tiare 72, 74
Tomas, Charles 311, 334
Townsend, Robert 16
Transpower 252
Trigon Ltd 190
Tru-Test 278–279, 340–343, 347, 358, 367
Tucker, Steve 25, 287, 305, 312, 313, 315, *320*, 321, 322, 346–347, 349–350, 351, 384, 386–387, 388, *390*, 391
Turkington, Don 340
Turners Auctions 252

Ubambo 286
Union Carbide 261
United Technologies (UTC) 29
Upton, Simon 248

Vedma, Jose 177
Veldman & Dijkstra 11, 23, 149–150, 156, 157, 161, 171, 190, 213, 217, 259, 270, 282, 286, 311, 312–313, 321, 344, 359 — see also Dijkstra, Dooitze; Dijkstra, Erik
Veldman, John 149, 150, *216* — see also Veldman & Dijkstra
Vodafone 382
Vogal Engineering 52, 69, 94

Waikato electric fence 92, 96–98, 126, 184
Waikouaiti 114
Wallace, LF 43, 46
Walley, John 209–210, 226, 227, 237, 261, 277, 279, 280, 288, 321
Watson, Eric 305
Watson, Les 178
Weir, John 276
WH Billings Ltd 126, 165–166, 168
Wilcox, Don 257
Wilkinson, Rob 298
Williams & Kettle 340
Williams electric fence 90
Williams, Gary 70
Williams, John 294–297, 298–299, 300, 302, 303, 304, 305, 306, 335
Williams, Reg 295–296
Williamson, Maurice 169, 252
Williamson, Owen 96, 98
Wilson, George 73
Wrightson 340

Yates 224
Yip In Tsoi group 302, 331
Young, Herbert *176*
Young, John 77